TRANSNATIONAL LITIGATION

IN A NUTSHELL

By

GEORGE A. BERMANN
Walter Gellhorn Professor of Law and
Jean Monnet Professor of European Union Law
Columbia Law School

THOMSON
WEST

Mat #40133921

610 Opperman Drive
P.O. Box 64526
St. Paul, MN 55164–0526
1–800–328–9352

ISBN 0–314–14584–2

TEXT IS PRINTED ON 10% POST CONSUMER RECYCLED PAPER

To my parents,
Mae Gordon Bermann
and Sigmund Dressler Berman

*

INTRODUCTION

As transactions increasingly entail cross-border elements, so too does the litigation that those transactions tend to generate. Although virtually all litigation arising out of international transactions takes place in one national court or another (if not in an international arbitral venue), that litigation is unlikely to proceed in exactly the same fashion as litigation over purely domestic disputes proceeds in that forum. Hence, this book and the law school courses for which it is designed.

This book employs the term "transnational litigation" to denote the materials covered, primarily to avoid confusion with the resolution of "international" disputes between States or between a State and an international organization. To that extent, "private" rather than "public" international law disputes are this book's subject.

The reader will soon discover that, while there is obviously both a federal and an international dimension to our subject, the field is far from completely addressed either by federal legislation (or federal rules of civil procedure) or by international treaties, or by a combination of the two. On the contrary, the sources of transnational litigation law in the US are multiple. The common law—both federal and state—has a role to play. So too does state legislation. Unsurprisingly in this situation, we will also encounter influential Restatements of the Law. Even they are several, notably the Restatements of Conflict of Laws and of the Foreign Relations Law of the United States.

Clearly, the conduct of transnational litigation in the US is governed, and governed pervasively, by the usual rules of civil procedure that obtain in the forum, state or federal. It is not the mission of this book, or the courses to which it corresponds, to cover the usual civil procedure ground. Students, particularly those trained overseas or otherwise not acquainted with American civil procedure, are advised to consult a civil procedure text so as to place the issues dealt with in this book in their conventional procedural context.

Notwithstanding the growth of transnational litigation in US courts, a significant volume of private international disputes are resolved not through adjudication in national (or sub-national) courts, but through international arbitral channels. Even if one wanted to, one could not ignore arbitration in a book of this sort—this, for the simple reason that courts have a significant role to play in many aspects of the international arbitral process, including compelling arbitration, awarding provisional relief in conjunction with arbitration, setting aside arbitral awards, and eventually recognizing and/or enforcing arbitral awards. On the other hand, the law of international arbitration presupposes a basic adjudicatory procedure that differs in fundamental ways from the conduct of litigation (including transnational litigation) in a national court system. It has also become exceedingly complex. Accordingly, international arbitration will be dealt with in only a preliminary fashion toward the end of this book, with a decided emphasis on the intersections between courts and arbitral tribunals. It is the subject of a separate Nutshell volume on "International Commercial Arbitration" prepared in conjunction with this one.

*

ACKNOWLEDGMENT

The author acknowledges with gratitude the research assistance of the team of Columbia Law School students who helped gather materials during the fall semester 2002: Christina Beharry, Jason Casey, Claire de Saint-Vincent, Estelle Dougier, Carine Dupeyron, Karen Eltis, Jose Manuel Garcia Represa, Ladan Fazlollahi, Amit Gupta, Erin Murray, Elizabeth Perez, Reimar Petursson, Kristen Santillo, Dan Thacker, and Joanne Wylomansksa. The Author also acknowledges with gratitude the editorial assistance of Karina Rodriguez.

*

OUTLINE

Page

INTRODUCTION V
ACKNOWLEDGMENTS IX
TABLE OF CASES XVII

Introduction 1
Chapter One. The Sources of Transnational Litigation Law 4
Federal Legislation and Rules 4
Treaties and International Agreements 7
The Federal Common Law 8
Restatements of the Law 11

Chapter Two. Jurisdiction Over Non–Nationals and Non–Residents 13
Forum Selection Clauses 14
Interpretation of forum selection clauses 14
Validity of forum selection clauses 17
(a) Contractual validity of the forum selection agreement 20
(b) Availability and adequacy of the chosen forum 23
(c) Non-alienability of the cause of action 26
Forum non conveniens and choice of forum clauses 29
Bremen in federal diversity cases 31

	Page
Jurisdiction in the Absence of a Selection	34
Statutory personal jurisdiction	35
(a) State courts	35
(b) Federal courts	37
The "due process" dimension	39
(a) General jurisdiction	44
(b) Specific jurisdiction	49
(c) Quasi-in-rem jurisdiction	51
The Internet and personal jurisdiction	53
"Aggregation" of national contacts	55
Piercing the jurisdictional veil	61
(a) "Alter ego" analysis	61
(b) Agency theory	65
Plaintiff's nationality	68
The Timing of Jurisdictional Objections	69
Chapter Three. Subject Matter Jurisdiction Over Transnational Disputes	70
Diversity and "Alienage" Jurisdiction	73
Federal Question Jurisdiction	77
General federal question jurisdiction	77
Specific federal question jurisdiction	79
Subject Matter and Personal Jurisdiction	82
Venue	83
Chapter Four. Parallel Litigation	86
International Forum Non Conveniens	89
General considerations	91
Available alternative forum	93
The Balance of considerations	95
Plaintiff's nationality	98
Change in applicable law	100
Conditions of dismissal	102

	Page
Federalism aspects	103
International Lis Pendens	106
Anti-Suit Injunctions	110
Chapter Five. "Sovereignty" Limitations on the Exercise of Jurisdiction	117
Foreign Sovereign Immunity	118
From common law to the FSIA	118
The FSIA	120
(a) The Legislative framework	120
(b) "States" and "agencies or instrumentalities"	124
(c) Exceptions to immunity	128
(i) Waiver	129
(ii) Commercial activity	132
(iii) Takings of property in violation of international law	138
(iv) Property rights acquired by succession or gift or pertaining to US real estate	140
(v) Non-commercial torts	140
(vi) Arbitral matters	146
(vii) Acts of terrorism	147
(viii) Admiralty	151
(d) Counterclaims	151
(e) Retroactivity of the FSIA	153
(f) Attachment of foreign sovereign property	154
(g) Suits by aliens against foreign states	160
(h) Default	161
Head of State or Government Immunity	162

Page

The Act of State Doctrine 167
Definitional aspects 170
Exceptions to the act of state doctrine 175
(a) Commercial exception 175
(b) The Bernstein exception 176
(c) Counterclaim exception 177
(d) Treaty exception 179
Congressional exclusion of the act of state doctrine 180
Political Questions and International Comity 183
The "Dormant" Foreign Affairs and Foreign Commerce Power 188
Foreign Sovereign Compulsion 192

Chapter Six. International Human Rights Cases 195
The Alien Tort Claim Statute 195
The Torture Victim Protection Act 204
Treaties and Customary International Law as a Source of Private Legal Claims 208
Universal Jurisdiction 210

Chapter Seven. Choice of Law and the Applicable Law 211
Choice of Law Clauses 215
Interpretation of choice of law clauses 215
Validity of the choice of law clause 217
(a) Whose law determines the validity of the clause? 218
(b) Limits on party autonomy 220
Choice of Law in the Absence of a Selection 223
Federal versus state law 224
Conflicts methodologies 226

Page

(a) The Second Restatement ... 227
(b) Forum public policy in the transnational context ... 229
Treaty law ... 231
Mandatory Rules of Law ... 232
Constitutional Limits on the Application of Forum Law ... 235
The "Extraterritorial" Application of US Law 237
Presumption against extraterritorial application of domestic law ... 237
(a) Narrowed statutory construction ... 238
(b) Balancing of factors ... 238
The "Timberlane" rule of reason ... 240
(a) Subject matter jurisdiction versus merits ... 243
(b) Subject matter jurisdiction versus comity ... 244
(c) Hartford Fire Ins. Co. v. California ... 246
Extraterritorial Causes of Action and Extraterritorial Application Of Constitutional Rights 247
The Application of Foreign Tax, Penal and "Public" Law ... 249
Pleading and Proof of Foreign Law ... 255

Chapter Eight. Transnational Service and Production of Evidence ... 262
Service of Documents Abroad ... 262
The Federal Rules ... 263
US service under foreign law ... 266
Service of Foreign Judicial Documents in the US ... 269
The Hague Service Convention ... 270

Page
Workings of the Convention 271
Scope and exclusivity of the Convention 274
Obtaining Evidence Abroad 277
The Federal Rules 278
Production by non-parties 283
Jurisdiction to order jurisdictional discovery 285
"Foreign Blocking Legislation" and its Effects 286
Conflicts Between US Discovery Orders and Foreign Law 289
Societe Internationale Pour Participations Industrielles et Commerciales v. Rogers 291
(a) Production order or not? 292
(b) Sanctions or not? 294
The Third Restatement 295
Production of Evidence for Use in Foreign Judicial Proceedings 300
The Hague Evidence Convention 304
Scope of the Evidence Convention 305
Exclusivity of the Convention 311

Chapter Nine. Transnational Provisional Relief 315
Ordering "Extraterritorial" Provisional Relief 316
Provisional Relief in Aid of Enforcing a Foreign Judgment 321

Chapter Ten. Recognition and Enforcement of Foreign Judgments 328
Foreign vs. Sister–State Judgments 330
The Uniform Foreign Country Money–Judgments Recognition Act 335
Reviewing Personal Jurisdiction and Notice 338
Impartiality, Procedural Due Process and Fraud 345
Judgments Contrary to Forum Public Policy 347

Page

Other Grounds for Non–Recognition and Non–Enforcement 350
Reciprocity 351
The Case of Foreign "Default" Judgments 351
Revenue and Penal Judgments 353
Enforcement of Non–Monetary Judgments 355
The Collateral Estoppel Effect of Foreign Judgments 356
Procedure in Enforcement Actions 357
The Currency of Foreign Judgments 359
Recognition and Enforcement of US Judgments Abroad 362
Treaty Regimes for the Enforcement of Foreign Judgments 363

Chapter Eleven. Judicial Intervention in International Commercial Arbitration 365
International Arbitral Institutions 366
The International Arbitration Framework in US Law 369
The Role of US Courts Prior to the Arbitral Procedure 373
  Compelling arbitration 374
    (a) Validity of the arbitration agreement 376
    (b) Interpretation of the arbitration agreement 380
      (i) Interpretation questions 381
      (ii) The Reach of the agreement to arbitrate: the First Options case 384
      (iii) Choice of law governing interpretation 385

Page

Federalism aspects of international arbitration in US courts 386
The Arbitrability of Statutory Claims 389
Judicial Intervention in the Arbitral Process 397
Judicial assistance in launching the arbitration 397
Interlocutory review of arbitral procedural rulings 401
Arbitral Choice of Law 402
Judicial Review of the Award 404
Confirmation and vacatur of arbitral awards 405
(a) Confirmation proceedings 405
(b) Vacatur of awards 406
Recognition and enforcement of foreign arbitral awards 409
(a) Convention grounds for non-recognition and non-enforcement 412
(b) US case law on recognition and enforcement of Convention awards 415

INDEX 423

TABLE OF CASES

References are to Pages

A

Aaron Ferer & Sons Ltd. v. Chase Manhattan Bank, Nat. Ass'n, 731 F.2d 112 (2nd Cir.1984), *224*

Abdi Jama v. United States I.N.S., 22 F.Supp.2d 353 (D.N.J. 1998), *201*

Abdulaziz v. Metropolitan Dade County, 741 F.2d 1328 (11th Cir.1984), *166*

Abdullah v. Sheridan Square Press, Inc., 154 F.R.D. 591 (S.D.N.Y.1994), *348*

Abdullahi v. Pfizer, Inc., 2002 WL 31082956 (S.D.N.Y.2002), *199*

Abdullah Sayid Rajab Al-Rifai & Sons W.L.L. v. McDonnell Douglas Foreign Sales Corp., 988 F.Supp. 1285 (E.D.Mo. 1997), *108*

Ackermann v. Levine, 788 F.2d 830 (2nd Cir.1986), *273, 340*

Adam v. Saenger, 303 U.S. 59, 58 S.Ct. 454, 82 L.Ed. 649 (1938), *331*

Afram Export Corp. v. Metallurgiki Halyps, S.A., 772 F.2d 1358 (7th Cir.1985), *50*

Aguinda v. Texaco, Inc., 142 F.Supp.2d 534 (S.D.N.Y.2001), *203*

Air Crash Disaster Near New Orleans, In re, 821 F.2d 1147 (5th Cir.1987), vacated on other grounds Pan American World Airways, Inc. v. Lopez, 490 U.S. 1032, 109 S.Ct. 1928, 104 L.Ed.2d 400 (1989), *93*

Air Disaster at Lockerbie, Scotland, In re, 928 F.2d 1267 (2nd Cir.1991), cert. denied Rein v. Pan American World Airways, Inc., 502 U.S. 920, 112 S.Ct. 331, 116 L.Ed.2d 272 (1991), *208*

Alcoa S. S. Co., Inc. v. M/V Nordic Regent, 654 F.2d 147 (2nd Cir.1980), cert. denied 449 U.S. 890, 101 S.Ct. 248, 66 L.Ed.2d 116 (1980), *99*

TABLE OF CASES

Alejandre v. Telefonica Larga Distancia, de Puerto Rico, Inc., 183 F.3d 1277 (11th Cir.1999), *158*

Alexander v. Gardner–Denver Co., 415 U.S. 36, 94 S.Ct. 1011, 39 L.Ed.2d 147 (1974), *392*

Alfadda v. Fenn, 159 F.3d 41 (2nd Cir.1998), *92*

Alfadda v. Fenn, 935 F.2d 475 (2nd Cir.1991), cert. denied Fenn v. Alfadda, 502 U.S. 1005, 112 S.Ct. 638, 116 L.Ed.2d 656 (1991), dismissed Alfadda v. Fenn, 159 F.3d 41 (2nd Cir. 1998), *244*

Alfred Dunhill of London, Inc. v. Republic of Cuba, 425 U.S. 682, 96 S.Ct. 1854, 48 L.Ed.2d 301 (1976), *171*

Alghanim & Sons v. Toys 'R' Us, Inc., 126 F.3d 15 (2nd Cir. 1997), cert. denied Toys 'R' Us, Inc. v. Yusuf Ahmed Alghanim & Sons, W.L.L., 522 U.S. 1111, 118 S.Ct. 1042, 140 L.Ed.2d 107 (1998), *407*

Allen v. Lloyd's of London, 94 F.3d 923 (4th Cir.1996), writ mandumus denied Allen, In re, 521 U.S. 1102, 117 S.Ct. 2497, 138 L.Ed.2d 1004 (1997), *223*

Allendale Mut. Ins. Co. v. Bull Data Systems, Inc., 10 F.3d 425 (7th Cir.1993), *115*

Allied Bank Intern. v. Banco Credito Agricola de Cartago, 757 F.2d 516 (2nd Cir.1985), cert. dismissed Banco Credito Agricola De Cartago v. Allied Bank International, 473 U.S. 934, 106 S.Ct. 30, 87 L.Ed.2d 706 (1985), *173*

Allied–Bruce Terminix Companies, Inc. v. Dobson, 513 U.S. 265, 115 S.Ct. 834, 130 L.Ed.2d 753 (1995), *375*

Allstate Ins. Co. v. Hague, 449 U.S. 302, 101 S.Ct. 633, 66 L.Ed.2d 521 (1981), *236*

ALS Scan, Inc. v. Digital Service Consultants, Inc., 293 F.3d 707 (4th Cir.2002), cert. denied ___ U.S. ___, 123 S.Ct. 868, 154 L.Ed.2d 773 (2003), *53*

Altmann v. Republic of Austria, 317 F.3d 954 (9th Cir.2002), *153*

Aluminum Co. of America, United States v., 148 F.2d 416 (2nd Cir.1945), *239*

Alvarez–Machain v. United States, 107 F.3d 696 (9th Cir.1996), cert. denied Berellez v. Alvarez–Machain, 522 U.S. 814, 118 S.Ct. 60, 139 L.Ed.2d 23 (1997), *205*

American Banana Co. v. United Fruit Co., 213 U.S. 347, 29 S.Ct. 511, 53 L.Ed. 826 (1909), *239*

American Const. Machinery & Equipment Corp. Ltd. v. Mechanised Const. of Pakistan Ltd., 659 F.Supp. 426 (S.D.N.Y.1987), affirmed 828 F.2d 117 (2nd Cir.1987), cert. denied Mechanised Const. of Pakistan Ltd. v. American Const. Machinery and Equipment Ltd., 484 U.S. 1064, 108 S.Ct. 1024, 98 L.Ed.2d 988 (1988), *419*

American Dredging Co. v. Miller, 510 U.S. 443, 114 S.Ct. 981, 127 L.Ed.2d 285 (1994), *104*

American Surety Co. v. Baldwin, 287 U.S. 156, 53 S.Ct. 98, 77 L.Ed. 231 (1932), *331*

Amoco Egypt Oil Co. v. Leonis Nav. Co., Inc., 1 F.3d 848 (9th Cir.1993), *45*

Amoco Overseas Oil Co. v. Compagnie Nationale Algerienne de Navigation ("C. N. A. N."), 605 F.2d 648 (2nd Cir.1979), *52*

Amoco (UK) Exploration Co v. Teesside Gas Transportation Ltd, 2001 WL 272910 (HL 2001), *116*

Amusement Equipment, Inc. v. Mordelt, 779 F.2d 264 (5th Cir.1985), *48*

Anderson v. Islamic Republic of Iran, 90 F.Supp.2d 107 (D.D.C. 2000), *159*

Antoine v. Atlas Turner, Inc., 66 F.3d 105 (6th Cir.1995), *125*

Apollo Computer, Inc. v. Berg, 886 F.2d 469 (1st Cir.1989), *381*

Appalachian Ins. Company v. Superior Court, 162 Cal.App.3d 427, 208 Cal.Rptr. 627 (Cal.App. 2 Dist.1984), *20*

Application of (see name of party)

Aquamar, S.A. v. Del Monte Fresh Produce N.A., Inc., 179 F.3d 1279 (11th Cir.1999), *129*

Arango v. Guzman Travel Advisors Corp., 621 F.2d 1371 (5th Cir.1980), *174*

Arbitration between Monegasque De Reassurances S.A.M., In re v. Nak Naftogaz of Ukraine, 311 F.3d 488 (2nd Cir.2002), *420*

Arco Electronics Control Ltd. v. Core Intern., 794 F.Supp. 1144 (S.D.Fla.1992), *341*

Argentine Republic v. Amerada Hess Shipping Corp., 488 U.S. 428, 109 S.Ct. 683, 102 L.Ed.2d 818 (1989), *128, 200*

Armendariz v. Foundation Health Psychcare Services, Inc., 99 Cal.Rptr.2d 745, 6 P.3d 669 (Cal.2000), *396*

Armstrong v. Virgin Records, Ltd., 91 F.Supp.2d 628 (S.D.N.Y. 2000), *250*

Arriaga v. Cross Country Bank, 163 F.Supp.2d 1189 (S.D.Cal. 2001), *396*

Artimm, S.r.l., In re, 278 B.R. 832 (Bkrtcy.C.D.Cal.2002), *325*

Asahi Metal Industry Co., Ltd. v. Superior Court of California, Solano County, 480 U.S. 102, 107 S.Ct. 1026, 94 L.Ed.2d 92 (1987), *41*

Asbestos Insurance, In re, [1985] 1 WLR 331 (H.L.1985), *308*

Asociacion de Reclamantes v. United Mexican States, 735 F.2d 1517, 237 U.S.App.D.C. 81 (D.C.Cir.1984), cert. denied 470 U.S. 1051, 105 S.Ct. 1751, 84 L.Ed.2d 815 (1985), *140*

Asta Medica, S.A., Application of, 981 F.2d 1 (1st Cir.1992), *304*

Attorney General of Canada v. R.J. Reynolds Tobacco Holdings, Inc., 268 F.3d 103 (2nd Cir.2001), cert. denied ___ U.S. ___, 123 S.Ct. 513, 154 L.Ed.2d 394 (2002), *252*

AT & T Technologies, Inc. v. Communications Workers of America, 475 U.S. 643, 106 S.Ct. 1415, 89 L.Ed.2d 648 (1986), *385*

AVC Nederland B.V. v. Atrium Inv. Partnership, 740 F.2d 148 (2nd Cir.1984), *27*

Avraham and Shigur Exp. Ltd., 1991 WL 177633 (S.D.N.Y.1991), *420*

B

Babanaft International Co SA v. Bassatne (CA 1988), *318*

Babcock v. Jackson, 240 N.Y.S.2d 743, 191 N.E.2d 279 (N.Y. 1963), *227*

Bachchan v. India Abroad Publications Inc., 154 Misc.2d 228, 585 N.Y.S.2d 661 (N.Y.Sup.1992), *348*

Baker v. Carr, 369 U.S. 186, 82 S.Ct. 691, 7 L.Ed.2d 663 (1962), *186*

Baker Marine (Nig.) Ltd. v. Chevron (Nig.) Ltd., 191 F.3d 194 (2nd Cir.1999), *415*

Baldwin v. Iowa State Traveling Men's Ass'n, 283 U.S. 522, 51 S.Ct. 517, 75 L.Ed. 1244 (1931), *331*

Balsys, United States v., 524 U.S. 666, 118 S.Ct. 2218, 141 L.Ed.2d 575 (1998), *249*

B. Altman & Co. v. United States, 224 U.S. 583, 32 S.Ct. 593, 56 L.Ed. 894 (1912), *209*

Banco Ambrosiano, S.P.A. v. Artoc Bank & Trust Ltd., 476 N.Y.S.2d 64, 464 N.E.2d 432 (N.Y.1984), *52*

Banco de Credito Indus., S.A. v. Tesoreria General, 990 F.2d 827 (5th Cir.1993), cert. denied Tesoreria General v. Banco de Credito Indus., S.A., 510 U.S. 1071, 114 S.Ct. 877, 127 L.Ed.2d 73 (1994), *258*

Banco Do Brasil, S.A. v. A.C. Israel Commodity Co., 239 N.Y.S.2d 872, 190 N.E.2d 235 (N.Y.1963), cert. denied 376 U.S. 906, 84 S.Ct. 657, 11 L.Ed.2d 605 (1964), *253*

Banco Frances e Brasileiro S. A. v. Doe, 370 N.Y.S.2d 534, 331 N.E.2d 502 (N.Y.1975), cert. denied Doe v. Banco Frances E Brasileiro, S.A., 423 U.S. 867, 96 S.Ct. 129, 46 L.Ed.2d 96 (1975), *254*

Banco Nacional de Cuba v. Chase Manhattan Bank, 658 F.2d 875 (2nd Cir.1981), *178*

Banco Nacional de Cuba v. Chemical Bank New York Trust Co., 658 F.2d 903 (2nd Cir.1981), *172*

Banco Nacional de Cuba v. First Nat. City Bank of New York, 270 F.Supp. 1004 (S.D.N.Y.1967), on appeal 431 F.2d 394 (2nd Cir.1970), vacated on other grounds First National City Bank v. Banco Nacional De Cuba, 400 U.S. 1019, 91 S.Ct. 581, 27 L.Ed.2d 630 (1971), affirmed Banco Nacional de Cuba v. First Nat. City Bank of New York, 442 F.2d 530 (2nd Cir.1971), on remand 478 F.2d 191 (2nd Cir.1973), *181*

Banco Nacional de Cuba v. Sabbatino, 376 U.S. 398, 84 S.Ct. 923, 11 L.Ed.2d 804 (1964), *10, 169*

Banco Para el Comercio Exterior de Cuba v. First Nat. City Bank, 744 F.2d 237 (2nd Cir.1984), *179*

Banco Para el Comercio Exterior de Cuba v. First Nat. City Bank, 658 F.2d 913 (2nd Cir.1981), *179*

Bandai America Inc. v. Bally Midway Mfg. Co., 775 F.2d 70 (3rd Cir.1985), cert. denied 475 U.S. 1047, 106 S.Ct. 1265, 89 L.Ed.2d 574 (1986), *347*

Bank Melli Iran v. Pahlavi, 58 F.3d 1406 (9th Cir.1995), cert. denied 516 U.S. 989, 116 S.Ct. 519, 133 L.Ed.2d 427 (1995), *345*

Bank of Montreal v. Kough, 612 F.2d 467 (9th Cir.1980), *351*

Bank of Montreal v. Kough, 430 F.Supp. 1243 (N.D.Cal.1977), affirmed 612 F.2d 467 (9th Cir.1980), *347*

Bank of Nova Scotia, United States v., 740 F.2d 817 (11th Cir.1984), cert. denied Bank of Nova Scotia v. United States, 469 U.S. 1106, 105 S.Ct. 778, 83 L.Ed.2d 774 (1985), *294*

Bank of Nova Scotia, United States v., 691 F.2d 1384 (11th Cir.1982), cert. denied Bank of Novia Scotia v. United States, 462 U.S. 1119, 103 S.Ct. 3086, 77 L.Ed.2d 1348 (1983), *294*

Bankston v. Toyota Motor Corp., 889 F.2d 172 (8th Cir.1989), *273*

Bank Tejarat v. Varsho–Saz, 723 F.Supp. 516 (C.D.Cal.1989), *179*

Banque Libanaise Pour le Commerce v. Khreich, 915 F.2d 1000 (5th Cir.1990), rehearing denied (1990), *337*

Bao Ge v. Li Peng, 201 F.Supp.2d 14 (D.D.C.2000), *201*

Barclays Bank PLC v. Franchise Tax Bd. of California, 512 U.S. 298, 114 S.Ct. 2268, 129 L.Ed.2d 244 (1994), *191*

Barclays Bank, S.A. v. Tsakos, 543 A.2d 802 (D.C.1988), *322*

Barkanic v. General Admin. of Civil Aviation of the People's Republic of China, 923 F.2d 957 (2nd Cir.1991), *123, 225*

Barrentine v. Arkansas–Best Freight System, Inc., 450 U.S. 728, 101 S.Ct. 1437, 67 L.Ed.2d 641 (1981), *392*

Base Metal Trading, Ltd. v. OJSC "Novokuznetsky Aluminum Factory", 283 F.3d 208 (4th Cir.2002), cert. denied ___ U.S. ___, 123 S.Ct. 101, 154 L.Ed.2d 30 (2002), *59, 420*

Basic v. Fitzroy Engineering, Ltd., 949 F.Supp. 1333 (N.D.Ill. 1996), affirmed without opinion 132 F.3d 36 (7th Cir.1997), *110*

Bata v. Bata, 39 Del.Ch. 258, 163 A.2d 493 (Del.Supr.1960), rehearing denied 39 Del.Ch. 548, 170 A.2d 711 (Del. Supr.1961), cert. denied 366 U.S. 964, 81 S.Ct. 1926, 6 L.Ed.2d 1255 (1961), *356*

Bayer AG, In re, 146 F.3d 188 (3rd Cir.1998), *304*

Beanal v. Freeport–McMoran, Inc., 197 F.3d 161 (5th Cir.1999), *200*

Beanal v. Freeport–McMoran, Inc., 969 F.Supp. 362 (E.D.La. 1997), affirmed on other grounds 197 F.3d 161 (5th Cir.1999), *206*

Becker Autoradio U.S.A., Inc. v. Becker Autoradiowerk GmbH, 585 F.2d 39 (3rd Cir.1978), *386*

Benton Graphics v. Uddeholm Corp., 118 F.R.D. 386 (D.N.J. 1987), *313*

Bergesen v. Joseph Muller Corp., 710 F.2d 928 (2nd Cir.1983), *372*

Bernstein v. N. V. Nederlandsche–Amerikaansche, Stoomvaart–Maatschappij, 210 F.2d 375 (2nd Cir.1954), *176*

Bersch v. Drexel Firestone, Inc., 519 F.2d 974 (2nd Cir.1975), cert. denied Bersch v. Arthur Andersen & Co., I.O.S., Ltd., 423 U.S. 1018, 96 S.Ct. 453, 46 L.Ed.2d 389 (1975), *244*

Bestfoods, United States v., 524 U.S. 51, 118 S.Ct. 1876, 141 L.Ed.2d 43 (1998), *65*

Bettis v. Islamic Republic of Iran, 315 F.3d 325, 354 U.S.App. D.C. 244 (D.C.Cir.2003), *150*

Bhatnagar v. Surrendra Overseas Ltd., 52 F.3d 1220 (3rd Cir. 1995), *94*

Biel v. Boehm, 94 Misc.2d 946, 406 N.Y.S.2d 231 (N.Y.Sup.1978), *330*

Birch Shipping Corp. v. Embassy of United Republic of Tanzania, 507 F.Supp. 311 (D.D.C.1980), *156*

Blackmer v. United States, 284 U.S. 421, 52 S.Ct. 252, 76 L.Ed. 375 (1932), *44, 268*

Blanco v. Banco Indus. de Venezuela, S.A., 997 F.2d 974 (2nd Cir.1993), *24, 100*

Bonny v. Society of Lloyd's, 3 F.3d 156 (7th Cir.1993), cert. denied 510 U.S. 1113, 114 S.Ct. 1057, 127 L.Ed.2d 378 (1994), *223*

Boosey & Hawkes Music Publishers, Ltd. v. Walt Disney Co., 145 F.3d 481 (2nd Cir.1998), *98*

Borden, Inc. v. Meiji Milk Products Co., Ltd., 919 F.2d 822 (2nd Cir.1990), cert. denied 500 U.S. 953, 111 S.Ct. 2259, 114 L.Ed.2d 712 (1991), *401*

Boshnjaku v. Federal Republic of Yugoslavia, 2002 WL 1575067 (N.D.Ill.2002), *131*

Bowen v. Amoco Pipeline Co., 254 F.3d 925 (10th Cir.2001), *407*

Boyd v. Grand Trunk Western R. Co., 338 U.S. 263, 70 S.Ct. 26, 94 L.Ed. 55 (1949), *27*

Boyle v. United Technologies Corp., 487 U.S. 500, 108 S.Ct. 2510, 101 L.Ed.2d 442 (1988), *10, 168*

Braka v. Bancomer, S.N.C., 762 F.2d 222 (2nd Cir.1985), *170*

Bridgeway Corp. v. Citibank, 45 F.Supp.2d 276 (S.D.N.Y.1999), affirmed 201 F.3d 134 (2nd Cir.2000), *345*

British Airways Board v. Laker Airways Ltd, [1984] 3 WLR 413, [1985] A.C. 58 (HL), *114*

Broughton v. Cigna Healthplans of California, 90 Cal.Rptr.2d 334, 988 P.2d 67 (Cal.1999), *396*

Brunette Mach. Works, Limited v. Kockum Industries, Inc., 406 U.S. 706, 92 S.Ct. 1936, 32 L.Ed.2d 428 (1972), *84*

Bryks v. Canadian Broadcasting Corp., 906 F.Supp. 204 (S.D.N.Y.1995), *145*

Bulova Watch Co., Inc. v. K. Hattori & Co., Ltd., 508 F.Supp. 1322 (E.D.N.Y.1981), *64*

Burger King Corp. v. Rudzewicz, 471 U.S. 462, 105 S.Ct. 2174, 85 L.Ed.2d 528 (1985), *41*

Burnham v. Superior Court of California, County of Marin, 495 U.S. 604, 110 S.Ct. 2105, 109 L.Ed.2d 631 (1990), *48*

Byrd v. Corporacion Forestal y Industrial de Olancho S.A., 182 F.3d 380 (5th Cir.1999), *127, 162*

C

Cabalceta v. Standard Fruit Co., 883 F.2d 1553 (11th Cir.1989), *74, 76*

Callejo v. Bancomer, S.A., 764 F.2d 1101 (5th Cir.1985), *173*

Calzaturificio Claudia v. Olivieri Footwear Ltd., 1998 WL 164824 (S.D.N.Y.1998), *231*

Cameco Industries, Inc. v. Mayatrac, S.A., 789 F.Supp. 200 (D.Md.1992), *52, 322*

Canada Malting Co. v. Paterson Steamships, 285 U.S. 413, 52 S.Ct. 413, 76 L.Ed. 837 (1932), *96*

Cannon Mfg. Co. v. Cudahy Packing Co., 267 U.S. 333, 45 S.Ct. 250, 69 L.Ed. 634 (1925), *62*

Cantieri Navali Riuniti v. M/V Skyptron, 802 F.2d 160 (5th Cir.1986), *259*

Capital Currency Exchange, N.V. v. National Westminster Bank PLC, 155 F.3d 603 (2nd Cir.1998), cert. denied 526 U.S. 1067, 119 S.Ct. 1459, 143 L.Ed.2d 545 (1999), *92*

Carbon Black Export, Inc. v. The Monrosa, 254 F.2d 297 (5th Cir.1958), cert. denied The Monrosa v. Carbon Black Export, Inc., 359 U.S. 180, 79 S.Ct. 710, 3 L.Ed.2d 723 (1959), *18*

Cardenas v. Solis, 570 So.2d 996 (Fla.App. 3 Dist.1990), review denied 581 So.2d 163 (Fla.1991), *324*

Carey v. Bahama Cruise Lines, 864 F.2d 201 (1st Cir.1988), *260*

Cargill, Inc. v. Hartford Acc. and Indem. Co., 531 F.Supp. 710 (D.Minn.1982), *112*

Cargill Intern. S.A. v. M/T Pavel Dybenko, 991 F.2d 1012 (2nd Cir.1993), *146*

Carl Marks & Co., Inc. v. Union of Soviet Socialist Republics, 841 F.2d 26 (2nd Cir.1988), cert. denied 487 U.S. 1219, 108 S.Ct. 2874, 101 L.Ed.2d 909 (1988), *153*

Carl Zeiss Stiftung v. V. E. B. Carl Zeiss, Jena, 293 F.Supp. 892 (S.D.N.Y.1968), modified 433 F.2d 686 (2nd Cir.1970), cert. denied V.E.B. Carl Zeiss Jena v. Carl Zeiss Stiftung, 403 U.S. 905, 91 S.Ct. 2205, 29 L.Ed.2d 680 (1971), *357*

Carnival Cruise Lines, Inc. v. Shute, 499 U.S. 585, 111 S.Ct. 1522, 113 L.Ed.2d 622 (1991), *23*

Carolina Power & Light Co. v. Uranex, 451 F.Supp. 1044 (N.D.Cal.1977), *327, 400*

Castillo v. Shipping Corp. of India, 606 F.Supp. 497 (S.D.N.Y. 1985), *151*

Central States, Southeast and Southwest Areas Pension Fund v. Reimer Express World Corp., 230 F.3d 934 (7th Cir.2000), cert. denied 532 U.S. 943, 121 S.Ct. 1406, 149 L.Ed.2d 348 (2001), *60*

Chase Manhattan Bank, N.A. v. Hoffman, 665 F.Supp. 73 (D.Mass.1987), *354*

Chicago Typographical Union No. 16 v. Chicago Sun–Times, Inc., 935 F.2d 1501 (7th Cir.1991), *421*

China Nat. Chemical Import & Export Corp. v. M/V Lago Hualaihue, 504 F.Supp. 684 (D.Md.1981), *151*

China Nat. Metal Products Import/Export Co. v. Apex Digital, Inc., 155 F.Supp.2d 1174 (C.D.Cal.2001), *327*

China Trade and Development Corp. v. M.V. Choong Yong, 837 F.2d 33 (2nd Cir.1987), *114*

Choi v. Kim, 50 F.3d 244 (3rd Cir.1995), *340*

Chromalloy Aeroservices v. Arab Republic of Egypt, 939 F.Supp. 907 (D.D.C.1996), *414*

Chuidian v. Philippine Nat. Bank, 912 F.2d 1095 (9th Cir.1990), *127*

Chukwu v. Air France, 218 F.Supp.2d 979 (N.D.Ill.2002), *136*

CIBC Mellon Trust Co. v. Mora Hotel Corp. N.V., 296 A.D.2d 81, 743 N.Y.S.2d 408 (N.Y.A.D. 1 Dept.2002), *349*

Cicippio v. Islamic Republic of Iran, 18 F.Supp.2d 62 (D.D.C. 1998), *159*

Circuit City Stores, Inc. v. Adams, 532 U.S. 105, 121 S.Ct. 1302, 149 L.Ed.2d 234 (2001), *395*

Circuit City Stores, Inc. v. Najd, 294 F.3d 1104 (9th Cir.2002), *389*

Clayco Petroleum Corp. v. Occidental Petroleum Corp., 712 F.2d 404 (9th Cir.1983), cert. denied 464 U.S. 1040, 104 S.Ct. 703, 79 L.Ed.2d 168 (1984), *171*

Cliffs–Neddrill Turnkey International–Oranjestad v. M/T Rich Duke, 734 F.Supp. 142 (D.Del.1990), *323*

Colorado River Water Conservation Dist. v. United States, 424 U.S. 800, 96 S.Ct. 1236, 47 L.Ed.2d 483 (1976), *107*

Commercial Ins. Co. of Newark, N. J. v. Pacific–Peru Const. Corp., 558 F.2d 948 (9th Cir.1977), *258*

Committee of United States Citizens Living in Nicaragua v. Reagan, 859 F.2d 929, 273 U.S.App.D.C. 266 (D.C.Cir.1988), *187, 209*

Commodity Futures Trading Com'n v. Nahas, 738 F.2d 487, 238 U.S.App.D.C. 93 (D.C.Cir.1984), *267*

Companía Mexicana De Aviacion, S.A. v. United States Dist. Court for Cent. Dist. of California, 859 F.2d 1354 (9th Cir. 1988), *122*

Compania Panemena Maritima v. J. E. Hurley Lbr. Co., 244 F.2d 286 (2nd Cir.1957), *402*

Competex, S.A. v. LaBow, 783 F.2d 333 (2nd Cir.1986), *361*

Complaint of (see name of party)

Contact Lumber Co. v. P.T. Moges Shipping Co. Ltd., 918 F.2d 1446 (9th Cir.1990), *92*

Container Corp. of America v. Franchise Tax Bd., 463 U.S. 159, 103 S.Ct. 2933, 77 L.Ed.2d 545 (1983), *191*

Continental Ore Co. v. Union Carbide & Carbon Corp., 370 U.S. 690, 82 S.Ct. 1404, 8 L.Ed.2d 777 (1962), *193*

Continental Service Life & Health Ins. Co. v. A.G. Edwards & Sons, Inc., 664 F.Supp. 997 (M.D.La.1987), *379*

Continental Time Corp. v. Swiss Credit Bank, 543 F.Supp. 408 (S.D.N.Y.1982), *109*

Cooper v. Ateliers de la Motobecane, S.A., 456 N.Y.S.2d 728, 442 N.E.2d 1239 (N.Y.1982), *400*

Cooper Industries, Inc. v. British Aerospace, Inc., 102 F.R.D. 918 (S.D.N.Y.1984), *282*

Core–Vent Corp. v. Nobel Industries AB, 11 F.3d 1482 (9th Cir.1993), *42*

Covington Industries, Inc. v. Resintex A. G., 629 F.2d 730 (2nd Cir.1980), *352*

Credit Agricole Indosuez v. Rossiyskiy Kredit Bank, 708 N.Y.S.2d 26, 729 N.E.2d 683 (N.Y.2000), *321*

Creighton Ltd. v. Government of State of Qatar, 181 F.3d 118, 337 U.S.App.D.C. 7 (D.C.Cir.1999), *121, 411*

Crosby v. National Foreign Trade Council, 530 U.S. 363, 120 S.Ct. 2288, 147 L.Ed.2d 352 (2000), *189*

Cryomedics, Inc. v. Spembly, Ltd., 397 F.Supp. 287 (D.Conn. 1975), *56*

CSR Ltd. v. Federal Ins. Co., 146 F.Supp.2d 556 (D.N.J.2001), *116*

CSR Ltd. v. Federal Ins. Co., 141 F.Supp.2d 484 (D.N.J.2001), *116*

CSR Ltd. v. Federal Ins. Co., 40 F.Supp.2d 559 (D.N.J.1998), *116*

Cunard S.S. Co. Ltd. v. Salen Reefer Services AB, 773 F.2d 452 (2nd Cir.1985), *340*

Cybersell, Inc. v. Cybersell, Inc., 130 F.3d 414 (9th Cir.1997), *53*

D

Dailey v. National Hockey League, 987 F.2d 172 (3rd Cir.1993), cert. denied 510 U.S. 816, 114 S.Ct. 67, 126 L.Ed.2d 36 (1993), *92*

Daliberti v. Republic of Iraq, 146 F.Supp.2d 19 (D.D.C.2001), *150*

Daliberti v. Republic of Iraq, 97 F.Supp.2d 38 (D.D.C.2000), *150*

Dames & Moore v. Regan, 453 U.S. 654, 101 S.Ct. 2972, 69 L.Ed.2d 918 (1981), *192*

Danjaq, S.A. v. Pathe Communications Corp., 979 F.2d 772 (9th Cir.1992), *76*

David L. Threlkeld & Co., Inc. v. Metallgesellschaft Ltd. (London), 923 F.2d 245 (2nd Cir.1991), cert. dismissed 501 U.S. 1267, 112 S.Ct. 17, 115 L.Ed.2d 1094 (1991), *378*

Davies v. Jobs & Adverts Online, GmbH, 94 F.Supp.2d 719 (E.D.Va.2000), *276*

Dayton v. Czechoslovak Socialist Republic, 834 F.2d 203, 266 U.S.App.D.C. 177 (D.C.Cir.1987), cert. denied 486 U.S. 1054, 108 S.Ct. 2820, 100 L.Ed.2d 921 (1988), *139*

Day & Zimmermann, Inc. v. Challoner, 423 U.S. 3, 96 S.Ct. 167, 46 L.Ed.2d 3 (1975), *214*

DeJames v. Magnificence Carriers, Inc., 654 F.2d 280 (3rd Cir. 1981), cert. denied 454 U.S. 1085, 102 S.Ct. 642, 70 L.Ed.2d 620 (1981), *56*

Delagi v. Volkswagenwerk A.G. of Wolfsburg, Germany, 328 N.Y.S.2d 653, 278 N.E.2d 895 (N.Y.1972), *67*

de la Mata v. American Life Ins. Co., 771 F.Supp. 1375 (D.Del. 1991), affirmed 961 F.2d 208 (3rd Cir.1992), *338*

De Letelier v. Republic of Chile, 748 F.2d 790 (2nd Cir.1984), cert. denied Morel De Letelier v. Republic of Chile, 471 U.S. 1125, 105 S.Ct. 2656, 86 L.Ed.2d 273 (1985), *157*

De Letelier v. Republic of Chile, 488 F.Supp. 665 (D.D.C.1980), *144*

Delta Foods Inc. v. Republic of Ghana, 265 F.3d 1068, 347 U.S.App.D.C. 336 (D.C.Cir.2001), *361*

de Pacanins v. Pacanins, 650 So.2d 1028 (Fla.App. 3 Dist.1995), *324*

Derby & Co Ltd v. Weldon (No.1), 1988 WL 622899 (CA 1988), *318*

DeRoburt v. Gannett Co., Inc., 733 F.2d 701 (9th Cir.1984), cert. denied Gannett Co., Inc. v. DeRoburt, 469 U.S. 1159, 105 S.Ct. 909, 83 L.Ed.2d 923 (1985), *173*

de Sanchez v. Banco Central De Nicaragua, 770 F.2d 1385 (5th Cir.1985), *138*

De Wit v. KLM Royal Dutch Airlines, N.V., 570 F.Supp. 613 (S.D.N.Y.1983), *75*

DiMercurio v. Sphere Drake Ins., PLC, 202 F.3d 71 (1st Cir. 2000), *376*

Doctor's Associates, Inc. v. Casarotto, 517 U.S. 681, 116 S.Ct. 1652, 134 L.Ed.2d 902 (1996), *375*

Dole Food Co. v. Patrickson, ___ U.S. ___, 123 S.Ct. 1655, ___ L.Ed.2d ___ (2003), *126*

Domingo, Estate of v. Republic of the Philippines, 694 F.Supp. 782 (W.D.Wash.1988), appeal dismissed Domingo, by Mast, Estate of, 895 F.2d 1416 (9th Cir.1990), *164*

Dow Chemical Co. v. Castro Alfaro, 786 S.W.2d 674 (Tex.1990), cert. denied Dow Chemical Co. v. Alfaro, 498 U.S. 1024, 111 S.Ct. 671, 112 L.Ed.2d 663 (1991), *105*

Dowling v. Richardson–Merrell, Inc., 727 F.2d 608 (6th Cir.1984), *101*

Dragon Capital Partners L.P. v. Merrill Lynch Capital Services Inc., 949 F.Supp. 1123 (S.D.N.Y.1997), *109*

Dresser Industries, Inc. v. Underwriters at Lloyd's of London, 106 F.3d 494 (3rd Cir.1997), *75*

Drexel Burnham Lambert Group Inc. v. Committee of Receivers for Galadari, 12 F.3d 317 (2nd Cir.1993), cert. denied 511 U.S. 1069, 114 S.Ct. 1644, 128 L.Ed.2d 365 (1994), *130*

Drexel Burnham Lambert Group Inc. v. Galadari, 777 F.2d 877 (2nd Cir.1985), *186*

Duffield v. Robertson Stephens & Co., 144 F.3d 1182 (9th Cir. 1998), cert. denied 525 U.S. 982, 119 S.Ct. 445, 142 L.Ed.2d 399 (1998), *396*

Dynamic Cassette Intern. Ltd. v. Mike Lopez & Associates, Inc., 923 F.Supp. 8 (E.D.N.Y.1996), *361*

E

Eckert Intern., Inc. v. Government of Fiji, 32 F.3d 77 (4th Cir.1994), *129*

E.E.O.C. v. Arabian American Oil Co., 499 U.S. 244, 111 S.Ct. 1227, 113 L.Ed.2d 274 (1991), *238*

E.E.O.C. v. Waffle House, Inc., 534 U.S. 279, 122 S.Ct. 754, 151 L.Ed.2d 755 (2002), *396*

Eisenfeld v. Islamic Republic of Iran, 172 F.Supp.2d 1 (D.D.C. 2000), *159*

El–Fadl v. Central Bank of Jordan, 75 F.3d 668, 316 U.S.App. D.C. 86 (D.C.Cir.1996), *127, 162*

El–Hadad v. United Arab Emirates, 216 F.3d 29, 342 U.S.App. D.C. 138 (D.C.Cir.2000), *145*

Eljer Mfg., Inc. v. Kowin Development Corp., 14 F.3d 1250 (7th Cir.1994), rehearing denied (1994), *408*

Employers Ins. of Wausau v. Banco De Seguros Del Estado, 199 F.3d 937 (7th Cir.1999), cert. denied El Banco de Seguros del Estado v. Employers Ins. of Wausau, 530 U.S. 1215, 120 S.Ct. 2218, 147 L.Ed.2d 251 (2000), *146*

Empresa Cubana Exportadora De Azucar y Sus Derivados v. Lamborn & Co., Inc., 652 F.2d 231 (2nd Cir.1981), *179*

Erie R. Co. v. Tompkins, 304 U.S. 64, 58 S.Ct. 817, 82 L.Ed. 1188 (1938), *8, 31*

Estate of (see name of party)

Euromepa, In re Application of, 51 F.3d 1095 (2nd Cir.1995), *302*

Europcar Italia, S.p.A. v. Maiellano Tours, Inc., 156 F.3d 310 (2nd Cir.1998), *413*

European Community v. RJR Nabisco, Inc., 186 F.Supp.2d 231 (E.D.N.Y.2002), *252*

Evergreen Marine Corp. v. Welgrow Intern. Inc., 954 F.Supp. 101 (S.D.N.Y.1997), *109*

Ex parte (see name of party)

Export Group v. Reef Industries, Inc., 54 F.3d 1466 (9th Cir. 1995), *129, 145*

F

Fagot Rodriguez v. Republic of Costa Rica, 297 F.3d 1 (1st Cir.2002), *140*

Fauntleroy v. Lum, 210 U.S. 230, 28 S.Ct. 641, 52 L.Ed. 1039 (1908), *331*

Faysound Ltd. v. United Coconut Chemicals, Inc., 878 F.2d 290 (9th Cir.1989), *75*

Feder v. Turkish Airlines, 441 F.Supp. 1273 (S.D.N.Y.1977), *52*

Feit & Drexler, Inc., In re, 760 F.2d 406 (2nd Cir.1985), *319*

Fendi S.r.l. v. Condotti Shops, Inc., 754 So.2d 755 (Fla.App. 3 Dist.2000), *22*

Ferdinand E. Marcos Human Rights Litigation, In re Estate of, 978 F.2d 493 (9th Cir.1992), cert. denied Marcos–Manotoc v.

Trajano, 508 U.S. 972, 113 S.Ct. 2960, 125 L.Ed.2d 661 (1993), *162, 196*

F. & H.R. Farman–Farmaian Consulting Engineers Firm v. Harza Engineering Co., 882 F.2d 281 (7th Cir.1989), *173*

Filanto, S.p.A. v. Chilewich Intern. Corp., 789 F.Supp. 1229 (S.D.N.Y.1992), appeal dismissed 984 F.2d 58 (2nd Cir.1993), *231, 327*

Filartiga v. Pena–Irala, 630 F.2d 876 (2nd Cir.1980), *196*

Filetech S.A.R.L. v. France Telecom, 978 F.Supp. 464 (S.D.N.Y. 1997), *185*

Filetech S.A.R.L. v. France Telecom, S.A., 212 F.Supp.2d 183 (S.D.N.Y.2001), affirmed 304 F.3d 180 (2nd Cir.2002), *185*

Fils et Cables d'Acier de Lens v. Midland Metals Corp., 584 F.Supp. 240 (S.D.N.Y.1984), *421*

Filus v. LOT Polish Airlines, 819 F.Supp. 232 (E.D.N.Y.1993), *266*

Fireman's Fund Ins. Co. v. Cho Yang Shipping Co., 131 F.3d 1336 (9th Cir.1997), cert. denied 525 U.S. 921, 119 S.Ct. 275, 142 L.Ed.2d 227 (1998), *29*

First Nat. Bank of Arizona v. British Petroleum Co., 324 F.Supp. 1348 (S.D.N.Y.1971), *259*

First Nat. Bank of Chicago, United States v., 699 F.2d 341 (7th Cir.1983), *293*

First Nat. City Bank v. Banco Nacional de Cuba, 406 U.S. 759, 92 S.Ct. 1808, 32 L.Ed.2d 466 (1972), *169*

First Nat. City Bank v. Banco Para El Comercio Exterior De Cuba, 462 U.S. 611, 103 S.Ct. 2591, 77 L.Ed.2d 46 (1983), *127*

First Nat. City Bank, United States v., 396 F.2d 897 (2nd Cir.1968), *293*

First Nat. City Bank, United States v., 379 U.S. 378, 85 S.Ct. 528, 13 L.Ed.2d 365 (1965), *319*

First Options of Chicago, Inc. v. Kaplan, 514 U.S. 938, 115 S.Ct. 1920, 131 L.Ed.2d 985 (1995), *375*

Flatow v. Islamic Republic of Iran, 999 F.Supp. 1 (D.D.C.1998), *149*

Florasynth, Inc. v. Pickholz, 750 F.2d 171 (2nd Cir.1984), *407*

Flores v. Southern Peru Copper Corp., 253 F.Supp.2d 510 (S.D.N.Y.2002), *200*

Foley Bros. v. Filardo, 336 U.S. 281, 69 S.Ct. 575, 93 L.Ed. 680 (1949), *237*

Foremost–McKesson, Inc. v. Islamic Republic of Iran, 905 F.2d 438, 284 U.S.App.D.C. 333 (D.C.Cir.1990), *130*

Forsythe v. Saudi Arabian Airlines Corp., 885 F.2d 285 (5th Cir.1989), *93, 161*

Franchise Tax Bd. of State of Cal. v. Construction Laborers Vacation Trust for Southern California, 463 U.S. 1, 103 S.Ct. 2841, 77 L.Ed.2d 420 (1983), *78*

Frolova v. Union of Soviet Socialist Republics, 761 F.2d 370 (7th Cir.1985), *142*

Frummer v. Hilton Hotels Intern., Inc., 60 Misc.2d 840, 304 N.Y.S.2d 335 (N.Y.Sup.1969), *260*

Frummer v. Hilton Hotels Intern., Inc., 281 N.Y.S.2d 41, 227 N.E.2d 851 (N.Y.1967), cert. denied Hilton Hotels (U K) Limited v. Frummer, 389 U.S. 923, 88 S.Ct. 241, 19 L.Ed.2d 266 (1967), *66*

F. T. C. v. Compagnie De Saint–Gobain–Pont-a–Mousson, 636 F.2d 1300, 205 U.S.App.D.C. 172 (D.C.Cir.1980), *267*

G

Galu v. Swiss Air Transport Co., Ltd., 873 F.2d 650 (2nd Cir. 1989), *172*

Garb v. Republic of Poland, 207 F.Supp.2d 16 (E.D.N.Y.2002), *153*

Garpeg Ltd. v. United States, 588 F.Supp. 1237 (S.D.N.Y.1984), *284*

Garpeg, Ltd. v. United States, 588 F.Supp. 1240 (S.D.N.Y.1984), *284*

Garpeg, Ltd. v. United States, 583 F.Supp. 789 (S.D.N.Y.1984), *284*

Gasperini v. Center for Humanities, Inc., 518 U.S. 415, 116 S.Ct. 2211, 135 L.Ed.2d 659 (1996), *230*

Gateway Technologies, Inc. v. MCI Telecommunications Corp., 64 F.3d 993 (5th Cir.1995), *421*

Gau Shan Co., Ltd. v. Bankers Trust Co., 956 F.2d 1349 (6th Cir.1992), appeal dismissed 966 F.2d 1452 (6th Cir.1992), *114*

Gelfand v. Tanner Motor Tours, Limited, 385 F.2d 116 (2nd Cir.1967), cert. denied Tanner Motor Tours, Limited v. Gelfand, 390 U.S. 996, 88 S.Ct. 1198, 20 L.Ed.2d 95 (1968), *67*

General Atomic Co. v. Exxon Nuclear Co., Inc., 90 F.R.D. 290 (S.D.Cal.1981), *294*

Gerling Global Reinsurance Corp. of America v. Low, 240 F.3d 739 (9th Cir.2001), *190*

Gianoli Aldunate, Application of, 3 F.3d 54 (2nd Cir.1993), cert. denied Foden v. Gianoli Aldunate, 510 U.S. 965, 114 S.Ct. 443, 126 L.Ed.2d 376 (1993), *304*

Gilmer v. Interstate/Johnson Lane Corp., 500 U.S. 20, 111 S.Ct. 1647, 114 L.Ed.2d 26 (1991), *393*

Glencore Grain Rotterdam B.V. v. Shivnath Rai Harnarain Co., 284 F.3d 1114 (9th Cir.2002), *420*

Gondre v. Silberstein, 744 F.Supp. 429 (E.D.N.Y.1990), *346*

Good Hope Chemical Corp., In re, 747 F.2d 806 (1st Cir.1984), cert. denied Good Hope Chemical Corporation Creditors' Committee v. Koerver & Lersch, 471 U.S. 1102, 105 S.Ct. 2328, 85 L.Ed.2d 845 (1985), *361*

Goodman Holdings v. Rafidain Bank, 26 F.3d 1143, 307 U.S.App. D.C. 79 (D.C.Cir.1994), cert. denied 513 U.S. 1079, 115 S.Ct. 728, 130 L.Ed.2d 632 (1995), *137*

Gould v. P.T. Krakatau Steel, 957 F.2d 573 (8th Cir.1992), cert. denied 506 U.S. 908, 113 S.Ct. 304, 121 L.Ed.2d 227 (1992), *51*

Government of India v. Cargill, Inc., 867 F.2d 130 (2nd Cir. 1989), *408*

Go–Video, Inc. v. Akai Elec. Co., Ltd., 885 F.2d 1406 (9th Cir.1989), *57, 84*

Grand Jury Subpoenas Duces Tecum Addressed to Canadian Intern. Paper Co., In re, 72 F.Supp. 1013 (S.D.N.Y.1947), *287*

Great Lakes Dredge & Dock Co. v. Harnischfeger Corp., 1990 WL 147066 (N.D.Ill.1990), *312*

Greenpeace, Inc. (U.S.A.) v. State of France, 946 F.Supp. 773 (C.D.Cal.1996), *138*

Green Tree Financial Corp.–Alabama v. Randolph, 531 U.S. 79, 121 S.Ct. 513, 148 L.Ed.2d 373 (2000), *393*

Grupo Mexicano de Desarrollo S.A. v. Alliance Bond Fund, Inc., 527 U.S. 308, 119 S.Ct. 1961, 144 L.Ed.2d 319 (1999), *320*

Grupo Protexa, S.A. v. All American Marine Slip, a Div. of Marine Office of America Corp., 20 F.3d 1224 (3rd Cir.1994), cert. denied 513 U.S. 986, 115 S.Ct. 481, 130 L.Ed.2d 395 (1994), *171*

Guinness PLC v. Ward, 955 F.2d 875 (4th Cir.1992), *358*

Gulf Oil Corp. v. Gilbert, 330 U.S. 501, 67 S.Ct. 839, 91 L.Ed. 1055 (1947), *96*

H

Haag v. Barnes, 216 N.Y.S.2d 65, 175 N.E.2d 441 (N.Y.1961), *223*

Haitian Refugee Center, Inc. v. Gracey, 600 F.Supp. 1396 (D.D.C. 1985), affirmed 809 F.2d 794, 257 U.S.App.D.C. 367 (D.C.Cir. 1987), *232, 249*

Haiti v. Duvalier (Mareva Injunction) (No.2), 1988 WL 624198 (CA 1988), *318*

Hanson v. Denckla, 357 U.S. 235, 78 S.Ct. 1228, 2 L.Ed.2d 1283 (1958), *40*

Hargrave v. Fibreboard Corp., 710 F.2d 1154 (5th Cir.1983), *63*

Harris v. Polskie Linie Lotnicze, 820 F.2d 1000 (9th Cir.1987), *224*

Harris v. VAO Intourist, Moscow, 481 F.Supp. 1056 (E.D.N.Y. 1979), *142*

Harrison v. Wyeth Laboratories, 510 F.Supp. 1 (E.D.Pa.1980), affirmed 676 F.2d 685 (3rd Cir.1982), *102*

Hartford Fire Ins. Co. v. California, 509 U.S. 764, 113 S.Ct. 2891, 125 L.Ed.2d 612 (1993), *246*

Haven v. Rzeczpospolita Polska, 215 F.3d 727 (7th Cir.2000), cert. denied Haven v. Republic of Poland, 531 U.S. 1014, 121 S.Ct. 573, 148 L.Ed.2d 490 (2000), *130*

Helicopteros Nacionales de Colombia, S.A. v. Hall, 466 U.S. 408, 104 S.Ct. 1868, 80 L.Ed.2d 404 (1984), *38*

Hercules Inc. v. Dynamic Export Corp., 71 F.R.D. 101 (S.D.N.Y. 1976), *75*

Her Majesty the Queen v. Gilbertson, 597 F.2d 1161 (9th Cir. 1979), *252, 353*

Heuft Systemtechnik,GmbH v. Videojet Systems Intern., Inc., 1993 WL 147506 (N.D.Ill.1993), *109*

Higgins v. The Islamic Republic of Iran, 2000 WL 33674311 (D.D.C.2000), *159*

Hilton v. Guyot, 159 U.S. 113, 16 S.Ct. 139, 40 L.Ed. 95 (1895), *184, 333*

Home Ins. Co. v. Dick, 281 U.S. 397, 50 S.Ct. 338, 74 L.Ed. 926 (1930), *236*

Honduras Aircraft Registry, Ltd. v. Government of Honduras, 129 F.3d 543 (11th Cir.1997), cert. denied Government of Honduras v. Honduras Aircraft Registry, 524 U.S. 952, 118 S.Ct. 2368, 141 L.Ed.2d 736 (1998), *176*

Howe v. Goldcorp Investments, Ltd., 946 F.2d 944 (1st Cir.1991), cert. denied 502 U.S. 1095, 112 S.Ct. 1172, 117 L.Ed.2d 418 (1992), *91*

Hudson v. Hermann Pfauter GmbH & Co., 117 F.R.D. 33 (N.D.N.Y.1987), *312*

Hugel v. Corporation of Lloyd's, 999 F.2d 206 (7th Cir.1993), *16*

Hunt v. BP Exploration Co. (Libya) Ltd., 492 F.Supp. 885 (N.D.Tex.1980), *344*

Hunt v. Coastal States Gas Producing Co., 583 S.W.2d 322 (Tex.1979), cert. denied 444 U.S. 992, 100 S.Ct. 523, 62 L.Ed.2d 421 (1979), *182*

Huntington v. Attrill, 146 U.S. 657, 13 S.Ct. 224, 36 L.Ed. 1123 (1892), *253*

Hwang Geum Joo v. Japan, 172 F.Supp.2d 52 (D.D.C.2001), *131, 187*

I

IIT, an Intern. Inv. Trust v. Cornfeld, 619 F.2d 909 (2nd Cir. 1980), *244*

Ikospentakis v. Thalassic S.S. Agency, 915 F.2d 176 (5th Cir. 1990), *92*

Illinois v. City of Milwaukee, Wis., 406 U.S. 91, 92 S.Ct. 1385, 31 L.Ed.2d 712 (1972), *78*

Industrial Inv. Development Corp. v. Mitsui & Co., Ltd., 671 F.2d 876 (5th Cir.1982), vacated on other grounds Mitsui & Co., Ltd. v. Industrial Investment Development Corporation, 460 U.S. 1007, 103 S.Ct. 1244, 75 L.Ed.2d 475 (1983), *92, 243*

Industrial Risk Insurers v. M.A.N. Gutehoffnungshutte GmbH, 141 F.3d 1434 (11th Cir.1998), cert. denied Nitram, Inc. v. M.A.N. Gutehoffnungshutte GmbH, 525 U.S. 1068, 119 S.Ct. 797, 142 L.Ed.2d 659 (1999), *372*

Ingersoll Mill. Mach. Co. v. Granger, 833 F.2d 680 (7th Cir.1987), *346*

In re (see name of party)

Instituto Per Lo Sviluppo Economico Dell' Italia Meridionale v. Sperti Products, Inc., 323 F.Supp. 630 (S.D.N.Y.1971), *258*

Instrumentation Associates, Inc. v. Madsen Electronics (Canada) Ltd., 859 F.2d 4 (3rd Cir.1988), *33*

Insurance Corp. of Ireland, Ltd. v. Compagnie des Bauxites de Guinee, 456 U.S. 694, 102 S.Ct. 2099, 72 L.Ed.2d 492 (1982), *40, 47, 285*

Interamerican Refining Corp. v. Texaco Maracaibo, Inc., 307 F.Supp. 1291 (D.Del.1970), *193*

Interamerican Trade Corp. v. Companhia Fabricadora De Pecas, 973 F.2d 487 (6th Cir.1992), *25*

Interbras Cayman Co. v. Orient Victory Shipping Co., S.A., 663 F.2d 4 (2nd Cir.1981), *378*

Intercontinental Dictionary Series v. De Gruyter, 822 F.Supp. 662 (C.D.Cal.1993), *139*

International Ass'n of Machinists and Aerospace Workers, (IAM) v. Organization of Petroleum Exporting Countries (OPEC), 649 F.2d 1354 (9th Cir.1981), cert. denied 454 U.S. 1163, 102 S.Ct. 1036, 71 L.Ed.2d 319 (1982), *170*

International Ass'n of Machinists and Aerospace Workers (IAM) v. Organization of Petroleum Exporting Countries (OPEC), 477 F.Supp. 553 (C.D.Cal.1979), affirmed 649 F.2d 1354 (9th Cir.1981), cert. denied 454 U.S. 1163, 102 S.Ct. 1036, 71 L.Ed.2d 319 (1982), *134*

International Shoe Co. v. State of Wash., Office of Unemployment Compensation and Placement, 326 U.S. 310, 66 S.Ct. 154, 90 L.Ed. 95 (1945), *40*

International Standard Elec. Corp. v. Bridas Sociedad Anonima Petrolera, Indus. Y Comercial, 745 F.Supp. 172 (S.D.N.Y. 1990), *420*

International Technologies Consultants, Inc. v. Euroglas S.A., 107 F.3d 386 (6th Cir.1997), *30*

Interocean Shipping Co. v. National Shipping & Trading Corp., 462 F.2d 673 (2nd Cir.1972), *378*

Interpool Ltd. v. Char Yigh Marine (Panama) S.A., 890 F.2d 1453 (9th Cir.1989), amended 918 F.2d 1476 (9th Cir.1990), *259*

Inter–Regional Financial Group, Inc. v. Hashemi, 562 F.2d 152 (2nd Cir.1977), cert. denied Hashemi v. Inter–Regional Financial Group, Inc., 434 U.S. 1046, 98 S.Ct. 892, 54 L.Ed.2d 798 (1978), *321*

Iran Aircraft Industries v. Avco Corp., 980 F.2d 141 (2nd Cir. 1992), *416*

Islamic Republic of Iran v. Boeing Co., 771 F.2d 1279 (9th Cir.1985), cert. dismissed 479 U.S. 957, 107 S.Ct. 450, 93 L.Ed.2d 397 (1986), *232*

Islamic Republic of Iran v. Pahlavi, 478 N.Y.S.2d 597, 467 N.E.2d 245 (N.Y.1984), cert. denied 469 U.S. 1108, 105 S.Ct. 783, 83 L.Ed.2d 778 (1985), *164*

I. T. A. D. Associates, Inc. v. Podar Bros., 636 F.2d 75 (4th Cir.1981), *326, 379*

Iwanowa v. Ford Motor Co., 67 F.Supp.2d 424 (D.N.J.1999), *187*

J

Japan Halon Co., Ltd. v. Great Lakes Chemical Corp., 155 F.R.D. 626 (N.D.Ind.1993), *282*

Japan Line, Ltd. v. Los Angeles County, 441 U.S. 434, 99 S.Ct. 1813, 60 L.Ed.2d 336 (1979), *190*

Javino, United States v., 960 F.2d 1137 (2nd Cir.1992), *246*

Jenco v. Islamic Republic of Iran, 154 F.Supp.2d 27 (D.D.C. 2001), affirmed Bettis v. Islamic Republic of Iran, 315 F.3d 325, 354 U.S.App.D.C. 244 (D.C.Cir.2003), *159*

Jensen v. Lane County, 222 F.3d 570 (9th Cir.2000), *201*

John Deere Ltd. v. Sperry Corp., 754 F.2d 132 (3rd Cir.1985), *303*

John Doe I v. Unocal Corp., 2002 WL 31063976 (9th Cir.2002), *199*

Joseph v. Office of Consulate General of Nigeria, 830 F.2d 1018 (9th Cir.1987), cert. denied Consulate General of Nigeria v. Joseph, 485 U.S. 905, 108 S.Ct. 1077, 99 L.Ed.2d 236 (1988), *145*

Jungquist v. Sheikh Sultan Bin Khalifa Al Nahyan, 115 F.3d 1020, 325 U.S.App.D.C. 117 (D.C.Cir.1997), *127, 162*

J. Zeevi and Sons, Ltd. v. Grindlays Bank (Uganda) Limited, 371 N.Y.S.2d 892, 333 N.E.2d 168 (N.Y.1975), cert. denied Grindlay's Bank Limited v. J. Zeevi & Sons, Ltd., 423 U.S. 866, 96 S.Ct. 126, 46 L.Ed.2d 95 (1975), *254*

K

Kadic v. Karadzic, 70 F.3d 232 (2nd Cir.1995), cert. denied Karadzic v. Kadic, 518 U.S. 1005, 116 S.Ct. 2524, 135 L.Ed.2d 1048 (1996), *124, 188, 196*

Kaepa, Inc. v. Achilles Corp., 76 F.3d 624 (5th Cir.1996), cert. denied Achilles Corp. v. Kaepa, Inc., 519 U.S. 821, 117 S.Ct. 77, 136 L.Ed.2d 36 (1996), *115*

Kahn Lucas Lancaster, Inc. v. Lark Intern. Ltd., 186 F.3d 210 (2nd Cir.1999), *375*

Kalamazoo Spice Extraction Co. v. Provisional Military Government of Socialist Ethiopia, 729 F.2d 422 (6th Cir.1984), *180*

Kelly v. Syria Shell Petroleum Development B.V., 213 F.3d 841 (5th Cir.2000), cert. denied Kelly v. Al Furat Petroleum Co., 531 U.S. 979, 121 S.Ct. 426, 148 L.Ed.2d 435 (2000), *126*

K & H Business Consultants Ltd. v. Cheltonian, Ltd., 567 F.Supp. 420 (D.N.J.1983), *75*

Kim Crest, S.A. v. M.V. Sverdlovsk, 753 F.Supp. 642 (S.D.Tex. 1990), *151*

Klaxon Co. v. Stentor Electric Mfg. Co., 313 U.S. 487, 61 S.Ct. 1020, 85 L.Ed. 1477 (1941), *9, 123, 214*

Klinghoffer v. S.N.C. Achille Lauro, 937 F.2d 44 (2nd Cir.1991), *124, 197*

Knowlton v. Allied Van Lines, Inc., 900 F.2d 1196 (8th Cir.1990), *45*

Koster v. (American) Lumbermens Mut.Cas. Co., 330 U.S. 518, 67 S.Ct. 828, 91 L.Ed. 1067 (1947), *96*

Koster v. Automark Industries, Inc., 640 F.2d 77 (7th Cir.1981), *340*

Kramer v. Smith Barney, 80 F.3d 1080 (5th Cir.1996), rehearing denied (1996), *393*

Kreimerman v. Casa Veerkamp, S.A. de C.V., 22 F.3d 634 (5th Cir.1994), cert. denied Casa Veerkamp, S.A. de C.V. v. Kreimerman, 513 U.S. 1016, 115 S.Ct. 577, 130 L.Ed.2d 492 (1994), *277*

L

Lafontant v. Aristide, 844 F.Supp. 128 (E.D.N.Y.1994), *163, 196*

Laker Airways Ltd. v. Pan American World Airways, 607 F.Supp. 324 (S.D.N.Y.1985), *284*

Laker Airways Ltd. v. Pan American World Airways, 568 F.Supp. 811 (D.D.C.1983), affirmed Laker Airways Ltd. v. Sabena, Belgian World Airlines, 731 F.2d 909, 235 U.S.App.D.C. 207 (D.C.Cir.1984), *92*

Laker Airways Ltd. v. Sabena, Belgian World Airlines, 731 F.2d 909, 235 U.S.App.D.C. 207 (D.C.Cir.1984), *106, 242*

Lamb v. Phillip Morris, Inc., 915 F.2d 1024 (6th Cir.1990), cert. denied 498 U.S. 1086, 111 S.Ct. 961, 112 L.Ed.2d 1048 (1991), *167*

Laminoirs–Trefileries–Cableries de Lens, S. A. v. Southwire Co., 484 F.Supp. 1063 (N.D.Ga.1980), *419*

Lander Co., Inc. v. MMP Investments, Inc., 107 F.3d 476 (7th Cir.1997), cert. denied MMP Investments, Inc. v. Lander Co., Inc., 522 U.S. 811, 118 S.Ct. 55, 139 L.Ed.2d 19 (1997), *372*

Landgraf v. United StatesI Film Products, 511 U.S. 244, 114 S.Ct. 1483, 128 L.Ed.2d 229 (1994), *153*

Lapine Technology Corp. v. Kyocera Corp., 130 F.3d 884 (9th Cir.1997), *421*

Laufer v. Westminster Brokers, Ltd., 532 A.2d 130 (D.C.1987), *329*

Lauritzen v. Larsen, 345 U.S. 571, 73 S.Ct. 921, 97 L.Ed. 1254 (1953), *238*

Lawford v. New York Life Ins. Co., 739 F.Supp. 906 (S.D.N.Y. 1990), *92*

Leasco Data Processing Equipment Corp. v. Maxwell, 468 F.2d 1326 (2nd Cir.1972), *244, 285*

Ledee v. Ceramiche Ragno, 684 F.2d 184 (1st Cir.1982), *375*

Lenchyshyn v. Pelko Elec., Inc., 281 A.D.2d 42, 723 N.Y.S.2d 285 (N.Y.A.D. 4 Dept.2001), *330*

Letter Rogatory From First Court of First Instance in Civil Matters, Caracas, Venezuela, In re, 42 F.3d 308 (5th Cir. 1995), *304*

Letters of Request From Supreme Court of Hong Kong, In re, 821 F.Supp. 204 (S.D.N.Y.1993), *303*

Libra Bank Ltd. v. Banco Nacional de Costa Rica, S. A., 676 F.2d 47 (2nd Cir.1982), *154*

Linear Products, Inc. v. Marotech, Inc., 189 F.Supp.2d 461 (W.D.Va.2002), *109*

Liu v. Republic of China, 892 F.2d 1419 (9th Cir.1989), cert, dismissed Republic of China v. Liu, 497 U.S. 1058, 111 S.Ct. 27, 111 L.Ed.2d 840 (1990), *123, 224*

Lord Day & Lord v. Socialist Republic of Vietnam, 134 F.Supp.2d 549 (S.D.N.Y.2001), *152*

Louring v. Kuwait Boulder Shipping Co., 455 F.Supp. 630 (D.Conn.1977), *52*

M

Ma v. Continental Bank N.A., 905 F.2d 1073 (7th Cir.1990), cert. denied Ma v. Continental Illinois Nat. Bank and Trust Co., 498 U.S. 967, 111 S.Ct. 430, 112 L.Ed.2d 414 (1990), *340*

MacArthur Area Citizens Ass'n v. Republic of Peru, 809 F.2d 918, 258 U.S.App.D.C. 77 (D.C.Cir.1987), vacated in part on other grounds 823 F.2d 606, 262 U.S.App.D.C. 198 (D.C.Cir. 1987), *140*

Macedo v. Boeing Co., 693 F.2d 683 (7th Cir.1982), *102*

Made in the USA Foundation v. United States, 242 F.3d 1300 (11th Cir.2001), cert. denied United Steelworkers of America, AFL–CIO, CLC v. United States, 534 U.S. 1039, 122 S.Ct. 613, 151 L.Ed.2d 536 (2001), *187*

Magness v. Russian Federation, 247 F.3d 609 (5th Cir.2001), cert. denied 534 U.S. 892, 122 S.Ct. 209, 151 L.Ed.2d 149 (2001), *125*

Magnolia Petroleum Co. v. Hunt, 320 U.S. 430, 64 S.Ct. 208, 88 L.Ed. 149 (1943), *331*

Malev Hungarian Airlines, Application of v. United Technologies Intern. Inc., 964 F.2d 97 (2nd Cir.1992), cert. denied United Technologies Intern., Inc., P & W Commercial Engine Business v. Malev Hungarian Airlines, 506 U.S. 861, 113 S.Ct. 179, 121 L.Ed.2d 125 (1992), *303*

Mannington Mills, Inc. v. Congoleum Corp., 595 F.2d 1287 (3rd Cir.1979), *171, 242*

Marc Rich & Co. A.G., In re, 739 F.2d 834 (2nd Cir.1984), *298*

Marc Rich & Co., A.G., In re, 736 F.2d 864 (2nd Cir.1984), *298*

Marc Rich & Co., A.G., Matter of, 707 F.2d 663 (2nd Cir.1983), cert. denied Marc Rich & Co., A.G. v. United States, 463 U.S. 1215, 103 S.Ct. 3555, 77 L.Ed.2d 1400 (1983), *285, 297*

Mareva Compania Naviera SA v. International Bulk Carriers SA (The Mareva), 1980 WL 149429 (CA 1975), *317*

Mar–Len of Louisiana, Inc. v. Parsons–Gilbane, 773 F.2d 633 (5th Cir.1985), *384*

Marriott v. Sedco Forex Intern. Resources, Ltd., 827 F.Supp. 59 (D.Mass.1993), *230*

Marsh v. Burrell, 805 F.Supp. 1493 (N.D.Cal.1992), *230*

Mastrobuono v. Shearson Lehman Hutton, Inc., 514 U.S. 52, 115 S.Ct. 1212, 131 L.Ed.2d 76 (1995), *375*

Matsushita Elec. Indus. Co., Ltd. v. Zenith Radio Corp., 475 U.S. 574, 106 S.Ct. 1348, 89 L.Ed.2d 538 (1986), cert. denied Zenith Radio Corp. v. Matsushita Elec. Indus. Co., Ltd., 481 U.S. 1029, 107 S.Ct. 1955, 95 L.Ed.2d 527 (1987), *240*

Matter of (see name of party)

Matusevitch v. Telnikoff., 159 F.3d 636, 333 U.S.App.D.C. 46 (D.C.Cir.1998), *348*

Maxwell Communication Corp. plc v. Societe Generale, 93 F.3d 1036 (2nd Cir.1996), *325*

McCord v. Jet Spray Intern. Corp., 874 F.Supp. 436 (D.Mass. 1994), *347*

McCreary Tire & Rubber Co. v. CEAT S. p. A., 501 F.2d 1032 (3rd Cir.1974), *326, 400*

McCulloch v. Sociedad Nacional de Marineros de Honduras, 372 U.S. 10, 83 S.Ct. 671, 9 L.Ed.2d 547 (1963), *237*

McDonnell Douglas Corp. v. Islamic Republic of Iran, 758 F.2d 341 (8th Cir.1985), cert. denied Islamic Republic of Iran v. McDonnell Douglas Corporation, 474 U.S. 948, 106 S.Ct. 347, 88 L.Ed.2d 294 (1985), *24*

McGee v. International Life Ins. Co., 355 U.S. 220, 78 S.Ct. 199, 2 L.Ed.2d 223 (1957), *40*

McGlinchy v. Shell Chemical Co., 845 F.2d 802 (9th Cir.1988), *242*

McKesson Corp. v. Islamic Republic of Iran, 185 F.R.D. 70 (D.D.C.1999), *314*

McKesson Corp. v. Islamic Republic of Iran, 138 F.R.D. 1 (D.D.C. 1991), reconsidered in part 1991 WL 178105 (D.D.C.1991), *299*

Meadows Indem. Co. Ltd. v. Baccala & Shoop Ins. Services, Inc., 760 F.Supp. 1036 (E.D.N.Y.1991), *391*

Mehinovic v. Vuckovic, 198 F.Supp.2d 1322 (N.D.Ga.2002), *206*

Melia v. Les Grands Chais de France, 135 F.R.D. 28 (D.R.I.1991), *275*

Mercier v. Sheraton Intern., Inc., 981 F.2d 1345 (1st Cir.1992), cert. denied 508 U.S. 912, 113 S.Ct. 2346, 124 L.Ed.2d 255 (1993), *30, 93*

Mesquite Lake Associates v. Lurgi Corp., 754 F.Supp. 161 (N.D.Cal.1991), *383*

Metropolitan World Tanker, Corp. v. P. N. Pertambangan, 427 F.Supp. 2 (S.D.N.Y.1975), *327*

Michaels v. Mariforum Shipping, S. A., 624 F.2d 411 (2nd Cir. 1980), *402*

Midland Bank Plc v. Laker Airways Ltd, 1985 WL 311095 (CA 1985), *114*

Milanovich v. Costa Crociere, S.p.A., 954 F.2d 763, 293 U.S.App. D.C. 332 (D.C.Cir.1992), *221*

Milhoux v. Linder, 902 P.2d 856 (Colo.App.1995), cert. denied (1995), *348*

Milliken v. Meyer, 311 U.S. 457, 61 S.Ct. 339, 85 L.Ed. 278 (1940), *44*

Ministry of Defense of Islamic Republic of Iran v. Gould Inc., 887 F.2d 1357 (9th Cir.1989), cert. denied Gould Inc. v. Ministry of Defense of Islamic Republic of Iran, 494 U.S. 1016, 110 S.Ct. 1319, 108 L.Ed.2d 494 (1990), *411*

Mitsubishi Motors Corp. v. Soler Chrysler–Plymouth, Inc., 473 U.S. 614, 105 S.Ct. 3346, 87 L.Ed.2d 444 (1985), *386*

Mobil Oil Indonesia Inc. v. Asamera Oil (Indonesia) Ltd., 56 A.D.2d 339, 392 N.Y.S.2d 614 (N.Y.A.D. 1 Dept.1977), *401*

MOL, Inc. v. Peoples Republic of Bangladesh, 736 F.2d 1326 (9th Cir.1984), cert. denied 469 U.S. 1037, 105 S.Ct. 513, 83 L.Ed.2d 403 (1984), *133*

Moore v. Mitchell, 30 F.2d 600 (2nd Cir.1929), affirmed on other grounds 281 U.S. 18, 50 S.Ct. 175, 74 L.Ed. 673 (1930), *251*

Moses H. Cone Memorial Hosp. v. Mercury Const. Corp., 460 U.S. 1, 103 S.Ct. 927, 74 L.Ed.2d 765 (1983), *107, 373*

M/S Bremen v. Zapata Off–Shore Co., 407 U.S. 1, 92 S.Ct. 1907, 32 L.Ed.2d 513 (1972), *19*

Mullane v. Central Hanover Bank & Trust Co., 339 U.S. 306, 70 S.Ct. 652, 94 L.Ed. 865 (1950), *331*

N

Nadd v. Le Credit Lyonnais, S.A., 804 So.2d 1226 (Fla.2001), *357*

Nahar v. Nahar, 656 So.2d 225 (Fla.App. 3 Dist.1995), review denied 664 So.2d 249 (Fla.1995), *324*

National Bank of Canada v. Interbank Card Ass'n, 666 F.2d 6 (2nd Cir.1981), *242*

National Broadcasting Co., Inc. v. Bear Stearns & Co., Inc., 165 F.3d 184 (2nd Cir.1999), *301*

National City Bank of New York v. Republic of China, 348 U.S. 356, 75 S.Ct. 423, 99 L.Ed. 389 (1955), *153*

National Equipment Rental, Limited v. Szukhent, 375 U.S. 311, 84 S.Ct. 411, 11 L.Ed.2d 354 (1964), *18*

Neuchatel Swiss General Ins. Co. v. Lufthansa Airlines, 925 F.2d 1193 (9th Cir.1991), *108*

Nippon Emo–Trans Co., Ltd. v. Emo–Trans, Inc., 744 F.Supp. 1215 (E.D.N.Y.1990), *341*

Nordin v. Nutri/System, Inc., 897 F.2d 339 (8th Cir.1990), *383*

Noriega, United States v., 117 F.3d 1206 (11th Cir.1997), cert. denied Noriega v. United States, 523 U.S. 1060, 118 S.Ct. 1389, 140 L.Ed.2d 648 (1998), *163*

Noriega, United States v., 746 F.Supp. 1506 (S.D.Fla.1990), *173*

Northrop Corp. v. Triad Intern. Marketing S.A., 811 F.2d 1265 (9th Cir.1987), cert. denied 484 U.S. 914, 108 S.Ct. 261, 98 L.Ed.2d 219 (1987), *419*

Nute v. Hamilton Mut. Ins. Co., 72 Mass. 174 (Mass.1856), *18*

O

Occidental of Umm al Qaywayn, Inc. v. A Certain Cargo of Petroleum 577 F.2d 1196 (5th Cir.1978), cert. denied Occidental of Umm al Qaywayn, Inc. v. Cities Service Oil Co., 442 U.S. 928, 99 S.Ct. 2857, 61 L.Ed.2d 296 (1979), *187*

Oceanic Transport Corp. of Monrovia v. Alcoa S. S. Co., 129 F.Supp. 160 (S.D.N.Y.1954), *398*

O'Connell Machinery Co., Inc. v. M.V. Americana, 734 F.2d 115 (2nd Cir.1984), cert. denied 469 U.S. 1086, 105 S.Ct. 591, 83 L.Ed.2d 701 (1984), *154*

Oetjen v. Central Leather Co., 246 U.S. 297, 38 S.Ct. 309, 62 L.Ed. 726 (1918), *169*

Oil Spill by Amoco Cadiz Off Coast of France on March 16, 1978, In re, 491 F.Supp. 161 (N.D.Ill.1979), *152*

Oil Spill by Amoco Cadiz Off Coast of France on March 16, 1978, Matter of, 954 F.2d 1279 (7th Cir.1992), rehearing denied (1992), *259, 360*

Olsen by Sheldon v. Government of Mexico, 729 F.2d 641 (9th Cir.1984), cert. denied United Mexican States v. Olsen by Sheldon, 469 U.S. 917, 105 S.Ct. 295, 83 L.Ed.2d 230 (1984), *142*

OMI Holdings, Inc. v. Royal Ins. Co. of Canada, 149 F.3d 1086 (10th Cir.1998), *43*

Omni Capital Intern., Ltd. v. Rudolf Wolff & Co., Ltd., 484 U.S. 97, 108 S.Ct. 404, 98 L.Ed.2d 415 (1987), *37*

Omron Healthcare, Inc. v. Maclaren Exports Ltd., 28 F.3d 600 (7th Cir.1994), *29*

O.N.E. Shipping Ltd. v. Flota Mercante Grancolombiana, S.A., 830 F.2d 449 (2nd Cir.1987), cert. denied 488 U.S. 923, 109 S.Ct. 303, 102 L.Ed.2d 322 (1988), *193*

Overseas Inns S.A. P.A. v. United States, 911 F.2d 1146 (5th Cir.1990), rehearing denied (1990), *349*

P

Pancotto v. Sociedade de Safaris de Mocambique, S.A.R.L., 422 F.Supp. 405 (N.D.Ill.1976), *230*

Parada Jimenez v. Mobil Oil Co. de Venezuela, S.A., 1991 WL 64186 (S.D.N.Y.1991), *330*

Parsons & Whittemore Overseas Co., Inc. v. Societe Generale De L'Industrie Du Papier (RAKTA), 508 F.2d 969 (2nd Cir.1974), *416*

Pere v. Nuovo Pignone, Inc., 150 F.3d 477 (5th Cir.1998), cert. denied Pere v. Nuovo Pignone S.p.A., 525 U.S. 1141, 119 S.Ct. 1033, 143 L.Ed.2d 42 (1999), *126*

Perez v. Alcoa Fujikura, Ltd., 969 F.Supp. 991 (W.D.Tex.1997), *230*

Perkins v. Benguet Consol. Min. Co., 342 U.S. 437, 72 S.Ct. 413, 96 L.Ed. 485 (1952), *46*

Perrier Bottled Water Litigation, In re, 138 F.R.D. 348 (D.Conn. 1991), *312*

Perry v. Thomas, 482 U.S. 483, 107 S.Ct. 2520, 96 L.Ed.2d 426 (1987), *375*

Persinger v. Islamic Republic of Iran, 729 F.2d 835, 234 U.S.App. D.C. 349 (D.C.Cir.1984), cert. denied 469 U.S. 881, 105 S.Ct. 247, 83 L.Ed.2d 185 (1984), *142*

Pfizer, Inc. v. Government of India, 434 U.S. 308, 98 S.Ct. 584, 54 L.Ed.2d 563 (1978), *68*

Phaneuf v. Republic of Indonesia, 106 F.3d 302 (9th Cir.1997), *129*

Philadelphia Gear Corp. v. Philadelphia Gear de Mexico, S.A., 44 F.3d 187 (3rd Cir.1994), *325*

Phillips Petroleum Co. v. Marathon Oil Co., 794 F.2d 1080 (5th Cir.1986), *382*

Phillips Petroleum Co. v. Shutts, 472 U.S. 797, 105 S.Ct. 2965, 86 L.Ed.2d 628 (1985), *236*

Pilkington Bros. P.L.C. v. AFG Industries Inc., 581 F.Supp. 1039 (D.Del.1984), *323*

Pinker v. Roche Holdings Ltd., 292 F.3d 361 (3rd Cir.2002), *59*

Piper Aircraft Co. v. Reyno, 454 U.S. 235, 102 S.Ct. 252, 70 L.Ed.2d 419 (1981), *98*

Pizzabiocche v. Vinelli, 772 F.Supp. 1245 (M.D.Fla.1991), *277*

PMS Distributing Co., Inc. v. Huber & Suhner, A.G., 863 F.2d 639 (9th Cir.1988), *326*

Pollux Marine Agencies, Inc. v. Louis Dreyfus Corp., 455 F.Supp. 211 (S.D.N.Y.1978), *383*

Posner v. Essex Ins. Co., Ltd., 178 F.3d 1209 (11th Cir.1999), *108*

Pravin Banker Associates, Ltd. v. Banco Popular del Peru, 9 F.Supp.2d 300 (S.D.N.Y.1998), *158*

Pravin Banker Associates, Ltd. v. Banco Popular Del Peru, 109 F.3d 850 (2nd Cir.1997), *184*

Price v. Socialist People's Libyan Arab Jamahiriya, 294 F.3d 82, 352 U.S.App.D.C. 284 (D.C.Cir.2002), *149*

Prima Paint Corp. v. Flood & Conklin Mfg. Co., 388 U.S. 395, 87 S.Ct. 1801, 18 L.Ed.2d 1270 (1967), *376*

Princz v. Federal Republic of Germany, 26 F.3d 1166, 307 U.S.App.D.C. 102 (D.C.Cir.1994), cert. denied 513 U.S. 1121, 115 S.Ct. 923, 130 L.Ed.2d 803 (1995), *131*

Psimenos v. E.F. Hutton & Co., Inc., 722 F.2d 1041 (2nd Cir. 1983), *243*

Pure Fishing, Inc. v. Silver Star Co., Ltd., 202 F.Supp.2d 905 (N.D.Iowa 2002), *330, 340*

Pyrenee, Ltd. v. Wocom Commodities, Ltd., 984 F.Supp. 1148 (N.D.Ill.1997), *61*

Q

Quackenbush v. Allstate Ins. Co., 517 U.S. 706, 116 S.Ct. 1712, 135 L.Ed.2d 1 (1996), *108*

R

Reagan, United States v., 453 F.2d 165 (6th Cir.1971), cert. denied Reagan v. United States, 406 U.S. 946, 92 S.Ct. 2049, 32 L.Ed.2d 334 (1972), *279*

Red Bull Associates v. Best Western Intern., Inc., 686 F.Supp. 447 (S.D.N.Y.1988), affirmed 862 F.2d 963 (2nd Cir.1988), *27*

Reebok Intern., Ltd. v. Marnatech Enterprises, Inc., 970 F.2d 552 (9th Cir.1992), *319*

Reinsurance Co. of America, Inc. v. Administratia Asigurarilor de Stat, 902 F.2d 1275 (7th Cir.1990), *299*

Renner v. Lanard Toys Ltd., 33 F.3d 277 (3rd Cir.1994), *42*

Republic of Argentina v. Weltover, Inc., 504 U.S. 607, 112 S.Ct. 2160, 119 L.Ed.2d 394 (1992), *121, 133*

Republic of Iraq v. First Nat. City Bank, 353 F.2d 47 (2nd Cir.1965), cert. denied 382 U.S. 1027, 86 S.Ct. 648, 15 L.Ed.2d 540 (1966), *172*

Republic of Kazakhstan v. Biedermann Intern., 168 F.3d 880 (5th Cir.1999), *301*

Republic of Mexico v. Hoffman, 324 U.S. 30, 65 S.Ct. 530, 89 L.Ed. 729 (1945), *119*

Republic of Nicaragua v. Standard Fruit Co., 937 F.2d 469 (9th Cir.1991), cert. denied 503 U.S. 919, 112 S.Ct. 1294, 117 L.Ed.2d 516 (1992), *377*

Republic of Peru, Ex parte, 318 U.S. 578, 63 S.Ct. 793, 87 L.Ed. 1014 (1943), *119*

Republic of the Philippines v. Marcos, 806 F.2d 344 (2nd Cir. 1986), cert. denied New York Land Co. v. Republic of Philippines, 481 U.S. 1048, 107 S.Ct. 2178, 95 L.Ed.2d 835 (1987), *165*

Republic of the Philippines v. Westinghouse Elec. Corp., 43 F.3d 65 (3rd Cir.1994), *183*

Republic of the Philippines v. Westinghouse Elec. Corp., 821 F.Supp. 292 (D.N.J.1993), reversed on other grounds 43 F.3d 65 (3rd Cir.1994), *252*

Republic of the Philippines v. Marcos, 888 F.2d 954 (2nd Cir. 1989), *292*

Republic of the Philippines v. Marcos, 862 F.2d 1355 (9th Cir. 1988), cert. denied Marcos v. Republic of Philippines, 490 U.S. 1035, 109 S.Ct. 1933, 104 L.Ed.2d 404 (1989), *163, 169, 174, 318*

Revell v. Lidov, 317 F.3d 467 (5th Cir.2002), *54*

Rhodes v. J.P. Sauer & Sohn, Inc., 98 F.Supp.2d 746 (W.D.La. 2000), *277*

Rhone Mediterranee Compagnia Francese Di Assicurazioni E Riassicurazoni v. Lauro, 712 F.2d 50 (3rd Cir.1983), *380*

Ricaud v. American Metal Co., 246 U.S. 304, 38 S.Ct. 312, 62 L.Ed. 733 (1918), *169*

Richards v. Lloyd's of London, 135 F.3d 1289 (9th Cir.1998), cert. denied 525 U.S. 943, 119 S.Ct. 365, 142 L.Ed.2d 301 (1998), *29, 223*

Richmark Corp. v. Timber Falling Consultants, 959 F.2d 1468 (9th Cir.1992), cert. denied Timber Falling Consultants, Inc. v. China Everbright Trading Co., 506 U.S. 948, 113 S.Ct. 454, 121 L.Ed.2d 325 (1992), *294*

Riggs Nat. Corp. & Subsidiaries v. Commissioner, 163 F.3d 1363, 333 U.S.App.D.C. 371 (D.C.Cir.1999), *170*

Riley v. Kingsley Underwriting Agencies, Ltd., 969 F.2d 953 (10th Cir.1992), cert. denied 506 U.S. 1021, 113 S.Ct. 658, 121 L.Ed.2d 584 (1992), *19, 386*

Rio Grande Transport, Inc., Complaint of, 516 F.Supp. 1155 (S.D.N.Y.1981), *137*

Rio Tinto Zinc Corp. v. Westinghouse Elec. Corp., [1978] AC 547, [1978] 1 All E.R. 434, *290, 308*

Risk v. Halvorsen, 936 F.2d 393 (9th Cir.1991), cert. denied Risk v. Kingdom of Norway, 502 U.S. 1035, 112 S.Ct. 880, 116 L.Ed.2d 784 (1992), *144*

Rivendell Forest Products, Ltd. v. Canadian Pacific Ltd., 2 F.3d 990 (10th Cir.1993), *98*

Robert v. Bell Helicopter Textron, Inc., 2002 WL 1268030 (N.D.Tex.2002), *203*

Roby v. Corporation of Lloyd's, 996 F.2d 1353 (2nd Cir.1993), cert. denied 510 U.S. 945, 114 S.Ct. 385, 126 L.Ed.2d 333 (1993), *27, 394*

Rockwell Intern. Systems, Inc. v. Citibank, N.A., 719 F.2d 583 (2nd Cir.1983), *24*

Rodriguez v. Fullerton Tires Corp., 115 F.3d 81 (1st Cir.1997), *42*

Rodriguez de Quijas v. Shearson/American Exp., Inc., 490 U.S. 477, 109 S.Ct. 1917, 104 L.Ed.2d 526 (1989), *392*

Romero v. International Terminal Operating Co., 358 U.S. 354, 79 S.Ct. 468, 3 L.Ed.2d 368 (1959), *239*

Roorda v. Volkswagenwerk, A. G., 481 F.Supp. 868 (D.S.C.1979), *63*

Rosenberg v. Merrill Lynch, Pierce, Fenner & Smith, Inc., 170 F.3d 1 (1st Cir.1999), *395*

Rosenberg Bros. & Co. v. Curtis Brown Co., 260 U.S. 516, 43 S.Ct. 170, 67 L.Ed. 372 (1923), *46*

Royal Bank of Canada v. Trentham Corp., 665 F.2d 515 (5th Cir.1981), *351*

Royal Bed and Spring Co., Inc. v. Famossul Industria e Comercio de Moveis Ltda., 906 F.2d 45 (1st Cir.1990), *30, 93*

Ruff v. St. Paul Mercury Ins. Co., 393 F.2d 500 (2nd Cir.1968), *258*

S

Saadeh v. Farouki, 107 F.3d 52, 323 U.S.App.D.C. 239 (D.C.Cir. 1997), *76*

S.A. Empresa de Viacao Aerea Rio Grandense (Varig Airlines), United States v., 467 U.S. 797, 104 S.Ct. 2755, 81 L.Ed.2d 660 (1984), *143*

Sale v. Haitian Centers Council, Inc., 509 U.S. 155, 113 S.Ct. 2549, 125 L.Ed.2d 128 (1993), *238*

Saltany v. Reagan, 702 F.Supp. 319 (D.D.C.1988), *163*

Sampson v. Federal Republic of Germany, 250 F.3d 1145 (7th Cir.2001), *131*

Santos v. Compagnie Nationale Air France, 934 F.2d 890 (7th Cir.1991), *137*

Sarei v. Rio Tinto PLC., 221 F.Supp.2d 1116 (C.D.Cal.2002), *201*

Saudi Arabia v. Nelson, 507 U.S. 349, 113 S.Ct. 1471, 123 L.Ed.2d 47 (1993), *134*

Sauer–Getriebe KG v. White Hydraulics, Inc., 715 F.2d 348 (7th Cir.1983), cert. denied White Hydraulics, Inc. v. Sauer–Getriebe, KG, 464 U.S. 1070, 104 S.Ct. 976, 79 L.Ed.2d 214 (1984), *327, 376*

Sawtelle v. Waddell & Reed, Inc., 754 N.Y.S.2d 264 (N.Y.A.D. 1 Dept.2003), *408*

S.C. Chimexim S.A. v. Velco Enterprises Ltd., 36 F.Supp.2d 206 (S.D.N.Y.1999), *344*

Scherk v. Alberto–Culver Co., 417 U.S. 506, 94 S.Ct. 2449, 41 L.Ed.2d 270 (1974), *373*

Scophony Corp. of America, United States v., 333 U.S. 795, 68 S.Ct. 855, 92 L.Ed. 1091 (1948), *63*

Scott v. Borg Warner Protective Services, 2003 WL 23315 (9th Cir.2003), *396*

S & Davis Intern., Inc. v. The Republic of Yemen, 218 F.3d 1292 (11th Cir.2000), *147*

Sealed Case, In re, 832 F.2d 1268, 266 U.S.App.D.C. 30 (D.C.Cir. 1987), *283*

Sealed Case, In re, 825 F.2d 494, 263 U.S.App.D.C. 357 (D.C.Cir. 1987), cert. denied Roe v. United States, 484 U.S. 963, 108 S.Ct. 451, 98 L.Ed.2d 391 (1987), *284*

Seattle Totems Hockey Club, Inc. v. National Hockey League, 652 F.2d 852 (9th Cir.1981), cert. denied Northwest Sports Enterprises, Ltd. v. Seattle Totems Hockey Club, Inc., 457 U.S. 1105, 102 S.Ct. 2902, 73 L.Ed.2d 1313 (1982), *113*

S.E.C. v. Banca Della Svizzera Italiana, 92 F.R.D. 111 (S.D.N.Y. 1981), *297*

S.E.C. v. Briggs, 234 F.Supp. 618 (N.D.Ohio 1964), *268*

S.E.C. v. International Swiss Investments Corp., 895 F.2d 1272 (9th Cir.1990), *319*

S.E.C. v. Tome, 833 F.2d 1086 (2nd Cir.1987), *266*

Securities Industry Ass'n v. Connolly, 883 F.2d 1114 (1st Cir. 1989), cert. denied Connolly v. Securities Industry Ass'n, 495 U.S. 956, 110 S.Ct. 2559, 109 L.Ed.2d 742 (1990), *388*

Sedco, Inc., Matter of, 543 F.Supp. 561 (S.D.Tex.1982), vacated in part on other grounds Sedco, Inc., Complaint of, 610 F.Supp. 306 (S.D.Tex.1984), *141*

Seetransport Wiking Trader v. Navimpex Centrala Navala, 989 F.2d 572 (2nd Cir.1993), *146*

Sequihua v. Texaco, Inc., 847 F.Supp. 61 (S.D.Tex.1994), *78, 185*

767 Third Ave. Associates v. Consulate General of Socialist Federal Republic of Yugoslavia, 218 F.3d 152 (2nd Cir.2000), *187*

Shaffer v. Heitner, 433 U.S. 186, 97 S.Ct. 2569, 53 L.Ed.2d 683 (1977), *51, 329*

Shapiro v. Republic of Bolivia, 930 F.2d 1013 (2nd Cir.1991), *130*

Sharon v. Time, Inc., 599 F.Supp. 538 (S.D.N.Y.1984), *174*

Shearson/American Exp., Inc. v. McMahon, 482 U.S. 220, 107 S.Ct. 2332, 96 L.Ed.2d 185 (1987), *393*

Sheets v. Yamaha Motors Corp., U.S.A., 891 F.2d 533 (5th Cir.1990), *276*

Shen v. Leo A. Daly Co., 222 F.3d 472 (8th Cir.2000), rehearing denied (2002), *358*

Sibaja v. Dow Chemical Co., 757 F.2d 1215 (11th Cir.1985), cert. denied 474 U.S. 948, 106 S.Ct. 347, 88 L.Ed.2d 294 (1985), *104*

Siderman de Blake v. Republic of Argentina, 965 F.2d 699 (9th Cir.1992), cert. denied Republic of Argentina v. Siderman de Blake, 507 U.S. 1017, 113 S.Ct. 1812, 123 L.Ed.2d 444 (1993), *138*

Siemer v. Learjet Acquisition Corp., 966 F.2d 179 (5th Cir.1992), cert. denied 506 U.S. 1080, 113 S.Ct. 1047, 122 L.Ed.2d 356 (1993), *45*

Simula, Inc. v. Autoliv, Inc., 175 F.3d 716 (9th Cir.1999), *327, 386*

Singh v. Daimler–Benz AG, 9 F.3d 303 (3rd Cir.1993), *75*

Slater v. Mexican Nat. R. Co., 194 U.S. 120, 24 S.Ct. 581, 48 L.Ed. 900 (1904), *254*

Smith v. Socialist People's Libyan Arab Jamahiriya, 101 F.3d 239 (2nd Cir.1996), *132*

Smith/Enron Cogeneration Ltd. Partnership, Inc. v. Smith Cogeneration Intern., Inc., 198 F.3d 88 (2nd Cir.1999), cert. denied Smith Cogeneration Intern., Inc. v. Smith/Enron Cogeneration Ltd. Partnership, Inc., 531 U.S. 815, 121 S.Ct. 51, 148 L.Ed.2d 20 (2000), *372*

Smith Kline & French Laboratories Ltd v. Bloch, 1982 WL 222260 (CA 1982), *112*

Smith, Valentino & Smith, Inc. v. Superior Court, 131 Cal.Rptr. 374, 551 P.2d 1206 (Cal.1976), *20*

Societe Internationale Pour Participations Industrielles Et Commerciales, S. A. v. Rogers, 357 U.S. 197, 78 S.Ct. 1087, 2 L.Ed.2d 1255 (1958), *291*

Societe Nationale Industrielle Aerospatiale v. United States Dist. Court for Southern Dist. of Iowa, 482 U.S. 522, 107 S.Ct. 2542, 96 L.Ed.2d 461 (1987), *311*

Society of Lloyd's v. Ashenden, 233 F.3d 473 (7th Cir.2000), rehearing denied (2000), *345*

Somportex Limited v. Philadelphia Chewing Gum Corp., 453 F.2d 435 (3rd Cir.1971), cert. denied Philadelphia Chewing Gum Corp. v. Somportex Limited, 405 U.S. 1017, 92 S.Ct. 1294, 31 L.Ed.2d 479 (1972), *352*

Somportex Limited v. Philadelphia Chewing Gum Corp., 318 F.Supp. 161 (E.D.Pa.1970), affirmed 453 F.2d 435 (3rd Cir. 1971), cert. denied Philadelphia Chewing Gum Corp. v. Somportex Limited, 405 U.S. 1017, 92 S.Ct. 1294, 31 L.Ed.2d 479 (1972), *9, 352*

South Carolina Insurance Co v. Assurantie Maatschappij De Zeven Provincien NV, 1986 WL 407667 (HL 1986), *304*

Southern Intern. Sales Co., Inc. v. Potter & Brumfield, 410 F.Supp. 1339 (S.D.N.Y.1976), *222*

South Ionian Shipping Co., Ltd. v. Hugo Neu & Sons Intern. Sales Corp., 545 F.Supp. 323 (S.D.N.Y.1982), *349*

Southland Corp. v. Keating, 465 U.S. 1, 104 S.Ct. 852, 79 L.Ed.2d 1 (1984), *373*

Southwest Livestock and Trucking Co., Inc. v. Ramon, 169 F.3d 317 (5th Cir.1999), *333*

Sphere Drake Ins. Ltd. v. All American Ins. Co., 256 F.3d 587 (7th Cir.2001), *379*

Spradlin v. Lear Siegler Management Services Co., Inc., 926 F.2d 865 (9th Cir.1991), *19*

Sprague & Rhodes Commodity Corp. v. Instituto Mexicano Del Cafe, 566 F.2d 861 (2nd Cir.1977), *343*

S & R Co. of Kingston v. Latona Trucking, Inc., 159 F.3d 80 (2nd Cir.1998), cert. dismissed 528 U.S. 1058, 120 S.Ct. 629, 145 L.Ed.2d 506 (1999), *376*

S & S Machinery Co. v. Masinexportimport, 706 F.2d 411 (2nd Cir.1983), cert. denied 464 U.S. 850, 104 S.Ct. 161, 78 L.Ed.2d 147 (1983), *155*

Stanton v. Paine Webber Jackson & Curtis, Inc., 685 F.Supp. 1241 (S.D.Fla.1988), *399*

Stewart Organization, Inc. v. Ricoh Corp., 487 U.S. 22, 108 S.Ct. 2239, 101 L.Ed.2d 22 (1988), *30*

Straub v. A P Green, Inc., 38 F.3d 448 (9th Cir.1994), *125*

Strawbridge v. Curtiss, 7 U.S. 267, 2 L.Ed. 435 (1806), *74*

Sugarman v. Aeromexico, Inc., 626 F.2d 270 (3rd Cir.1980), *135*

Sun v. Taiwan, 201 F.3d 1105 (9th Cir.2000), cert. denied Taiwan v. Sun, 531 U.S. 979, 121 S.Ct. 427, 148 L.Ed.2d 435 (2000), *135*

Sutherland v. Islamic Republic of Iran, 151 F.Supp.2d 27 (D.D.C. 2001), *159*

Swiss American Bank, Ltd., United States v., 191 F.3d 30 (1st Cir.1999), *60*

Swiss American Bank, Ltd., United States v., 274 F.3d 610 (1st Cir.2001), *57*

T

Tachiona v. Mugabe, 234 F.Supp.2d 401 (S.D.N.Y.2002), *202*

Tachiona v. Mugabe, 216 F.Supp.2d 262 (S.D.N.Y.2002), *164, 199, 203*

Tachiona v. Mugabe, 169 F.Supp.2d 259 (S.D.N.Y.2001), *164*

Teledyne, Inc. v. Kone Corp., 892 F.2d 1404 (9th Cir.1989), *377*

Tel–Oren v. Libyan Arab Republic, 726 F.2d 774, 233 U.S.App. D.C. 384 (D.C.Cir.1984), cert. denied 470 U.S. 1003, 105 S.Ct. 1354, 84 L.Ed.2d 377 (1985), *197*

Texas Trading & Mill. Corp. v. Federal Republic of Nigeria, 647 F.2d 300 (2nd Cir.1981), cert. denied Federal Republic of Nigeria v. Texas Trading & Milling Corp., 454 U.S. 1148, 102 S.Ct. 1012, 71 L.Ed.2d 301 (1982), *132*

The Antelope, 23 U.S. 66, 6 L.Ed. 268 (1825), *251*

The Paquete Habana, 175 U.S. 677, 20 S.Ct. 290, 44 L.Ed. 320 (1900), *208*
The Schooner Exchange v. McFaddon, 11 U.S. 116, 3 L.Ed. 287 (1812), *118*
Thomas v. General Motors Corp., 522 U.S. 222, 118 S.Ct. 657, 139 L.Ed.2d 580 (1998), *331*
Thorsteinsson v. M/V Drangur, 891 F.2d 1547 (11th Cir.1990), *340*
Ticketmaster–New York, Inc. v. Alioto, 26 F.3d 201 (1st Cir. 1994), *43*
Timberlane Lumber Co. v. Bank of America, N.T. and S.A., 549 F.2d 597 (9th Cir.1976), *171, 240*
Topf v. Warnaco, Inc., 942 F.Supp. 762 (D.Conn.1996), *395*
Toronto–Dominion Bank v. Hall, 367 F.Supp. 1009 (E.D.Ark. 1973), *348*
Torres v. Southern Peru Copper Corp., 965 F.Supp. 899 (S.D.Tex.1996), *79*
Torres v. Southern Peru Copper Corp., 965 F.Supp. 895 (S.D.Tex.1995), *79*
Tramontana v. S. A. Empresa De Viacao Aerea Rio Grandense, 350 F.2d 468, 121 U.S.App.D.C. 338 (D.C.Cir.1965), cert. denied Tramontana v. Varig Airlines, 383 U.S. 943, 86 S.Ct. 1195, 16 L.Ed.2d 206 (1966), *230*
Transunion Corp. v. PepsiCo, Inc., 811 F.2d 127 (2nd Cir.1987), *92*
Transure, Inc. v. Marsh and McLennan, Inc., 766 F.2d 1297 (9th Cir.1985), *75*
Triad Financial Establishment v. Tumpane Co., 611 F.Supp. 157 (N.D.N.Y.1985), *222*
Turner Entertainment Co. v. Degeto Film GmbH, 25 F.3d 1512 (11th Cir.1994), *109*
Twohy v. First Nat. Bank of Chicago, 758 F.2d 1185 (7th Cir.1985), *260*

U

Umbenhauer v. Woog, 969 F.2d 25 (3rd Cir.1992), *264*
Underhill v. Hernandez, 168 U.S. 250, 18 S.Ct. 83, 42 L.Ed. 456 (1897), *168*
Union Carbide Corp. Gas Plant Disaster at Bhopal, India, In re, 809 F.2d 195 (2nd Cir.1987), cert. denied Union of India v.

Union Carbide Corp., 484 U.S. 871, 108 S.Ct. 199, 98 L.Ed.2d 150 (1987), *103*

Union Carbide Corp. Gas Plant Disaster at Bhopal, India, In re, 634 F.Supp. 842 (S.D.N.Y.1986), *94*

United Elec., Radio and Mach. Workers of America v. 163 Pleasant Street Corp., 960 F.2d 1080 (1st Cir.1992), *62*

United Nuclear Corp. v. General Atomic Co., 96 N.M. 155, 629 P.2d 231 (N.M.1980), *191*

United Paperworkers Intern. Union, AFL–CIO v. Misco, Inc., 484 U.S. 29, 108 S.Ct. 364, 98 L.Ed.2d 286 (1987), *418*

United States v. ______ (see opposing party)

United World Trade, Inc. v. Mangyshlakneft Oil Production Ass'n, 33 F.3d 1232 (10th Cir.1994), cert. denied 513 U.S. 1112, 115 S.Ct. 904, 130 L.Ed.2d 787 (1995), *137*

Upton v. Empire of Iran, 459 F.Supp. 264 (D.D.C.1978), affirmed 607 F.2d 494, 197 U.S.App.D.C. 180 (D.C.Cir.1979), *142*

Uranium Antitrust Litigation, In re, 480 F.Supp. 1138 (N.D.Ill. 1979), *279*

V

Vagenas v. Continental Gin Co., 988 F.2d 104 (11th Cir.1993), cert. denied Allied Products Corp. v. Vagenas, 510 U.S. 947, 114 S.Ct. 389, 126 L.Ed.2d 337 (1993), *332*

Van Cauwenberghe v. Biard, 486 U.S. 517, 108 S.Ct. 1945, 100 L.Ed.2d 517 (1988), *97*

Van Dusen v. Barrack, 376 U.S. 612, 84 S.Ct. 805, 11 L.Ed.2d 945 (1964), *90*

Vencedora Oceanica Navigacion, S.A. v. Compagnie Nationale Algerienne De Navigation (C.N.A.N.), 730 F.2d 195 (5th Cir. 1984), *136*

Verdugo–Urquidez, United States v., 494 U.S. 259, 110 S.Ct. 1056, 108 L.Ed.2d 222 (1990), *248*

Verlinden B.V. v. Central Bank of Nigeria, 461 U.S. 480, 103 S.Ct. 1962, 76 L.Ed.2d 81 (1983), *74, 161*

Verlinden B.V. v. Central Bank of Nigeria, 488 F.Supp. 1284 (S.D.N.Y.1980), affirmed 647 F.2d 320 (2nd Cir.1981), reversed on other grounds 461 U.S. 480, 103 S.Ct. 1962, 76 L.Ed.2d 81 (1983), *130*

Vermeulen v. Renault, U.S.A., Inc., 985 F.2d 1534 (11th Cir. 1993), cert. denied Regie Nationale Des Usines Renault S.A.

v. Vermeulen, 508 U.S. 907, 113 S.Ct. 2334, 124 L.Ed.2d 246 (1993), *64*

Vetco Inc., United States v., 691 F.2d 1281 (9th Cir.1981), cert. denied Vetco, Inc. v. United States, 454 U.S. 1098, 102 S.Ct. 671, 70 L.Ed.2d 639 (1981), *283*

Victory Transport Inc. v. Comisaria General de Abastecimientos y Transportes, 336 F.2d 354 (2nd Cir.1964), cert. denied Comisaria General de Abastecimientos y Transportes v. Victory Transport Inc, 381 U.S. 934, 85 S.Ct. 1763, 14 L.Ed.2d 698 (1965), *120*

Victrix S.S. Co., S.A. v. Salen Dry Cargo A.B., 825 F.2d 709 (2nd Cir.1987), *419*

Victrix S.S. Co., S.A. v. Salen Dry Cargo A.B., 65 B.R. 466 (S.D.N.Y.1986), affirmed 825 F.2d 709 (2nd Cir.1987), *329*

Vimar Seguros y Reaseguros, S.A. v. M/V Sky Reefer, 515 U.S. 528, 115 S.Ct. 2322, 132 L.Ed.2d 462 (1995), *393*

Virtual Defense and Development Intern., Inc. v. Republic of Moldova, 133 F.Supp.2d 1 (D.D.C.1999), *175*

Vishipco Line v. Chase Manhattan Bank, N.A., 660 F.2d 854 (2nd Cir.1981), cert. denied Chase Manhattan Bank, N.A. v. Vishipco Line, 459 U.S. 976, 103 S.Ct. 313, 74 L.Ed.2d 291 (1982), *173, 260*

Vitamins Antitrust Litigation, In re, 120 F.Supp.2d 45 (D.D.C. 2000), *312*

Volkswagenwerk Aktiengesellschaft v. Beech Aircraft Corp., 751 F.2d 117 (2nd Cir.1984), *62*

Volkswagenwerk Aktiengesellschaft v. Schlunk, 486 U.S. 694, 108 S.Ct. 2104, 100 L.Ed.2d 722 (1988), *275*

Volt Information Sciences, Inc. v. Board of Trustees of Leland Stanford Junior University, 489 U.S. 468, 109 S.Ct. 1248, 103 L.Ed.2d 488 (1989), *373*

W

Wagner v. Islamic Republic of Iran, 172 F.Supp.2d 128 (D.D.C. 2001), *159*

Waterside Ocean Nav. Co., Inc. v. International Nav. Ltd., 737 F.2d 150 (2nd Cir.1984), *419*

Weidner Communications, Inc. v. H.R.H. Prince Bandar Al Faisal, 859 F.2d 1302 (7th Cir.1988), *21*

Weinstein v. Islamic Republic of Iran, 184 F.Supp.2d 13 (D.D.C. 2002), *159*

West v. Multibanco Comermex, S.A., 807 F.2d 820 (9th Cir.1987), cert. denied 482 U.S. 906, 107 S.Ct. 2483, 96 L.Ed.2d 375 (1987), *182*

Whirlpool Financial Corp. v. Sevaux, 96 F.3d 216 (7th Cir.1996), *258*

White v. Paulsen, 997 F.Supp. 1380 (E.D.Wash.1998), *209*

Wilko v. Swan, 346 U.S. 427, 74 S.Ct. 182, 98 L.Ed. 168 (1953), *392*

Wiwa v. Royal Dutch Petroleum Co., 226 F.3d 88 (2nd Cir.2000), cert. denied Royal Dutch Petroleum Co. v. Wiwa, 532 U.S. 941, 121 S.Ct. 1402, 149 L.Ed.2d 345 (2001), *67, 97, 203*

Wolf v. Federal Republic of Germany, 95 F.3d 536 (7th Cir.1996), cert. denied 520 U.S. 1106, 117 S.Ct. 1112, 137 L.Ed.2d 313 (1997), *141*

World Wide Minerals Ltd. v. Republic of Kazakhstan, 116 F.Supp.2d 98 (D.D.C.2000), affirmed in part 296 F.3d 1154, 353 U.S.App.D.C. 147 (D.C.Cir.2002), cert. denied ___ U.S. ___, 123 S.Ct. 1250, 154 L.Ed.2d 1019 (2003), *121*

World–Wide Volkswagen Corp. v. Woodson, 444 U.S. 286, 100 S.Ct. 559, 62 L.Ed.2d 490 (1980), *41*

W.S. Kirkpatrick & Co., Inc. v. Environmental Tectonics Corp., Intern., 493 U.S. 400, 110 S.Ct. 701, 107 L.Ed.2d 816 (1990), *174*

Y

Yahoo!, Inc. v. La Ligue Contre Le Racisme et L'Antisemitisme, 169 F.Supp.2d 1181 (N.D.Cal.2001), *54, 348*

Young v. New Haven Advocate, 315 F.3d 256 (4th Cir.2002), *53*

Z

Zappia Middle East Const. Co. Ltd. v. Emirate of Abu Dhabi, 215 F.3d 247 (2nd Cir.2000), *139*

Zicherman v. Korean Air Lines Co., Ltd., 516 U.S. 217, 116 S.Ct. 629, 133 L.Ed.2d 596 (1996), *226*

Zipfel v. Halliburton Co., 832 F.2d 1477 (9th Cir.1987), cert. denied Halliburton Co. v. Zipfel, 486 U.S. 1054, 108 S.Ct. 2819, 100 L.Ed.2d 921 (1988), *92*

Zippo Mfg. Co. v. Zippo Dot Com, Inc., 952 F.Supp. 1119 (W.D.Pa.1997), *54*

Zoelsch v. Arthur Andersen & Co., 824 F.2d 27, 262 U.S.App. D.C. 300 (D.C.Cir.1987), *244*

Zschernig v. Miller, 389 U.S. 429, 88 S.Ct. 664, 19 L.Ed.2d 683 (1968), *10, 189*

*

TRANSNATIONAL LITIGATION

IN A NUTSHELL

*

INTRODUCTION

As transactions increasingly entail cross-border elements, so too does the litigation that those transactions tend to generate. Although virtually all litigation arising out of international transactions takes place in one national court or another (if not in an international arbitral venue), that litigation is unlikely to proceed in exactly the same fashion as litigation over purely domestic disputes proceeds in that forum. Hence, this book and the law school courses for which it is designed.

This book employs the term "transnational litigation" to denote the materials covered, primarily to avoid confusion with the resolution of "international" disputes between States or between a State and an international organization. To that extent, "private" rather than "public" international law disputes are this book's principal subject.

The reader will soon discover that, while there is obviously both a federal and an international dimension to our subject, the field is far from completely addressed either by federal legislation (or federal rules of civil procedure) or by international treaties, or by a combination of the two. On the contrary, the sources of transnational litigation law in the US are multiple. The common law—both federal and state—has a role to play. So too does state legislation. Unsurprisingly in this situation, we will also encounter influential Restatements of the Law. Even they are several, notably the Restatements of Conflict of Laws and of the Foreign Relations Law of the United States.

Clearly, the conduct of transnational litigation in the US is governed, and governed pervasively, by the usual rules of civil procedure that obtain in the forum, state or federal. It is not the mission of this book, or the courses to which it corresponds, to cover the usual civil procedure ground. Students, particularly those trained overseas or otherwise not acquainted with American civil procedure, are advised to consult a civil procedure text so as to place the issues dealt with in this book in their conventional procedural context.

Notwithstanding the growth of transnational litigation in US courts, a significant volume of private international disputes are resolved not through adjudication in national (or sub-national) courts, but through international arbitral channels. Even if one wanted to, one could not ignore arbitration in a book of this sort—this, for the simple reason that courts have a significant role to play in many aspects of the international arbitral process, including compelling arbitration, awarding provisional relief in conjunction with arbitration, setting aside arbitral awards, and eventually recognizing and/or enforcing arbitral awards. On the other hand, the law of international arbitration presupposes a basic adjudicatory procedure that differs in fundamental ways from the conduct of litigation (including transnational litigation) in a national court system. It has also become exceedingly complex. Accordingly, international arbitration will be dealt with in only a preliminary fashion toward the end of this book, with a decided emphasis on the intersections between courts and arbitral tribunals. It is the subject of a separate Nutshell volume on "International Commercial Arbitration" prepared in conjunction with this one.

CHAPTER ONE

THE SOURCES OF TRANSNATIONAL LITIGATION LAW

Transnational litigation in the US is marked by a remarkable multiplicity of sources. Although it might be desirable to have a common federal legislative regime for the conduct of transnational litigation in the US, the reality is that no such regime exists. Thus, the rules and principles governing such litigation are drawn from both federal and state law and from legislation, treaties and the common law alike. Before embarking on a consideration of any of the salient issues in transnational litigation, it will be useful to canvass the range of sources of transnational litigation law.

FEDERAL LEGISLATION AND RULES

Congress has unquestionable authority, acting pursuant to the commerce clause and/or Congress' power to legislate over foreign affairs, to address many of the issues that concern us in transnational litigation. It has occasionally exercised that power, examples of which we find in the 1976 Foreign Sovereign Immunities Act (see Chapter 5 *infra*) and in the statutory provisions on assistance to foreign tribunals in the service of documents and the obtaining of evidence found in 28 U.S.C.A. secs. 1696 and 1782, respectively (see Chapter 8 *infra*). Whether these statutes apply only to litigation in the federal courts or to state and federal litigation alike can only be determined by examining their language and purpose, as well as general principles for delineating the proper lines of demarcation between state and federal law. Thus, it is clear both from the language and purpose of the Sovereign Immunities Act that actions in the state and federal courts are equally affected. (The Act even provides for the removal from state to federal court of all actions that are subject to it.) On the other hand, the US Code provisions on transnational service and evidence-gathering, by their terms, have exclusive application to the federal courts. The provisions say nothing about the availability of such assistance from the state courts; absent an appropriate treaty, the assistance available from them is presumably determined by state procedural law alone.

The Federal Rules of Civil Procedure obviously play a central role in transnational litigation in the federal courts. Though adopted by delegation, the Rules are expressly authorized by Congress in the Rules Enabling Act of 1938, and transnational cases are as fully governed by them (for example on issues like joinder of parties, motion practice and summary judgment) as is any other category of federal court litigation. On occasion, the Federal Rules contain provisions that expressly address transnational scenarios. A good example is Rule 4(i) on service of summonses and complaints (see Chapter 8 *infra*), or Rule 44.1 on the pleading and proof of foreign law (see Chapter 7 *infra*). But these are the exception. For example, provisional relief in transnational cases in the federal courts (see Chapter 9 *infra*) is governed by Federal Rules of Civil Procedure 64 and 65, just as in domestic cases. All in all, due to the range of litigation issues they address, the Federal Rules are a proper starting point for understanding the procedural context of transnational litigation. But by the same token, and by their nature, they only have application to transnational litigation as conducted in the federal, as opposed to the state, courts.

Even where the Federal Rules provide a procedural rule, that rule may not be an entirely autonomous one. Take, as an example, Federal Rule of Civil Procedure 4(e). According to that Rule, service of a complaint in a federal action may be made according to the procedure laid down in any relevant federal statute and, failing that, "pursuant to the law of the state in which the district court is located, or in which service is effected. . . ." Similarly, the rules governing prejudgment attachment in federal courts are, according to Rule 64, largely derivative of state procedural law.

Clearly, Congress has not chosen to occupy the field of transnational litigation—not even in the federal courts.

TREATIES AND INTERNATIONAL AGREEMENTS

Similarly, the Executive Branch may, as a constitutional law matter (and subject to Senate consent, as constitutionally required), enter into treaties and other international agreements on a broad range of transnational litigation issues. By virtue of the Supremacy Clause, such agreements necessarily take priority over any inconsistent state law. Once again, however, the international agreements that obtain in this field are relatively few and relatively narrow. Prototypical are the Hague Conventions of 1965 and 1970 on service of process and obtaining evidence abroad, respectively (see Chapter 8 *infra*), and the 1958 New York Convention on the Recognition and Enforcement of Foreign Arbitral Awards (see Chapter 11 *infra*). And, once again, these instruments themselves ordinarily tell us whether only federal or, instead, both federal and state litigation, are affected.

The sources of international law in the US include, in addition to treaties and international agreements, customary international law, by which is meant the rules and principles by which States consider themselves bound even in the absence of a formal written international agreement to that effect. While customary international law will on occasion furnish substantive rules that bear on the merits of transnational cases, as under the Alien Tort Claim Statute (see Chapter 6 *infra*), it rarely addresses questions that go to the procedural aspects of transnational litigation. We shall therefore only infrequently have occasion to evoke customary international law in this volume.

The reasons for the fragmentary treatment of transnational litigation in US legislation and treaties are several. The issues that are salient in the field are not ones that necessarily occupy a high rank on the federal legislative or executive agendas. Nor does there appear to be a strong constituency for codification of transnational litigation law at any level, be it state or federal. Finally, it may be that the courts are considered thus far to have performed reasonably well in the transnational litigation gap-filling role that has necessarily fallen to them.

THE FEDERAL COMMON LAW

As has just been implied, the federal courts may endeavor to strengthen the federal presence in the field of transnational litigation by developing a "federal common law" on certain recurring issues. There is arguably a sufficient federal interest in at least some of these issues to justify the federal courts in elaborating the relevant rules and principles and applying them as appropriate.

There is nothing strictly inconsistent between the elaboration of a federal common law of transnational litigation and the principle of *Erie Railroad Co. v. Tompkins* (S.Ct.1938). The rule in *Erie*, to the effect that a federal court sitting in a diversity case should apply the substantive common law of the state in which it sits, seeks essentially to preserve the place of federal law, even in diversity cases, in governing issues that are basically procedural. *Erie* leaves the federal courts sitting in diversity scope for applying not only the Federal Rules of Civil Procedure, but also unwritten common law rules of a profoundly procedural character, some of which may play a prominent role in transnational litigation. Take, for example, the rule of *forum non conveniens* (see Chapter 4 *infra*). Under *Erie*, this federal common law "abstention" doctrine presumably applies to all federal court actions, including diversity cases, but is not binding as such on the state courts. (When and if state courts apply a *forum non conveniens* doctrine, they ordinarily do so as a matter of state procedural law and in accordance with the state law version of that doctrine.)

The opening that *Erie* creates for federal courts to establish procedural common law in diversity cases should not, however, be exaggerated. There are certain issues crucial to transnational litigation that will be deemed committed under the *Erie* doctrine to state law. As examples, take the rules governing choice of law in transnational litigation (see *Klaxon Co. v. Stentor Elec. Mfg. Co.* (S.Ct. 1941)), discussed in Chapter 7 *infra*, or the rules governing the recognition and enforcement of foreign judgments (see *Somportex, Ltd. v. Philadelphia Chewing Gum Corp.* (E.D.Pa.1970)), discussed in Chapter 10 *infra*. On both matters, by virtue of *Erie*, federal courts in diversity cases apply the law of the state in which they sit. Differences among state choice of law or recognition of judgment policies commonly cause the outcome of transnational litigation in diversity cases to vary according to the state in which the federal district court sits.

Second and more far-reaching, *Erie* merely held that there is no federal "general" common law. It did not rule out the recognition of narrower federal common law rules in "a few areas, implicating 'uniquely federal interests.'" See *Boyle v. United Technologies Corp.* (S.Ct.1988). Where such interests are at stake, and the federal courts have elaborated a common law rule to accommodate them, that rule may be binding in both federal and state court and, by virtue of the supremacy of federal law, may preempt any inconsistent state law. It is in this sense that we may best understand federal court case law establishing an "act of state doctrine," shielding from review the legality of acts of foreign governments taken on their own territory (*Banco Nacional de Cuba v. Sabbatino* (S.Ct.1964)), or a "dormant" foreign affairs power, barring states from acting so as to impede the US interest in speaking "with one voice" in foreign affairs (*Zschernig v. Miller* (S.Ct.1968)), both treated in Chapter 5 *infra*. The common law principles that these cases announce are not merely procedural rules that continue to apply in federal diversity cases under *Erie*; rather, they are rules that embody a distinct federal interest and are, as such, applicable in state and federal court alike.

Despite the impressive arguments that may be made in favor of developing and applying a comprehensive federal common law in this field, the federal courts have not energetically pursued that strategy. The reader will observe, over the course of this book, how relatively few are the doctrines that the federal courts have propounded in the name of federal common law—either as part of *Erie*'s "procedural law" exception or as an expression of a paramount federal interest. Indeed, even when a federal common law rule can be discerned, it is not always apparent which of these roles the rule is performing, and therefore whether the rule applies in the state as well as the federal courts.

RESTATEMENTS OF THE LAW

All in all, we observe that federal laws or treaties address transnational litigation issues only to a very limited extent, and that the door is correspondingly open to the possibility of applying either a rule of federal common law or a "borrowed" rule of state law. Under these circumstances, Restatements of the Law have a particularly important role to play.

In addition to the Restatement of Conflict of Laws (which by its nature addresses international as fully as it does interstate cases), the American Law Institute has produced an influential Restatement of the Foreign Relations Law of the United States. The current Restatement—the Third—provides a rule of decision or a framework of analysis for state and federal courts on a great many transnational litigation issues on which there is neither a relevant federal statute or treaty, nor an obviously applicable and binding rule of state law. The Restatement has influentially addressed, for example, the question of the scope of application of federal legislation to scenarios that are in whole or in part extraterritorial (see Chapter 6 *infra*), as well as the question of the consequences to be drawn from a litigant's refusal to produce evidence in reliance on a foreign country's so-called "blocking legislation" (see Chapter 8 *infra*). In sum, the Restatements have understandably exerted a strong influence on state and federal courts as they seek to fill the very considerable interstices that characterize the law of transnational litigation.

As a reading of this book will reveal, a study of the most salient issues in transnational litigation will entail an examination of the fully panoply of sources of law that have been identified in this chapter.

CHAPTER TWO

JURISDICTION OVER NON-NATIONALS AND NON-RESIDENTS

Issues of personal jurisdiction typically arise in transnational litigation in the US when the defendant is not a US national or resident. It is true that, unlike lack of subject matter jurisdiction (see Chapter 3 *infra*), lack of personal jurisdiction is considered waivable in US law. However, unless the defendant has submitted to jurisdiction, either by waiver of jurisdictional objections or by a valid choice of forum clause, personal jurisdiction may be a serious issue. Precisely for this reason, when parties to international transactions wish to ensure the availability of a US forum for potential claims against a non-national or non-resident defendant, they often negotiate and conclude a forum selection clause. This chapter accordingly begins with issues surrounding forum selection agreements, and only then considers the situation where no such agreement has been concluded, or where such an agreement has been concluded, but is found to be invalid or otherwise unenforceable.

FORUM SELECTION CLAUSES

A forum selection clause represents an agreement by which the parties to a contract designate in advance the court or courts before which disputes arising out of or related to that contract may or must be brought. It is designed to introduce a measure of certainty and predictability concerning the proper forum for eventual litigation. (While the usual forum selection agreement is entered into on a pre-dispute basis, parties are also generally free to conclude such an agreement after a dispute has already arisen.) As a contractual provision, forum selection agreements are of course susceptible to the same questions of interpretation and validity as those to which party agreements are customarily subject.

Interpretation of forum selection clauses

The fact that the parties have agreed to submit a certain class of disputes to a designated court will not necessarily render that court the "exclusive" forum for resolving them. The clause may merely serve to render the selected court competent in personal jurisdiction terms, and therefore "available." In that event, the possibility remains open that other courts may and will exercise jurisdiction over such a dispute to the extent that they are otherwise competent to do so. Where the parties to a forum selection clause intend the designated forum to become the exclusive forum, to the prejudice of any and all otherwise competent fora, their clause should contain language of exclusivity (e.g. "all disputes ... shall be brought in ..."). Agreements that designate an exclusive forum are commonly known as "derogation clauses" precisely because they operate to displace or "oust" the otherwise competent fora. Agreements that merely identify a forum in which claims "may" be brought are known as "prorogation clauses."

As might be expected, whether an agreement constitutes a derogation or a prorogation clause is principally a matter of party intention and therefore of contract interpretation. Unfortunately, parties often use language that is ambiguous on this point, and they may be surprised to learn that as plaintiff, for example, they are precluded from bringing suit in a court that would otherwise have been competent, or that as defendant they may still be sued in a court other than the one designated. Even so, the courts exhibit a tendency to treat forum selection clauses as exclusive rather than non-exclusive.

Another matter subject to contract interpretation is the scope of disputes to which a forum selection agreement is applicable. US law recognizes no strong presumption in favor either of a broad or narrow construction of forum selection clauses. A typical clause purports to cover all disputes "arising out of" and/or "related to" the contract in which it is found. The latter phrase is generally deemed to denote a broader range of cases than does the former, which may possibly be understood as encompassing only claims sounding in contract as such, and not claims that sound in other theories such as tort, products liability, property or unjust enrichment, or statutory causes of action that happen to bear some relation to the underlying contract. In order to help ensure that covered claims are not limited to contract claims, parties to forum selection agreements should not confine themselves to use of the "arising under" language. In *Hugel v. Corporation of Lloyd's* (7th Cir.1993), an "arising under" clause was found to encompass claims for breach of contract, breach of fiduciary duty, invasion of privacy, and tortious interference because all arose or were related to the contractual relationship. But, to better ensure that result, parties should consider using "or related to" language as well or, better yet, referring to "all claims arising out of or related to this agreement, *including, but not limited to*, claims sounding contract."

Lastly, questions increasingly arise as to whether a forum selection clause should be understood, exceptionally, to bind parties who are not themselves signatories of the contract containing the forum selection clause. Who, in other words, beside the signatory parties, is bound by or may invoke a forum selection agreement? Whether, for example, third party beneficiaries or close corporate affiliates or so-called "alter-egos" are bound, or may themselves invoke the agreement, may be a contested matter, to be determined by the law that the forum considers to be applicable to that issue. It is safe to say that most bodies of US law recognize a strong presumption both against treating non-contracting parties as bound by a contractual choice of forum clause and against permitting them to invoke the clause against a contracting party. But almost all recognize exceptional circumstances where justice requires that non-contracting parties be bound by, or be permitted to invoke, such a clause.

To the extent that the meaning or effect of a forum selection clause is in issue, there also arises a choice of law question, namely the question of the jurisdiction whose law should govern the interpretation of the clause. Courts are seldom explicit about their choice of law for purposes of interpreting a choice of forum agreement. Some appear to interpret the clause in light of the law stipulated in the contract's choice of law clause, if any, or in light of the law applicable to the interpretation of the contract generally. Others—perhaps the majority—appear to apply forum law for these purposes, or to cite no particular body of law at all. On the last-mentioned interpretive question above—applicability of the clause to non-signatories—the forum will most likely consider that the law applicable to that issue is either forum law (as if the issue were procedural) or the law (possibly a law other than that of the forum) that most properly governs the relationship between the related entities.

Validity of forum selection clauses

Forum selection agreements are subject not only to questions of interpretation and application, but also validity. A jurisdiction might conceivably regard forum selection clauses as invalid in general, because they tamper with judicial jurisdiction, a matter deemed to lie beyond the scope of party autonomy. The traditional attitude of the US federal courts toward forum selection clauses—prorogation and derogation alike—was indeed one of hostility. Over 150 years ago, a state Supreme Court opined: "The rules to determine in what courts and counties actions may be brought are fixed, upon considerations of general convenience and expediency, by general law; to allow them to be changed by the agreement of parties would disturb the symmetry of the law, and interfere with such convenience." *Nute v. Hamilton Mut. Ins. Co.* (Mass. 1856). The federal courts long maintained much the same view. See, e.g., *Carbon Black Export, Inc. v. The Monrosa* (5th Cir.1958).

When lower federal courts relaxed this attitude, they received cautious support from dicta by the Supreme Court in the case of *National Equip. Rental, Ltd. v. Szukhent* (S.Ct.1964), from the Model Choice of Forum Act adopted in 1968 by the National Conference of Commissioners on Uniform State Laws, and from the Restatement (Second) of Conflict of Laws, section 80.

The Model Act, 17 Am. J. Comp. L. 292 (1969), basically calls on the forum to decline jurisdiction by virtue of a forum selection clause favoring another forum, unless (1) the forum is required by its own law to hear the case, (2) effective relief is unavailable in the chosen forum other than for reasons of delay in bringing the action, (3) the chosen forum is a substantially less convenient place for trial, (4) the choice of forum clause was obtained by misrepresentation, duress or unconscionable means, or (5) enforcement would otherwise be unfair or unreasonable, (Conversely, the Model Act calls on the chosen forum to accept jurisdiction under a forum selection clause, even if it has no independent jurisdictional basis, unless it lacks subject matter jurisdiction, is not a reasonably convenient place for trial, the agreement was obtained by improper means, or the defendant was not adequately served). Likewise, the Restatement (Second) of Conflict of Laws (sec. 80) calls upon courts to enforce choice of forum clauses, unless unfair or unreasonable.

If a forum selection clause designating a foreign court is valid and enforceable (and exclusive), then the party invoking it in federal court may be able to win a dismissal of the action for lack of subject matter jurisdiction, improper venue, or failure to state a cause of action under Federal Rules 12(b)(1), (3) or (6), respectively. If appealed, the court's determination will ordinarily be subject to *de novo* review (*Hugel v. Corporation of Lloyd's*, *supra*; *Riley v. Kingsley Underwriting Agencies, Ltd.* (10th Cir.1992)), though some courts are prepared to review the determination under an abuse of discretion standard (*Spradlin v. Lear Siegler Mgt. Servs. Co., Inc.* (9th Cir.1991)).

Eventually, the Supreme Court broadly embraced forum selection clauses in its decision in *The Bre-*

men v. Zapata Off–Shore Co. (S.Ct.1972), as have the great majority of state courts. See, e.g., *Smith, Valentino & Smith, Inc. v. Superior Court* (Cal. 1976). According to *Bremen*, forum selection clauses are entitled to great respect, particularly in international contracts, where it may be sound and reasonable for the parties to decide that their disputes will be resolved in courts other than those of the US. The Supreme Court laid particular emphasis on the value in these situations of jurisdictional certainty and predictability. However, as the discussion that follows shows, the respect owing to choice of forum clauses is by no means absolute. Such clauses are generally enforceable, but only subject to certain conditions.

Notwithstanding *Bremen,* a handful of states continue to regard forum selection clauses designating an out-of-state forum as unenforceable in principle, either statutorily or as a matter of public policy, at least under some circumstances. They also will not necessarily insulate jurisdiction based on a forum selection clause from the possibility of dismissal on *forum non conveniens* grounds. (See Chapter 4 *infra.*) See, e.g., *Appalachian Ins. Co. v. Superior Court* (Cal.App.1984).

(a) Contractual validity of the forum selection agreement

One way to avoid a forum selection clause is, of course, to impugn it as a matter of contract law. *Bremen* expressly opens up this possibility, for example, by a showing of fraud or overreaching. Any standard ground for denying enforcement of a contract—e.g. incapacity, duress or overreaching, fraud, mutual mistake, unconscionability, even (however unlikely it may be) absence of consideration—may presumably be advanced to render the clause unenforceable. These attempts are occasionally successful. See, e.g., *Weidner Communic., Inc. v. H.R.H. Prince Bandar Al Faisal* (7th Cir.1988), barring a party from invoking the forum selection clause due to contractual bad faith.

In determining the validity of a choice of forum clause under *Bremen*, courts again have a number of possibilities by way of choice of law. One possibility is to subject the *validity* of the clause to the same law that governs the clause's *interpretation*, as discussed immediately above. In doing so, a court may choose to apply to this issue the same law that governs the interpretation and validity the law of the contract as a whole, whether by virtue of a contractual choice of law clause or of the choice of law rules applicable in the forum in the absence of a valid forum selection clause. Another possibility is simply to apply the law of the forum to the question of the validity of the forum selection clause (whatever the law applicable to the rest of the contract), on the theory that the issue, broadly viewed, is more procedural than substantive in nature, and that applying forum law to them more closely corresponds to the parties' probable intentions, if any. There are reported court decisions that illustrate both of these approaches. For a recent discussion, at the state level, see *Fendi v. Condotti Shops, Inc.* (Fla.App.2000).

We have assumed that any validity challenge will be directed specifically to the choice of forum clause. But sometimes a party does not challenge the validity of that clause in particular, but rather the validity of the contract as a whole. In that situation, arguably, the challenger is bound to submit the question to the forum designated by the clause. However, requiring resort to the chosen court for these purposes has an obvious "bootstrapping" quality to it. For this reason, courts commonly determine the meaning and validity of a forum selection clause as a threshold matter, even if they are not the chosen forum, assuming of course that they are otherwise competent to do so.

A related question arises when the underlying contract is found by the chosen court to be invalid, but that court would not otherwise have been a competent one. It is logically problematic for a court whose competence derives solely from a forum selection clause to validly determine that the contract containing that clause is unenforceable. However, under the prevailing "separability doctrine," the choice of forum clause is deemed severable for these purposes from the main contract—with the result that the chosen forum does not by declaring the contract invalid thereby automatically lose its jurisdiction to make that very determination.

On the merits, challenges to the validity of forum selection clauses may be difficult to maintain. In

Carnival Cruise Lines, Inc. v. Shute (S.Ct.1991), a divided Supreme Court enforced a clause whereby a cruise ship passenger living in the State of Washington had consented, through non-negotiable language on the ticket, to the exclusive jurisdiction of the courts of Florida (place of business of the cruise line) for all claims arising out of or related to the contract. Treating the case as one in admiralty, the Court applied the federal common law governing the enforceability of forum selection clauses (essentially the rule of *Bremen*). It ruled that even a clause found in a consumer contract is not to be considered unreasonable merely because non-negotiable, because entered into by parties of unequal bargaining power, and because not the subject of genuine bargaining. On the contrary, the Court considered it reasonable for the cruise line to have limited the fora in which it was answerable and to have selected Florida as the exclusive forum, as well as not unjust for the passenger to be bound by that selection. Inequality of bargaining power alone is accordingly unlikely to result in the invalidity of a forum selection clause. Nor is a party's failure to read the forum selection clause—though the result may be otherwise where that party lacked any reasonable notice of the clause.

(b) Availability and adequacy of the chosen forum

Another way to avoid a forum selection clause is, of course, to demonstrate that the chosen forum is in fact unavailable or, if available, is corrupt, biased or dysfunctional, a result that was achieved in *Rockwell Int'l Systems v. Citibank* (2d Cir.1983), but that ordinarily fails. See, e.g., *Blanco v. Banco Indust. de Venezuela, S.A.* (2d Cir.1993). But the broadest argument, and one specifically invited by the *Bremen* decision, is that the forum selection clause is unreasonable or unjust.

One reason for which a forum selection clause may be found unreasonable or unjust, and denied enforcement, is that the chosen forum is so seriously inconvenient a place for the litigation that enforcement of the clause would mean that the plaintiff "will for all practical purposes be deprived of his day in court." See, e.g., *McDonnell Douglas Corp. v. Islamic Republic of Iran* (8th Cir.1985). Naturally, a party that has subscribed to a forum selection clause bears a heavy burden of showing why it should be excused from litigating in a forum to whose jurisdiction it had by prior contractual agreement freely submitted. It would almost certainly be necessary to show unusual circumstances, such as seriously unequal bargaining power between the parties or wholly unforeseeable developments, subsequent to the choice of forum, which rendered the chosen forum untenable.

While courts may, very rarely, disregard forum selection clauses on grounds of gross inconvenience, it should not be supposed that they impose a requirement of minimum contacts between the chosen forum, on the one hand, and the parties or the transaction, on the other. Parties are presumably free, as an exercise of party autonomy, to select a forum irrespective of its contacts with the underlying contract or the parties, and indeed irrespective of the forum's convenience or lack thereof. See e.g., *Interamerican Trade Corp. v. Companhia Fabricadora de Pecas,* (6th Cir.1992). But under some circumstances, particularly where the choice of a "remote" or "alien" forum cannot be justified on grounds of forum neutrality or expertise, and where inconvenience is decidedly present, the choice of a forum lacking any relationship to the case may be denied effect. Even the *Bremen* court allowed, by way of dictum, the possibility that an agreement between two Americans to resolve their essentially local disputes abroad might be disregarded. Needless to say, if the parties choose a wholly unrelated forum, and that forum then elects not to hear the case (due to inconvenience, for example), the clause will be deemed to have failed in its essential purpose, and all otherwise competent fora will "regain" their competence, the choice of forum clause notwithstanding.

A final adequacy issue has to do with remedy. Under *Bremen*, forum selection clauses may also be denied enforcement if their effect would be to deprive the plaintiff of any adequate remedy for his or her claim. (While it is commonly the plaintiff who seeks to avoid the chosen forum, it may also conceivably be the defendant who does so, arguing that the chosen forum fails to afford it a minimally adequate opportunity to present its defense.) The *Bremen* case itself illustrates the point. The plaintiff there sought to show that the court selected contractually by the parties (*viz.* the High Court of London) would have enforced a contractual clause exculpating the defendant for its own negligence, whereas the court where the plaintiff sued (*viz.* federal district court in Tampa, Florida) would not have enforced it. Ordinarily, such efforts are unavailing. In *Bremen*, the Court remanded so that the lower court could determine whether the balance of convenience weighed strongly enough in the US court's favor to justify allowing the case to proceed there, notwithstanding the forum selection clause indicating London. But it ruled that the fact that the chosen foreign court would enforce the contract's exculpatory clause was not sufficient to render the choice of forum unfair or unreasonable in the context of an international towage contract.

(c) Non-alienability of the cause of action

An aspect of the enforceability of a forum selection agreement is of course its legality. Even under *Bremen* and the state courts that have followed it, a legislature has the right to vest exclusive jurisdiction over certain statutory causes of action in the local courts, so that forum selection clauses designating a foreign forum will be ineffective as far as those causes of actions are concerned. (In other words, as to those causes of action, the forum's jurisdiction is non-waivable). The clearest example would be a federal or state law which creates a specific statutory cause of action and proceeds to vest in a local court exclusive jurisdiction to entertain such actions. For instance, language in the Federal Employer's Liability Act (45 U.S.C.A. sec. 56) has been read as precluding suit under the Act in any place other than the place of the defendant's residence. *Boyd v. Grand Trunk W. R.R. Co.* (S.Ct. 1949). (The analogous question as to whether legislatures may validly declare causes of action non-arbitrable is a matter dealt with in Chapter 11 *infra.*)

It is possible that, even in the absence of statutory language creating exclusive local jurisdiction over statutory claims, a court may find that public policy requires a given statutory claim to be asserted, if at all, locally. Lower federal courts have on occasion held that particular statutory claims, even in the absence of such language, may not be validly subjected to forum selection clauses in favor of foreign fora. See, e.g., *Red Bull Assocs. v. Best Western Int'l* (S.D.N.Y.1988) (refusal to transfer to contractual forum an action alleging racial discrimination). Just as often, however, they give such clauses effect even as to important federal statutory claims. See, e.g., *AVC Nederland BV v. Atrium Inv. Partnership* (2d Cir.1984) (federal securities laws).

A particularly influential decision pointing in the latter direction is *Roby v. Corporation of Lloyd's* (2d Cir.1993). There, US citizens and residents who had invested in Lloyd's underwriting syndicates sued Lloyd's (and certain of its members, agents and entities) in federal district court for violation of the federal securities laws and RICO, which expressly preclude waiver of the substantive rights that they afford. The plaintiffs brought the action in the US, notwithstanding the contract's having designated the English courts as the exclusive forum for resolving disputes relating to membership in and underwriting at Lloyd's, coupled with a contractual designation of English law as the governing law. (It was undisputed that no English court would enforce the US securities laws.) The Court of Appeals conceded that it would violate the public policies underlying the securities laws and RICO for a claim properly brought in the US under those laws to be remitted to a foreign court for application, in lieu of US law, of foreign legislation that inadequately protects US investors.

However, the court in *Roby* found that the plaintiffs had failed to show that a UK court applying UK law would not afford an adequate remedy for achieving the protective purposes underlying the US securities laws and RICO. On the contrary, it concluded that the common law claims that a UK court could be expected to enforce (*viz.* common law deceit and misrepresentation, the Misrepresentation Act of 1967, and breach of fiduciary duties) were adequate, even if they required proof by the plaintiffs of actual misconduct and reliance, as well as a stronger showing of causation, and did not make as broad a range of defendants answerable as US law would have done. The unavailability in the UK of punitive damages (provided for by RICO), and the reduced deterrent quality of UK law, did not alter the court's opinion. This is now the dominant view among the circuits. *See e.g., Richards v. Lloyd's of London* (9th Cir.1998) *(en banc)*. To similar effect, see *Omron Healthcare Inc. v. Maclaren Exports Ltd.* (7th Cir.1994) (trademark infringement suit); *Fireman's Fund Ins. Co. v. Cho Yang Shipping Co.* (9th Cir.1997) (Carriage of Goods by Sea Act).

States, too, on occasion purport to make certain statutory causes of action (typically causes of action protecting the weaker party to commercial transactions) exclusively enforceable in their own courts. As directives from the state legislature to the state courts, such provisions presumably bind the latter. Doubts as to the efficacy of this kind of legislation arise only where suit under the statute is brought in federal court sitting in diversity. While the federal court might well show deference to the state's public policy by refusing to treat such claims as subject to a forum selection clause designating the courts of a different state or country, it is also possible that the federal court will disregard the state policy on forum selection clauses and instead treat the clause's enforceability as governed entirely by federal procedural common law, i.e. *Bremen*. (See the discussion below of *Erie* and choice of forum clauses.)

Forum non conveniens and choice of forum clauses

We have assumed in this discussion that if an exclusive forum selection clause is valid and enforceable, it will be determinative, and most courts do reason in that fashion. Thus, faced with an exclusive forum selection clause designating another jurisdiction, a court ordinarily either enforces the clause (by declining jurisdiction) or disregards it as unenforceable (and asserts jurisdiction if otherwise competent). But, as noted in *Stewart Organization, Inc. v. Ricoh Corp.* (S.Ct.1988), the court sometimes also faces a motion for dismissal on *forum non conveniens* grounds. In that event it has to decide how much weight to give to the choice of forum clause in the overall *forum non conveniens* analysis. In most cases, as in *Ricoh*, a forum selection clause designating a foreign court will be a weighty factor pointing toward dismissal in favor of the selected forum. For examples in the international context, see *Mercier v. Sheraton Int'l, Inc.* (1st Cir.1992); *Royal Bed & Spring Co. v. Famossul Industria* (1st Cir.1990). From time to time, courts, even in the face of a clause designating a foreign court, expressly inquire into whether their own assertion of jurisdiction would be reasonable. But for them, too, the parties' choice of a foreign forum will clearly be a major factor in determining that the forum's exercise of jurisdiction is unreasonable. See e.g., *International Technologies Consultants, Inc. v. Euroglas, S.A.* (6th Cir.1997).

Conversely, should a court ever stay or dismiss a case on *forum non conveniens* grounds in the face of a forum selection clause designating *it* as the competent forum? We take up this question in Chapter 4, but note as of now that the Model Choice of Forum Act (page 18 *supra*) expressly contemplates this possibility. On the other hand, a legislature may act so as to make a forum selection clause in favor of the local forum absolutely binding on the local courts, thus ruling out a dismissal on *forum non conveniens* grounds. New York General Obligations Law, section 5–1402, for example, entitles any person to maintain an action in the New York courts against a foreign corporation pursuant to a forum selection clause, provided (a) the claim arises out of a contractual obligation in an amount in excess of one million dollars and (b) the contract designates New York law as the governing law. The stated purpose is precisely to insulate any action within the scope of the provision from stay or dismissal on *forum non conveniens* grounds. (Obviously, the provision cannot insulate the action from a jurisdictional due process challenge, though the presence of a forum selection clause would make a due process challenge difficult to maintain.)

Bremen in federal diversity cases

The enforceability of forum selection clauses also raises choice of law problems under *Erie Railroad Co. v. Tompkins* (S.Ct.1938). The *Bremen* case is not itself a particularly good indication, since it was an admiralty (hence a federal question) case, and thus a candidate for application of a federal common law on the enforceability of forum selection clauses. Predictably, *Bremen* has been applied to federal statutory causes of action as well. See e.g., *Riley v. Kingsley Underwriting Agencies, Ltd., supra* (federal and state securities laws).

Lower courts are divided, however, as to whether *Bremen* should be applied more broadly. There are several possibilities. *Bremen* may be interpreted as constituting a rule of federal *procedural* common law, thus binding in all federal cases, federal question and diversity alike, though not in state courts. This is the dominant view. It may also be considered as a rule of *substantive* federal common law binding in federal question cases in federal court, but not in diversity cases. However, it may also be considered—as the act of state doctrine (see Chapter 5 *infra*) sometimes is—as expressing a substantive common law of such importance that it should be treated as binding under the supremacy clause in all cases and in all courts, state and federal alike. There is even the possibility of applying to the question of the enforceability of a forum selection clause the substantive law of the contract containing the clause. (This could, for example, be the law designated in the contract's choice of law clause, if any.) While there is no consensus among courts about the proper reach of *Bremen*, most seem to consider that *Bremen* is binding in all federal court actions, but in them alone.

The reality is that even when state or federal courts do not consider themselves strictly bound by *Bremen* in the case before them, they are nevertheless likely to apply the reasoning of *Bremen* as highly persuasive. Indeed, the broad similarity between federal and most state common law rules on the subject has helped courts avoid deciding the choice of law issue head on. Frequently enough, a court enforces a forum selection clause without opting clearly for one body of US law or another (or indeed a body of foreign law) on the enforceability of forum selection clauses. See, e.g., *Instrumentation Assocs., Inc. v. Madsen Elec. Ltd.* (3d Cir.1988). Still, as noted, the *Erie* issue matters because the law of some states is much less hospitable to forum selection agreements than the rule in *Bremen* would suggest.

Two things are clear, however. There is no written federal law on the subject, and the *Bremen* decision has been unusually influential. While a federal statute, 28 U.S.C.A. sec. 1404(a), governs the transfer of cases from one federal district court to another, that provision is necessarily limited to domestic transfers. Interestingly, while Section 1404(a) speaks to the matter of transfers for convenience, rather than transfers by reason of forum selection agreements, the Supreme Court has nevertheless specifically addressed the importance of forum selection clauses in deciding cases under Section 1404(a). In *Stewart Organization, Inc. v. Ricoh Corp., supra*, the Supreme Court ruled that the presence of a forum selection clause, while only one factor in the overall balance of convenience under Section 1404(a), is nevertheless a very important one. By incorporating forum selection clauses centrally into the analysis of district-to-district transfers under Section 1404(a), the Court in *Ricoh* succeeded in establishing a uniform federal rule for such cases. Ironically, though, this rule cannot apply in international forum selection clause cases—

the cases where, due to potential foreign relations implications, it would be most useful of all to have a uniform federal approach—precisely because Section 1404(a) only contemplates transfers between US federal district courts.

JURISDICTION IN THE ABSENCE OF A SELECTION

The presence of a forum selection clause binding a non-national or non-resident defendant will usually be determinative of personal jurisdiction. As the *Bremen* case shows, the burden of demonstrating that a clause is so burdensome or unfair to the defendant that it should not be enforced is an extremely heavy one.

Where no forum selection agreement is present and applicable, the existence of personal jurisdiction depends on the ordinarily applicable jurisdictional rules. The personal jurisdiction that may be exercised by state courts in the US is, in the first instance, a matter of state law, either statutory or common law, as the case may be. Jurisdiction in transnational litigation is likely to turn on the state's long-arm statute and its judicial interpretation. By virtue of Federal Rule 4(k)(1)(A), the personal jurisdiction of federal courts over non-nationals is ordinarily derivative of state law, the federal court "borrowing" the long-arm statute (and its interpretation) from the law of the state in which it sits. This is true not only of actions brought in federal court on grounds of diversity of citizenship, but also of federal question cases. Of course, Congress, in enacting special statutory causes of action, may specifically vest jurisdiction in certain federal courts. In that event, federal jurisdiction ceases to be derivative of, and dependent on, state law.

As in domestic litigation, the fact that a court enjoys state statutory or common law jurisdiction over a defendant is not the end of the inquiry. Due process requires a further inquiry, namely whether the court's assertion of personal jurisdiction over a non-local defendant comports with fundamental fairness and thereby due process. The following discussion of personal jurisdiction covers, in turn, each of these two phases of the inquiry.

Statutory personal jurisdiction

An exercise of personal jurisdiction by US courts, whether state or federal, requires at a minimum that the relevant statutory conditions are met. These conditions are laid down in legislation, and occasionally in court rules, within the jurisdiction. It is important to distinguish between the statutory personal jurisdiction of the state and the federal courts.

(a) State courts

Each state has enacted legislation or rules defining the personal jurisdiction of that state's courts over out-of-state (i.e. non-resident) defendants. These are commonly known as "long-arm" statutes, precisely because they identify the circumstances in which a party, though not "present" within the jurisdiction, will nevertheless be deemed to be subject to the personal jurisdiction, or adjudicatory reach, of the state's courts. Typically, long-arm statutes refer simply to "non-residents," or the like, without distinguishing between residents of sister-states and residents (or nationals) of foreign countries. In fact, these statutes are equally applicable to both classes of non-residents.

Long-arm statutes and rules vary from state to state, but nevertheless follow certain patterns. In some states, they recite a catalogue of more or less specific circumstances permitting the assertion of personal jurisdiction over non-residents, with the defendant in each such circumstance having one or another significant contact or "nexus" with the state in question. Typical long-arm provisions authorize the exercise of personal jurisdiction over non-residents on the basis of a tort committed by the defendant within the state, a contract to be performed within the state, or the location within the state of real property whose ownership is the subject of dispute. Rather than establish a catalogue of this sort, another group of states has enacted legislation giving their courts statutory personal jurisdiction over non-residents to the full extent permitted by the due process clause of the US Constitution (or, alternatively, of the US and the State Constitutions). Such long-arm statutes in effect conflate the statutory and constitutional inquiries into personal jurisdiction, with the result that if an exercise of personal jurisdiction is constitutionally permissible, it is also necessarily statutorily authorized. As state law enactments, these statutes are subject to authoritative interpretation by the respective state courts. However, to the extent that they incorporate federal due process criteria, they are for all practical purposes subject to the constitutional understandings developed by the federal courts.

Satisfaction of a long-arm basis of personal jurisdiction, though essential to the exercise of jurisdiction over a non-resident, is not sufficient to establish it. Service is invariably also necessary, not only as a constitutional but also as a statutory matter. (Service in transnational litigation is treated in Chapter 8 *infra.*)

(b) Federal courts

Like state courts, federal courts may exercise personal jurisdiction only to the extent that such an exercise is specifically statutorily authorized. The fact that an exercise of jurisdiction would not offend due process is not enough. See *Omni Capital Int'l v. Rudolf Wolff & Co., Ltd.* (S.Ct.1987). However, unlike state court systems, the federal court system does not possess a general long-arm statute regime of its own.

In place of a general federal long-arm statute, the Federal Rules of Civil Procedure basically "borrow" the existing personal jurisdiction of the state courts. Thus, by virtue of Federal Rule 4(k), replacing former Rule 4(e)), the long-arm jurisdiction of the federal courts is basically derivative of the long-arm jurisdiction of the courts of the state in which they sit. Rule 4(k)(1)(A) provides that a federal court has personal jurisdiction over any person "who could be subjected to the jurisdiction of a court of general jurisdiction in the state in which the district court is located." This borrowing applies to all exercises of federal court jurisdiction, whether based on diversity of citizenship, federal question or alienage. The proper interpretation of the "borrowed" state long-arm statute is manifestly a matter of state law. See *Helicopteros Nacionales de Colombia, S.A. v. Hall* (S.Ct.1984). But assuming an exercise of jurisdiction over a non-resident is authorized by a state long-arm statute, the question may still arise whether that exercise comports with federal due process. We deal with that aspect of the problem below.

In addition, the Federal Rules contemplate the possibility of specific federal statutory grants of personal jurisdiction. Rule 4(k)(1)(D) recognizes personal jurisdiction "when authorized by a statute of the United States." Examples of federal legislation authorizing the exercise of personal jurisdiction, as well as out-of-state service of process, include the Foreign Sovereign Immunities Act, the Clayton Antitrust Act, the Securities Acts and RICO (the Racketeering–Influenced and Corrupt Organizations Act).

Rule 4 contains a third personal jurisdiction provision, as to claims arising under federal law, targeting all persons who fall outside Rule 4(k)(1)(A) in that they are *not* subject to the courts of general jurisdiction of *any* state in the US. As to such claims (and subject to proper service), Rule 4(k)(2) renders subject to federal district court jurisdiction "any defendant who is not subject to the jurisdiction of the courts of general jurisdiction of any state." However, it contains the following crucial proviso: "[i]f the exercise of jurisdiction is consistent with the Constitution ... of the United States." As we shall see in connection with the notion of "aggregation of national contacts" (page 55 *infra*), this means at a minimum that the defendant's contacts with the US as a whole must be such as to make the assertion of jurisdiction fair and reasonable. Moreover, while Rule 4(k)(2) is seemingly broad enough in its terms to permit any federal district court to exercise jurisdiction over such a defendant, the plaintiff's precise choice of federal district may be limited in the interest of due process. We return to this problem below. For now it is sufficient to note that Rule 4(k)(2) apparently authorizes, as to federal causes of action, the exercise of jurisdiction over covered defendants to the fullest extent that due process will allow.

The above-mentioned categories of federal personal jurisdiction are limitative. If a federal court's exercise of personal jurisdiction over a non-resident cannot be justified by reference to one or more of them, it is improper. *Omni Capital Int'l*, *supra*.

The "due process" dimension

As noted, an exercise of personal jurisdiction by any court—state or federal—is valid only if it satisfies both the relevant statutory and constitutional criteria. The constitutionality of a state court's exercise of personal jurisdiction depends on its satisfying the 14th Amendment, whose "due process" clause has been held by the United States Supreme Court to require that the defendant have at least "minimum contacts" with the state in question. The seminal decision is *International Shoe Co. v. Washington* (S.Ct.1945), according to which a state court may constitutionally exercise personal jurisdiction over persons located outside the territory of the state only if they "have certain minimum contacts with it such that the maintenance of the suit does not offend traditional notions of fair play and substantial justice." The Court subsequently predicated this requirement on "the individual liberty interest preserved by the Due Process Clause." *Insurance Corp. of Ireland v. Compagnie des Bauxites de Guinee* (S.Ct.1982).

Cases involving jurisdiction over non-nationals are largely an extension of the sister-state jurisdictional due process cases with which students are likely already familiar. Accordingly they entail variations on the "minimum contacts" theme, for example "a contract which had substantial connection with that state" (*McGee v. International Life Ins. Co.* (S.Ct.1957)) or purposeful availment of the privileges of conducting business in the forum (*Hanson v. Denckla* (S.Ct.1958)). Particularly influential in the development of jurisdictional due process case law were the Court's rulings in *World–Wide Volkswagen Corp. v. Woodson* (S.Ct.1980), and *Burger King Corp. v. Rudzewicz* (S.Ct.1985), positing that due process requires not only purposefully-created minimum contacts between the defendant and the forum, but also overall reasonableness. *World–Wide Volkswagen* in particular established the notion that while a state may assert personal jurisdiction "over a corporation that delivers its products into the stream of commerce with the expectation that they will be purchased by consumers in the forum State," something more than the mere foreseeability of effects within the forum is required. That something presumably must amount to purposeful availment.

In fact, some of the Supreme Court's most influential rulings on the constitutional limits on state court exercises of personal jurisdiction arose out of cases in which the defendant is not merely out-of-state, but actually out-of-country, without, however, the international character of those cases necessarily drawing particular attention from the Court.

In *Asahi Metal Indus. Co. v. Superior Court* (S.Ct. 1987), four members of the Court once again underscored the necessity, in order to meet the minimum contacts requirement, that the out-of-state defendant have purposefully availed itself of the benefits of the forum. But for them, a mere awareness that one's products might enter a "stream of commerce" ultimately placing it in the forum is not enough. Some form of targeting of the forum state needs to be shown. For four other members, such knowledge would suffice. This division has led in turn to a division among the circuits. Compare *Renner v. Lanard Toys, Ltd.* (3d Cir.1994), with *Rodriguez v. Fullerton Tires Corp.* (1st Cir.1997).

The entire Supreme Court agreed in *Asahi*, however, that even if there is purposeful availment, and therefore "minimum contacts," an exercise of jurisdiction may nevertheless be "unreasonable" under the circumstances and therefore fail to satisfy due process. *Asahi* entailed an indemnity action in California state court by a Japanese tire producer against a Taiwanese component part manufacturer, the former having settled a tort action brought against it in that court by the victims of a motorcycle accident allegedly caused by a defect in the product. The Court ruled that, while the principal action against the tire producer belonged in a California court, the indemnity action between the Japanese and Taiwanese parties did not, stressing the burdens on defendants of litigating in a foreign forum and the forum's lack of interest in the outcome. By treating convenience as a central factor in the overall assessment of jurisdictional reasonableness, *Asahi* gives non-US nationals—all else being equal—a greater chance than US nationals of defeating a US court's assertion of jurisdiction. To this effect, see *Core–Vent Corp. v. Nobel Indus., A.B.* (9th Cir.1993). This will particularly be so where the claimant, as in *Asahi*, is likewise a non-US national. More generally, some courts have taken to describing minimum contacts and reasonableness as situated on a "sliding scale": the stronger the contacts, the more it will take to establish unreasonableness; the weaker the contacts, the easier to establish unreasonableness. See e.g., *O.M.I. Holdings, Inc. v. Royal Ins. Co.* (10th Cir.1998), citing *Ticketmaster–New York, Inc. v. Alioto* (1st Cir. 1994).

The case of *Helicopteros Nacionales de Colombia, supra*, found the Supreme Court strongly endorsing a basic distinction between "specific" and "general" personal jurisdiction. "General" jurisdiction requires real or constructive "presence," whether through nationality, residence or incorporation, or through a pattern of ongoing and continuous activity in the forum, such as by maintaining an office or a representative there or advertising there. Under general jurisdiction, the defendant may be sued in the forum on any cause of action, including one unrelated to the forum state or the defendants' contacts with it. But even if not subject to the forum's general jurisdiction, the defendant may still be subject to its jurisdiction on account of one or more specific contacts with the forum, not rising to the level of real or constructive presence, provided of course that they manifest the required purposeful availment and render the exercise of jurisdiction otherwise reasonable. Such "specific" jurisdiction, however, will only entitle the forum to entertain actions arising out of or related to those contacts. General and specific jurisdiction therefore differ both in their requirements and their consequences. In *Helicopteros*, the parties apparently conceded the absence of specific jurisdiction, and the Court found that the defendant's contacts with Texas were not sufficiently "continuous and systematic" to sustain an exercise of general jurisdiction.

(a) General jurisdiction

General jurisdiction, in the sense just described, may arise in a number of different ways. It may arise from a general and ordinarily permanent relationship between the defendant and the forum, e.g. from the defendant's having the nationality of the forum or having domicile or residence there. Although nationality may come first to mind as typifying such a relationship, actually few state long-arm statutes expressly provide for jurisdiction based solely on nationality, at least where natural persons are concerned. However, where a state long-arm statute authorizes, or is read as authorizing, jurisdiction to the full limits of due process, nationality will suffice to create general jurisdiction. Nationality-based general jurisdiction has been endorsed as constitutional by the US Supreme Court (*Blackmer v. United States* (S.Ct.1932)). See also Restatement (Third) of Foreign Relations Law, sec. 421(2)(d). Domicile figures much more prominently in state long-arm statutes as a basis of general jurisdiction, and its use for this purpose is indisputably constitutional in principle. See *Milliken v. Meyer* (S.Ct. 1940); Restatement, sec. 421(2)(b). The same may be said for residence. Restatement, sec. 421(2)(c).

In the case of a business entity, nationality, domicile and residence ordinarily translate into incorporation within the forum. Restatement, sec. 421(2)(e). However, state legislation typically also confers on courts personal jurisdiction over business entities incorporated elsewhere, provided they are registered or qualified to do business within the forum. (An enterprise "does business" within a state other than its state of incorporation when it conducts substantial and continuous activities there.) Whether the resulting general jurisdiction is truly "general," in the sense of conferring jurisdiction over all actions, whether or not related to the business conducted in the forum state, or less than general, in the sense of restricted to actions arising out of activities within the state, depends on the language and interpretation of the state statute and, of course, the circumstances.

Moreover, even if a state considers that having a license to do business there ordinarily justifies an assertion of general jurisdiction, the federal courts may question whether, under the circumstances of a given case, that satisfies due process. Compare, e.g., *Knowlton v. Allied Van Lines, Inc.* (8th Cir. 1990), with *Siemer v. Learjet Acquisition Corp.* (5th Cir.1992). More generally, even where the defendant's activities within the forum rise to a level that warrants general jurisdiction, a particular exercise of personal jurisdiction may arguably be unreasonable and thus considered as inconsistent with due process. See, for example, *Amoco Egypt Oil Co. v. Leonis Navig. Co., Inc.* (9th Cir.1993).

A distinctive feature of the US law of jurisdiction, however, is the possibility of general jurisdiction arising not from nationality, domicile or residence, but from a pattern of conduct linking the defendant with the forum. In the usual parlance, where the defendant conducts "continuous and systematic" activity in the forum, it may be deemed to be "doing business" there—i.e., present, and thus subject to the forum's general jurisdiction. Many state long-arm statutes expressly so provide; others do as much by authorizing (or being read to authorize) jurisdiction to the full limits of due process, since the Supreme Court has ruled the assertion of general jurisdiction based on "doing business" as in principle constitutional. See *Perkins v. Benguet Consol. Mining Co.* (S.Ct.1952); *Rosenberg Bros. & Co. v. Curtis Brown Co.* (S.Ct.1923). See also Restatement (Third) of Foreign Relations Law, sec. 421(2)(h). Clearly, then, a non-resident alien defendant can become subject to US jurisdiction without having physically entered the forum, provided its activities abroad have substantial or relevant enough effects within the forum. Equally clearly, if personal jurisdiction results, it is more likely to be specific than general, though both are possible.

The threshold of contacts with the forum state required to establish "doing business" jurisdiction is necessarily uncertain, and the courts are divided in their application of the test. Among frequent indicia of doing business are maintaining an office or general bank account within the forum, regularly soliciting business or advertising there, or engaging employees or agents there. However, none of these factors necessarily guarantees a finding of general jurisdiction, and the decisions are not entirely consistent. What is clear is that merely occasional or sporadic activity in the forum will not suffice. Nor, ordinarily, will isolated acts of shipping products into the forum, ordering products from the forum, or sending agents into the forum. The same may be said of entering into contracts with forum residents. The most that such activity is likely in itself to generate is "specific" jurisdiction (see below).

Two other possible bases of general jurisdiction require mention. One is consent or waiver. The defendant may consent to the general jurisdiction of the forum, either expressly or impliedly, and either in advance of or subsequent to the emergence of a dispute. Consent or waiver, if valid, will be constitutionally sufficient to justify the exercise of jurisdiction. See *Insurance Corp. of Ireland v. Compagnie des Bauxites de Guinee* (S.Ct.1982). An example of waiver is consent to a forum selection clause. Waiver may also result from a failure to raise jurisdictional objections at the stage required under forum procedural law. It is necessary to bear in mind, however, that the scope of the jurisdiction conferred by consent or waiver depends on the terms of the consent or the circumstances of the waiver, and that consent or waiver will ordinarily give rise only to specific rather than general personal jurisdiction.

The second, and far more controversial jurisdictional basis is "tag" or "transient" jurisdiction, i.e.

jurisdiction based on the bare fact that the defendant was, and could lawfully be, served with a summons (or a summons and complaint) in the forum, and without any other contacts. Although it remains subject to harsh critiques and has been disavowed by the Restatement (Third) of Foreign Relations Law (sec. 421, reporters note 5), the practice of tag jurisdiction has been upheld as constitutional by the Supreme Court. *Burnham v. Superior Court* (S.Ct.1990). For some members of the Court, it is by definition consistent with due process. For others, it is consistent with due process only if its exercise under the circumstances is, once again, reasonable and fair. Tag or transient jurisdiction is presumably no less valid in international than in sister-state cases. Only in rare circumstances—physical presence in the forum procured by fraud or duress, or due strictly to litigation or settlement negotiation activity—can tag jurisdiction be considered excluded as a matter of constitutional law.

Tag jurisdiction operates in a reasonably straightforward manner where jurisdiction over natural persons is concerned. The workings of tag jurisdiction over legal persons are less obvious. In *Amusement Equipment, Inc. v. Mordelt* (5th Cir.1985), the plaintiff "tagged" an officer of the defendant German corporation while he was attending a trade show within the state. The court treated service on the officer as giving rise to general jurisdiction over him. However, to the extent that the claim (like the lawsuit itself) was against the corporation rather than against him, personal jurisdiction was not perfected. See also *Siemer v. Learjet Acquisition Corp., supra.* Other courts under like circumstances, however, have found that tagging a corporate officer creates general jurisdiction over the corporation as well as the officer.

(b) Specific jurisdiction

In order to be effective, a US court's personal jurisdiction need not be general, in the sense of entitling the court to entertain any and all actions against the defendant. Personal jurisdiction may also be "specific." General and specific jurisdiction differ not only as to the circumstances needed to justify jurisdiction, but also as to the consequences of jurisdiction, and more particularly the range of disputes as to which such jurisdiction may be exercised. In principle, when a court's jurisdictional basis is specific rather than general, it may only entertain actions against the defendant that arise out of or relate to the circumstances (or contacts) that underlie the exercise of jurisdiction. Clearly, specific jurisdiction is more easily established than general jurisdiction, but at the same time its jurisdictional effects are narrower.

Like general jurisdiction, specific jurisdiction must be both statutorily authorized and constitutionally defensible. Depending on the state, long-arm statutes either set out particular bases of specific jurisdiction or are to be read as authorizing all exercises of specific jurisdiction that due process will allow. The basis of specific jurisdiction that is relevant to a particular exercise of jurisdiction will depend on the cause of action being asserted. For example, a breach of contract action may be brought in the forum against a non-resident defendant by virtue of the fact that the particular contract in question was to be performed there; a tort action may be brought against a non-resident defendant by virtue of the fact that the alleged tort was committed there, etc.

Determining whether a tort or contract scenario presents sufficient contacts with the forum to justify an exercise of specific jurisdiction over a tort or contract claim, respectively, is not as simple as it may appear. In a leading domestic law case, the Supreme Court ruled that the fact that an out-of-state defendant concluded a contract with a forum state resident is not in itself sufficient even to vest the forum with specific jurisdiction over the former, but that additional connections with the forum state—such as place of negotiations, payment, delivery, inspection, service, or notification—might make a difference. *Burger King Corp. v. Rudzewicz, supra*. For a case where sufficient additional elements were present to permit the exercise of contract-based specific jurisdiction, see *Afram Export Corp. v. Metallurgiki Halyps, S.A.* (7th Cir.1985).

Product liability cases are also commonly predicated on specific jurisdiction, more particularly on the ground that the non-resident defendant placed the defective product in the so-called "stream of commerce" leading to the forum state, the place of injury. The foundation case is *World–Wide Volkswagen Corp. v. Woodson, supra,* where the Supreme Court ruled that a manufacturer cannot be said to place goods in the stream of commerce for these purposes unless it purposefully availed itself of the benefits and protections of the forum's laws (and the exercise of jurisdiction is otherwise reasonable). The foreseeability of effects within the forum would not suffice. Despite a division in the Court, the *Asahi* case, *supra* page 41, seems to have reinforced this view. See also *Gould v. P.T. Krakatau Steel* (8th Cir.1992). Unless the stream of commerce is broad and deep enough to constitute "doing business" within the forum, the jurisdiction flowing from that stream is presumably specific only, in the sense that it will only justify suits arising out of or related to the "stream."

(c) Quasi-in-rem jurisdiction

The constitutional requirement of due process applies even in cases where the jurisdiction sought to be obtained is not *in personam*, but rather *quasi-in-rem.* (*Quasi-in-rem* jurisdiction is jurisdiction based on the attachment of property in the forum belonging to an out-of-state defendant, thus permitting the forum to entertain an action against the defendant up to the value of the property attached, even though the property is unrelated to the cause of action being asserted.) In *Shaffer v. Heitner* (S.Ct.1977), the Supreme Court ruled that *quasi-in-rem* jurisdiction is subject to the same general test of "fair play and substantial justice" as applies to the assertion of jurisdiction *in personam*. (In *Shaffer*, the Court ruled that the defendants' holding of shares in a Delaware corporation does not constitute a sufficient contact with Delaware to support the exercise of *quasi-in-rem* jurisdiction over them by the Delaware courts.) In some cases, the contacts are found to be sufficient to support *quasi-in-rem* jurisdiction, even when the local property is unrelated to the cause of action. See, e.g., *Feder v. Turkish Airlines* (S.D.N.Y.1977). Still, when there is some relation between the property and the underlying claim, the likelihood that an exercise of *quasi-in-rem* jurisdiction will be found constitutional is increased. In any case, courts seem generally readier to find contacts sufficient for due process purposes where *quasi-in-rem* rather than *in personam* jurisdiction is in issue. *Cameco Indus., Inc. v. Mayatrac, S.A.* (D.Md.1992); *Banco Ambrosiano S.p.A. v. Artoc Bank & Trust Ltd.* (N.Y.1984).

The *Shaffer* opinion contained a significant footnote (number 37) disclaiming any intention to decide whether the mere presence of the defendant's property in a state might be a sufficient basis for jurisdiction when no other forum would be available to the plaintiff. Most courts assume that this exception would apply only if the defendant were amenable to suit nowhere else in the world (see *Amoco Overseas Oil Co. v. Compagnie Nationale Algerienne de Navigation* (2d Cir.1979)), but others consider it sufficient that the defendant may not be sued anywhere else in the US (see *Louring v. Kuwait Boul-*

der Shipping Co. (D.Conn.1977)). The Court in *Shaffer* also declined to decide whether a state in which property is located should have jurisdiction to attach that property as security for a judgment being sought in another forum whose exercise of jurisdiction would comport with due process. (We revisit the latter question in Chapter 9 of this book on transnational provisional relief.)

The Internet and personal jurisdiction

US courts have had some difficulty applying the existing jurisdictional principles to internet-based activity. When does a foreign party subject itself to US court jurisdiction by virtue of the fact that persons located in the US have access to its website which, though maintained abroad, is fully accessible here? Assuming the foreign party may subject itself to US court jurisdiction in this fashion, when is that jurisdiction "general," in the sense in which we have used that term, and when is it "specific"?

Most courts have sought to apply the traditional standards, inquiring notably whether and to what extent the defendant specifically targeted a forum audience. See *ALS Scan, Inc. v. Digital Serv. Consultants, Inc.* (4th Cir.2002); *Cybersell, Inc. v. Cybersell, Inc.* (9th Cir.1997). Thus, in *Young v. New Haven Advocate* (4th Cir.2002), the court ruled that Virginia lacked personal jurisdiction over Connecticut newspapers for purposes of a defamation action arising from an article about the housing of Connecticut prisoners in Virginia, since the newspapers did not through purposeful conduct manifest an intent to aim their websites at a Virginia audience. The court was uninfluenced by the fact that the article itself had a specific Virginia focus. Other courts have suggested that the presence of such a focus might make a difference for jurisdictional due process purposes. See. e.g., *Revell v. Lidov* (5th Cir.2002). Still other decisions lay emphasis on the extent to which the defendant operates an "active" or a "passive" website. See *Zippo Mfg. Co. v. Zippo Dot Com, Inc.* (W.D.Pa.1997), proposing a "sliding scale" between the use of a website for entering into contracts or otherwise doing business with residents of the forum state, at the one end, and merely posting information on the website, at the other.

The problem presents some urgency because foreign jurisdictions may assert personal jurisdiction over US companies that allegedly cause injury on their territory traceable to the companies' websites being accessible (and being accessed) abroad. A high-profile example is the ruling by a Paris, France, court asserting jurisdiction over the US company, Yahoo!, on account of the fact that French users could access via the Yahoo! website certain displays of Nazi memorabilia in violation of French penal law. The French court issued an injunction forbidding Yahoo! from making such internet displays available to users in France. (The opinion in which a US court subsequently announced that it would not recognize or enforce the French injunction—*Yahoo!, Inc. v. La Ligue Contre Le Racisme et*

L'Antisemitisme (N.D.Cal.2001)—is discussed at page 348 *infra*.)

"Aggregation" of national contacts

Students will be accustomed to gauging the fairness of an exercise of personal jurisdiction over a non-local defendant by reference to the latter's "contacts" with the state in which the state or federal court, as the case may be, is sitting. It is assumed that, by definition, every US domiciliary may be found for general jurisdictional purposes in at least one state, the state of domicile. In order to justify "haling" such a person into the courts of another state, due process requires minimum contacts with that other state.

In transnational litigation, however, the defendant may well have no US domicile or residence. The question has arisen whether, in such a case, it is appropriate to continue measuring the defendant's contacts on a state-by-state basis, or whether it is preferable instead to assess the defendants's contacts with the US as a whole. In the latter event, a court—after establishing that it has statutory jurisdiction over the defendant—would inquire whether the defendant's "national" or "aggregate" contacts are such as to justify in fairness the assertion of jurisdiction.

The prospects of aggregating national contacts will differ according to whether the forum is a state or federal court. No state court—certainly no state court entertaining a state law cause of action—has taken the position that the existence of minimum contacts of the defendant for due process purposes may be gauged on an aggregated, as opposed to a state-wide, basis. This does not mean, however, that the court may never take the defendant's contacts with other states into account. This is especially so insofar as the court is determining whether the state's exercise of jurisdiction is "reasonable" in the more general sense.

The idea behind aggregating contacts is to permit the exercise of jurisdiction over non-residents who lack sufficient contacts with any single state to meet the usual due process standard, but whose contacts overall with the United States are sufficient. The underlying assumption is that non-US-resident defendants generally have a reduced interest in being "haled" into one particular state's courts rather than another's.

Prior to adoption of Federal Rule 4(k)(2), courts took a variety of approaches to this question. Some courts insisted that non-domiciliaries and non-nationals be treated on exactly the same terms as domiciliaries and nationals, i.e. requiring that those parties have minimum contacts with the particular state in which the court sits. See, e.g., *DeJames v. Magnificence Carriers, Inc.* (3d Cir.1981). Others took the position that, at least where a federal cause of action is concerned, the fairness of a federal court's exercise of personal jurisdiction should depend on nationally aggregated contacts. See, e.g., *Cryomedics, Inc. v. Spembly, Ltd.* (D.Conn.1975). Still others courts—in fact a majority—adopted an intermediate position according to which national contacts could be aggregated for due process purposes where the federal cause of action being asserted was based upon a federal statute which expressly authorizes the nation-wide or world-wide service of process, but not otherwise. A leading decision to that effect is *Go–Video, Inc. v. Akai Elec. Co., Ltd.* (9th Cir.1989), involving the Clayton Act, a statute which provides both a federal cause of action and authorizes world-wide service of process. The Supreme Court in effect endorsed this approach, holding that since the Commodity Exchange Act does not authorize nation-wide or world-wide service of process, aggregation of national contacts is not statutorily authorized. *Omni Capital Int'l, supra.* Courts aggregating contacts in federal question cases (with or without reliance on statutory language authorizing nation-wide or world-wide service of process) have emphasized that due process limitations on the exercise of personal jurisdiction by federal courts are determined by the Fifth rather than the Fourteenth Amendment, and therefore need not parallel the due process limitations on the exercise of jurisdiction by state courts. See, e.g., *United States v. Swiss Am. Bank, Ltd.* (1st Cir. 2001).

The Federal Rules, as amended, now appear to address the issue, so far as the federal courts are concerned. After reciting in subsection (k)(1)(A) that federal court jurisdiction may be exercised over a defendant "who could be subjected to the jurisdiction of a court of general jurisdiction in the state in which the district court is located,'' Rule 4 provides, in subsection (k)(2) that:

> If the exercise of jurisdiction is consistent with the Constitution and laws of the United States, serving a summons or filing a waiver of service is also effective, with respect to claims arising under federal law, to establish personal jurisdiction over the person of any defendant who is not subject to the jurisdiction of the courts of general jurisdiction of any state.

Rule 4(k)(2) was adopted in recognition of the fact that there may be non-residents who do not meet the statutory and constitutional conditions for the exercise of personal jurisdiction in any single state, but whose contacts with the US as a whole otherwise make it reasonable to subject them to suit in the US. If, absent an applicable specific statutory basis of federal jurisdiction over the person, federal court jurisdiction over such persons were entirely dependent on satisfying the statutory and due process conditions applicable to the exercise of jurisdiction of one or more individual states, they could escape the jurisdiction of US courts altogether—something a US resident, by definition, could not do.

Under Rule 4(k)(2), once it is determined that the defendant is not subject to the courts of general jurisdiction of *any* state, that defendant essentially becomes subject to the jurisdiction of the courts of *every* state, provided the exercise of jurisdiction does not otherwise offend due process. As is ordinarily the case, the personal jurisdiction that results from an aggregation of contacts may subject the defendant to either general or specific jurisdiction, depending on the strength and character of the contacts. See, e.g., *United States v. Swiss Am. Bank, Ltd., supra.* (Curiously, notwithstanding the advent of Rule 4(k)(2), some federal courts, in aggregating national contacts, continue to emphasize that the plaintiff's claim is based on a federal statute authorizing nationwide service of process. See, e.g., *Pinker v. Roche Holdings Ltd.* (3d Cir.2002).)

In general, the plaintiff has the burden of proving that the defendant is not subject to any state's general jurisdiction, and that the defendant's contacts with the US as a whole support the exercise of jurisdiction. *Base Metal Trading, Ltd. v. OJSC Novokuznetsky Alum. Factory* (4th Cir.2002). But the courts have developed more refined variations on the burden of proof. Recognizing the difficulty of establishing that the defendant is not amenable to jurisdiction in any US state, one court has ruled as follows. The plaintiff must first demonstrate the presence of a federal question, the inapplicability of any specific statutory basis of jurisdiction, and the sufficiency of aggregated national contacts. However, as to the unavailability of general jurisdiction in any state, the plaintiff need only assert that such is the case to the best of its knowledge. The defendant then has the burden of showing that it comes within the general jurisdiction of one or more states. If the defendant fails to do that, the court will assume that no state has general jurisdiction over the defendant, so that Rule 4(k)(2) may be used. If, however, the defendant claims that it *is* within the jurisdiction of a state, it must identify the state, at which point the plaintiff may either sue in that state or seek to prove that the defendant is not subject to that state's general jurisdiction, so as to justify suing the defendant elsewhere. *United States v. Swiss Am. Bank, Ltd.* (1st Cir.1999).

Authorization to aggregate contacts on a national basis under Rule 4(k)(2) does not therefore guarantee that, in any given case, due process will thereby be satisfied. An exercise of personal jurisdiction would presumably offend due process if the defendant's contacts with the US, even taken in the aggregate, do not satisfy a "minimum contacts" standard or would otherwise be unreasonable or unfair. *Central States, Southeast and Southwest Areas Pension Fund v. Reimer Express World Corp.* (7th Cir.2000); *Base Metal Trading, Ltd., supra.* Theoretically, a defendant's nationwide contacts may be too sparse to support jurisdiction in the federal courts of any state. Moreover, an exercise of jurisdiction may still offend due process if, for example, the defendant is sued under Rule 4(k)(2) in a significantly and needlessly inconvenient US forum. Thus courts, even while aggregating contacts (and finding the aggregated contracts sufficient), may find that the exercise of personal jurisdiction by a particular federal court would not, under the circumstances, be fair or reasonable. Finally, a court may have adequate jurisdiction in all respects on an aggregated contacts basis, but nevertheless decline jurisdiction on other valid grounds, such as *forum non conveniens*. See, e.g., *Pyrenee, Ltd. v. Wocom Commods., Ltd.* (N.D.Ill.1997).

Piercing the jurisdictional veil

We have in a sense already broached the "alter ego" question by noting (*supra* pages 16–17) the possibility that a non-signatory might in some circumstances be bound by, as well as invoke, a forum selection agreement. More generally, though, even in the absence of such a clause, a non-national, non-domiciliary may be found to be "present" in a US jurisdiction, due to the activities of a closely related party that is itself present or is otherwise subject to the court's jurisdiction.

US courts have recognized a number of theories on which jurisdiction may validly be predicated in a sense vicariously.

(a) "Alter ego" analysis

One such theory is precisely that of corporate fiction. For example, a local company may be so closely tied to a foreign parent that it is regarded as the latter's "alter ego" and capable, on account of its own contacts with the forum, of bringing the latter within the court's personal jurisdiction. This result is not, of course, to be presumed, even in the case of a 100%-owned corporate subsidiary, due to the fact that corporations are deemed presumptively to have an identity that is separate both from the shareholders and from related corporate entities.

Although most alter ego cases involve reaching a foreign parent through the activities of a local subsidiary, the reverse situation is also possible, so that personal jurisdiction may be acquired over a foreign subsidiary due to the activities of its local parent.

Any exercise of personal jurisdiction on this theory must be justified both statutorily and constitutionally. As to the former, since state long-arm statutes rarely address the question, guidance must be found in state common law. Unfortunately, there is little clarity as to the state whose law on the "alter ego" question is properly applied in making this determination. It might be the law of the state of incorporation of one of the entities, or the law of the state having the most significant contacts with the case, or, much more often than not, the forum's own law. Where a federal court is sitting in diversity, the forum law for these choice of law purposes will be the law of the state where the court sits. *Volkswagenwerk AG v. Beech Aircraft Corp.* (2d Cir.1984). In federal question cases, it will be federal common law. *United Elec., Radio & Mach. Workers v. 163 Pleasant St. Corp.* (1st Cir.1992). Sometimes, the forum avoids stating any clear choice of law preference at all.

Ultimately, whether the corporate veil may be pierced for jurisdictional purposes will depend on the forum's assessment of the fairness of doing so, within the meaning of due process. A leading precedent is *Cannon Mfg. Co. v. Cudahy Packing Co.* (S.Ct.1925), where the Supreme Court held that it is not enough, for these purposes, to show that the parent completely dominates its subsidiary, even to the point that the latter functions no differently than were it a branch of the parent. It is necessary to show that even the corporate formalities—separate books, separate boards, etc.—were disrespected. Scholars are divided over whether *Cannon* is truly a constitutional law, or merely a common law, decision. Moreover, in a later decision, *United States v. Scophony Corp. of Amer.* (S.Ct.1948), the Court expressly held that neither the federal legislation in question (the Clayton Act) nor due process prevented the assertion of jurisdiction over a parent company on account of its "constant supervision and intervention [of the subsidiary] beyond the normal exercise of shareholders' rights," even though corporate formalities were apparently respected. The outcome of the piercing exercise in any given case tends to turn on the pervasiveness and "day-to-day-ness" of the parent company's intervention and control. See, e.g., *Roorda v. Volkswagenwerk A.G.* (D.S.C.1979), calling into question whether *Cannon*'s strict standards still represent good law.

The point may be illustrated by *Hargrave v. Fibreboard Corp.* (5th Cir.1983), a case in which the Fifth Circuit ruled that, under a proper interpretation of the state long-arm statute, a UK company could not be made to answer in US court for the actions of its US subsidiary because, while enjoying complete authority over the latter's general policy decisions, the parent left the subsidiary free to make its day-to-day business and operational determinations. The question whether due process would have permitted the exercise of jurisdiction was thus left unanswered.

Even if a parent-subsidiary relationship does not meet the prevailing test for piercing the corporate veil, its contacts with the subsidiary, and therefore indirectly with the forum where the subsidiary does business, may be relevant in assessing the strength of the parent's own contacts with the forum and, more particularly, in determining whether the parent purposefully availed itself of the privilege of conducting business in the forum. Some courts thus tend to put the parent-subsidiary relationship into a larger business context, inquiring whether, overall, the parent and subsidiary functions as if they were an integrated whole, or whether the subsidiary formed an integral part of a business operation strategy put in place by the parent. A leading example is *Bulova Watch Co. v. K. Hattori & Co. Ltd.* (E.D.N.Y.1981). This may lead to an assertion of jurisdiction, even where the parent does not exercise pervasive day-to-day control over the subsidiary, much less show disrespect for corporate formalities. If jurisdiction over the parent results, that jurisdiction is, of course, likely to be "specific" rather than "general," in the sense of only permitting the adjudication of claims that arise out of or relate to the business conducted in the forum. For an example, see *Vermeulen v. Renault, U.S.A., Inc.* (11th Cir.1993).

It should not in any event be assumed that a party that is deemed amenable to US jurisdiction on veil-piercing grounds will thereby necessarily also be subject to liability on veil-piercing grounds. Courts have generally applied a stricter test to the "vicarious" imposition of liability than to the "vicarious" subjection to suit. See *Hargrave v. Fibreboard Corp., supra.* For vicarious liability in this context, the common law in most US jurisdictions requires not only an actual disregard of the corporate formalities, but also the perpetration of a fraud on a third party. See *United States v. Bestfoods* (S.Ct.1998).

(b) Agency theory

An alternative basis for obtaining jurisdiction over a non-resident entity on account of another entity's activities in the forum is agency. In other words, even if two entities do not constitute corporate "alter egos," they may nevertheless stand in a principal/agent relationship to one another. The agent's presence may then be imputable to the principal, at least with regard to causes of action related to the subject of the agency. As with the parent-subsidiary relationship, courts do not always (or indeed even very often) distinguish between whether the exercise of agency-based jurisdiction is, on the one hand, authorized by state law and, on the other hand, permitted by due process. The two inquiries are more often than not conflated.

A question obviously apt to arise in this context is the meaning of agency and, indeed, the law that the forum should apply in deciding whether or not an agency relationship exists. Where state law is specifically consulted, the forum has the possibility of applying either the forum law of agency, or agency principles of the law of the place where the relationship that is claimed to represent an agency is centered, or indeed the law of some other jurisdiction deemed to have the most significant contacts with the case or the greatest interest in having its law applied to that issue. Not surprisingly, courts rarely make an explicit and determined choice among these various jurisdictions' agency law—perhaps because the broad outlines of agency are not altogether dissimilar from jurisdiction to jurisdiction.

Generally speaking, an agency does not arise for jurisdictional purposes unless the alleged agent acted for the account and benefit of the alleged principal, with the latter's knowledge and consent, and subject to the latter's control. In any event, the agent must have acted within the scope of its authority. Parties need not be corporate affiliates in order to stand in a principal-agent relationship. On the other hand, corporate affiliation may make it more likely that the required elements of agency just mentioned will be found. In the well-known case of *Frummer v. Hilton Hotels International* (N.Y.1967), the court found that Hilton Hotels (UK) Ltd. subjected itself to the jurisdiction of a New York court by making regular use of the New York-based Hilton Reservation Service for the purpose of taking reservations. The court treated the Service as the agent of Hilton UK for purposes of establishing New York jurisdiction over the latter. Of particular significance was the fact that the Service both directly accepted and confirmed room reservations at the London Hilton. See also *Wiwa v. Royal Dutch Petroleum Co.* (2d Cir.2000); *Gelfand v. Tanner Motor Tours, Ltd.* (2d Cir.1967).

Once again, it may be uncertain whether an agency relationship, once proven, gives rise to "specific" or "general" jurisdiction. The plaintiff in *Frummer* did not allege that the Reservation Service had anything whatsoever to do with his case; in order to provide jurisdiction over his claim, the agency-based jurisdiction must therefore have been, to that extent at least, general. In several cases, the question was whether Volkswagen AG of Germany was generally amenable to the jurisdiction of US courts due to its agency relationship with a franchised and wholly-owned wholesale distributor in the US which itself engages in a regular and systematic course of business in a US state. See, e.g., *Delagi v. Volkswagenwerk AG* (N.Y.1972), where jurisdiction was found lacking because the auto accident in question did not arise out of the franchisee's operations and because there was not sufficient evidence of agency and control. Whether general or specific jurisdiction is created presumably depends on the range and substantiality of the agency relationship. Closely related to agency is the notion that, through some other relationship—a distributorship, for example—

an out-of-state defendant may have rendered itself subject to the forum's jurisdiction.

Again, vicarious jurisdiction does not necessarily imply vicarious liability. A principal/agent relationship may permit imputing the presence of the agent in the forum to the non-present principal, without making them interchangeably liable.

Plaintiff's nationality

In keeping with US jurisdictional principles generally, it is essentially the *defendant's* contacts with the forum which determine whether an exercise of personal jurisdiction is statutorily and constitutionally proper. The *plaintiff's* contacts are fundamentally irrelevant to that inquiry. The question arises whether different presumptions should operate in the transnational, as opposed to the sister-state, context.

Although arguments could be made in favor of restricting aliens' access to US courts, no such barrier exists. Rather, foreign persons have in principle full access to US courts. Congress may of course, in creating a new statutory cause of action, limit that cause of action to plaintiffs who are citizens (or residents) of the US, and the courts will presumably respect that, subject to treaty undertakings. The statute's grant of subject matter jurisdiction will then be correspondingly limited. But Congress is not presumed to have intended to limit causes of action to US nationals. The rule is no different where the foreign plaintiff is a foreign state (or instrumentality) itself. See *Pfizer, Inc. v.*

Government of India (S.Ct.1978), recognizing foreign states' standing under the antitrust laws.

If the plaintiff's nationality and residence are basically irrelevant to a court's subject matter jurisdiction, they may nevertheless be relevant to the court's determination whether to exercise that jurisdiction. As the next chapter shows, for example, the readiness of a US court to dismiss a transnational case on *forum non conveniens* grounds may well turn on the plaintiff's nationality or residence.

THE TIMING OF JURISDICTIONAL OBJECTIONS

The claim that a court lacks personal jurisdiction is usually asserted at the threshold of litigation. Particularly in transnational litigation, however, such an objection may re-surface at the stage when a judgment of State X is brought for recognition and enforcement in State Y. Indeed, the defendant may not have interposed that objection in State X in the first place. Because a court's consideration of jurisdictional objections is understandably somewhat different when raised at the recognition or enforcement stage—whether or not previously raised—we defer its treatment to Chapter 10, which deals with problems arising at that point in time.

CHAPTER THREE

SUBJECT MATTER JURISDICTION OVER TRANSNATIONAL DISPUTES

The previous chapter dealt with personal jurisdiction over non-nationals and non-residents. US courts, state and federal alike, also of course need to have subject matter jurisdiction in order validly to entertain a case, and are required to verify its existence whether or not a party raises the issue. While one might have supposed that the federal courts in the US would necessarily enjoy subject matter jurisdiction over transnational disputes, that is by no means the case. It is entirely possible that a piece of transnational litigation may be heard in the US, if at all, only in state court. This is because the jurisdiction of the state courts in the US is in principle plenary, while the jurisdiction of the federal courts is not. At the same time, as we shall see, "transnational law cases" is simply not, as such, a category of federal court jurisdiction. Moreover, subject matter jurisdiction (unlike personal jurisdiction) is regarded as affecting the court's very power to hear a case, and cannot be waived by the parties or the court.

Not only is the federal courts' subject matter jurisdiction limited, but it does not necessarily cover all disputes we would regard as transnational. We can establish this by examining the various components of federal subject matter jurisdiction. In the first place, Article III contemplates federal court jurisdiction of claims "arising under" federal law (commonly known as "federal question" jurisdiction). Although many cases that we would consider to be transnational do in fact arise under the US Constitution, a federal statute or a treaty, not all of them do. The fact that a dispute contains a foreign element—even an important one—does not necessarily suffice to render the dispute a "federal question" case within the meaning of Article III.

Second, Article III gives the federal courts constitutional subject matter jurisdiction over disputes between citizens of different states, as well as between a state or a citizen of a state and a foreign State or one of its citizens. This is commonly known as "diversity jurisdiction." Diversity jurisdiction (especially "alienage jurisdiction," covering suits between a US national and a non-national) will encompass a good many transnational disputes, but, again, certainly not all.

Third, Article III specifically grants federal court jurisdiction over a number of matters, some of which are inherently international, for example cases involving ambassadors and consuls (over which federal jurisdiction is exclusive) and admiralty and maritime cases. But this represents a relatively narrow range of disputes.

Except where the Constitution or a federal statute states the contrary, federal question cases may be brought in state as well as federal court. However, when the case is one over which a federal court would have had original jurisdiction, the defendant has a right of removal of the case to federal court (28 U.S.C.A. sec. 1141). This is subject to an important exception: removal of diversity cases is available only when none of the defendants is a citizen of the forum state (*id.* sec.1441(b)).

From examining the scope of Article III, we therefore see that cases having important foreign or international elements may arise without triggering federal court jurisdiction. If such cases are to be heard in the US, they will be heard in a court of one of the states and handled no differently procedurally than more routine state court cases. However, to the extent that substantive federal law (statutory, common law, treaty and of course the Constitution) nevertheless proves relevant to the disposition of the case, it will of course come into play in the state court adjudication.

Article III merely authorizes legislative grants of subject matter jurisdiction to be made; it does not itself make them. Congress must enact legislation establishing such jurisdiction before it can arise. In fact, Congress has enacted both general and specific legislation giving effect to the constitutional grant of judicial jurisdiction under Article III. By way of general authorization, 28 U.S.C.A. secs. 1331 and 1332, respectively, vest in federal district courts jurisdiction over federal question and diversity (including "alienage") cases. As noted, these may indeed cover transnational disputes. Congress has also made a very large number of grants of specific subject matter jurisdiction, many of which (the antitrust acts, for example) may well have application to transnational cases. See, e.g., 28 U.S.C.A. sec. 1337. Some of this legislation makes federal court jurisdiction exclusive, so that actions thereunder may not be brought in state court. These include admiralty, bankruptcy, and patent and copyright claims (28 U.S.C.A. secs. 1333, 1334 and 1338, respectively), as well as suits against foreign diplomatic and consular officers (28 U.S.C.A. sec. 1351). But two statutory grants are particularly relevant to transnational cases. They are, in order of enactment, the Alien Tort Claim Statute and the Foreign Sovereign Immunities Act, dealt with briefly below and in greater depth in Chapters 6 and 5 *infra*, respectively.

DIVERSITY AND "ALIENAGE" JURISDICTION

The branch of diversity jurisdiction that most concerns us is "alienage" jurisdiction, i.e. jurisdiction over cases "between a State, or the citizens thereof, and foreign States, Citizens or Subjects," to borrow the language of Article III of the Constitution. These cases were considered especially appropriate for federal jurisdiction in the interest of avoiding unfair treatment of foreign nationals by state courts and, more generally, embarrassment to US foreign relations. The current statutory authorization for such suits is found in 28 U.S.C.A. sec. 1332(a)(2) and (3).

Subsection 2 vests the federal district courts with original jurisdiction over civil actions involving more than $75,000 between "citizens of a State and citizens or subjects of a foreign State." As in the case of sister-state diversity (*Strawbridge v. Curtiss* (S.Ct.1806)), "complete" diversity is required. If aliens figure among the parties on both sides of a dispute, diversity is destroyed. *Cabalceta v. Standard Fruit Co.* (11th Cir.1989). *A fortiori*, alienage jurisdiction does not encompass suits between aliens. *Verlinden BV v. Central Bank of Nigeria* (S.Ct.1983). Indeed, the Court in *Verlinden* reached this result as a matter of constitutional and not merely statutory interpretation. On the other hand, it should be noted that Section 1332, as amended in 1988, provides that an alien who is admitted to the US as a permanent resident "shall be deemed a citizen of the State in which such alien is domiciled."

28 U.S.C.A. sec. 1332(a)(3) permits a different result in certain cases. Added in 1948, it confers original jurisdiction in suits between "citizens of different States ... in which citizens or subjects of a foreign state are additional parties," for the purpose of preventing the presence of an alien on one side of a dispute between citizens of sister-states from destroying the diversity that would otherwise

exist. Although the statutory language suggests that the same result should obtain where aliens are present on both sides of a dispute between citizens of sister-states, the courts are in disagreement as to that. Under the prevailing view there is diversity even then. See e.g., *Dresser Indus., Inc. v. Underwriters at Lloyd's* (3d Cir.1997); *Transure, Inc. v. Marsh & McLennan, Inc.* (9th Cir.1985); But see *Faysound Ltd. v. United Coconut Chems., Inc.* (9th Cir.1989); *Hercules Inc. v. Dynamic Export Corp.* (S.D.N.Y.1976). Some courts that permit alienage jurisdiction to survive the presence of aliens on both sides nevertheless require complete diversity between the aliens on the two sides (see e.g., *DeWit v. KLM Royal Dutch Airlines, N.V.* (S.D.N.Y.1983), but the majority do not (see e.g., *K & H Business Consultants Ltd. v. Cheltonian, Inc.* (D.N.J.1983)). In any case, subsection (3) is unavailable unless there are genuinely parties from different states on both sides of the dispute, and there is complete diversity as to them.

Matters are complicated by the 1988 amendment referred to above, deeming a permanent resident alien to be a citizen of the state of that person's domicile. The amendment can affect alienage jurisdiction in different ways. Some courts have inferred that the amendment creates new opportunities for federal jurisdiction by allowing aliens to be treated as citizens of a state for diversity purposes (and thus entitled to sue another alien in federal court). See e.g., *Singh v. A.G. Daimler–Benz* (3d Cir.1993). But others have held otherwise, on the ground that the amendment was meant to contract, not expand, diversity jurisdiction. See e.g., *Saadeh v. Farouki* (D.C.Cir.1997). In any event, the amendment may remove alienage jurisdiction where suit is between a US citizen and a permanent alien resident in the same state.

Section 1332(c) introduces a further complication by positing that a corporation shall be deemed "a citizen of any State by which it has been incorporated and of the State where it has its principal place of business," i.e. a dual citizen. If section 1332(c) applies to foreign corporations, then it may operate so as render a foreign corporation a non-alien by virtue of the fact that it has its principal place of business in a US state. If that state is also the state of citizenship of an opposing party, then diversity will be destroyed. But a foreign corporation that has its principal place of business in the US is also nonetheless an alien. Since the presence of an alien on both sides destroys diversity, this may prove fatal to alienage jurisdiction. *Danjaq, S.A. v. Pathe Communic. Corp.* (9th Cir.1992); *Hercules Inc. v. Dynamic Export Corp., supra.* However, a domestic corporation with its principal place of business abroad is not an alien so as to defeat diversity when the other party is an alien. *Cabalceta v. Standard Fruit Co.* (11th Cir.1989).

Suits *by* foreign governments may be regarded as a species of diversity cases, since 28 U.S.C.A. sec. 1332(a)(4) provides for federal jurisdiction when the plaintiff is a foreign state, within the meaning of the Foreign Sovereign Immunities Act (FSIA), discussed in Chapter 5 *infra*, and the defendants are "citizens of a State or of different States." The FSIA also introduced a separate basis of federal jurisdiction for suits *against* foreign governments by adding 28 U.S.C.A. section 1330(a), which is noted below as a species of federal question jurisdiction and discussed in greater detail in Chapter 5.

FEDERAL QUESTION JURISDICTION

Federal question jurisdiction opens the way for transnational litigation to take place in the federal courts irrespective of the alienage of one or more of the parties. That the dispute "arises under [the] Constitution, the Laws of the United States, and Treaties made, or which shall be made, under their authority" (to quote Article III of the Constitution) is constitutionally sufficient.

General federal question jurisdiction

Notwithstanding the language of Article III, Congress did not statutorily grant general federal question jurisdiction to the district courts until 1875. The relevant jurisdictional statute is found in 28 U.S.C.A. sec. 1331, which provides that "district courts shall have original jurisdiction of all civil actions arising under the Constitution, laws, or treaties of the United States."

The great majority of federal question cases arise under specific federal statutes, advancing causes of action that those statutes specifically create. (Many such statutes—such as the antitrust and securities laws—themselves contain an express grant of federal court subject matter jurisdiction, thus rendering section 1331 duplicative.) However, claims based upon federal common law (i.e. non-statutory federal claims) likewise constitute claims arising under federal law for Section 1331 purposes. *Illinois v. Milwaukee* (S.Ct.1972).

International cases present no peculiar difficulties as far as general federal question jurisdiction is concerned. As with federal question cases generally, the complaint must itself present a claim created by federal, as opposed to state, law, either as the basis of the cause of action or as a substantial and necessary element of a non-federal cause of action. *Franchise Tax Bd. v. Construction Laborers Vacation Trust* (S.Ct.1983). It is not enough that the defendant asserts a federal law by way of defense to a non-federal claim.

While it is true that a non-federal claim does not become subject to federal question jurisdiction merely because the defendant happens to raise a defense based on federal law, the courts have nevertheless given the notion of a federal question a reasonably broad interpretation. Thus, for example, the courts have treated as falling within federal question jurisdiction a claim based entirely on a state law cause of action (e.g. contract or tort), provided the case necessarily implicates important federal interests. A good example is *Sequihua v. Texaco, Inc.* (S.D.Tex.1994), where a federal court entertained certain state law causes of action by residents of a foreign country due to the fact that resolution of the claims being asserted would "affect ... international law and the relationship between United States and foreign governments," and thus necessarily entail the application of federal common law. By such reasoning, courts have occasionally found a case that could not otherwise be said to arise under federal law to do so on account of the inevitable necessity of entertaining application of the act of state doctrine (discussed in Chapter 5). (The federal court in *Sequihua*, having assumed jurisdiction on federal question grounds, then proceeded to dismiss the case on grounds of international comity and *forum non conveniens*. A similar scenario arose in *Torres v. Southern Peru Copper Corp.* (S.D.Tex.1995), (S.D.Tex.1996)).

Specific federal question jurisdiction

While Congress did not establish general federal question jurisdiction until 1875, it created specific federal question jurisdiction much earlier. The Judiciary Act of 1789 granted the district courts subject matter jurisdiction over admiralty and maritime cases and cases involving foreign consuls. Through what has come to be known as the Alien Tort Claim Statute (ATCS), codified at 28 U.S.C.A. sec. 1350, it also granted them jurisdiction over "any civil action by an alien for a tort only, committed in violation of the law of nations or a treaty of the United States." (The ATCS is treated in Chapter 6 *infra*.)

In the intervening years, Congress has created many new federal statutory causes of action and, in so doing, expressly vested jurisdiction to hear them in the federal district courts. Once again, the federal antitrust and securities laws are prime examples. Unlike the availability of general bases of federal jurisdiction, the availability of these specific bases depends on whether the claim being advanced falls within the scope of application of the specific legislation in question, with the consequence that it may sometimes be difficult to distinguish the question of subject matter jurisdiction from the merits of the case.

Perhaps the most "general" of the specific grants of federal question jurisdiction is found in the 1976 Foreign Sovereign Immunities Act (FSIA), treated at length in Chapter 5 *infra*. This statute, which is principally codified at 28 U.S.C.A. secs. 1601–11, creates federal subject matter jurisdiction over all civil cases against foreign governments and their instrumentalities as to which those entities are not immune according to the substantive provisions of the FSIA. See 28 U.S.C.A. sec. 1330(a). Thus, unlike other specific statutory grants of subject matter jurisdiction, the FSIA's grant of federal jurisdiction is not tied to a particular cause of action, but rather to the identity of the defendant. Furthermore, the grant is directly linked to the immunity question: there is subject matter jurisdiction in suits against such defendants only to the extent that the latter do not enjoy immunity. (As discussion of the FSIA in Chapter 5 will show, there is also statutory personal jurisdiction over sovereign defendants whenever they do not enjoy immunity under the terms of the FSIA.)

The *Verlinden* case, *supra*, required the Supreme Court to find a proper constitutional basis for the FSIA's grant of subject matter jurisdiction in cases between an alien plaintiff and a foreign government. The plaintiff, a Dutch corporation, brought a breach of contract action in the US against Nigeria's central bank, asserting jurisdiction under the FSIA (and, more particularly, the FSIA's exception from immunity for commercial acts performed abroad having substantial effects in the US). The Court found that application of the FSIA under these circumstances could not be justified under the diversity jurisdiction branch of Article III because the latter does not authorize suits between aliens. However, the Court ruled that "federal question" jurisdiction under Article III was present because the FSIA was a valid exercise of congressional authority to regulate foreign affairs. Accordingly, cases brought under the FSIA could therefore properly be considered as cases "arising under" federal law. This was so, even if the underlying cause of action (as in the *Verlinden* case itself) was a state rather than a federal law cause of action. The *Verlinden* case demonstrates that adequate federal question jurisdiction exists where suits are statutorily authorized by legislation validly adopted pursuant to Congress' legislative authority under Article I of the Constitution.

Despite the arguments that could be made in favor of exclusive federal subject matter jurisdiction under the FSIA, that jurisdiction is not exclusive. Foreign states may be sued in state court as readily as in federal court (though only, of course, where one of the FSIA's own exceptions to the rule of immunity is applicable). The statute, however, specifically gives the defendant a right of removal of the case from state to federal court.

SUBJECT MATTER AND PERSONAL JURISDICTION

We return in conclusion to the interplay between federal subject matter jurisdiction, on the one hand, and personal jurisdiction, on the other. In order for a federal court's exercise of jurisdiction to be valid—whether in domestic or transnational cases—it must enjoy both types of jurisdiction. Note that a cause of action may be statutorily authorized in regard to subject matter jurisdiction, but nevertheless unconstitutional in terms of personal jurisdiction. This may be the case, for example, in a common law action by a US plaintiff against a non-resident, non-national defendant. Subject matter jurisdiction will be satisfied due to diversity (or, more particularly, alienage), but personal jurisdiction not, if, as may well be the case, the defendant lacks minimum contacts with the forum. It is even possible that a state or federal court would have both subject matter jurisdiction and statutory personal jurisdiction over a foreign sovereign (due to the fact that the one of FSIA's statutory exceptions to sovereign immunity—the commercial act exception, for example—is applicable), and yet the foreign sovereign's contacts with the US might be insufficient to satisfy constitutional due process.

VENUE

Transnational, like domestic, litigation requires proper venue as well as proper subject matter jurisdiction. We can tell from most federal venue provisions that their purpose is to identify the court, within the competent jurisdictional system, which is the most convenient one for trying a case falling within the subject matter jurisdiction of the federal courts.

At the federal level, there are both general and specific venue statutes. In diversity and federal question cases, venue lies in the judicial district where (1) any defendant resides (providing all the defendants reside in the same state), (2) where a substantial part of the events or omissions giving rise to the claim occurred or where the property that is the subject of the action is situated, or (3) where, failing both of the above, any defendant is subject to personal jurisdiction. 28 U.S.C.A. sec. 1391(a), (b). (The venue statute was amended in 1990 to eliminate the option in diversity suits of suing at the plaintiff's residence.)

Where the defendant is not a US national (which can of course easily be the case in transnational litigation), venue is specifically governed by the

Alien Venue Statute, 28 U.S.C.A. sec. 1391(d), which provides that aliens may be sued in "any" district (meaning any district having personal jurisdiction over them). This simplifies the not uncommon scenario in which co-defendants include both US and non-US nationals. Particular federal statutes may contain their own venue provisions, which generally prevail in cases arising under those statutes. However, in order to preserve the advantages of liberal venue in suits against aliens, the Alien Venue Statute has been construed as prevailing over such specialized provisions. *Brunette Mach. Works, Ltd. v. Kockum Indus., Inc.* (S.Ct.1972); *Go–Video, Inc. v. Akai Elec. Co., Ltd.* (9th Cir.1989). Thus, where alien defendants are concerned, the specificity of the Alien Venue Statute in effect trumps the specificity of specialized statutory venue provisions. (Needless to say, the fact that an alien may, as a matter of venue, be sued in "any" district does not mean that the exercise of personal jurisdiction over the alien in any given case is either statutorily or constitutionally proper. Venue is determined only after personal jurisdiction has been properly and independently established.)

Only the FSIA has been found to displace the Alien Venue Statute, chiefly because it contains a specialized venue provision covering a particular category of aliens (namely, foreign states and their agencies or instrumentalities). As amended by the FSIA, the general federal venue statute provides for suit against a foreign state to be brought in specified federal judicial districts, including the district in which a substantial part of the events or omissions giving rise to the claim occurred or in which the property in question in the action is located, the district court for the District of Columbia (in actions against the state or a political subdivision of it), or the district where an agency or instrumentality of a foreign state is licensed to do, or does, business (in actions against an agency or instrumentality). 28 U.S.C.A. sec. 1391(f).

CHAPTER FOUR

PARALLEL LITIGATION

By its very nature, transnational litigation lends itself to a multiplicity of fora. The more jurisdictions having an interest in, or even merely a point of contact with, a transaction or relationship, the greater the number of potential fora for the resolution of disputes arising out of or related to that transaction or relationship. In a world of increased mobility, where business and personal transactions transcend national boundaries, the jurisdiction of a number of different fora may easily be invoked in a single or a set of related disputes. The possibility of litigating in a variety of jurisdictions raises issues as complex as they are controversial, most notably where each party seeks a "home field advantage" or access to a forum seemingly "friendlier" to it. International "forum shopping" is an obvious prospect.

Multiple fora are less of a problem when they arise within a single jurisdiction. Any such jurisdiction has it within its power to establish rules for determining, as among potentially competing fora within that jurisdiction, which one that will enjoy competence. Within the US, for example, the Full Faith and Credit Clause of the Constitution holds out some promise in this regard by requiring that "Full Faith and Credit shall be given in each State

. . . to the Judicial Proceedings of every other State. . . ." (US Const. Art. IV, sec. 1).

Federal law also provides for the transfer of cases from one federal district to another for reasons of convenience (28 U.S.C.A. sec. 1404(a)). Even so, not all interstate jurisdictional conflicts in the US are thereby avoided or solved. But when the potential fora are found in separate and distinct legal systems, the opportunity for any such regulation is still further reduced.

This chapter deals with three scenarios that arise with frequency in transnational litigation in US courts. In the first scenario, only one forum has been invoked, but that forum has serious doubts as to whether it is the most appropriate forum in which to have the claim at issue adjudicated. In many jurisdictions around the world, this is a non-problem because the availability of a more appropriate forum elsewhere—even a vastly more appropriate one—is simply not a valid ground for declining to exercise jurisdiction over a dispute. Most civil law jurisdictions are quite unfamiliar with, and find odd, the notion of dismissals or stays for *forum non conveniens*; they tend to address problems of parallel litigation, if at all, through other instruments discussed below. But, in the US, as in numerous other common law jurisdictions, the discretionary doctrine of *forum non conveniens* is well established and frequently applied.

Second, the same or related litigation may have in fact been instituted in the courts of two or more jurisdictions. Judicial economy, orderliness and the need to avoid inconsistent rulings all suggest that the litigation should go forward in only one of the courts whose jurisdiction has been invoked. Within many legal systems there prevails a so-called doctrine of *lis pendens*, according to which all courts other than the first one seised should decline to exercise jurisdiction. Its chief objective is to avoid the conduct of parallel proceedings in different courts, with the attendant waste of resources and risk of inconsistent outcomes. The *lis pendens* doctrine presupposes that priority in the timing of the filing of litigation merits decisive consideration. Accordingly, it is sometimes referred to as a "first-in-time rule," taking the time of filing rather than the time of judgment as critical, and allowing only the court "first seised" of a dispute to proceed with it. While the notion and practice of *lis pendens* is firmly anchored in domestic practice within civil law systems, adherence to it by those systems in the international context is considerably weaker. Within the US, *lis pendens* is less firmly anchored even domestically, much less internationally.

Third, sometimes a court, far from declining jurisdiction in favor a more convenient or appropriate foreign forum (or a foreign court seised earlier in time), may consider that it is itself so much the more convenient or appropriate forum that the parties should be prevented from submitting their claims to the courts of any other jurisdiction. At the same time, it may lack confidence that the courts of those other jurisdictions will themselves decline jurisdiction on *forum non conveniens*, *lis pendens*, or some other jurisdiction-declining ground. The stage is then set for the court to adopt a more assertive posture, in the form of an "anti-suit injunction," by which is meant the issuance of an order to a party to refrain from instituting or maintaining litigation in the other forum.

Of all the instruments that may be deployed to deal with parallel litigation, the latter is by far the most controversial, often enough unleashing jurisdictional conflict rather than jurisdictional cooperation. This will explain why, in the interest of international comity, even when courts do issue anti-suit injunctions, they address them to litigants (and only to litigants who are subject to the enjoining court's jurisdiction), and not directly to the foreign court. It will also explain the stated reluctance with which courts resort to this device. Understandably, however, such precautions have hardly defused the controversy associated with anti-suit injunctions when issued.

INTERNATIONAL *FORUM NON CONVENIENS*

Students of American civil procedure are not accustomed to attaching great significance to the *forum non conveniens* doctrine. It is commonly assumed that, while considerations of convenience might heavily counsel in favor of a dismissal on *forum non conveniens* grounds, neither the applicable procedural rules nor the applicable substantive law is likely to change dramatically as a consequence of a dismissal. Transfers of venue for convenience in the federal courts, expressly provided for by 28 U.S.C.A. sec. 1404(a), are common. Minimizing the substantive consequences is the fact that the transferee court applies the substantive law that the transferor court would have applied had it retained jurisdiction. *Van Dusen v. Barrack* (S.Ct. 1964).

Any assumption that dismissal for convenience in the transnational context will have little procedural or substantive consequence would be quite misplaced. With the movement of a case to an internationally different forum are likely to come into play significant and possibly outcome-determinative changes in the applicable procedural or substantive law, including available causes of action, and remedies. Even where two systems have the same textual rules in place, the same result may not obtain due to differences in interpretation of these rules or in the respective courts' characterizations of the facts.

Thus, *forum non conveniens* may prove to be quite a high-stakes game indeed when deployed in the transnational litigation context. It is little wonder that dismissal motions on convenience grounds have become a staple of the practice and are likely to be vigorously contested by the opposing party. Interestingly, transfers for convenience within the federal court system under Section 1404(a) are not infrequently followed in transnational cases almost immediately by a motion to dismiss to another country's courts on *forum non conveniens* grounds.

General considerations

Unlike domestic *forum non conveniens*, which in the federal courts is governed by a specific statutory provision (sec. 1404(a)), international *forum non conveniens* has no express statutory basis. As applied in the transnational context, *forum non conveniens* is thus a common law doctrine, and one generally traced to Scottish judicial practice.

The *forum non conveniens* doctrine is applied, in proper circumstances, to statutory as well as common law claims. Illustrative is *Howe v. Goldcorp Investments, Ltd.* (1st Cir.1991), where the court dismissed an action by a US shareholder under the US securities laws against a Canadian corporation and its Canadian officers and advisors arising out of the defendants' alleged attempts to take over two other Canadian companies. The court concluded that, although the US court had jurisdiction, and although the US statutes contained a special venue provision, dismissal was proper. The court concluded that the case had many more points of contact with Canada than with the US, and was appropriately dismissed in deference to a Canadian forum.

Where recognized, the *forum non conveniens* doctrine is presumably available in all cases in which the legislature has not precluded its application. But do there exist any federal statutory claims that are immune from the possibility of a *forum non conveniens* stay or dismissal? Although, as a matter of principle, the legislature may expressly forbid *forum non conveniens* stays or dismissals of certain claims, Congress has never done so. The fact remains that courts sometimes inquire as to whether, even in the absence of any such language, forum public policy might nevertheless bar a *forum non conveniens* motion from being entertained, and have answered in the affirmative. This has occurred with the federal antitrust laws (e.g., *Industrial Inv. Dev. Corp. v. Mitsui & Co.* (5th Cir.1982); *Laker Airways Ltd. v. Pan American World Airways* (D.D.C.1983)), and very occasionally other statutes. See, e.g., *Zipfel v. Halliburton Co.* (9th Cir.1987) (the Jones Act). See also *Lawford v. New York Life Ins. Co.* (S.D.N.Y.1990) (ERISA).

However, most courts now consider these and other federal statutory claims to be subject, in appropriate circumstances, to *forum non conveniens*. These include COGSA (see, e.g., *Contact Lumber Co. v. P.T. Moges Shipping Co., Ltd.* (9th Cir. 1990)), ERISA (see, e.g., *Dailey v. National Hockey League,* (3d Cir.1993)), the Jones Act (see, e.g., *Ikospentakis v. Thalassic S.S. Agency* (5th Cir. 1990)), RICO (see, e.g., *Transunion Corp. v. PepsiCo, Inc.* (2d Cir.1987)), and the federal securities laws (see, e.g., *Alfadda v. Fenn* (2d Cir.1998)). Lately, even antitrust suits have been dismissed on convenience grounds (see, e.g., *Capital Currency Exch. N.V. v. National Westminster Bank, PLC* (2d Cir.1998)). As discussed in Chapters 5 and 6 *infra*, even actions under the FSIA and the Alien Tort Claim Statute are amenable to *forum non conve-*

niens dismissal. See, e.g., *Forsythe v. Saudi Arabian Airlines Corp.* (5th Cir.1989).

A *forum non conveniens* motion will be greatly compromised when the forum where suit was brought is *itself* the forum designated a forum selection clause entered into by the parties. The presence of a choice of forum clause will only raise further the already high hurdle facing the movant for a *forum non conveniens* stay or dismissal. But the possibility of a convenience-based dismissal probably cannot be entirely ruled out. (The Model Choice of Forum Act, page 30 *supra*, establishes that possibility.) On the other hand, where there is a choice of forum clause designating a *foreign* forum, that will certainly heavily favor a *forum non conveniens* stay or dismissal (assuming the court does not stay or dismiss the case on the strength of the choice of forum clause alone). For such a case, see *Mercier v. Sheraton Int'l, Inc.* (1st Cir.1992); *Royal Bed & Spring Co. v. Famossul Industria* (1st Cir.1990).

Faced with a *forum non conveniens* motion, a court must conduct a number of different analyses.

Available alternative forum

A case will not be stayed or dismissed on *foreign non conveniens* grounds unless the plaintiff is shown to have an available alternative forum elsewhere. *In re Air Crash Disaster Near New Orleans* (5th Cir.1987). On this, the moving party bears the burden of proof. *Mercier v. Sheraton Int'l, Inc., supra.*

A number of factors affect the assessment of an alternative forum's adequacy. The statute of limitations abroad may have run, or the foreign court may lack either subject matter or personal jurisdiction over the defendant. While, as we shall see, waiver of these defenses may be made a condition of stay or dismissal, it is possible that they will be considered non-waivable by the foreign court. Occasionally, doubts will be raised as to the integrity or impartiality of the foreign court (based, for example, on suspicions of corruption or bias in favor of local nationals), as to the fairness of its judicial procedures, or as to its basic operational efficiency (due, for example, to lack of resources, congestion and delay, or interfering circumstances such as civil unrest). In one noted case, the Second Circuit found that delays of "up to a quarter of a century" rendered the foreign forum—India—inadequate for these purposes. *Bhatnagar v. Surrendra Overseas, Ltd.* (3d Cir.1995).

A well-known example is *In re Union Carbide Corp. Gas Plant Disaster at Bhopal, India* (S.D.N.Y. 1986), in which the district court rejected plaintiff's argument that the Indian courts were incapable of handling the complex litigation arising out of the catastrophic toxic gas leakage at Union Carbide's Bhopal, India, plant. (The plaintiff, the Government of India, suing *parens patriae*, was in the unusual position of questioning the efficacy of its own civil justice system.) The district court concluded that the Indian courts were capable of adequately adjudicating the dispute, and dismissed the case. (As we shall see below, the decision was reversed as to certain conditions on which the dismissal was made contingent.)

More problematic in principle is the question of the adequacy of the available remedies in the foreign forum. The question arises because plaintiffs, in resisting a *forum non conveniens* stay or dismissal, not infrequently urge that the foreign system, even if fair and adequate in general, will not afford them a fair and adequate opportunity to make out their claim or defense. As we shall see below, the courts have repeatedly stated that the plaintiff should not be remitted on convenience grounds to a court when the available remedy is "so clearly inadequate or unsatisfactory that it is no remedy at all." On the other hand, the fact that the remedy is less generous or the procedures more onerous will not render the foreign forum inadequate for *forum non conveniens* purposes. We return to this problem below.

The Balance of considerations

It is not enough that there be an alternative available forum (and that it afford at least a minimally adequate remedy). For dismissal on *forum non conveniens* grounds to be had, it must be shown that, all things considered, the weight of convenience tips heavily in favor of the foreign forum. Despite the difference in context, US courts have broadly transposed the analysis of convenience-based dismissal motions from the domestic to the transnational scene.

After endorsing the *forum non conveniens* notion in admiralty cases (see *Canada Malting Co. v. Paterson S.S. Ltd.* (S.Ct.1932)), the Supreme Court expressly embraced the doctrine more generally in two 1947 decisions, *Gulf Oil Corp. v. Gilbert* (S.Ct. 1947), and *Koster v. (American) Lumbermens Mut. Casualty Co.* (S.Ct.1947). Under *Gulf Oil* (which, being a domestic case in federal court, would be governed today by the federal transfer of venue statute, 28 U.S.C.A. sec. 1404(a)), courts are to conduct a broadly-gauged weighing of the "private" and the "public" interest factors in assessing the case for stay or dismissal on convenience grounds. The private interest factors to be considered include, among other things, access to sources of documents and witnesses, availability of compulsory process (in the case of unwilling witnesses), and ease of enforceability of judgments, although ease of international transportation and communication has tended to lessen the weight of these considerations. A range of other considerations—the availability of discovery, contingent fee representation, recovery of attorneys fees, a jury trial, and non-compensatory damages, to name just a few—may all come into play. Public interest factors include the burden on congested courts (and on local jurors), the possible difficulty of establishing foreign law, the putative advantage of "having localized controversies decided at home," and the relative strength of the various jurisdictions' interests in having their own courts allowed to adjudicate a given dispute.

Unless consideration of all these factors causes the court to tilt heavily in favor of a foreign forum, the plaintiff's choice of forum (much as in domestic cases) will not be disturbed. Since *forum non conveniens* outcomes depend on a large number of factors which often point in different directions, and since the weight to be given to them is ultimately a matter of judgment, the doctrine lends itself to seemingly conflicting and often unpredictable results. This is certainly no less the case in international than in domestic cases. Therefore, while the *forum non conveniens* doctrine brings flexibility to the conflict of jurisdiction analysis, it is also characterized by a pronounced lack of predictability traceable to the high degree of discretion vested in the courts. This in turn explains its general lack of favor in civil law jurisdictions which tend to place a high value on jurisdictional predictability.

The decision to grant or deny *forum non conveniens* dismissal is generally committed to the trial court's discretion, and a denial of a *forum non conveniens* motion is not subject to immediate appeal. *Van Cauwenberghe v. Biard* (S.Ct.1988). When review does take place, it is conducted on the basis of an abuse of discretion standard, and the disposition will more often than not be upheld. The appellate court will reverse only if it finds that the trial court failed to consider or give reasonably adequate weight to an especially relevant factor. See, e.g., *Wiwa v. Royal Dutch Petroleum Co.* (2d Cir.2000).

A prominent feature of transnational litigation in this context is the prospect of the applicability of foreign law. The Supreme Court itself noted in *Piper Aircraft Co. v. Reyno* (S.Ct.1981), that the need to apply foreign law is a factor tending to favor dismissal, and it does play an influential role in the *forum non conveniens* cases. Conversely, the applicability of US law operates to favor retention of jurisdiction. See *Rivendell Forest Prods. v. Canadian Pac. Ltd.* (10th Cir.1993). But the applicable law—domestic or foreign—is far from being in itself the decisive factor. Following the Court's lead in *Piper*, courts have ruled that if a case is otherwise not ripe for *forum non conveniens* stay or dismissal, the applicability of foreign law as governing law will not in itself change the result. See, e.g., *Boosey & Hawkes Music Pub., Ltd. v. Walt Disney Co.* (2d Cir.1998).

From both district court rulings and court of appeal review of those rulings, we find that transnational cases have a tendency to highlight certain other recurring considerations. We consider at length below two such factors—first, the plaintiff's nationality (or, to be more precise, non-nationality) and, second, the likelihood that an international change of forum will result in the application of a body of substantive law that is significantly less favorable to the plaintiff than the substantive law that the court where the action was initially filed would have applied.

Plaintiff's nationality

US courts have repeatedly remarked that a plaintiff's non-nationality is a factor that courts are entitled to count heavily in consideration of a *forum non conveniens* motion. Indeed, a failure to gave that factor sufficient weight in the overall *forum non conveniens* analysis has been held to constitute reversible error. In the *Piper* decision, *supra*, the Supreme Court expressly stated that a foreign plaintiff's choice of a US forum deserves less deference than a choice to that effect by a US national or resident. The Court considered it reasonable to assume that US nationals or residents generally sue in the US because it is convenient to do so, while foreigners are likely to sue in the US on account of strategic considerations—procedural and substantive alike—such as contingent fee representation, jury trials, discovery, higher damage levels, and a more favorable body of substantive law.

Consideration of nationality as a weighty *forum non conveniens* factor has stirred controversy due to the discriminatory aspect of any jurisdictional preference for US plaintiffs. Preferential treatment of US plaintiffs is not, however, categorical. The Supreme Court in *Piper* stopped well short of categorically protecting US nationals and residents from application of the *forum non conveniens* doctrine. Lower courts have accordingly on occasion applied the doctrine to stay or dismiss claims by US nationals. See, e.g., *Alcoa S.S. Co. v. M/V Nordic Regent* (2d Cir.1980) (*en banc*).

The question has arisen whether bilateral friendship, commerce, and navigation (FCN) treaties (which typically reciprocally guarantee access to the courts) might bar US courts from showing greater deference to a US national's than a foreign national's choice of a US forum. A number of US courts have so ruled. See, e.g. *Blanco v. Banco Industrial de Venezuela, SA* (2d Cir.1993); *Alcoa S.S. Co. v. M/V Nordic Regent, supra*. Needless to say, foreign nationals, even under such agreements, have no greater protection from *forum non conveniens* stays or dismissals from US courts than US nationals do.

Change in applicable law

As noted, changes in venue, whether for *forum non conveniens* or other reasons, may produce a change in the applicable substantive law to the benefit of one party and detriment of another. The question then arises whether the prospect of such a change (to the plaintiff's disadvantage, let us say) should count in the determination whether or not to dismiss.

In *Piper*, the Supreme Court ruled that, in principle, stay or dismissal on *forum non conveniens* grounds may be granted even though the law applicable in the alternative forum is less favorable to the plaintiff. The Court clearly admonished lower courts not to give undue weight to the fact that a convenience-based stay or dismissal will bring about a change in the applicable law that is disadvantageous to the plaintiff. Such a change is a factor "not [to] be given conclusive or even substantial weight in the forum non conveniens inquiry." *Piper*, *supra*. According to *Piper*, a change in the applicable rules of substantive law is to be given substantial weight only where the alternative forum provides a remedy that "is so clearly inadequate or unsatisfactory that it is no remedy at all." As it is sometimes put, the remedy available abroad must be so deficient as to as to deprive the plaintiff effectively of its "day in court."

Once a court concludes that the foreign forum does not furnish an adequate remedy in this sense, a *forum non conveniens* motion is almost certain to be denied, whatever the balance of convenience. But deciding whether the remedy abroad is or is not adequate can be a more delicate question. For example, sometimes the foreign court will entertain some of the plaintiff's claims, but not all of them. Sometimes the foreign court will award a form of relief, but deny other forms of relief. Even if it awards damages, it may exclude certain "heads" of damages or impose a monetary ceiling of some sort. It may construe the applicable cause of action as requiring elements that the plaintiff cannot establish, or it may recognize formidable affirmative defenses. It is clearly difficult to determine at what point a remedial system (whether in substantive or procedural respects, or both) ceases to be merely disadvantageous and actually becomes "inadequate."

However, it appears that a foreign forum will not be deemed inadequate for these purposes merely because it does not recognize certain legal theories of recovery (see *Dowling v. Richardson–Merrell, Inc.* (6th Cir.1984); *Mercier v. Sheraton Int'l, Inc.*, *supra*, or because the measure of damages will be substantially lower than they would be in the US. In almost all instances, suggestions that, in a case that is otherwise suitable for *forum non conveniens* dismissal, dismissal should not be ordered due exclusively to procedural differences between US and foreign litigation are unavailing (see, e.g., *Macedo v. Boeing Co.* (7th Cir.1982)). On the other hand, such differences (e.g. discovery, jury trial, cross-examination, contingent fee representation, blocking statutes) may be pertinent to the convenience question.

Conditions of dismissal

Customarily, *forum non conveniens* stays or dismissals are ordered subject to certain conditions designed to ensure effective access to the foreign court. The defendant will commonly be asked to consent to service of process and to the personal jurisdiction of the foreign court, as well as asked to waive any applicable statute of limitations or other technical defenses ordinarily available in the foreign forum. These conditions raise few problems. In addition, however, the defendant may be required to produce certain documents or witnesses in the foreign jurisdiction (even at its own expense) and to consent in advance to pay any judgment that the foreign court may enter. See, e.g., *Harrison v. Wyeth Laboratories* (E.D.Pa.1980).

Such conditions are much more problematic. On appeal in the *Bhopal* case, *supra*, the Court of Appeals affirmed the district court's *forum non conveniens* dismissal, but threw out two of the conditions imposed, namely that the defendant submit to discovery in India pursuant to the Federal Rules of Civil Procedure and that it consent in advance to satisfy any monetary judgment rendered against it by the Indian court. *In re Union Carbide Corp. Gas Plant Disaster at Bhopal, India* (2d Cir. 1987). The first condition was disapproved as an attempted intrusion by the US judiciary into the prospective foreign proceedings, and the second as an attempt to short-circuit the serious questions that may ordinarily be raised (and that due process may require to be raised) when enforcement of a foreign judgment in sought in the US.

Federalism aspects

Since state courts commonly apply notions broadly similar to the *forum non conveniens* doctrine recognized in *Gulf Oil*, *Koster*, and *Piper*, it has not often been considered necessary to decide whether the federal doctrine should be regarded primarily as (a) a common law procedural rule binding in all actions (diversity as well as federal question) in federal court under *Erie*, or as (b) a true principle of federal common law also binding on state courts under the principle of federal supremacy.

An argument could be made that federal courts sitting in diversity cases should follow the *forum non conveniens* principles of the state in which they sit. (In *Piper*, having decided that federal and state law principles of *forum non conveniens* were similar, the Supreme Court was not called upon to decide this question.) However, *forum non conve-*

niens is almost always considered to be a matter of procedural law, with the result that the federal version of the doctrine will be applicable in federal courts, in diversity and federal question cases alike. See *Rivendell Forest Prods., supra.*

As to whether *forum non conveniens* is a principle of federal common law also binding on state courts under the principle of federal supremacy, the weight of opinion suggests that it is not. Accordingly, state courts are free—even in transnational cases—to apply their own notions (assuming they have them, as some evidently do not) of dismissal on grounds of convenience. This assumption is supported by *American Dredging Co. v. Miller* (S.Ct. 1994), where the Supreme Court held that, where an admiralty action (i.e. a federal question case) is heard in state court, state law principles of *forum non conveniens* apply, due to those principles' essentially procedural character. Most lower courts indeed consider *forum non conveniens* motions in diversity cases in federal courts to be governed by federal rather than state law, again due to their procedural character. See *In re Air Crash Disaster Near New Orleans, supra*; *Sibaja v. Dow Chem. Co.* (11th Cir.1985). The federal forum's interest in self-regulation is commonly invoked in this context as weightier than the interest in avoiding forum shopping as between federal and state court. In no reported decision has a court declared *forum non conveniens* to be a substantive federal common law principle, and thus binding, under the supremacy clause, in actions in state court.

While most states have adopted a version of *forum non conveniens*, only a small number have codified it. For the rest, *forum non conveniens* remains a common law doctrine, in whose elaboration and application the *Gulf Oil* and *Koster* cases have been influential. Still, the states are presumably free to craft their own *forum non conveniens* doctrines. Some, by statute or case law, have rejected the application of *forum non conveniens*, at least in some situations. Section 71.031 of the Texas Civil Practice and Remedies Code, for example, provided that, subject to certain conditions, a personal injury action "may be enforced in the courts of [Texas]" even where the plaintiff is a non-US national and the tort occurred abroad. A divided Texas Supreme Court interpreted that language as statutorily precluding the *forum non conveniens* dismissal of such an action. *Dow Chem. Co. v. Castro Alfaro* (Tex. 1990). The Texas legislature subsequently enacted a statute allowing state courts to freely apply the *forum non conveniens* doctrine where a non-resident of the US sues in state court for personal injury or death. By contrast, the *forum non conveniens* doctrine may not be applied to any plaintiff in a personal injury or death action who is US resident, provided the underlying act or omission occurred in the US, and it may not be applied at all to a plaintiff who is a Texas resident. Tex. Civ. Proc. & Rem. Code sec. 71.051(a) (2002). The legislation responds to a belief that forum shopping by foreign plaintiffs was contributing to unreasonably heavy state court dockets. Other states restrict *forum non conveniens* to actions involving non-residents or to actions arising outside the state.

INTERNATIONAL *LIS PENDENS*

The same factors that explain the prominence of *forum non conveniens* in transnational litigation also explain the frequency of actual parallel litigation. As we have seen, transnational litigation by definition may be instituted in multiple jurisdictions, and the procedural and substantive law differences among fora commonly give each party to a dispute a strong incentive to prefer a different forum.

In very general terms, a court presented with a dispute already pending in a foreign court may either (1) defer to the foreign proceeding by staying or dismissing its own, or (2) entertain the action, thus permitting both to proceed concurrently. (The next section takes up a third and more aggressive option, *viz.* enjoining the foreign action so that the forum suit, and it alone, may proceed.) The traditionally dominant approach in US practice is to the let the actions proceed in parallel. See *Laker Airways, Ltd. v. Sabena Belgian World Airlines,* (D.C.Cir.1984).

At the same time there exists a general notion of *lis pendens*, according to which the pendency of an action in the courts of one jurisdiction is reason for the courts of another jurisdiction to decline to entertain the same, and possibly even a related, legal action, thereby promoting judicial orderliness and consistency of judgments. However, the status of *lis pendens* in international cases in US courts is uncertain at best. US courts do on occasion decline to exercise jurisdiction because the same or a closely related cause of action is already pending in a foreign forum, and they have occasionally indicated that they expect foreign courts to do likewise. To the extent that they identify a source of law for the practice, federal courts tend to cite federal case law, while state courts tend to cite state law, implying that the matter is properly viewed as procedural. But *lis pendens* is still generally considered to be nothing more than a discretionary instrument that courts may, out of deference to a prior-filed action abroad, deploy, or that they may, where they find good reason to persist in the exercise of jurisdiction, elect not to deploy.

Even in the domestic context, the Supreme Court has shown a preference for allowing litigation to proceed in multiple fora until one case reaches judgment. See *Colorado River Water Conservation District v. United States* (S.Ct.1976), where the Court treated the stay of a federal district court action in deference to a prior-filed state court action as highly exceptional. (In *Colorado River*, the Court distinguished stays of a federal district court action in deference to an action previously filed in another federal district court, describing entertainment of such an action as duplicative.) A later ruling of the Court (*Moses H. Cone Memorial Hosp. v. Mercury Constr. Corp.* (S.Ct.1983)), specifies several relevant factors (including the relative convenience of the alternative fora, the timing of filing, extent of progress of pending actions, avoidance of piecemeal litigation, protection of litigants' rights in the alternative fora, the good faith of the parties, and possibly extenuating circumstances), but still weights the balance heavily in favor of the exercise of federal jurisdiction. More recently, in *Quackenbush v. Allstate Ins. Co.* (S.Ct.1996), still in the federal-state context, the Court once again tightened the standard. The Court described abstention as an available course of action only if the relief sought is equitable or otherwise discretionary, although it stressed that in that case it was addressing outright dismissals only and not mere stays of proceedings. *Quackenbush* has caused some federal courts in transnational cases to rule out dismissal unless the action seeks equitable or otherwise discretionary relief. *Abdullah Sayid Rajab Al–Rifai & Sons, W.L.L. v. McDonnell Douglas Foreign Sales Corp.* (E.D.Mo.1997). But other courts prefer to confine *Quackenbush* to the federal-state context. See, e.g., *Posner v. Essex Ins. Co., Ltd.* (11th Cir.1999).

In the transnational context, the place of *lis pendens* is very difficult to gauge. Some federal courts have taken a particularly restrictive view, insisting that they are presumptively under an obligation to exercise the jurisdiction conferred on them by Congress. See, e.g., *Neuchatel Swiss Gen. Ins. Co. v. Lufthansa Airlines* (9th Cir.1991). But other federal courts have preferred to treat prior-filed foreign proceedings much like actions previously filed in another federal district, that is to say, without any predisposition against the issuance of a stay under the *lis pendens* doctrine. See, e.g., *Turner Entertainment Co. v. Degeto Film GmbH* (11th Cir.1994); *Continental Time Corp. v. Swiss Credit Bank* (S.D.N.Y.1982). Indeed, recent decisions in international cases explicitly take into account "the sovereigns' relative interests in the litigation," at least where policy considerations appear to be prominent, as in *Linear Prods., Inc. v. Marotech, Inc.* (W.D.Va. 2002).

As with *forum non conveniens*, courts in *lis pendens* sometimes dismiss, and sometimes merely stay, the local action. There is no clear pattern to be observed in the courts' preferences as between the two. Similarly, the practice of *lis pendens* is highly discretionary, entailing the balancing of various factors (such as similarity of parties and issues, judicial efficiency, adequacy of relief abroad, fairness and convenience), but with a decided emphasis on how far the first-filed foreign action has already progressed. See, e.g., *Turner Entertainment Co., supra*; *Evergreen Marine Corp. v. Welgrow Int'l, Inc.* (S.D.N.Y.1997); *Dragon Cap. Partners L.P. v. Merrill Lynch Cap. Servs. Inc.* (S.D.N.Y.1997); *Heuft Systemtechnik GmbH v. Videojet Syst. Int'l, Inc.* (N.D.Ill.1993). This contrasts with the rather more strict approach observed in civil law systems jurisdictions and, more particularly, within the European Union. Among EU Member States, the court whose jurisdiction has first been invoked is generally permitted to determine its own competence; if it finds in favor of its own competence, other courts within the system must decline to exercise jurisdiction over a case involving the same parties and the same subject matter.

General rules of *lis pendens* in transnational litigation are becoming especially hard to come by, as parties seek more and more to accelerate the race to litigation through such devices as actions for "reverse" declaratory relief, notably a declaration of non-liability, thereby instituting the "first-filed" action. They may even seek a declaration of the unenforceability of the eventual foreign country judgment. An example of this preemptive strategy is *Basic v. Fitzroy Eng., Ltd.* (N.D.Ill.1996), where a party asked a US court for a declaration that a New Zealand proceeding could not yield a valid judgment because the court lacked personal and subject matter jurisdiction, because of claim preclusion, and because the cause of action violated US public policy. Partly out of comity, the US court deferred to the New Zealand proceedings.

ANTI-SUIT INJUNCTIONS

Anti-suit injunctions are orders addressed by courts to parties enjoining them from introducing, maintaining or prosecuting a given action in another court. Notwithstanding their seemingly overreaching character, anti-suit injunctions have been issued with some frequency by US courts, both in the domestic and the international context. Especially in the latter context, they have provoked intense opposition and, on occasion, outrage.

Notwithstanding the practice of addressing anti-suit injunctions to litigants rather than courts, the remedy is understandably viewed as an act of judicial interference with the power of another court, including the court of another "sovereign." The highest profile cases, as we shall see, are those in which the enjoining court justifies the remedy in terms of protecting its "public policy" with the result (and often the purpose) of frustrating the public policy of the other state involved.

As with *lis pendens*, the use of anti-suit injunctions tends not to be addressed by statute either at the federal or state level. Courts have issued such orders in consideration of their own general equitable powers over persons subject to their jurisdiction. Again as with *lis pendens*, courts seem to treat the matter as wholly procedural, so that, to the extent that they cite authority for the issuance of anti-suit injunctions, state and federal courts tend to cite, respectively, state and federal case authority.

A common anti-suit scenario is one that may be likened to a "reverse" *forum non conveniens* case. A US court may find itself to be so clearly the more convenient or otherwise appropriate forum for adjudicating a given transnational dispute that it considers it necessary and appropriate to enjoin the defendant in that action from even attempting to have that case heard elsewhere. In such cases, anti-suit injunctions effectively convert convenience arguments from a "shield" into a "sword." US courts on occasion do issue anti-suit injunctions on this ground, sometimes describing the introduction or maintenance of foreign litigation as oppressive or vexatious. See *Cargill, Inc. v. Hartford Accident & Indemnity Co.* (D.Minn.1982). So, too, do courts of other common law countries. See, e.g., *Smith Kline & French Laboratories Ltd. v. Bloch* (Ct.App.1982).

In a related scenario, the plaintiff, having instituted litigation in the US, asks the same (or possibly a different) court to enjoin the defendant from instituting "mirror-image" litigation in the courts of another country. The plaintiff may take a similar step upon winning judgment in the US forum, with a view to preventing relitigation of the dispute in a foreign court. As just noted, mirror-image litigation is becoming especially common in transnational litigation, with one Party X to a transaction seeking to impose liability on Party Y in forum A, and Party Y seeking a declaration of non-liability to Party X in forum B.

Convenience arguments are not the only ones that have triggered the issuance of international anti-suit injunctions. Quite apart from convenience or inconvenience, a US court may come to the conclusion that a compelling public interest recognized by US law will be frustrated if a case is heard in other than a US forum. Anti-suit injunctions have accordingly been justified on grounds of the paramountcy of US antitrust law, with the result that parties are enjoined from pursuing a contract remedy abroad based on a contract that is or may be the subject of a US antitrust action. See *Seattle Totems Hockey Club, Inc. v. National Hockey League* (9th Cir.1981).

Sometimes, finally, anti-suit injunctions have been used as a remedy for the enforcement of contract or contract-like undertakings. Thus, courts may enjoin a party from pursuing an action in a foreign court where bringing the foreign action violated an undertaking not to sue, or to sue exclusively in a different court (as pursuant to a derogation clause), or to refer the dispute in question exclusively to an arbitral tribunal.

The very prospect that a party might seek and obtain an anti-suit injunction may be enough to cause the other party to take preemptive action in the form of a "counter-anti-suit injunction," by which is meant an order forbidding the other party from seeking an anti-suit injunction in the first place. Counter-anti-suit injunctions are sometimes justified on the ground that they seek to do nothing more than prevent or neutralize the anti-suit injunction that an opposing party is seeking or likely to seek, and are to be viewed as essentially defensive or self-protective.

Whether they happen to grant or deny an anti-suit injunction in the case before them, courts invariably describe themselves as deeply cautious and hesitant about this instrument. Some seem disposed never to issue an anti-suit injunction, absent a threat from abroad to the court's own exercise of jurisdiction (thus justifying a counter-anti-suit injunction) or the evasion by a party of a fundamental public policy of the forum. A leading example is *Laker Airways, Ltd. v. Sabena, supra.* Freddie Laker claimed that his "low-cost, no-frills" transatlantic airline service was threatened by predatory pricing on the part of the major airlines and their collusion with Laker's creditors. Upon his filing of a US action under the antitrust laws, British Airways obtained an order from a UK court enjoining maintenance of that suit, at which point the US court, at *Laker*'s request, issued an injunction of its own forbidding the other antitrust defendants from seeking to obtain similar anti-suit injunctive relief in the UK. Both the UK and US injunctive relief was affirmed in the two countries' respective courts of appeal, and the impasse not overcome until the House of Lords vacated the UK injunction as unwarranted. *British Airways Board v. Laker Airways Ltd.* (H.L.1985). But a parallel UK anti-suit injunction protecting Laker's UK creditor from similar US antitrust proceedings stood. *Midland Bank v. Laker Airways* (Ct.App.1985)

The court in *Laker* underlined the narrowness of the circumstances—the need for a court to protect its own jurisdiction—that warrant an anti-suit injunction. Other circuits have joined in adopting that stance. See also *Gau Shan Co., Ltd. v. Bankers Trust Co.*, and especially *China Trade & Dev. Corp. v. M.V. Choong Yong* (2d Cir.1987), where the court concluded:

> The equitable factors relied upon by the District Court in granting the anti-suit injunction are not sufficient to overcome the restraint and caution required by international comity. Because the Korean litigation poses no threat to the jurisdiction of the District Court or to any important public policy of this forum, we conclude that the District Court abused its discretion by issuing the injunction.

However, other courts entertain anti-suit injunction applications more liberally, granting them where the case rests mainly on convenience grounds or where the stated purpose is simply to avoid duplicative litigation and the risk of inconsistent results. *Kaepa, Inc. v. Achilles Corp.* (5th Cir.1996); *Seattle Totems Hockey Club, Inc. v. National Hockey League, supra*; *Cargill, Inc. v. Hartford Accident & Indemnity Co., supra.* A noted example is *Allendale Mut. Ins. Co. v. Bull Data Sys., Inc.* (7th Cir.1993), where the court, in affirming the lower court's issuance of an injunction, specifically cited the possibility that a US insurance company would not receive full and fair consideration of its arson defense to an insurance claim if the case were to be heard in French court. The court also expressed some concern over the character of the proceedings in the French commercial court, which it considered to function more along the lines of an arbitral tribunal than a court. The case ended up being heard in the US, notwithstanding the fact that the loss occurred in France, much of the physical evidence was located there, and the claim was to be adjudicated under principles of French insurance law.

As the *Laker* case shows, although US courts are the most frequent issuers of anti-suit injunctions, they have themselves on occasion been its targets. In one case, the London High Court concluded that Texas was not a "natural" forum for hearing a suit on a claim that was already pending in London, and issued an *ex parte* injunction to prevent the defendant in the UK action from maintaining a "mirror image" action in Texas seeking a declaration of non-liability. The UK plaintiffs eventually won a judgment against Amoco. *Amoco (UK) Exploration Co. v. Teesside Gas Transp. Ltd.* (H.L.2001).

The chronology was somewhat different in *CSR Ltd. v. Federal Ins. Co.* (D.N.J.1998), (D.N.J.2001) (April 24), (D.N.J.2001) (May 25). There, an Australian asbestos manufacturer first brought an insurance claim against its insurers in the US, whereupon the insurers obtained an anti-suit injunction in Australia, coupled with a declaration of non-liability on the claim. However, the Australian injunction was reversed on appeal. That reversal played a role in the US court's eventual rejection of the claim that it should decline jurisdiction on *forum non conveniens* grounds in deference to Australian jurisdiction.

CHAPTER FIVE

"SOVEREIGNTY" LIMITATIONS ON THE EXERCISE OF JURISDICTION

Parallel litigation is only one of several scenarios in which a US court may consider declining an exercise of judicial jurisdiction that it indubitably possesses, *forum non conveniens* and *lis pendens* being the prime examples. There are a range of other abstention doctrines that characterize the US law of transnational litigation. The act of state doctrine and, more generally, the political question doctrine and international comity also play an important prudential role in this field.

The sovereign immunity doctrine has particular importance in this context. Historically, the notion that foreign sovereigns should be spared having to appear, and possibly incur liability, before US courts might have been viewed as yet another self-imposed limitation on the exercise of jurisdiction. Seemingly required neither by the Constitution nor by legislation, immunity was granted, if at all, in consideration of political factors and as a matter of common law. This, as we shall see, is no longer an apt way of conceiving of sovereign immunity in the US. With the enactment of the Foreign Sovereign

Immunities Act of 1976 (FSIA), US courts are instructed to consider themselves lacking in both subject matter jurisdiction and personal jurisdiction in actions against foreign governments and their instrumentalities, unless the case at hand falls within one of the statutorily enumerated "exceptions" to sovereign immunity. The question of sovereign immunity thus now goes to the jurisdiction of the court, and not merely to the question whether such jurisdiction as exists should possibly not be exercised.

Precisely because sovereign immunity affects a court's jurisdiction, we begin with that subject. The chapter then considers a series of other sovereignty-related issues of a more discretionary character: act of state, the political question doctrine, international comity, the "dormant" foreign affairs and commerce powers and, finally, foreign sovereign compulsion as a rule of substantive law.

FOREIGN SOVEREIGN IMMUNITY

From common law to the FSIA

The FSIA takes the notion of sovereign immunity as its starting point, declaring foreign states and their instrumentalities immune to suit in both state and federal courts except to the extent that the FSIA itself provides otherwise. 28 U.S.C.A. sec. 1604. To this extent, the FSIA represents a continuation of common law doctrine. In *The Schooner Exchange v. McFaddon* (S.Ct.1812), Chief Justice

Marshall had stated that "[the] perfect equality and absolute independence of sovereigns, and [their] common interest impelling them to mutual intercourse, and an exchange of good offices with each other," precluded the exercise by one sovereign state of judicial jurisdiction over another. In its common law version, sovereign immunity was considered absolute, in the sense of covering both the governmental and the commercial acts of foreign states.

Over time, the courts modified the common law of sovereign immunity by allowing the executive branch to express, and indeed following, its opinion on the opportuneness of according or denying sovereign immunity in a particular case. They effectively treated the State Department's "suggestion" of sovereign immunity or non-immunity, both in commercial and governmental cases, as conclusive. See *Republic of Mexico v. Hoffman* (S.Ct.1945); *Ex parte Peru* (S.Ct.1943). In 1952, the State Department announced a general policy (in the so-called "Tate Letter," named for the State Department's then Legal Adviser), based upon a traditional distinction between a sovereign state's public or governmental acts (acts *jure imperii*), on the one hand, and its private or commercial acts (acts *jure gestionis*), on the other. According to this "restrictive" theory of immunity, states are immune as to the former, but not as to the latter. The Department's "suggestions" thereafter largely reflected that approach. The courts also followed that distinction even in the absence of a specific "suggestion" on the part of the

State Department. See, e.g., *Victory Transport Inc. v. Comisaria General de Abastecimientos y Transportes* (2d Cir.1964). Although the Tate Letter was never enacted into law, the courts displayed deference to the State Department both as to general principles and as to the appropriateness of according or not according immunity in any given case.

The FSIA

Ultimately, however, courts were not comfortable permitting their exercise of jurisdiction to be dictated, directly or indirectly, by State Department notions as to the appropriateness or convenience of bringing foreign governments or their instrumentalities to account in US courts. When Congress enacted the FSIA in 1976 (inserted in the US Code at 28 U.S.C.A. secs. 1330, 1332, 1391(f), 1441(d), 1602–11), it essentially restored to the courts the authority to make sovereign immunity determinations, while at the same time establishing a framework and set of principles for their doing so. The Act proceeded by reaffirming (in section 1604) the presumption of immunity, while engrafting on it (in section 1605) a number of more or less specific exceptions which, in some measure, reflect the distinction between commercial and non-commercial acts.

(a) The Legislative framework

We have already in Chapter 2 identified the FSIA as among the specific statutory bases of federal subject matter jurisdiction, and among the most salient in transnational litigation. The jurisdiction thereby created extends to all claims as to which foreign states and their instrumentalities do not enjoy sovereign immunity under the FSIA's "substantive" provisions (28 U.S.C.A. sec. 1330(a)). Basically the same may be said about personal jurisdiction; its exercise over foreign states and their instrumentalities is statutorily authorized in all circumstances in which those states and instrumentalities lack sovereign immunity under the FSIA (28 U.S.C.A. sec. 1330(b)), provided they have been properly served. (It may also be necessary, however, to ensure that any exercise of that authority comports with jurisdictional due process, measured by minimum contacts and reasonableness.)

Although the Supreme Court in *Republic of Argentina v. Weltover, Inc.* (S.Ct.1992), questioned whether the due process aspect of personal jurisdiction applies to suits against foreign states, most courts continue to act on the assumption that it does. See, e.g., *Creighton Ltd. v. Government of Qatar* (D.C.Cir.1999). Others, however, exclude foreign states as defendants from this form of due process protection. See, e.g., *World Wide Minerals Ltd. v. Republic of Kazakhstan* (D.D.C.2000). As a practical matter, minimum contacts are almost invariably found to be satisfied once the nexus required by the applicable exception s found to be met.

Even where immunity under the FSIA does not obtain, the sovereign's exposure to litigation and liability is limited in various ways. By its terms, the FSIA bars the use of jury trials (28 U.S.C.A. sec. 1441(d)) and, in the case of actions against a foreign state rather than against one of its agencies or instrumentalities (*id.* sec. 1606), the award of punitive damages. (A 1998 amendment to the FSIA permitted punitive damages to be recovered in cases under the new "terrorist acts" exception (see below), subject to the possibility of a waiver proclaimed by the President of the US, as indeed occurred. However, this limited allowance of punitive damages was subsequently repealed by Public Law 106–386, enacted in 2000.)

The FSIA does not make federal court jurisdiction exclusive, but does provide for removal from state court (*id.* sec. 1441(d)). Not only the Act's principles of non-immunity, but also its procedural and quasi-procedural provisions apply equally in federal and state court. For example, Section 1608(d) provides that in an FSIA action in federal or state court, a foreign state has 60 days after service of the complaint in which to serve an answer or other responsive pleading. On the other hand, the FSIA's venue provision (sec. 1391(f)), designating the federal district in which suit may be brought, naturally refers to FSIA actions in federal court only. If a motion to dismiss under the FSIA is denied, an interlocutory appeal may be taken. *Compania Mexicana de Aviacion S.A. v. U.S. Dist. Ct.* (9th Cir.1988).

Regardless of all else that it does, the FSIA does not, however, create a cause of action. In terms of substantive liability, the Act does no more than declare the foreign state liable "to the same extent as a private individual under like circumstances" (28 U.S.C.A. sec. 1606). This means that the action must find its substantive legal basis elsewhere, presumably in a statutory or common law cause of action, be it federal or state.

Choosing the substantive law applicable to the cause of action requires an exercise in choice of law. At least one court (*Liu v. Republic of China* (9th Cir.1989)), has held that, since the FSIA is a federal statute, and since there is an interest in uniformity of results in FSIA cases, this choice should be made in accordance with federal common law rules of choice of law, rather than (as in diversity cases, under the rule of *Klaxon v. Stentor Elec. Mfg. Co.* (S.Ct.1941)) in accordance with the choice of law rules of the state in which the federal court sits. Curiously, though, even if a federal choice of law rule were to be applied to all FSIA cases, this would still not produce uniform results, since the federal choice of law rule will result in the application of different bodies of substantive law depending on the facts of each FSIA case.

Still, the prevailing view is that in FSIA cases, all issues that would ordinarily be governed by state substantive law are to be determined in accordance with the choice of law rule of the state where the court sits. This is so, even if the substantive law to which the relevant state choice of law rule points is the law of the defendant nation. *Barkanic v. Gener-*

al Adm'n of Civil Aviation of the People's Republic of China (2d Cir.1991). Even under this view, however, federal common law rules of choice of law would be applicable where the underlying cause of action arises out of federal law.

(b) "States" and "agencies or instrumentalities"

The term "foreign state" is not defined with any precision in the FSIA, although the Act does expressly include within this notion both "a political subdivision" and "an agency or instrumentality" of a foreign state. The Restatement (Third) of Foreign Relations Law (sec. 201) defines a "state" as "an entity that has a defined territory and a permanent population, under the control of its own government, and that engages in, or has the capacity to engage in, formal relations with other such entities." In *Klinghoffer v. S.N.C. Achille Lauro* (2d Cir.1991), the Palestine Liberation Organization (PLO) was found not to meet the criteria. On the other hand, there appears to be no requirement that the US government have recognized an entity as a state in order for it to qualify as a foreign state for FSIA purposes. *Kadic v. Karadzic* (2d Cir.1995). As a practical matter, the views of the State Department are likely to be decisive.

"Agency or instrumentality" is, however, defined in the FSIA, namely as an entity which (1) has separate legal personality from the state and (2) either constitutes an "organ" of the state (or of one of its subdivisions) or is majority-owned by the state (or, again, by one of its subdivisions). The definition expressly excludes citizens of a state of the US and entities created under the laws of a third country. 28 U.S.C.A. sec. 1603(a)(3).

The distinction between foreign states and their agencies and instrumentalities is an important one in various respects under the FSIA regime. 28 U.S.C.A. sec. 1608 establishes different procedures for service of process, depending on whether service is upon a foreign state or its political subdivision, on the one hand, or an agency or instrumentality of the foreign state, on the other. Courts have drawn on this distinction with respect to the adequacy of service. *Magness v. Russian Federation* (5th Cir. 2001). As noted, under Section 1606, punitive damages are available in a proper case against an agency or instrumentality, but not against a foreign state as such. The courts are divided over the question whether the FSIA's rules on service of default judgments in Section 1608(e) apply only to judgments against foreign states or also to judgments against their agencies and instrumentalities. Compare *Antoine v. Atlas Turner, Inc.* (6th Cir.1995), with *Straub v. A.P. Green, Inc.* (9th Cir.1994). The Act also distinguishes between states and instrumentalities with regard to attachment in execution of judgments. (See below.) Unfortunately, the line between states and their agencies or instrumentalities is not an entirely clear one. Courts sometimes consider the extent to which the entity in question is an integral part of the foreign government's political and administrative structure, and whether the entity functions chiefly for governmental or commercial purposes.

A still further question relates to the time at which the agency or instrumentality status of an entity is to be determined. Although Section 1603(b) uses the present tense ("is"), the general practice has been also to apply the FSIA if the defendant was a state-owned company at the time the acts complained of occurred, even if it had become privately owned by the time of suit. *Pere v. Nuovo Pignone, Inc.* (5th Cir.1998). However, the Supreme Court has ruled that the purposes of the FSIA will be best served by determining agency or instrumentality status strictly as of the time of filing of the complaint. *Dole Food Co. v. Patrickson* (S.Ct.2003).

Note that an entity can be an "agency or instrumentality," within the meaning of the FSIA, without necessarily being a corporation a majority of whose shares are owned by the state. The public functions that it serves may suffice to render an entity having personality separate from the state an "agency or instrumentality" of that state. See, e.g., *Kelly v. Syria Shell Petroleum Dev. B.V.* (5th Cir. 2000). However, a US court may on occasion find that an entity's legal separateness from the state is purely fictional. In that event, the entity will be treated as if it were the state itself. A fine example is *First Nat'l City Bank v. Banco Para El Comercio Exterior de Cuba* (S.Ct.1983), where the Supreme Court held that when a Cuban bank that was ostensibly separate from the Cuban government brought suit against the United States, the US was permitted to file a counterclaim against Cuba in the same action. (As noted below, the FSIA permits a US court to exercise jurisdiction over a foreign state in the form of a counterclaim to a US court action brought by that state.) The presumptive separateness of the bank from the state was thus overcome for purposes of the counterclaim.

Courts have also sometimes interpreted the FSIA as protecting individuals who act in an official capacity for a foreign government, treating them effectively as an agency or instrumentality of the state. See, e.g., *Chuidian v. Philippine Nat'l Bank* (9th Cir.1990), dismissing a suit against a member of the Philippine Presidential Commission under the FSIA on the assumption that, as an official acting within the scope of office, he was effectively an instrumentality of the state and entitled to invoke immunity under the FSIA. See also *Byrd v. Corporacion Forestal y Industrial de Olancho S.A.* (5th Cir.1999); *Jungquist v. Sheikh Sultan Bin Khalifa Al Nahyan* (D.C.Cir.1997); *El–Fadl v. Central Bank of Jordan* (D.C.Cir.1996).

While the FSIA clearly applies to claims against instrumentalities of foreign states, doubt subsists over its applicability to subsidiaries of those instrumentalities. While some courts have been willing to treat "instrumentalities of instrumentalities" as entitled to sovereign immunity, the Supreme Court has ruled otherwise. The foreign state must itself directly own a majority of shares of the entity in question. *Dole Food Co. v. Patrickson, supra.*

(c) Exceptions to immunity

The heart of the FSIA lies in its exceptions to sovereign immunity. Section 1605 sets these statutory exceptions out with some particularity, and the Supreme Court has confirmed that they are exclusive. *Argentine Republic v. Amerada Hess Shipping Corp.* (S.Ct.1989). Unless one of them applies, the state remains immune under 28 U.S.C.A. section 1604. In holding the FSIA to be the sole basis for suing a foreign state in the courts of the US, the Court implicitly found that no other federal law—whether statutory (e.g., the Alien Tort Claim Statute) or common law (e.g., general maritime law)—could be interpreted as intended to subject foreign states to suit. Therefore, at present, unless an FSIA exception applies, the foreign state remains immune. Generally, the foreign state or instrumentality has the burden of presenting a *prima facie* case of sovereign status. See, e.g., *Export Group v. Reef Indus., Inc.* (9th Cir.1995). If the plaintiff then produces evidence that an FSIA exception to immunity is applicable, the burden of persuasion on that issue reverts to the defendant, which must prove, by a preponderance of the evidence, that the exception is not applicable. *Aquamar S.A. v. Del Monte Fresh Produce N.A., Inc.* (11th Cir.1999); *Phaneuf v. Republic of Indonesia* (9th Cir.1997).

(i) Waiver

A first basis for non-immunity (and, in the FSIA's logic, for subject matter and personal jurisdiction as well) is waiver, either express or implied (28 U.S.C.A. sec. 1605(a)(1)). While a choice of forum clause would appear to constitute an express waiver, the situation is less clear with a choice of law clause. While there might be various reasons for including a choice of US substantive law in a contract which do not imply a submission to the judicial jurisdiction of US courts, courts have been largely willing to treat such as a clause as an implied waiver of immunity, and the FSIA's own legislative history supports them. See, e.g., *Eckert Int'l, Inc. v. Government of Fiji* (4th Cir.1994). However, courts do not generally read choice of law clauses designating *non-US law* as constituting submissions to US judicial jurisdiction, even when there is no reason to doubt a US court's willingness to respect the choice of law clause and to apply the designated foreign law.

Courts frequently admonish that implied waiver is not lightly to be found. See, e.g., *Drexel Burnham Lambert Group Inc. v. Committee of Receivers for Galadari (A.W.)* (2d Cir.1993); *Foremost-McKesson, Inc. v. Islamic Republic of Iran* (D.C.Cir.1990). For example, the fact that a foreign state brings suit in the US does not in itself constitute an implied waiver of immunity from the jurisdiction of that court—though the FSIA's important provisions on counterclaims (see below) may result in subjecting the state to suit, particularly on related claims. See, e.g., *Shapiro v. Republic of Bolivia* (2d Cir.1991). Without question, the most promising scenario of implied waiver arises when the defendant appears and pleads to the merits, without raising a sovereign immunity objection. *See, e.g., Haven v. Rzeczpospolita Polska* (7th Cir.2000).

As with any waiver, it may be necessary to determine its scope. For example, a choice of forum clause contained in a contract presumably functions as a waiver of immunity only as to claims arising out of or related to that contract. Moreover, it may not be obvious from a particular waiver that it constitutes waiver of immunity to suit *in a US court*. A choice of forum clause designating a non-US forum, or an arbitral forum, may not reasonably be construed as implying submission to the jurisdiction of a US court, at least not as to the merits of the dispute. *Verlinden B.V. v. Central Bank of Nigeria* (S.D.N.Y.1980). Indeed, in the absence of any contact whatsoever between the dispute at hand and the US, an assertion of US judicial jurisdiction over a foreign state could conceivably be regarded as unconstitutional, as in violation of due process.

The other principal basis of waiver—express or implied—is treaty. However, establishing that a treaty entails a waiver of immunity to suit has not proved simple. According to the Supreme Court, a foreign state "cannot waive its immunity . . . by signing an international agreement that does not mention a waiver of immunity to suit in United States courts or even the availability of a cause of action in the United States." *Argentine Republic v. Amerada Hess, supra.* In other words, the fact that a treaty establishes substantive rules of conduct does not itself denote submission to private lawsuits in US courts. *Foremost–McKesson, Inc., supra.* Thus, claimants have been unsuccessful in arguing that execution of a human rights treaty constitutes an implied waiver to immunity from human rights claims (*Boshnjaku v. Federal Republic of Yugoslavia* (N.D.Ill.2002)), or that Japan's post-war treaty with the US constituted an implied waiver of immunity by Japan to claims arising out of wartime atrocities (*Hwang Geum Joo v. Japan,* (D.D.C. 2001)). Courts have also repeatedly been invited to rule that waiver of immunity under the FSIA may be based upon a State's violation of a peremptory norm of international law (*ius cogens*), within the meaning of Article 53 of the Vienna Convention on Treaties. They have uniformly declined to do so. *Sampson v. Federal Republic of Germany* (7th Cir. 2001); *Princz v. Federal Republic of Germany*

(D.C.Cir.1994); *Smith v. Socialist People's Libyan Arab Jamahiriya* (2d Cir.1996).

The FSIA's waiver exception produces an interesting result. A foreign state that would otherwise enjoy immunity may forfeit it by waiver, for example through an appearance coupled with a failure to assert immunity under the Act. Thus, the defendant would seem to be allowed in effect to "confer" on a court not only personal jurisdiction, but also subject matter jurisdiction, where it would otherwise be lacking. This runs counter to the usual understandings in the US concerning the non-waivability of subject matter jurisdiction limitations.

(ii) Commercial activity

By any measure, the principal exception to immunity under the FSIA is the so-called "commercial acts" or "commercial activity" exception. Application of this exception of course necessitates a definition of "commercial." While the term "commercial" is unfortunately not usefully defined in the FSIA, Section 1603)(d), supported by legislative history, does provide that the "commerciality" of an act or activity is to be determined by reference to its nature and not its purpose. See *Texas Trading and Milling Corp. v. Federal Republic of Nigeria* (2d Cir.1981).

There is abundant case law on the question of whether a given act or activity is or is not "commercial" within the meaning of the FSIA. Much of it cites the proposition, just referred to, that the commercial or non-commercial character of an activity depends not on the purpose for which the activity is conducted, but rather on the nature of the activity itself. More frequently than not, therefore, courts inquire whether or not the activity out of which the claim arose is one in which private parties may or do customarily engage. See again *Texas Trading, supra.* The Supreme Court has had only one occasion to construe the term "commercial" in this context. In *Republic of Argentina v. Weltover, Inc.* (S.Ct.1992), the Court unanimously ruled that when Argentina issued bonds in an effort to stabilize its currency, it issued a debt instrument much like private parties do. The fact that its motive in doing so may have reflected a "sovereign" interest in currency stability was irrelevant to the nature of the exercise and did not lessen the commercial nature of the underlying activity.

Notwithstanding the nature/purpose distinction, lower courts have on occasion found that an activity is non-commercial even when the activity has a counterpart in the private sector, provided the foreign state has, or appears to have, a special "interest" or "stake" in the activity or when the activity has special importance for that state's public interest. A leading example is *MOL, Inc. v. Peoples Republic of Bangladesh* (9th Cir.1984), where the Ninth Circuit ruled that Bangladesh's unique interest in the conservation of local animal species, as a form of natural resource, rendered it immune from suit on a breach of contract for the cultivation and export of those animals. According to the Court, those factors rendered the underlying contract non-commercial by nature. Such rulings have proven controversial.

The applicability of the exception requires that the claim in question be "based upon" a commercial act or activity having the necessary US nexus. This requires that two further questions be asked. Is the claim indeed "based upon" a commercial activity or an act in connection with a commercial activity? If so, was the activity or act in question performed in the US or otherwise have the requisite effect in the US?

Whether a claim is "based upon" a given act or activity may depend on the breadth with which the act or activity is defined. An act or activity may be defined narrowly or broadly, thus plausibly giving rise, respectively, to a narrow or broad range of claims. For a broad notion, see *International Assn. of Machinists v. Organization of Petroleum Exporting Countries (OPEC)* (C.D.Cal.1979). Yet, in *Saudi Arabia v. Nelson* (S.Ct.1993), the Supreme Court adopted a narrower one. It had to decide whether the plaintiff's claim of unlawful detention and torture as a "whistle-blower" by Saudi authorities was "based upon" the state's admittedly commercial activity of engaging personnel as hospital monitor system engineers. The Court held in effect that, while recruitment and employment of such personnel constituted a commercial activity, it was not upon those activities—but rather upon a non-commercial activity, viz. the law enforcement activities of Saudi authorities who allegedly illegally questioned and abused the plaintiff—that the claim was based. The mere "connection" between the conduct of the police and penal officers, on the one hand, and the commercial activity of the government in recruiting and employing the plaintiff, on the other, was deemed insufficient. The court did not take seriously the independent claim that Saudi Arabia had violated in the US a duty to warn about the risks of employment in that country, thus providing an act within the US in connection with a commercial activity abroad. However, lower courts consider that such an argument might be taken seriously on different facts. See, e.g., *Sun v. Taiwan* (9th Cir. 2000).

It is not enough that a claim be based upon an act or activity that is "commercial." The act or activity upon which it is based must itself have a certain nexus with the United States. By the FSIA's own terms, the claim must arise *either* out of a commercial activity carried on by the foreign state in the US, *or* out of an act performed in the US in connection with the foreign state's commercial activity elsewhere, *or* out of an act performed outside the US in connection with the foreign state's commercial activity outside the US, but causing a direct effect in the US. 28 U.S.C.A. sec. 165(a)(2).

Even the seemingly simple question whether the relevant commercial activity was carried on in the US can prove highly contestable. In *Sugarman v. Aeromexico, Inc.* (3d Cir.1980), the court decided that the negligent operation of a flight in Mexico, resulting in physical and emotional injury to a US passenger, had a sufficient nexus with the US because related to a course of commercial activity in the US. The fact that the specific injury-causing events all occurred in Mexico made no difference. (The court left open on remand the question of the applicable law.) *See also Chukwu v. Air France* (N.D.Ill.2002). On the other hand, where the liability-generating activity is not related to an ongoing commercial activity in the US, the nexus will not be met. See, e.g., *Vencedora Oceanica Navigacion, S.A. v. Compagnie Nationale Algerienne De Navigation* (5th Cir.1984).

If there is neither a commercial act in the US nor an act in the US in connection with a commercial activity abroad, the only possibility for establishing a commercial act exception is to find a commercial act abroad having a "direct effect" in the US. It is not unusual for such an effect to be found. See, e.g., *Texas Trading*, *supra*. In *International Assoc. of Machinists v. OPEC*, *supra*, the court concluded that the alleged price-fixing both was commercial and had a direct effect in the US, though it still dismissed the action on act of state doctrine grounds.

The Supreme Court addressed the "direct effect" question in the *Weltover* case, *supra*, where a unanimous Court ruled that Argentina's rescheduling of debt had such an effect in the US. While disagreeing with the Court of Appeals' conclusion that the effect of the debt rescheduling on New York City's status as world financial center constituted a sufficient direct effect in the US, the Court nevertheless considered it sufficient that New York bank accounts had been designated, and had in the past functioned, as the place of payment of the debt in question. But courts are not quick to find a nexus sufficient to justify direct effect merely because an act of payment under a contract was to have occurred in the US or because the damages resulting from a wrongful act continue to be suffered in the US. See, e.g., *Princz v. Federal Republic of Germany, supra*; *United World Trade, Inc. v. Mangyshlakneft Oil Prod. Assn.* (10th Cir.1994); *Goodman Holdings v. Rafidain Bank* (D.C.Cir.1994).

Assuming there is a commercial act or activity having the requisite US nexus, a question arises as to how "general" is the personal jurisdiction thereby created. More specifically, in order to be entertained, must a claim against a foreign state arise out of or relate to the act or activity constituting the US nexus, or may the state be sued on a claim having nothing to do with that act or activity? Most, but not all, courts that have faced this question take the more restrictive position, thus making "general jurisdiction" over foreign states virtually unattainable. See, e.g., *Santos v. Compagnie Nationale Air France* (7th Cir.1991). A less common view is illustrated by *In re Rio Grande Transp., Inc.* (S.D.N.Y.1981), where the court interpreted the phrase "commercial activity" to encompass a foreign state's world-wide shipping operations and found the suit at hand to be "based upon" them, within the meaning of Section 1605(a)(2). The matter has to be regarded as still open. Whether or not the FSIA permits the exercise of general jurisdiction over foreign states, any exercise—be it general or specific—must presumably also comport with due process, in the minimum contacts and reasonableness sense.

Finally, although the losses claimed under the exception are most often commercial losses, that need not be the case. Moreover, while the exception requires a commercial act or activity, it does not require that the cause of action be a commercial one in nature. See *Siderman de Blake v. Republic of Argentina* (9th Cir.1992).

(iii) Takings of property in violation of international law

28 U.S.C.A. § 1605(a)(3) provides an exception from sovereign immunity for claims based on a taking of property in violation of international law. Generally speaking, in order for a taking of property not to violate international law, the taking must serve a public purpose, not discriminate against aliens, and be accompanied by payment of just compensation. *Greenpeace, Inc. (U.S.A.) v. France* (C.D.Cal.1996). The requirement that discrimination against aliens be shown means that a state's expropriation of property of its own nationals is not covered by the exception. *Chuidian v. Philippine Nat'l Bank, supra*; *de Sanchez v. Banco Central de*

Nicaragua (5th Cir.1985). The courts are not in perfect agreement as to whether and under what circumstances the taking of intangible interests—such as contract or trademark rights—falls within the exception. Some courts have been willing for the sake of argument to assume that they are covered (see, e.g., *Zappia Middle East Constr. Co., Ltd. v. Emirate of Abu Dhabi* (2d Cir.2000)). Others have suggested that they are not. See, e.g., *de Sanchez, supra*; *Intercontinental Dictionary Series v. De-Gruyter* (C.D.Cal.1993). The expropriation exception in particular applies only if the property in question (or any property exchanged for it) is either (a) present in the United States in connection with a commercial activity carried on in the US, or is (b) owned or operated by an agency or instrumentality of foreign state engaged in a commercial activity in the US. *Dayton v. Czechoslovak Socialist Republic,* (D.C.Cir.1987). These conditions were satisfied in *Siderman de Blake v. Republic of Argentina, supra.*

Significantly, at the jurisdictional stage, courts need not decide whether a taking actually violated international law, as long as the claim is substantial and non frivolous. Still, even for these purposes, at least a superficial look at the merits of the underlying international law claim will need to be taken. See *Siderman, supra,* where, on remand, the district court was invited to take a closer look at whether the exception's conditions were satisfied.

(iv) Property rights acquired by succession or gift or pertaining to US real estate

28 U.S.C.A. section 1605(a)(4) provides an exception to foreign sovereign immunity when rights in property in the US have been acquired by succession or gift, or where rights in immovable property in the US are at stake. The exception is applicable only to disputes that directly involving property rights. The exception must not be construed so broadly as to "abrogate immunity for any action touching upon real estate." *See e.g. MacArthur Area Citizens Assn. v. Republic of Peru*,, where Peru's operation of its chancery in a residential area of District of Columbia was held not to fall within the FSIA's "immovable property" exception because alleged zoning violations in the use of property do not entail direct claims to interest or rights in property. See also *Asociacion de Reclamantes v. United Mexican States* (D.C.Cir.1984) (claim for compensation for taking not a claim for rights in property); *Fagot Rodriguez v. Republic of Costa Rica* (1st Cir.2002) (trespass not a claim of ownership, use or possession).

(v) Non-commercial torts

The FSIA, borrowing language from the US Federal Tort Claims Act (FTCA), makes foreign states amenable to suit in tort where personal injury, death, or damage to or loss of property result in the US due to a tortious act or omission by a foreign state or by one of its employees acting within the scope of employment (28 U.S.C.A. sec. 1605(a)(5)). While the FSIA's legislative history suggests that Congress principally had in mind garden-variety automobile and personal injury accidents on US territory, the exception is drafted more broadly. Moreover, the exception is assumed to cover tortious conduct unrelated to any commercial act by the foreign state. Indeed it is sometimes called the "non-commercial torts" exception, precisely because it is assumed that a "commercial" tort claim could in any event be advanced under the commercial acts exception.

Under the tort exception, the injury caused by the tortious act or omission must have occurred "in the United States." In *In re Sedco, Inc.* (S.D.Tex.1982), a federal court dismissed an action against a Mexican government agency for pollution of the Texas shores of the Gulf of Mexico, on the ground that while the damage complained of may have been sustained in Texas, the underlying allegedly tortious conduct occurred in Mexico or Mexican territorial waters, and thus outside the US. The court relied on legislative history for the proposition that the exception requires that the underlying tortious conduct itself have occurred in the US. Indeed, according to the court, the tortious conduct must in fact have "wholly" occurred in the US. This limitation is regularly applied. See, e.g., *Wolf v. Federal Republic of Germany* (7th Cir.1996). However, read closely, the statutory language requires that the "injury," and not necessarily the "conduct," have occurred in the US. Other courts have resolved the apparent contradiction between the statutory language and the legislative history by holding the exception to be applicable where both the injury and at least some of the tortious conduct occurred in the US. *Olsen v. Government of Mexico* (9th Cir.1984).

Even when courts, following the statutory language, lay emphasis on the place of injury (as distinct from the place of tortious conduct), they tend to distinguish fairly sharply between the place of injury, on the one hand, and the place where the effects of the injury are felt, on the other. See, e.g., *Frolova v. Union of Soviet Socialist Republics* (7th Cir.1985); *Persinger v. Islamic Republic of Iran* (D.C.Cir.). The Supreme Court lent strong support to this distinction in the case of *Argentine Republic v. Amerada Hess Shipping Corp.*, *supra*, where it underscored that, while a commercial act abroad with direct effect in the US satisfies the commercial acts exception, the tort exception requires that the injury itself, and not merely its effects, be localized in the US. US courts struggle with the distinction between injury and effects, within the meaning of the FSIA's tort exception. In a series of cases, they have concluded that when US tourists suffer injury in accidents abroad, the fact that the personal effects of the injury continue to be felt, even substantially, upon the tourist's return to the US is insufficient to satisfy the exception. See, e.g., *Harris v. VAO Intourist, Moscow* (E.D.N.Y.1979); *Upton v. Empire of Iran* (D.D.C.1978).

The FSIA does not indicate what substantive body of tort law a US court should apply in an action entertained under this exception (any more than the waiver or commercial acts exception indicates the applicable substantive law). Since the injury resulting from the tortious act or omission, by definition, must have occurred in the US, US tort law is likely to be applied. But there are certainly circumstances when the foreign state's law, or indeed a third country's law, could conceivably be applied, as, for example, where the underlying tortious conduct exceptionally took place there.

The non-commercial torts exception is in turn subject to two exceptions. First, the exception does not reach claims based on certain so-called intentional torts, such as malicious prosecution, libel, or misrepresentation (an exception derived from the FTCA). Second, it is subject to a general "discretionary function" exception (likewise derived from the FTCA), according to which an act of a foreign sovereign will be shielded from review under the FSIA if it is grounded in social, economic and political policy and deemed to involve the exercise of policy judgment. *See, e.g., United States v. S.A. Empresa de Viacao Aerea Rio Grandense (Varig Airlines)* (S.Ct.1984); *MacArthur Area Citizens Ass'n v. Republic of Peru, supra.*

In the *Sedco* case, *supra*, the court regarded the discretionary function exception as an alternative basis for treating the Mexican government agency as immune, largely because it understood Mexico's exploration and exploitation of its natural resources to be inherently "discretionary." Other courts have given the discretionary function exception a more restrictive interpretation. A particularly interesting decision is *De Letelier v. Republic of Chile* (D.D.C. 1980). It was held there that, however high-ranking and politically "discretionary" it may have been, a foreign government's decision to commit a political assassination cannot be said to fall within the scope of a state's discretion and therefore to be shielded as a discretionary act ("[T]here is no discretion to commit ... an illegal act"). In the course of its decision, the court expressly rejected the notion that the tort exception should be limited to commercial, as opposed to non-commercial, torts. Occasionally, the "exception to the exception" is applied, as when the alleged tort arose out of a foreign state's issuance of travel documents to one of its nationals to enable her and her children to return to the country, even though the children's return was in violation of a US court custody order. *Risk v. Halvorsen & Kingdom of Norway* (9th Cir.1991).

Arguably, the tort allegedly committed in *De Letelier*, being an illegal act, might have been considered as outside the "scope of employment" within the meaning of the FSIA's tort exception, thus leaving the immunity of the sovereign intact. Such an argument was expressly made in *Liu v. Republic of China, supra*, a case involving a claim that the head of a Chinese government agency within the Defense Ministry had orchestrated the political assassination of a dissident journalist living in California. The Ninth Circuit decided that the choice of law applicable to the question whether the agency head had acted within the scope of employment under the FSIA (being a federal statute) should be determined in accordance with federal common law rules of choice of law, and that the latter called for application of the law of California as the place where the injury occurred. The court concluded that the agency head had acted within the scope of employment because the act was "incident to" his duties, even if neither required nor even foreseeable, and that that was sufficient under California law to place him within the scope of employment. (As in *De Letelier*, the court found the discretionary function exception to the tort exception to be unavailable.) For a similar result, see *Joseph v. Office of the Consulate General of Nigeria* (9th Cir.1987).

The courts have largely kept the commercial activity exception (sec. 1605(a)(2)) and the tort exception (sec. 1605(a)(5)) analytically separate. In *Export Group v. Reef Indus., Inc.* (9th Cir.1995), it was held that a tortious interference with contract claim could be maintained under the commercial activities exception even though barred under the tort exception. Similarly, a claim based on commercial activity is not subject to the tort exception's own exception for libel and slander. *El–Hadad v. United Arab Emirates* (D.C.Cir.2000). For a rare opinion holding the two exceptions to be mutually exclusive, see *Bryks v. Canadian Broadcasting Corp.* (S.D.N.Y. 1995), refusing to limit the tort exception proviso for "libel" to the non-commercial tort exception, and applying it as well to claims in tort under the commercial acts exception.

(vi) Arbitral matters

Having entered into an arbitration agreement to arbitrate a dispute in the territory of a country that, like the US, was party to the 1958 New York Convention on the Recognition and Enforcement of Arbitral Awards (see Chapter 11 *infra*), a foreign state might be found to have impliedly waived its immunity to an enforcement action in the US on the resulting award under the FSIA's waiver exception. See, e.g., *Seetransport Wiking Trader v. Navimpex Centrala Navala,* (2d Cir.1993).

In order to eliminate any doubt on that score, Congress amended the FSIA in 1988 to deny foreign state immunity in actions to enforce arbitration agreements and to confirm (or enforce) arbitral awards. However, in doing so, the Act still preserved the requirement of a nexus with the US. Thus, Section 1605(a)(6) requires at least one of the following: (a) that the US be the place of arbitration, (b) that the agreement or award be subject to a treaty to which the US is a party and which governs the recognition and enforcement of arbitral awards, or (c) that the underlying claim be one that, but for the arbitration agreement, could ordinarily have been maintained in a US court under the FSIA. See *Cargill Int'l S.A. v. M/T Pavel Dybenko* (2d Cir.1993), and *Employers Ins. of Wausau v. Banco De Seguros Del Estado* (7th Cir.1999), treating the New York Convention on Recognition and Enforcement of Foreign Arbitral Awards and the Inter–American Convention on International Commercial Arbitration, respectively, as just the sort of treaties referred to by the Section 1605(a)(6) exception. Since the New York Convention, as implemented in the US, applies to all awards rendered in a signatory state, it does not matter whether the foreign sovereign that was a party to that arbitration and is the defendant in the enforcement action is also a signatory. *S & Davis Int'l, Inc. v. Republic of Yemen* (11th Cir.2000); *Creighton Ltd. v. Government of Qatar, supra.* The arbitration amendment overrules prior law holding that an arbitration clause does not constitute a waiver of immunity to suit to enforce an award unless the state had agreed to arbitrate in the US.

(vii) Acts of terrorism

The FSIA exceptions were most recently expanded in 1996, by the Antiterrorism and Effective Death Penalty Act (AEDPA), through the addition of an exception (sec. 1605(a)(7)) for suits for damages for personal injury or death caused by an act of torture, extrajudicial killing, aircraft sabotage, or hostage taking (or abetting such acts) on the part of an official, employee or agent of a foreign state acting within the scope of office, employment or agency.

This exception is limited in important ways, however. In order to trigger the section 1605(a)(7) exception, the claimant must prove that (i) the defendant foreign state is designated as a state sponsor of terrorism under Section 6(j) of the Export Administration Act of 1979 (50 U.S.C.A.App. sec. 2405(j)) or Section 620A of the Foreign Assistance Act of 1961 (22 U.S.C.A. sec. 2371), or came to be so designated as a result of the act giving rise to the claim, (ii) that he or she was a US national at the time of the terrorist act and, (iii) that the act occurred on the territory of the defendant state and that the claimant offered that state a reasonable opportunity to arbitrate the claim "in accordance with accepted international rules of arbitration." States certified as state sponsor of terrorism have included Cuba, Iran, Iraq, Libya, Syria, Sudan and North Korea.

The new exception (along with new exceptions to immunity from attachment discussed below) represents a response to the perceived threat of terrorism against Americans abroad. The idea was to go beyond the provisions of the Torture Victim Protection Act (TVPA), enacted in 1991, which expressly excluded claims by persons injured abroad and only allowed recovery from individual defendants. (On the TVPA, see Chapter 6 *infra*.)

Enactment of the FSIA's terrorist acts amendment generated some controversy between Congress and the Administration. Both the Departments of State and Justice questioned the efficacy of the new provisions, doubting (a) that foreign states would appear before US courts to be judged for acts committed on their country, (b) that significant commercial assets belonging to those states would be present in the US, and (c) that judgments under the exception would be enforceable abroad. Complicating matters were concerns over disclosures that might jeopardize national security. In response to the latter concern, the FSIA was amended to authorize the Attorney General, in actions under Section 1605(a)(7), to request the court to stay any discovery request addressed to the US that "would significantly interfere with a criminal investigation or prosecution, or a national security operation, related to the incident."

The new exception was soon applied in *Flatow v. Islamic Republic of Iran* (D.D.C.1998), where Iran failed to appear to answer an FSIA claim arising out of its alleged sponsorship of anti-Israeli terrorism, and was condemned in a default judgment to pay over $225 million in compensatory and punitive damages for a terrorist incident. Other suits arising out of state-sponsored terrorism—against Libya, Cuba, Iraq and Iran—have followed. At the same time, these judgments have faced real difficulties of execution. (See below.)

The question has arisen whether, contrary to the accepted notion that the FSIA does not itself create a federal cause of action against foreign states, the FSIA does actually create such a cause of action for terrorist acts. In *Flatow, supra*, the court styled the action as one sounding in wrongful death, but nevertheless explicitly stated that the 1996 amendment adding Section 1605(a)(7) created a federal cause of action for personal injury or death resulting from state-sponsored terrorists acts. However, in other cases (e.g., *Price v. Socialist People's Libyan Arab*

Jamahiriya (D.C.Cir.2002), and *Bettis v. Islamic Republic of Iran* (D.C.Cir.2003)), that question has been deliberately left open. The possibility also must be reckoned with that a claim stated under this exception may fail for want of adequate personal jurisdiction, due to the absence of minimum contacts with the US. In one case, Iraq maintained that application of the terrorist acts exception to it would violate jurisdictional due process. The court entertained, but rejected, the assertion in *Daliberti v. Republic of Iraq* (D.D.C.2000), and eventually found Iran liable (D.D.C.2001).

The terrorist acts exception is not to be read as a general human rights exception. Unless a human rights claim against a foreign government falls within this, or some other, exception, jurisdiction will be lacking. In *Sampson v. Federal Republic of Germany*, *supra*, the court underscored that Congress had not created an exception to sovereign immunity for violation of *ius cogens* international norms, and thus dismissed a claim for compensation for enslavement during World War II. See also *Boshnjaku v. Federal Republic of Yugoslavia*, *supra*, which likewise declined to treat execution of a human rights treaty as an implied waiver of immunity. To similar effect, see *Hwang Geum Joo v. Japan*, *supra*, involving claims of Japan's forcible abduction and sexual slavery of Chinese women during World War II.

(viii) Admiralty

Section 1605(b) provides for an exception to sovereign immunity "in any case in which a suit in admiralty is brought to enforce a maritime lien against a vessel or cargo of the foreign state, which maritime lien is based upon a commercial activity of the foreign state." In determining whether the activity of the vessel is commercial, courts are guided by understandings of that term within meaning of the more general commercial activity exception. See, e.g., *China Nat'l Chem. Import & Export Corp. v. M/V Lago Hualaihue* (D.Md.1981).

Availability of the admiralty exception is subject to two conditions relating to service and timing of notice. Notice of suit must be given to the person or agent having possession of the vessel, followed within ten days by notice to the foreign state itself. The courts will determine whether proper and timely notice in both respects was given (see, e.g. *China Nat'l Chem. Import & Export Corp., supra*; *Kim Crest, S.A. v. M.V. Sverdlovsk* (S.D.Tex.1990)) and failure of notice will in fact defeat FSIA jurisdiction under the exception (see, e.g., *Castillo v. Shipping Corp. of India* (S.D.N.Y.1985)).

(d) Counterclaims

According to the FSIA (sec. 1607(b)), if a foreign state or instrumentality brings an action in the US, the court has jurisdiction over related counterclaims, without any limitation on recovery, even though the counterclaim would ordinarily have been subject to immunity. The idea behind the exception is to require that foreign States accept the "bitter" with the "sweet," while at the same time favoring adjudication of multiple claims in a single proceeding. (A counterclaim may also of course be brought on matters for which the foreign state would not in any event be entitled to immunity under the FSIA.) The courts have entertained counterclaims liberally, requiring only that the two claims, or their underlying facts or issues, share a "logical relationship." *Lord Day & Lord v. Socialist Republic of Vietnam* (S.D.N.Y.2001).

A good example is *In re Oil Spill by Amoco Cadiz* (N.D.Ill.1979), where the claimant foreign states were unsuccessful in seeking dismissal of counterclaims and third-party claims in consolidated actions arising out of an oil tanker disaster off the coast of the foreign states. The court found that the claims, counterclaims and third-party claims arose from the same transaction or occurrence within the meaning of section 1607, and that substantially the same evidence would support or refute them. Sovereign immunity therefore did not prevent the counterclaims and third-party claims from being entertained.

Where the counterclaim is unrelated to the principal claim, the FSIA (28 U.S.C.A. sec. 1607(c)) permits its maintenance, but limits recovery on the counterclaim to the amount recovered on the claim, as if a set-off. This "compromise" reflects a codification of pre-FSIA case law. *National City Bank v. Republic of China* (S.Ct.1955). As noted, *supra* page 178, in *First Nat'l City Bank v. Banco Para El Comercio Exterior de Cuba*, the Supreme Court, by veil-piercing, even permitted a claim against Cuba to be set off against an unrelated claim brought by a Cuban government instrumentality.

(e) Retroactivity of the FSIA

The issue of the FSIA's retroactivity has often arisen. Initially, the courts held that the FSIA could not be applied to claims arising prior to 1976. *Carl Marks & Co., Inc. v. Union of Soviet Socialist Repubs.* (2d Cir.1988). Following general indications given by the Supreme Court on the circumstances in which federal statutes might appropriately be applied retroactively (see *Landgraf v. USI Film Prods.* (S.Ct.1994)), the courts have now taken a range of views. Compare *Princz v. Federal Republic of Germany*, *supra*, and *Altmann v. Republic of Austria* (9th Cir.2002) (retroactivity), with *Garb v. Republic of Poland* (E.D.N.Y.2002) (non-retroactivity).

When Congress added the terrorist acts exception to the FSIA (28 U.S.C.A. sec. 1605(a)(7)), *supra* page 147, it expressly directed that that exception be applied retroactively (Pub. L. No. 104–132, sec. 221(c)). The courts have followed that direction, even while admitting that retroactive application of statutes to pre-enactment conduct is ordinarily disfavored.

(f) Attachment of foreign sovereign property

The FSIA separately addresses the question of the attachment of foreign government property. According to Section 1609, such property is presumptively immune from attachment, subject only to international agreement or to another section of the FSIA. Other sections of the FSIA contemplate attachment in two scenarios only.

First, according to Section 1610(d), *prejudgment* attachment of property for purposes of securing satisfaction of an eventual judgment is permitted only insofar as the foreign state has explicitly waived immunity from attachment for that purpose. (For good measure, section 1610(d) categorically excludes prejudgment attachment of property for purposes of obtaining jurisdiction).

It has been held that where a state by contract "irrevocably and unconditionally waives any right or immunity from legal proceedings, including suit, judgment or execution on grounds of sovereignty which it or its property may now or hereafter enjoy . . .," such waiver constitutes an explicit waiver of immunity from prejudgment attachment, even though prejudgment attachment was not specifically mentioned in the waiver. *Libra Bank Ltd. v. Banco Nacional de Costa Rica, S.A.* (2d Cir.1982). Other cases have declined to go that far. See, e.g., *O'Connell Mach. Co., Inc. v. M.V. Americana* (2d Cir.1984). Moreover, a state's waiver by treaty of "immunities from suit or execution of judgment or other liability in the territory of the other Party with respect to commercial or financial transactions'' was deemed not sufficiently explicit to permit prejudgment attachment. *S & S Mach. Co. v. Masinexportimport* (2d Cir.1983).

Second, the FSIA permits the attachment of foreign government property for purposes of executing a final judgment already rendered against a foreign state under the FSIA, i.e *post-judgment* attachment. Post-judgment attachment is allowed more broadly, though still only via a court order (sec. 1610). Attachment is proper in prescribed circumstances only: (i) where immunity from attachment has been waived either explicitly or implicitly (sec. 1610(a)(1)); (ii) where, in the case of a judgment predicated on the FSIA's commercial activity exception, the property sought to be attached was used for purposes of the commercial activity that gave rise to the underlying claim (sec. 1610(a)(2)); (iii) where the execution relates to certain judgments establishing rights in property (sec. 1610(a)(3), (4)); (iv) where the property consists of proceeds to indemnify or hold the state harmless under an insurance policy covering the claim; (v) where the judgment is based on an order confirming an arbitral award rendered against the foreign state (sec. 1610(a)(6)); and (vi) where the judgment relates to a claim for which the foreign state is not immune under the terrorist acts exception (sec. 1610(a)(7)). In the case of judgments under the terrorist acts exception, the FSIA specifically permits attachment ''regardless of whether the property is or was involved with the act upon which the claim is based.''

In 1998, the FSIA's exceptions to immunity from attachment were further expanded by the addition of a new sub-section 1610(f), which specifically makes certain other property—in particular assets blocked under specific federal laws—available for execution of any judgment relating to a claim under the terrorist acts exception. The amendment also entitles a judgment creditor in such a case to cooperation by the Treasury and State Departments in locating and executing against available property of the judgment debtor.

The attachment of assets of agencies or instrumentalities is more relaxed. In addition to the possibilities of attachment described above, the property of an agency or instrumentality may, in cases falling under the exceptions of sections 1605(a)(2), (3) and (5), as well as (7), be attached without the property also having been used for the activity upon which the claim is based.

Thus, certain of these post-judgment attachment provisions require execution on property related to the claim, while others do not. The requirement that, in the absence of waiver, the property attached be used for the purpose of the commercial activity that generated the claim has given rise to particular difficulties. In *Birch Shipping Corp. v. Embassy of United Republic of Tanzania* (D.D.C. 1980), the court not only found an implicit waiver of immunity from attachment, but also found that there was a sufficient nexus between the property and the claim, and the fact that the property was not used solely for that purpose made no difference.

Certain special categories of property belonging to a foreign state (including property of a foreign central bank or monetary authority held for its own account, and certain property used in connection with a military activity) are categorically immune from attachment (sec. 1611). The FSIA contains more liberal rules for the attachment of property of an agency or instrumentality engaging in commercial activity in aid of execution of a judgment against that agency or instrumentality (sec. 1610(b)).

The structure of the FSIA makes it possible for a state to lose its sovereign immunity from suit, but nevertheless enjoy immunity from execution of the resulting judgment. In commercial acts, this can happen when there has been no waiver (even implicit) and there is no available commercial property related to the liability-generating activity. It can happen even more easily with regard to claims predicated on the FSIA's tort exception, since in such a case there may well not even be a commercial activity in connection with which one might seek to attach "related" property. In *DeLetelier v. Republic of Chile* (2d Cir.1984), Chile was condemned to pay damages for commission of a tort within the US (namely, a political assassination in Washington DC), but the judgment could not be satisfied since there was no waiver and, by definition (since jurisdiction was not predicated on a commercial activity) no related commercial property. The court also refused to authorize attachment of commercial assets belonging to Chile's national airline, even though those assets could conceivably have been related to the claim, since the airline had not been sued or had a judgment rendered against it. The court refused to "pierce the veil" for attachment purposes, since it found that Chile had not abused the airline's separate corporate identity. By the court's admission, "[u]nder the circumstances at issue in this case, Congress did in effect create a right without a remedy." Successful FSIA plaintiffs have from time to time failed in attaching the assets of state instrumentalities to execute a judgment rendered against a foreign state precisely because they could not establish the instrumentality's own involvement in the violation or overcome the presumption that government instrumentalities enjoy a separate juridical status. *Alejandre v. Telefonica Larga Distancia de Puerto Rico, Inc.* (11th Cir. 1999); *Pravin Banker Assocs., Ltd. v. Banco Popular del Peru* (S.D.N.Y.1998).

In *the Flatow* case, *supra* page 149, the plaintiffs had enormous difficulty recovering their 225 million dollar judgment. The courts declined to enforce the judgment against property owned by a foundation that they did not consider to be the foreign state's alter ego or agent. (D.Md.1999). They also declined to issue a writ against the US attaching all property of Iran held by the US, as in violation of the US government's own sovereign immunity. (D.D.C. 1999). Finally, they declined to enforce the judgment against three properties owned by Iran in Washington DC (a former embassy building and residences of the Minister for Cultural Affairs and the Military Attaché) and two bank accounts, on the ground that they were immune from attachment under the FSIA because not used for a commercial activity in the US. The court so ruled, notwithstanding the 1998 FSIA amendment referred to earlier, allowing judgment creditors under Section 1605(a)(7) to attach foreign government property in the US if it had been blocked or frozen by the executive branch, the reason being that the president had waived this provision, as he was authorized to do, in the interest of national security. (D.D.C.1999).

Likewise, US teachers and journalists kidnapped in Beirut won large FSIA judgments, but failed to get them enforced. *See, e.g.*, *Cicippio v. Islamic Republic of Iran* (D.D.C.1998); *Anderson v. Islamic Republic of Iran* (D.D.C.2000); *Eisenfeld v. Islamic Republic of Iran* (D.D.C.2000); *Sutherland v. Islamic Republic of Iran* (D.D.C.2001); *Jenco v. Islamic Republic of Iran* (D.D.C.2001); *Weinstein v. Islamic Republic of Iran* (D.D.C.2002); *Wagner v. Islamic Republic of Iran* (D.D.C.2001). See also *Higgins v. Islamic Republic of Iran* (D.D.C.2000).

In response to all these difficulties, Congress enacted the Victims of Trafficking and Violence Protection Act of 2000, Pub. L. No. 106–386, 114 Stat. 1464, section 2002(a)(1), which permits certain victims of terrorist acts to collect the entirety of their compensatory (but none of their punitive) damages from the US government and compels the US to seek reimbursement from the foreign state. Pursuant to this provision, the Treasury Department paid Flatow $26 million (the compensatory portion of the judgment, plus post-judgment interest), on condition that he give up his right to execute against property blocked or frozen under US law. (D.C.Cir. 2002).

Attachment in execution poses a particular problem when the underlying claim against the sovereign is not one that a US court adjudicated under the FSIA (through an assertion of personal jurisdiction that satisfied the conditions of both the FSIA and due process), but rather a claim that was subject to adjudication in a foreign court or international arbitral tribunal. Arguably, the US court cannot assert jurisdiction to enforce the foreign judgment or arbitral award in the absence of personal jurisdiction under both the FSIA and due process. See, e.g., *Creighton Ltd. v. Government of Qatar, supra*, where the terms of the arbitration exception to the FSIA were met, but jurisdictional due process was found not to be, and the enforcement action was accordingly dismissed.

(g) Suits by aliens against foreign states

Although the FSIA does not limit the jurisdiction of US courts to suits by US nationals, arguably the US Constitution does. Article III authorizes the exercise of federal subject matter jurisdiction in diversity cases only in suits between "a State, or the Citizens thereof, and foreign States, Citizens or Subjects." The US Supreme Court has nevertheless ruled that the Constitution permits application of the FSIA to suits by aliens because, while such cases do not fall within Article III's diversity jurisdiction, they do fall within the scope of "federal question" jurisdiction. The Court reasoned that FSIA suits arise out of federal legislation (*viz.* the FSIA itself), which was constitutionally enacted pursuant to Congress' Article I power over foreign affairs. *Verlinden B.V. v. Central Bank of Nigeria* (S.Ct.1983).

Suits by aliens against foreign states inevitably raise *forum non conveniens* and other litigation strategy issues. Forum shopping is a distinct possibility, since even if US forum were to apply foreign law to the underlying cause of action, the determination of damages would be treated as procedural, giving claimants the benefit of generally high US damages levels. In fact, suits under the FSIA have, on rare occasion, been dismissed on *forum non conveniens* grounds. See, e.g., *Forsythe v. Saudi Arabian Airlines Corp.* (5th Cir.1989).

(h) Default

The FSIA permits default judgments, but only on condition that the claimant establish its claim or right to relief by evidence satisfactory to the court (28 U.S.C.A. sec. 1608(e)). This most definitely includes proof that an exception to FSIA immunity applies, for the simple reason that the court's subject matter jurisdiction depends on such a showing, and is not waivable. Notice of the default judgment is required to be delivered in the same manner as service was made.

HEAD OF STATE OR GOVERNMENT IMMUNITY

The FSIA addresses only the immunity of foreign states, and their agencies and instrumentalities, and would appear not to address the immunity of individuals. However, as noted (*supra* page 127, the question has arisen whether an individual official could possibly constitute an "agency or instrumentality" of a foreign state under the FSIA. The court in *Chuidian v. Philippine Nat'l Bank*, *supra*, dismissed a suit against a member of the Philippine Presidential Commission under the FSIA on the assumption that, as an official acting within the scope of office, he was effectively an instrumentality of the state and entitled to invoke immunity under the FSIA. See also *Byrd v. Corporacion Forestal y Industrial de Olancho S.A.* (5th Cir.1999); *Jungquist v. Sheikh Sultan Bin Khalifa Al Nahyan* (D.C.Cir.1997); *El–Fadl v. Central Bank of Jordan* (D.C.Cir.1996). However, courts have drawn the line at the point where the foreign government official could be said to have acted beyond the scope of authority. See, e.g., *Trajano v. Marcos (In re Estate of Ferdinand E. Marcos Human Rights Litig.)* (9th Cir.1992). A foreign official may also step outside the scope of authority when the acts undertaken are sufficiently violative of international law. See, e.g., *Republic of the Philippines v. Marcos* (9th Cir.1988).

Assuming a case is not subsumed under the FSIA, the question whether a head of state or government, or other foreign public official, enjoys immunity is presumably a matter of common law. By tradition, a head of state immunity is recognized for the official head of state or government, as conclusively determined by the US executive. *Saltany v. Reagan* (D.D.C.1988). An example of its application is *Lafontant v. Aristide* (E.D.N.Y.1994). There, the wife of a political opponent of the Haitian regime sued the then recently elected President Aristide, in exile in the US, for having ordered her husband's execution while in prison. The US government, having by then recognized Aristide as Haiti's lawfully elected head of state despite his overthrow, filed a suggestion of immunity on account of US foreign policy interests. The court applied common law immunity principles to hold that, absent waiver by statute or by the relevant foreign government, Aristide, as Haiti's head of state recognized by the United States, was absolutely immune from the exercise of jurisdiction by US courts. On the other hand, following clear directions from the executive branch, the court denied to Nicaragua's President Manuel Noriega immunity from prosecution for drug-related offenses based on head of state immunity. *United States v. Noriega* (11th Cir.1997). The court cited the facts, among others, that Noriega was not the constitutionally designated head of state, that the government of Nicaragua had not sought immunity for him, and that he had been charged with private acts in pursuit of personal enrichment. These examples demonstrate the great influence of the State Department "suggestions" regarding immunity. In any case, former heads of state are ordinarily denied head of state immunity. See, e.g., *Islamic Republic of Iran v. Mohammed Reza Pahlavi* (N.Y.1984); *Estate of Domingo v. Republic of the Philippines* (W.D.Wash.1988).

Some courts, in an apparent application of head of state immunity, maintain the view that heads of state and government are immune even from claims of international law violations, such as torture, terrorism, and summary execution, under the Alien Tort Claim Statute and the Torture Victim Protection Act (see Chapter 6 *infra*). Indeed, that immunity has occasionally been extended to certain high officials close to the head of state. This occurred in *Tachiona v. Mugabe* (S.D.N.Y.2001), involving high officials of the government of Zimbabwe. (Immunity was found not to extend, however, to the ruling Zimbabwean political party itself, of which those officials were members, and the party was eventually held liable. (S.D.N.Y.2002); (S.D.N.Y.2001).) As described in Section 66 of the Restatement (Second) of Foreign Relations Law, this immunity is a limited one. According to it, "the immunity of a foreign state ... extends ... to its heads of state and any person designated by him as a member of his official party and ... ; its head of government and any person designated by him as a member of his official party; [and] any other public minister, official or agent of the state with respect to acts performed in its official capacity if the effect of the rule exercising jurisdiction would be to enforce a rule of law against the state." A case citing the Second Restatement is *Republic of the Philippines v. Marcos* (2d Cir.1986).

The Restatement (Third) of Foreign Relations Law (secs. 464–465) also mentions a more restricted immunity for diplomatic and consular agents, both of which are addressed by international treaties ratified by the US, specifically the Vienna Convention on Diplomatic Relations, 500 UNTS 95, 23 UST 3227 (1961), and the Vienna Convention on Consular Relations, 596 UNTS 262, 21 UST 78 (1963). To the extent that a person enjoys immunity under one of these conventions, the US Diplomatic Relations Act, 22 U.S.C.A. sec. 254, requires dismissal of the action.

Under the Diplomatic Relations Convention (art. 31), diplomatic agents, while enjoying full immunity from the criminal jurisdiction of the receiving state, enjoy only limited immunity from civil or administrative jurisdiction. Immunity, which may be waived by the sending state, attaches only to acts within the scope of the diplomat's official functions, and is subject to certain narrow exceptions. The US Diplomatic Relations Act, 22 U.S.C.A. sec. 254, gives "members of a mission" of a non-party to the Vienna Diplomatic Relations Convention the same privileges and immunities as provided for by that Convention, subject to the President's authority to raise or lower the level of protection as to them. The Vienna Consular Relations Convention (art. 43) immunizes consular officials from civil as well as criminal liability with respect to acts performed in the exercise of consular functions, again subject to exceptions. Whether an individual enjoys diplomatic or consular status for these purposes is typically determined by the State Department. *Abdulaziz v. Metropolitan Dade Co.* (11th Cir.1984). Subject to these immunities, the district courts enjoy original and exclusive subject matter jurisdiction under 28 U.S.C.A. sec. 1351 in civil actions against consuls, vice-consuls and members of a mission (or members of the latter's families).

Besides amending the FSIA with respect to the liability of states for terrorist acts (and attachments in execution of resulting judgments), Congress in 1996 enacted the Civil Liability for Acts of State Sponsored Terrorism Act, Pub. L. No. 104–208, 110 Stat. 3009–172, sec. 589, 28 U.S.C.A. sec. 1605 note, otherwise known as the "*Flatow* amendment," after the case of that name (see pages 149 *supra.*) The statute applies only to officials, employees and agents of foreign states that have been designated as a state sponsor of terrorism under Section 6(j) of the Export Administration Act of 1979, provided they were acting within the scope of office, employment or agency. The statute renders any such person liable to a US national for personal injury or death arising out of acts for which sovereign immunity of the foreign state is waived under Section 1605(a)(7), and permits recovery of economic damages, pain and suffering, and punitive damages. The FSIA's specific statute of limitations and rules on discovery in claims under Section 1605(a)(7), as set out in Sections 1605(f) and (g), apply equally here.

THE ACT OF STATE DOCTRINE

Whether or not a foreign government or its instrumentality is named as defendant, a claim in US court may effectively call into question the legality or propriety of its official acts. Indeed, the very aim of the litigation may be to avoid the legal effects of those acts. According to the "act of state doctrine," no US court will pass upon the validity of official public acts taken by a foreign government on its own territory. Doing so is thought to risk interference with the federal executive's prerogatives in the management of US foreign relations and possible embarrassment to those relations. Presumably, the party invoking the act of state doctrine bears the burden of proving its applicability. *Lamb v. Phillip Morris, Inc.* (6th Cir.1990). On the other hand, even if a state or other party fails to appear, or appears but fails to invoke the doctrine, the court may raise the issue on its own.

There is no agreement on the exact nature of the act of state doctrine. It seems to operate, variously, as a defense, as a jurisdictional barrier, as a choice of law rule, as a rule of issue preclusion, or merely as a rule of evidence. Perhaps the most accurate way to view it is as an abstention doctrine. Because of its chameleon character, we find the doctrine being raised at various points in litigation—sometimes at the very threshold, sometimes only when a particular argument is sought to be made. Similarly, its effects will vary. In some cases, it will cause an entire action to be dismissed, while at other times it will merely cause a line of argument to be excluded. In any case, its application is not restricted to cases in which foreign states or their officials are a party.

Unlike foreign sovereign immunity, the act of state doctrine is not predicated on any enactment by Congress. It is essentially a common law, and more specifically a substantive federal common law, creation. As such, it is presumably binding on state courts, since touching on "uniquely federal interests." See generally *Boyle v. United Technologies Corp.* (S.Ct.1988). Only rarely is the act of state doctrine, as such, addressed in federal legislation. One example is the Second Hickenlooper Amendment, discussed below. Another is the Federal Arbitration Act, 9 U.S.C.A. sec. 15, which, as amended in 1988, provides that the act of state doctrine has no application in actions for the enforcement of international arbitration agreements or awards. (See Chapter 11 *infra.*)

The act of state doctrine is often traced to the Supreme Court's decision in *Underhill v. Hernandez* (S.Ct.1897), where the Court announced that "the courts of one country will not sit in judgment on the acts of the government of another, done within its own territory." In two subsequent rulings—*Oetjen v. Central Leather Co.* (S.Ct.1918), and *Ricaud v. American Metal Co.* (S.Ct.1918)—the Court chiefly predicated the act of state doctrine on notions of international comity, although it also suggested that the doctrine might be thought of simply as an international choice of law rule.

The fundamental modern case is *Banco Nacional de Cuba v. Sabbatino* (S.Ct.1964), which reaffirmed the act of state doctrine as a "federal law" doctrine, while giving it an additional foundation, namely the constitutional separation of powers and, more particularly, the avoidance of judicial intrusion into matters of foreign affairs, which are entrusted to the political branches of government. This additional foundation is frequently echoed in the act of state cases. See, e.g., *First Nat'l City Bank v. Banco Nacional de Cuba* (S.Ct.1972); *Republic of Philippines v. Marcos* (9th Cir.1988). In *Sabbatino*, the Court ruled that the act of state doctrine is applicable even when the foreign government act was allegedly taken in violation of international law.

The Restatement (Third) of Foreign Relations Law, section 443, broadly endorses the act of state doctrine in the following terms: "In the absence of a treaty or other unambiguous agreement regarding controlling legal principles, courts in the United States will generally refrain from examining the validity of a taking by a foreign state of property within its own territory, or from sitting in judgment on other acts of a governmental character done by a foreign state within its territory and applicable there." Application of the doctrine does not appear to vary according to the norms—US law, foreign law, or international law—against which the validity of the foreign government act is sought to be challenged, or according to the cause of action—common law or statutory—in the context of which it is raised.

The act of state doctrine is not infrequently applied. Good examples are *International Association of Machinists v. OPEC* (9th Cir.1981) (shielding the OPEC states from an antitrust action for fixing the price of crude oil and declining to treat the OPEC action as commercial, based on the inappropriateness of a domestic court instructing a foreign state as to the disposition of its natural resources), *Braka v. Bancomer, S.N.C.* (2d Cir.1985) (shielding Mexico from suit on a certificate of deposit because its default of payment on the debt was due to foreign exchange control regulations), and *Riggs Nat'l Corp. v. Commissioner of Internal Rev. Serv.* (D.C.Cir.1999) (barring inquiry into the validity of Brazilian government determination that taxes are due). It is not uncommon for suits that a foreign state fails to get dismissed for want of jurisdiction under the FSIA to end up being dismissed on the basis of the act of state doctrine or international comity. Such was the case in both the *OPEC* and *Braka v. Bancomer* cases, *supra*.

Definitional aspects

By definition, only acts deemed by their nature to be "public," or "governmental" are protected from review. Many of the leading cases involved acts of expropriation, which are routinely considered "public" or" governmental." But no formulation of the doctrine has limited it to that category of cases. The frontiers of the notion of act of state are difficult to define. Leading cases have held the doctrine inapplicable to an alleged misuse of foreign judicial procedures (*Timberlane Lumber Co. v. Bank of Am.* (9th Cir.1976)) and to the issuance of a foreign patent (*Mannington Mills, Inc. v. Congoleum Corp.* (3d Cir. 1979)), yet applicable to bribery (*Clayco Petroleum Corp. v. Occidental Petroleum Corp.* (9th Cir.1983)) and price fixing (*International Assoc. of Machinists v. OPEC, supra*).

The only further guidance on this issue from the Supreme Court comes from the plurality opinion of the Court in *Alfred Dunhill of London, Inc. v. Republic of Cuba* (S.Ct.1976), holding that a measure or policy can be considered an act of state only if it is supported by a "statute, decree, order or resolution" of the foreign state. (There, a refusal by the Cuban government to reimburse the plaintiff for sums of money that the latter allegedly mistakenly paid to it for merchandise shipped by a private Cuban company prior to its official expropriation by the Cuban government was held not to be an act of state, because not supported by any such "statute, decree, order or resolution.") Lower court decisions seem to lay emphasis on the extent of evidence of "official" authorization. See *Grupo Protexa, S.A. v.*

All Am. Marine Slip (3d Cir.1994); *Galu v. Swiss Air Transp. Co.* (2d Cir.1989). The rank of the government actor may therefore be a relevant factor. Indeed some courts have in a sense "codified" this requirement by recognizing a "ministerial" exception for what they consider to be routine government decisions, such as the issuance of a patent. See, e.g., *Mannington Mills, Inc. v. Congoleum Corp., supra.* Whether an alleged act of state has the requisite "official" or "governmental" character is ultimately a matter for the court to determine. See *World Wide Minerals Ltd. v. Republic of Kazakhstahn, supra.*

Also by definition, an act of a foreign government may be shielded by the act of state doctrine only to the extent that it is deemed to have been "taken" on the territory of the foreign state. The doctrine does not therefore extend to takings outside the territory of the state concerned. See *Republic of Iraq v. First Nat'l City Bank* (2d Cir.1965), where the court noted that when the property seized is situated in the US, the taking will be given effect only if consistent with US law. *See also Banco Nacional de Cuba v. Chemical Bank New York Trust Co.* (2d Cir.1981).

The territorial requirement has given rise to questions about the "situs" of a foreign government act, particularly where intangible property is concerned. In *Braka v. Bancomer, supra,* the act of state doctrine was ruled applicable because the alleged act of state (*viz.* repudiation of a government debt in the form of a certificate of deposit) could only have been taken in Mexico, the place where payment under the contract was required to be made. The court reconciled the result with its earlier ruling in *Allied Bank Int'l v. Banco Credito Agricola de Cartago* (2d Cir.1985) (*rehearing en banc*), finding the debt situs to have been in the US, on the ground that the underlying obligation in the *Allied Bank* case was capable of being performed in the US. See also *Vishipco Line v. Chase Manhattan Bank, N.A.* (2d Cir.1981), involving claims by the Saigon branches of various US and French banks that they could not honor deposits by Vietnamese nationals due to a revolutionary government decree, issued the day after the South Vietnamese government fell, confiscating those branches as "organs of US imperialism." Obviously, situating an intangible is still more difficult where the parties have not designated a specific place of performance in their contract. In those cases, courts often tend toward a multi-factor "center of gravity" analysis. See, e.g., *F. & H.R. Farman–Farmaian Consulting Engineers Firm v. Harza Eng. Co.* (7th Cir.1989); *Callejo v. Bancomer, S.A.* (5th Cir.1985).

Predictably, the courts have taken different approaches to the question whether the act of an individual official should be ascribed to the state for act of state doctrine purposes. Courts have, however, been reluctant to accord act of state status to individual misconduct by government officers, such as financial crimes or drug trafficking. See, e.g., *DeRoburt v. Gannett Co. Inc.* (9th Cir.1984); *United*

States v. Noriega (S.D.Fla.1990); *Sharon v. Time, Inc.* (S.D.N.Y.1984). They also have refused to extend it to the acts of ex-chiefs of state. See, e.g., *Republic of Philippines v. Marcos* (9th Cir.1988).

Recent Supreme Court case law confirms a third definitional limitation. Foreign governmental acts are sheltered from review only as to their *validity*. In its decision in *W.S. Kirkpatrick & Co., Inc. v. Environmental Tectonics Corp., Int'l* (S.Ct.1990), the Court ruled unanimously that the act of state doctrine is not implicated except to the extent that the validity of a foreign government act is actually put in question. There, a party had sought to show in its US antitrust and RICO action against a competitor that the latter had won a contract from the government of Nigeria through the payment of bribes. The defendant invoked the act of state doctrine in order to bar the plaintiff from asserting the defendant's collusion with the Nigerian government. The Court rejected the doctrine's application to that case, largely because it was not the *validity* of the acts of the Nigerian government, but at most their *motivation*, that was being questioned. Among the matters incidentally clarified by *Kirkpatrick* was that the act of state doctrine is a "principle of decision binding on federal and state courts alike." In a related vein, courts have held that, while the act of state doctrine may insulate foreign sovereign acts from review as to their validity, it does not necessarily protect private parties from liability for conduct prompted by those acts. See, e.g., *Arango v. Guzman Travel Advisors Corp.* (5th Cir.1980).

Exceptions to the act of state doctrine

Besides underscoring certain definitional restrictions on the act of state doctrine, case law has narrowed the scope of application of the act of state doctrine in a variety of ways commonly and perhaps misleadingly described as "exceptions." Thus, even within the proper realm of acts of state, as defined, the doctrine may not apply. The status of these so-called unwritten exceptions to the unwritten act of state doctrine is quite uncertain.

(a) Commercial exception

A first possible exception is a so-called "commercial exception," in some ways paralleling the commercial acts exception to sovereign immunity. A plurality of the Supreme Court in the *Alfred Dunhill* case, *supra*, recognized such an exception, holding that even if the refusal of payment had constituted a public or governmental act, "the concept of an act of state should not be extended to include the repudiation of a purely commercial obligation owed by a foreign sovereign or by one of its commercial instrumentalities." Whether the "commerciality" of an act were treated as an exception, or simply served to negate the "public" or "governmental" element required for an act to constitute an act of state, it would result in an important restriction on the doctrine. The exception has been widely applied (see, e.g., *Virtual Defense & Dev. Int'l, Inc. v. Republic of Moldova* (D.D.C.1999)). However, because it commanded the affirmative support of only four members of the Court, it has not been uniformly accepted. In *Honduras Aircraft Registry, Ltd. v. Government of Honduras* (11th Cir.1997), the court found that it had jurisdiction under the commercial exception to the FSIA, but it nevertheless barred the claim under the act of state doctrine, which the court found to be subject to no analogous exception. Moreover, as in the sovereign immunity context, the notion of "commercial" is problematic in its application.

Even under a commercial exception, the fact that a case arises in a commercial context is not decisive. In *Callejo v. Bancomer, supra*, and *Braka v. Bancomer, supra*, two courts of appeal refused to examine the validity of a Mexican regulation requiring all Mexican bank deposits to be repaid in pesos at a specific below-market exchange rate, because the regulation remained a sovereign act even though applied in a commercial context.

(b) The Bernstein exception

The so-called *Bernstein* exception takes its name from a case in which a US claimant, who had been deprived of property by the Nazi government of Germany during World War II, secured a letter from the State Department to the effect that judicial entertainment of the claim would not disrupt US foreign relations, and that the act of state doctrine accordingly need not be applied. *Bernstein v. N.V. Nederlandsche–Amerikaansche Stoomvaart–Maatschappij* (2d Cir.1954). In its only decision on this exception, the Supreme Court declined to apply the act of state doctrine, but the "*Bernstein* exception" as such won the affirmative support of only three justices of the Court. *First Nat'l City Bank v. Banco Nacional de Cuba, supra.* The status of the exception thus remains unsettled. Executive branch "suggestions" on the matter—one way or the other—are most safely regarded as no more than a relevant factor.

The Restatement (Third) of Foreign Relations Law, drawing upon *Sabbatino* and other cases, notes that if the State Department issues a *Bernstein* letter requesting the courts not to review the validity of a particular act, such a letter will be highly persuasive, though not binding. On the other hand, a *Bernstein* letter to the effect that the Department has no objection to judicial determination of the validity of a foreign act will leave the courts free to apply the doctrine or not, while taking the executive branch's views into account. Restatement (Third) of Foreign Relations Law, sec. 443, rptrs note 8.

(c) Counterclaim exception

Courts have largely rejected the existence of a "counterclaim" exception that would permit courts, when faced with a claim by a foreign state, to entertain a counterclaim ordinarily falling within the act of state doctrine. In *Sabbatino*, the Supreme Court held that any counterclaim whose success depends on a showing of the invalidity of a foreign act of state must necessarily fail. However, the Second Circuit, in a series of cases, has sought to mitigate the position of the Court by holding that, while the act of state doctrine barred a US bank from asserting a counterclaim against Cuba, the bank could invoke its claim as a set-off against recovery on a successful claim by Cuba against it. *Banco Nacional de Cuba v. Chase Manhattan Bank* (2d Cir.1981). In the latter case, the court applied the same basic rule as the Supreme Court had laid down in *First Nat'l City Bank v. Banco Nacional de Cuba, supra*. In order for a counterclaim not to be barred by the act of state doctrine, several conditions would have to be met: (1) the Executive Branch would need to furnish a *Bernstein* letter to the effect that the act of state doctrine need not be applied, (2) adjudication of the claim would need to be shown not to interfere with delicate foreign relations, and (3) the claim against the foreign sovereign would need to be asserted by way of counterclaim and not exceed the value of the sovereign's own claim.

In *First Nat'l City Bank v. Banco Para El Comercio, supra*, the issue before the Supreme Court was whether Citibank could set the value of its expropriated Cuban assets off against a claim by *Bancec*, notwithstanding the fact that *Bancec* was juridically separate from the Cuban government which had expropriated Citibank's property. The Court of Appeals, reversing the district court, had previously disallowed the setoff, holding that the Cuban bank's juridical separateness from the Cuban government had to be respected, at least where the claim in question arose from acts of the government unrelated to the operations of the bank. (2d Cir.1981). In its judgment in *First Nat'l City Bank v. Banco Para El Comercio*, the Supreme Court applied "principles of equity common to international law and federal common law" to permit the setoff. (The Second Circuit thereafter affirmed the district court judgment dismissing the claim by the Cuban bank as fully offset by the counterclaim. (2d Cir.1984).)

Notwithstanding the result in the *First Nat'l City Bank* case, it would be wrong to assume that, absent a *Bernstein* letter, the setoff would have been allowed. In *Bank Tejarat v. Varsho–Saz* (C.D.Cal. 1989), the defendant sought to defeat a fraud action government-controlled Iranian bank by bringing an offsetting confiscation claim against Iran. The Iranian bank successfully asserted the act of state doctrine, and the court refused to permit the offsetting counterclaim to proceed, rejecting the notion of a "mere setoff exception to the act of state doctrine." In other situations, too, absent a *Bernstein* letter, the act of state doctrine has barred an offsetting counterclaim. See, e.g., *Empresa Cubana Exportadora de Azucar y sus Derivados v. Lamborn & Co.* (2d Cir.1981).

(d) Treaty exception

A "treaty" exception, based on language in the *Sabbatino* decision ("in the absence of a treaty or other unambiguous agreement regarding controlling legal principles"), was successfully invoked to avoid the act of state doctrine in the case of *Kalamazoo Spice Extraction Co. v. Provisional Military Government of Socialist Ethiopia* (6th Cir.1984). The court entertained an action arising out of Ethiopia's expropriation of a US-owned company, on the ground that Ethiopia had entered into a bilateral treaty with the US prohibiting the taking of property except for a public purpose and upon just and effective compensation. To the extent that the act of state doctrine rests on international comity, it should arguably also be subject to a more general "waiver" exception, but courts have rarely found a waiver outside the treaty (or express contractual language) context.

A recurring difficulty with several of the exceptions—including the commercial and the treaty exceptions—is that not all courts treat them as categorical exceptions, but rather simply as factors to be taken into account in an overall balancing process. A balancing approach results in lessened predictability, but obviously permits a nuanced application of the doctrine. *See. e.g., Callejo v. Bancomer, supra,* where the court ruled, on the basis of "pragmatic considerations" that Mexico's alleged violation of the International Monetary Fund Agreement through exchange controls on dollars did not bring the treaty exception into play so as to render the act of state doctrine inapplicable.

Congressional exclusion of the act of state doctrine

As a rule of federal common law, the act of state doctrine is presumably subject to congressional modification. On the other hand, the doctrine is, at least to some extent, based on constitutional considerations, and therefore may not be fully modifiable by Congress. An important example of such legislation is the so-called "Second Hickenlooper Amendment," 22 U.S.C.A. sec. 2370(e)(2), by which Congress, following the Supreme Court's *Sabbatino* ruling, prohibited US courts from applying the act of state doctrine to claims of title to property within the US based upon acts of a foreign state taken in violation of international law—subject, however, to the President's right to declare in any given case that US foreign policy interests necessitated the doctrine's application. (Congress had international expropriations in mind.) The Amendment is echoed by the Restatement (Third) of Foreign Relations Law, section 444.

The Hickenlooper Amendment has been narrowly construed, however. In *Banco Nacional de Cuba v. First Nat'l City Bank of New York* (S.D.N.Y.1967), the district court found the confiscation of a US bank's property in Cuba to be in violation of international law, while finding that the successor Cuban bank and the government of Cuba to be one and the same. On appeal, the Second Circuit ruled that the act of state doctrine applied and that the Hickenlooper Amendment came into play only with respect to the claimant's property within the US that had been specifically nationalized, and not to other assets of the nationalizing country located within the jurisdiction of the court. (The Second Circuit reaffirmed this interpretation in proceedings at a later stage in the case.) The Supreme Court reversed, with a plurality of the Court (three justices) finding that the *Bernstein* exception applied. *First Nat'l City Bank v. Banco Nacional de Cuba, supra.* On remand, the Court of Appeals affirmed the original district court judgment, finding that the confiscation violated international law and that the Cuban bank and the government of Cuba were to be considered as a single entity. See also *Banco Nacional de Cuba v. Chase Manhattan Bank*, *supra*, where the court also limited the right of counterclaim under the Hickenlooper Amendment to claims advanced by the defendant in the same capacity in which it was sued.

Although some state courts have held the Amendment inapplicable to the expropriation of contract rights (see e.g., *Hunt v. Coastal States Gas Producing Co.* (Tex.1979)), the federal courts have since ruled otherwise. See, e.g., *West v. Multibanco Comermex, S.A.* (9th Cir.1987), treating government regulations requiring dollar-denominated certificates of deposit to be converted to pesos at below-market rates as subject to the Amendment, but ultimately not in violation of international law.

For another example of an override of the act of state doctrine, see the Helms–Burton legislation (discussed at page 247 *infra*). Yet another example is the Federal Arbitration Act, 9 U.S.C.A. sec. 15 (discussed at page 370 *infra*), specifically barring the act of state doctrine in suits to enforce arbitration agreements or to confirm or enforce foreign arbitral awards. Arguably, the doctrine is also antithetical to certain specifically-created causes of action whose purposes its application would tend to frustrate. See, e.g., *Daliberti v. Republic of Iraq*, *supra*, finding that the FSIA's terrorist acts exception contemplates the kind of action brought, and considering that application of the act of state doctrine would actually impair, rather than promote, US foreign policy.

POLITICAL QUESTIONS AND INTERNATIONAL COMITY

The act of state doctrine reflects judicial sensitivity to the impact that litigation may have on the conduct of US foreign relations. In that sense, it may be regarded, at least in part, as an expression of international comity. But international comity has a broader range of application. Thus, for example, litigation may risk embarrassment to our foreign relations even though no issue of the legality of an act of a foreign government is presented to the court. It certainly may do so, even though the act of state doctrine is not itself technically applicable, due to the absence of one or more of its preconditions, for example, the situs requirement. A good example is *Republic of the Philippines v. Westinghouse Elec. Corp.* (3d Cir.1994), a case in which the court dismissed on comity grounds a suit for injunctive relief against a foreign state enjoining its own conduct on its own territory.

International comity has been defined as "the recognition which one nation allows within its own territory to the legislative, executive or judicial acts of another nation." See *Pravin Banker Assocs., Ltd. v. Banco Popular del Peru* (2d Cir.1997), citing *Hilton v. Guyot* (S.Ct.1895). It is considered a manifestation of deference paid to the policies and interests of other states, even in the absence of any international obligation to do so. In determining whether an exercise of international comity is warranted in a given case, courts inevitably consider whether and to what extent there is a conflict between domestic and foreign law. A standard balancing test may be found in Section 403 of the Restatement (Third) of Foreign Relations Law, according to which:

> Where two states have jurisdiction to prescribe and enforce rules of law and the rules they may prescribe require inconsistent conduct upon the part of a person, each state is required by international law to consider, in good faith, moderating the exercise of its enforcement jurisdiction in light of such factors as:
>
> (a) vital national interest of each of the states,
>
> (b) the extent and the nature of the hardship that inconsistent enforcement of actions would impose upon the person,
>
> (c) the extent to which the required conduct is to take place in the territory of the other state,

(d) the nationality of the person, and

(e) the extent to which enforcement by action of either state can reasonably be expected to achieve compliance with the rules prescribed by that state.

In *Filetech S.A.R.L. v. France Telecom* (S.D.N.Y. 1997), the district court found that a French corporation and its US subsidiary could not invoke the antitrust laws of the US to complain of conduct by an entity of France occurring almost entirely in France without violating international comity. After the appeals court reversed the act of state finding (due to the absence of a showing of conflict), the district court again dismissed the case on sovereign immunity grounds on account of the absence of a sufficient nexus with the US. (S.D.N.Y.2001). Its decision was upheld. International comity served, however, as the basis for dismissing a suit by Ecuadorean nationals against Texaco for pollution in Ecuador. Curiously, the same basic consideration—*viz.* opposition to the suit by the government of Ecuador—which caused the court to find that the suit, though based on a state law cause of action, came within federal question jurisdiction, also caused the court to dismiss the case on grounds of international comity. See *Sequihua v. Texaco, Inc.* (S.D.Tex.1994).

Not surprisingly, international comity, even where applicable, must yield to overriding US public policy when a conflict emerges. This has not infrequently occurred. See, e.g., *Pravin*, *supra*;

Drexel Burnham Lambert Group Inc. v. Galadari, (2d Cir.1985).

Another instrument for keeping the courts out of highly sensitive international cases is the political question doctrine. Even though subject matter and personal jurisdiction might be present, a case could conceivably be regarded as politically non-justiciable because potentially disruptive of, or embarrassing to, the conduct of US foreign relations. Most courts believe that political non-justiciability should be decided on a strictly case by case basis, in consideration of the factors laid down in the Supreme Court's "political question" ruling in *Baker v. Carr* (S.Ct.1962).

> [A]ll questions touching foreign relations are political questions. Not only does resolution of such issues frequently turn on standards that defy judicial application, or involve the exercise of a discretion demonstrably committed to the executive or legislature; but many such questions uniquely demand single-voiced statement of the Government's views. Yet it is error to suppose that every case or controversy which touches foreign relations lies beyond judicial cognizance. Our cases in this field seem invariably to show a discriminating analysis of the particular question, posed in terms of the history of its management by the political branches, of its susceptibility to judicial handling in the light of its nature and posture in the specific case, and of the possible consequences of judicial action.

The political question doctrine, which has been tied to Article III of the Constitution, because it seeks to keep courts from deciding controversies that are more appropriately committed to the political branches of government, has on occasion been applied to keep internationally sensitive cases out of court. See, e.g., *Made in the USA Fdtn. v. United States* (11th Cir.2001); *Iwanowa v. Ford Motor Co.* (D.N.J.1999) (reparations claim for forced labor as Nazi prisoner during world War II); *Occidental of Umm al Qaywayn, Inc. v. A Certain Cargo of Petroleum* (5th Cir.1978); *Hwang Geum Joo v. Japan* (D.D.C.2001). In *Committee of U.S. Citizens Living in Nicaragua v. Reagan* (D.C.Cir.1988), the district court dismissed as involving non-justiciable political questions a complaint alleging physical, economic, and other injuries inflicted on persons opposed to United States policy in Central America and seeking injunctive and declaratory relief. On appeal, the complaint was ruled justiciable, but was nevertheless found to fail to state a claim on which relief could be granted, and was dismissed. Another example is *767 Third Ave. Assocs. v. Consulate General of the Socialist Federal Rep. of Yugoslavia* (2d Cir. 2000), where the court refused to override the position of the State Department that the liability of the former Yugoslavia did not automatically pass to the new states created from it as "successor states," and concluded that such questions are best left to international negotiation. On other occasions, the political question doctrine has not been a barrier. *Klinghoffer v. S.N.C. Achille Lauro*, *supra*; *Sharon v. Time, Inc., supra*; *Kadic v. Karadzic* (2d Cir. 1995), *supra.*

The political question doctrine can arise in FSIA cases. In a very recent example, the US government intervened in fall 2002 in the FSIA suits against Saudi Arabia filed by families of the victims of September 11, accusing members of the royal Saudi family of ties to Al Qaeda. The government was fearful of the effect of damages Saudi–US relations at a time when the US envisaged a war against Iraq. On the other hand, like the act of state doctrine, the political question doctrine is by no means confined to suits to which foreign states or their officials are a party.

THE "DORMANT" FOREIGN AFFAIRS AND FOREIGN COMMERCE POWER

Tying the political question doctrine to Article III, which addresses only federal courts, raises the prospect that a state court might be left free to entertain such cases. However, in all likelihood, other doctrines would operate to keep out of state courts the cases that the political question doctrine keeps out of federal court. The principal such instrument is sometimes known as the "dormant" foreign affairs doctrine, which bears some affinity to the better-known "dormant" commerce clause doctrine. Both of these play a role in limiting state legislative and judicial involvement in matters in which the

US has a substantial foreign affairs or international commerce interest.

The dormant foreign affairs cases are few, but important. An early precedent is the case of *Zschernig v. Miller* (S.Ct.1968). There, the Supreme Court ruled that an Oregon statute, which made an alien's right to inherit real property situated in Oregon conditional upon an Oregon resident's having the right to inherit real property in the alien's home state, offended the federal interest in the conduct of foreign affairs, mainly because the reciprocity requirement invited a state court to make a negative assessment of foreign political and judicial systems. More recently, in *Crosby v. National Foreign Trade Council* (S.Ct.2000), the Court held that Massachusetts could not validly enact a law barring companies from doing business with the state if they also conducted business with Myanmar (formerly Burma). This time, rather than suggest that federal law completely preempted the states from enacting any such legislation, the Court cited evidence to the effect that Congress had considered, and rejected, legislation imposing economic sanctions on Burma and on companies doing business in Burma. To that extent, *Burma* is less a foreign affairs preemption case than a foreign affairs supremacy case.

The outcome of such cases may depend on the extent of the state's actual interference with US foreign relations. Where California required all insurers that had sold Holocaust-era insurance policies to persons living in Europe (or were related to companies that did so) to furnish information about such policies before doing business in California, that was held not to burden the foreign affairs power to such an extent as to run afoul of the Constitution. *Gerling Global Reinsur. Corp. v. Low* (9th Cir.2001). (The court also based its result on a finding that Congress knew, and failed to disapprove of, these types of state laws when it passed federal legislation establishing a commission to study related problems.)

This handful of cases echoes a broader line of cases to the effect that the states overstep their bounds when they act in such a way as to compromise the federal government's capacity to "speak with one voice" in the conduct of international commercial relations. A fundamental decision is *Japan Line, Ltd. v. County of Los Angeles* (S.Ct.1979), where the Court found that a local tax imposed on shipping containers used in foreign commerce violated the dormant commerce clause because it created a substantial risk of interstate multiple taxation and, as such, prevented the federal government from "speaking in one voice when regulating commercial relations with foreign governments." While the decision was plainly influenced by domestic dormant commerce clause cases, the Court indicated in *Japan Line* that state laws would be subjected to stricter scrutiny when alleged to interfere with foreign, rather than merely interstate, commerce.

The Court has qualified the teachings of *Japan Line* in a pair of dormant foreign affairs power cases arising out of state income taxation of international enterprises. In *Container Corp. of America v. Franchise Tax Bd.* (S.Ct.1983), the Court sustained a California statute using companies' worldwide business as a basis for computing state income taxation, on the grounds that the operations taxed bore a substantial relationship to California and that the tax was fairly apportioned, did not discriminate against interstate or foreign commerce, and did not create a substantial risk of international multiple taxation or otherwise impair the federal government's ability to "speak with one voice." In *Barclays Bank PLC. v. Franchise Tax Bd.* (S.Ct. 1994), the Court further limited the reach of the dormant foreign commerce clause analysis by recognizing that congressional silence in the face of a known potential irritant to US foreign relations (in the circumstances, state use of worldwide corporate income figures for state tax purposes) may constitute a ratification of state policy on the matter, thus rendering dormant commerce considerations inapposite.

Although state courts rarely appear to have confronted the issue, by definition, the Court's dormant commerce clause jurisprudence is binding, as far as it goes, in state as well as federal courts. Those state courts that have confronted it have been guided by the case law discussed above. *See, e.g., United Nuclear Corp. v. General Atomic Co.* (N.M.1980).

Rarely, the US government will itself act to nullify claims (and possibly also attachments and judgments) in federal and state court against foreign governments, where the class of disputes in question has been submitted to a negotiated bilateral settlement system. The President issued just such an executive order as part of a 1981 deal with Iran for the release of American hostages. All covered claims were remitted to binding arbitration before an Iran–US Claims Tribunal. When challenged, the executive orders were upheld as statutorily authorized under the International Emergency Economic Powers Act, 50 U.S.C.A. sec. 1702(a)(1)(B). *Dames & Moore v. Regan* (S.Ct.1981).

FOREIGN SOVEREIGN COMPULSION

In a similar vein, and as a matter of common law, US courts have excused persons from certain obligations under US law when compliance would necessitate their violating the law of another country. Section 441 of the Restatement (Third) of Foreign Relations Law recognizes a limited substantive "foreign sovereign compulsion" defense. It generally prohibits states from requiring anyone to perform an act *in a foreign state* that is forbidden either by the law of that state or by the law of the state of that person's nationality, or from requiring anyone to refrain from performing an act *in a foreign state* that is required either by the law of that state or by the law of that person's nationality. On the other hand, it generally allows a state to require a foreigner to perform an act *in that state*, even if it is prohibited by the law of the state of that person's nationality, or to require a foreigner to refrain from performing an act *in that state*, even if it is required by the law of the state of that person's nationality. Linked as it is to the act of state doctrine, foreign sovereign compulsion is arguably a substantive federal common law rule binding on all US courts, federal and state. State courts appear to be of this view. See, e.g., *United Nuclear Corp. v. General Atomic Co., supra.*

A finding of foreign sovereign compulsion obviously requires a finding of compulsion. In *Interamerican Refining Corp. v. Texaco Maracaibo, Inc.* (D.Del.1970), foreign sovereign compulsion was recognized as a defense in an action charging the defendant with engaging in a boycott in violation of the antitrust laws. The court found in favor of the defendant on the ground that the boycott had been compelled by the Venezuelan authorities. The defense was also successfully asserted in *O.N.E. Shipping Ltd. v. Flota Mercante Grancolombiana, S.A.* (2d Cir.1987).

But not every act of a foreign government entails compulsion. A government may authorize or even entitle a party to act in a certain without necessarily compelling that action. Similarly, it may excuse a party from conduct without necessarily prohibiting it. In such cases, courts have declined to recognize foreign sovereign compulsion as a defense. See, e.g., *Continental Ore Co. v. Union Carbide & Carbon Corp.* (S.Ct.1962); *Mannington Mills, Inc. v. Congoleum Corp., supra.*

Thus, whether or not a foreign sovereign act is compulsory may require inquiry. In *United States v. Watchmakers of Switzerland Information Center* (S.D.N.Y.1962), an antitrust action against Swiss companies, the latter asserted that their agreements had been entered into in accordance with Swiss law and were effectively orders of the Swiss government. The district court initially found no compulsion, but when the Swiss government eventually took further regulatory action, the court reversed its judgment to make it clear that it was not purporting to prohibit any defendant from performing acts required by Swiss law or from refraining from acts barred by Swiss law. (S.D.N.Y.1965). In order to convince a US court of the foreign sovereign compulsion defense, a party may have to show that non-compliance with the foreign government prohibition or order will entail sanctions. At all events, courts are sensitive to claims that the party invoking foreign sovereign compulsion may have invited or "courted" the compulsion.

CHAPTER SIX

INTERNATIONAL HUMAN RIGHTS CASES

While sovereign immunity, the act of state doctrine, and related notions sometimes operate to limit the jurisdiction of US courts in internationally sensitive disputes, recent developments have widened the availability of those courts to hear and decide international human rights cases. This is due partly to application of the FSIA's exceptions to sovereign immunity (discussed in Chapter 5), partly to the recent invigoration of the Alien Tort Claim Statute (referred to in Chapter 3), and partly to federal legislation implementing the Convention against Torture, to which the US is a party. The latter two enactments are the subject of the present chapter.

THE ALIEN TORT CLAIM STATUTE

As mentioned in Chapter 3, the 1789 Judiciary Act vested the district courts with non-exclusive jurisdiction in suits brought by aliens in tort for violation of international law, including treaties of the US. As currently worded, the relevant provision refers to "civil action[s] by an alien for a tort only, committed in violation of the law of nations or a treaty of the United States." 28 U.S.C.A. sec. 1350.

While little use was made of the Alien Tort Claim Statute (ATCS) for nearly two centuries, the 1980 ruling of the Court of Appeals for the Second Circuit in *Filartiga v. Pena–Irala* (2d Cir.1980), opened up new prospects by treating the statute as a proper basis for a suit by a Paraguayan national against a former Paraguayan police official for the alleged torture and murder of the claimant's Paraguayan relative, on the theory that official torture constitutes a violation of customary international law. On remand, the district court, applying international rather than Paraguayan law, found a violation and awarded both compensatory and punitive damages.

Numerous international human rights cases against foreign officials or former foreign officials have since been brought in federal court on this basis, among them *Kadic v. Karadzic* (2d Cir.1995); *In re Estate of Ferdinand E. Marcos Human Rights Litig.* (9th Cir.1992); and *Lafontant v. Aristide* (E.D.N.Y.1994). In *Kadic*, the plaintiffs (a group of Croats and Muslims resident in the former Yugoslavia) were permitted to sue Karadzic, president of the self-proclaimed Bosnian–Serbian Republic, for genocide, war crimes and crimes against humanity, based on allegations of rape, forced prostitution, torture and summary execution. The court predicated personal jurisdiction on personal service on Karadzic while an invitee of the United Nations, and found subject matter jurisdiction in the ATCS, on the theory that the claimed offenses were condemned by international law. It also refused to dismiss the claim as non-justiciable under the "political question" doctrine (see Chapter 5 *infra.*)

Another court took a more restrictive view of the statute. In *Tel–Oren v. Libyan Arab Republic* (D.C.Cir.1984), the court upheld the dismissal of an action against the Palestinian Liberation Organization (PLO) for terrorist killings in Israel. (Only one member of the court took the view that the Act both conferred subject matter jurisdiction and created a cause of action; however, he found that the PLO was not a state as required under the Act. A second member felt the US courts were in any event incapable of handling such a case. A third took the view that the Alien Tort Claim Statute merely establishes federal subject matter jurisdiction, but does not create a cause of action. The latter is certainly a minority view.)

Although the language of the Alien Tort Claim Statute is not itself clear on the point, the cases demonstrate that the tort claim sued upon need not have arisen within the US. Indeed ordinarily it will have arisen abroad. See, e.g., *Klinghoffer v. S.N.C. Achille Lauro* (2d Cir.1991). Nor apparently need the plaintiff be a US national or domiciliary. What is required, if only by virtue of the due process clause of the Constitution, is that the defendant be within the court's jurisdiction. As the *Kadic* case, *supra*, shows, even tag jurisdiction (see Chapter 2 *supra*) would be enough. No case has been brought under the Alien Tort Claim Statute where the defendants were not arguably within the jurisdiction of the US courts, and any such attempt would be constitutionally suspect.

The Alien Tort Claim Statute does not define a "violation of the law of nations." As noted in the Restatement (Third) of Foreign Relations Law, sec. 102(2), the law of nations is said to result from a general and consistent practice of states which they follow from a sense of legal obligation. While international human rights treaties, such as the International Covenant on Civil and Political Rights may not be self-executing or create a private right of action in US courts, they may nevertheless serve as benchmarks for norms of international law, within the meaning of the ATCS. Other sources include the usage of nations, judicial opinions and the works of jurists. Importantly in this context, the law of nations can apply to relations between a State and its own nationals.

Filartiga attempted to limit the application of the ATCS to "universally recognized norms of international law," such as genocide, slavery, torture and murder. Considering the admittedly dynamic nature of customary international law, however, this list cannot be exhaustive. Debates thus ensue as to the propriety of bringing various other offenses within the sphere of "universally recognized norms" for purposes of the ATCS. It is clear that all such "norms" must be universal. As emphasized in *Filartiga*, "it is only where the nations of the world have demonstrated that the wrong is of mutual and not merely several, concern, by means of express international accords, that a wrong generally recognized becomes an international law violation within the meaning of the statute." Such norms must also be specific and obligatory, meaning that there must exist sufficient criteria to determine whether a given action amounts to the prohibited act and the prohibition must be non-derogable and binding at all times. *Tachiona v. Mugabe* (S.D.N.Y.2002). When considering motions to dismiss ATCS claims for lack of subject matter jurisdiction, courts typically engage in a more searching preliminary review of the merits than they ordinarily do under a statutory "arising under" formulation.

A range of international law violations have been found to be cognizable under the ATCS. These include repeated acts of terror and violence that are so systematic and gross as to violate the rights of association, assembly, expression and political participation (*Tachiona v. Mugabe, supra*), as well as administering experimental medication, or lower doses of medication than is the recognized standard of care for research purposes, without informed consent (*Abdullahi v. Pfizer, Inc.* (S.D.N.Y.2002)). In *John Doe I v. Unocal* (9th Cir.2002), the Court of Appeals permitted an ATCS action to go forward on grounds of forced labor, murder and rape, but—only for want of an adequate evidentiary basis—not on torture.

On the other hand, other decisions have concluded that certain objectionable acts, even when taken under color of foreign law, are *not* encompassed by the prohibition of the ATCS. For example, it has been held that the seizure of a citizen's property by a government is not a violation of customary international law. *See Tachiona v. Mugabe, supra.* Conduct causing environmental harms within a State's borders, even if detrimental to human life, health and development, has been determined not to fall with the reach of the ATCS. See e.g., *Flores v. S. Peru Copper Corp.* (S.D.N.Y.2002) (claims of violations of rights to life, health and sustainable development based on diseases caused by mining and refinery operations dismissed); *Beanal v. Freeport McMoran Copper & Gold, Inc.* (5th Cir.1999) (claims of environmental abuses by mining corporation dismissed).

The Alien Tort Claim Statute does not by its terms identify who is a proper defendant. All cases thus far have been brought against persons who were foreign government officials at the time of the actions complained, or were arguably acting under "color" of foreign authority. A good example is the class action litigation against the estate of the former president of the Philippines for human rights abuses by the military under his command. *Hilao v. Estate of Marcos* (9th Cir.1996). However, a foreign government (or government instrumentality) cannot itself be sued under the Alien Tort Claim Statute. According to the Supreme Court, the FSIA is the exclusive statutory basis for suits against foreign states and their instrumentalities. *Argentine Republic v. Amerada Hess Shipping Corp.* (S.Ct.

1989); *Abdi Jama v. United States INS* (D.N.J. 1998).

Acts by private individuals satisfy the ATCS requirements if they are performed "under color" of foreign authority. However, courts have differed as to which theory of responsibility should be used when private actors are implicated in the alleged violations. Some courts have used a "joint participation" theory, requiring "a sufficiently close nexus between the state and the private actor" so that action of latter can be fairly treated as one of the state. *See Sarei v. Rio Tinto* (C.D.Cal.2002); *Abdullahi v. Pfizer, Inc., supra*; *Jensen v. Lane County* (9th Cir.2000); *Ge v. Peng* (D.D.C.2000). Courts have also found state action present when private parties aided and abetted a government in its actions by affording practical assistance or encouragement, with substantial effect on perpetration of the violation. Some courts have looked to the rulings of international criminal tribunals in determining this issue. Others have looked by analogy to the US Civil Rights Act, 42 U.S.C.A. sec. 1983, to determine whether the "under color" requirement is met. Punitive as well as compensatory damages are regularly, but not invariably, awarded in ATCS cases.

Still, there exist a "handful of crimes" for which apparently no state action is required for ATCS liability. Judge Edwards' concurrence in *Tel–Oren* singled out piracy and slave trading. *Kadic* added genocide and war crimes to the list, but not acts of rape, torture, and summary execution, unless committed in connection with genocide or war crimes. As to those claims requiring state action, the court in *Kadic* remanded to permit a showing that the Bosnian–Serb entity met the definition of a state or, alternatively, that acting in concert with the government of the former Yugoslavia would itself constitute state action. More recently, forced labor was determined to be a modern variant of slavery, and thus within the prohibition of the ATCS even without state action. *John Doe I v. Unocal Corp., supra.* It remains to be seen how expansive the "handful" of international law violations not requiring state action will become.

Choice of law analysis plays an important role in ATCS claims. Different courts have applied international law, the law of the state where the underlying events occurred, or forum law, or some combination of these. In *Filartiga*, the court held that if the law of the foreign state would not permit relief appropriate to the ATCS, a court may consider applying instead the principles of its own law or of international law. *Unocal* asserted that where only *ius cogens* violations are alleged, it may be preferable to apply international law, reasoning that by definition, the law of any particular state is either identical to *ius cogens* norms or is invalid. The district court in *Tachiona v. Mugabe* (S.D.N.Y. 2002), also surveyed the possibilities, concluding that in principle the local law of the state where the wrongs and injuries occurred should apply, insofar as it is consistent with federal common law and international law and provides a remedy consonant with the ATCS and the relevant international norms. Failing that, according to the court, a court should fashion a remedy from analogous principles of forum or federal law, or from the domestic law of the foreign jurisdiction. (In so holding the court retreated from its earlier view in *Tachiona, supra,* that the choice of law should be determined through an openended balancing of contacts and interests, which pointed in that case to the application of Zimbabwean law, Zimbabwe being the place of nationality of the parties and of the acts. (S.D.N.Y. 2002).)

The doctrine of *forum non conveniens* has been widely used by district courts to dismiss cases brought under the Alien Tort Claim Statute. *See Abdullahi v. Pfizer, Inc., supra*; *Robert v. Bell Helicopter Textron, Inc.* (N.D.Tex.2002); *Aguinda v. Texaco, Inc.* (S.D.N.Y.2001). Needless to say, it is not always successfully invoked. See, e.g., *Wiwa v. Royal Dutch Petroleum Co.* (2d Cir.2000). In addition, Alien Tort Claim Statute cases can raise serious political question doctrine and comity issues. *See Sarei v. Rio Tinto, supra,* refusing a *forum non conveniens* dismissal, but dismissing on various non-justiciability grounds (act of state, international comity and political question). Yet other courts have opined that the act of state doctrine should rarely operate to defeat an ATCS claim. Moreover, the courts do not consider the ATCS as limited to situations where no relief would otherwise be available under domestic law. See, e.g., *Abdi Jama v. United States INS, supra.*

Filartiga and the subsequent ATCS jurisprudence signal an important advance for international human rights adjudication in US court. In *Filartiga*, the court specifically refused to draw a distinction between an alien and a citizen for purposes of customary international law, thus recognizing that there exist certain fundamental and universal human rights that an individual possesses vis-a-vis his or her government. The court also underscored the principle that courts must interpret customary international law as it exists today, not as it existed at the time the ATCS was enacted. It characterized customary international law as a fluid concept, thus pointing to the possibility of an expanded use of the ATCS in the future.

THE TORTURE VICTIM PROTECTION ACT

While controversy swelled over the proper scope of the Alien Tort Claim Statute, Congress in 1992 enacted the Torture Victim Protection Act (TVPA), 28 U.S.C.A. § 1350 note, in implementation of the 1984 Convention Against Torture and Other Cruel, Inhuman or Degrading Treatment or Punishment. 23 I.L.M. 1027 (1984). The TVPA responded to the suggestion by Judge Bork in *Tel–Oren, supra,* that in the absence of "affirmative action by Congress," the ATCS should not be applied in human rights litigation that the drafters of the Act could not have contemplated. Congress provided such "affirmative action" through the TVPA. Congress did not expressly provide that the TVPA should be applied retroactively, but the courts have been willing to do so, on the ground that the TVPA did not impose new duties or liabilities; the legal duty to refrain from torture predated the TVPA's enactment, dating back as far as the enactment of the Alien Tort Claim Statute. See *Alvarez–Machain v. United States* (9th Cir.1996).

The TVPA not only establishes federal jurisdiction over at least certain types of claims previously brought under the Alien Tort Claim Statute, but likewise guarantees to victims of torture and like acts a cause of action. The Act makes persons acting "under actual or apparent authority, or color of law, of any foreign nation" liable for damages to any person whom they have subjected to torture or to the legal representative or survivor of the victim of an extrajudicial killing (while at the same time defining both "torture" and "extrajudicial killing"). According to the rationale of *Amerada Hess*, *supra*, foreign states and their instrumentalities would not themselves be proper defendants. The standards for determining whether a person acted under "color" of foreign authority under the TVPA are presumably similar to those applicable to ATCS claims. They should also be subject to similar justiciability and choice of law principles.

However, liability under the TVPA is defined more narrowly than under the ATCS. Liability is limited to acts by individuals under authority or color of a *foreign* nation. Unlike the ATCS, then, actions chiefly implicating the United States government do not fall within the reach of the TVPA. Further, the TVPA establishes a ten-year statute of limitations and imposes a requirement of exhaustion of local remedies not found in the ATCS. *See Sarei v. Rio Tinto, supra.*

The Act does not specify who is a proper plaintiff. Presumably, a person of any nationality or residence may assert a claim. Who is a proper defendant seems to be more questionable. It has been held that the TVPA applies only to individuals as defendants and not to corporations. *Beanal v. Freeport–McMoran, Inc.* (E.D.La.1997).

Increasingly, claimants invoke both the ATCS and the TVPA. In *Kadic, supra*, the court concluded that the TVPA creates a cause of action, though not subject matter jurisdiction; it based subject matter jurisdiction on the ATCS (without needing to decide whether jurisdiction could also be based on general federal question jurisdiction, 28 U.S.C.A. sec. 1331), on the theory that customary international law forms part of federal law. Likewise, in *Mehinovic v. Vuckovic* (N.D.Ga.2002), liability was imposed on a soldier under both the ATCS and the TVPA for carrying out torture, imprisonment and cruel, inhuman and degrading treatment in furtherance of the Bosnian–Serb government's policy of ethnic cleansing under color of state law. Both compensatory and punitive damages were awarded. Finding no evidence that the laws of Bosnia–Herzegovina differ from those of the state of Georgia (both the forum state and the state of defendant's domicile), the court also predicated liability on the common law of assault and battery, false imprisonment, intentional infliction of emotional distress and conspiracy, all under Georgia state law.

The ramifications of the Torture Victim Protection Act for the Alien Tort Claim Statute remain unclear. Most commentators argue that the TVPA merely supplements the ATCS, thus allowing courts to recognize causes of action under the ATCS for customary international law violations other than torture and extrajudicial killing. The court in *Kadic*, citing Congress, stressed that "torture and summary executions do not exhaust the list of actions that may appropriately be covered [by the ATCS]," and that the ATCS "should remain intact to permit suits based on other norms that already exist or may ripen in the future into rules of customary international law." (quoting H.R. Rep. No. 367, 102d Cong., 2d Sess., at 4 (1991)). Some scholars have argued that the limitations expressed in the TVPA indicate Congress' rejection of the open-ended *Filartiga* approach to the judicial incorporation of customary international law into federal law, but the courts have generally not followed that reasoning. A related question is whether the ATCS may be used to circumvent some of the limitations of the TVPA, including the exhaustion requirement or the statute of limitations. The majority of courts have rejected the view that the TVPA provides the sole cause of action for torture or extrajudicial killing and, to that extent, supersedes the ATCS.

TREATIES AND CUSTOMARY INTERNATIONAL LAW AS A SOURCE OF PRIVATE LEGAL CLAIMS

Both the Alien Tort Claim Statute (as interpreted) and the Torture Victim Protection Act (as drafted) create federal causes of action for violation of at least some international human rights norms. The question then arises whether international human rights claims may be asserted in US court independently of those statutes. The obvious source of any such claim would be international law, most likely in the form of treaty or customary law, or possibly in the form of general principles common to the major legal systems of the world. It is long-established that "[i]nternational law is part of our law, and must be ascertained and administered by the courts of justice of appropriate jurisdiction, as often as questions of right depending upon it are duly presented for their determination." *The Paquete Habana* (S.Ct.1900).

To start with treaties, Article VI of the Constitution declares them to be federal law. Moreover, 28 U.S.C.A. sec. 1331 expressly creates subject matter jurisdiction over cases arising under treaties. If a treaty were to give rise to a private legal claim, such a claim would thus necessarily fall within the federal courts' subject matter jurisdiction. *In re Air Disaster at Lockerbie, Scotland* (2d Cir.1991); Restatement (Third) of Foreign Relations Law, sec. 111. For these purposes, the courts have assimilated to treaties other forms of international agreement, such as congressional-executive agreements (executive agreements authorized or approved by Congress) and sole executive agreements (agreements made solely by the President). *B. Altman & Co. v. United States* (S.Ct.1912). However, due to the tendency of US courts to regard international human rights treaties as non-self-executing, direct reliance on treaties by human rights plaintiffs in US courts is extremely rare. US courts have not in any event rallied to the notion that private domestic causes of action may be inferred from the violation of treaties.

Arguably, private legal claims could also be predicated on customary international law. But here the prospects are even more slight. Customary international law is highly uncertain not only as to its content, but also as to the question whether it creates individual legal rights. Accordingly, courts have not been willing to predicate liability directly on the violation of customary norms of international law. When invited to do so, courts tend to cite the adequacy of existing domestic law remedies (including of course the ATCS and the TVPA, which to varying degrees incorporate international law) and the primacy of the legislative and executive branches in foreign affairs. See, e.g., *White v. Paulsen* (E.D.Wash.1998). Certainly, treaties and customary international law cannot be invoked to override congressional enactments. *Committee of United States Citizens Living in Nicaragua v. Reagan* (D.C.Cir.1988).

UNIVERSAL JURISDICTION

Some academic literature, as well as a number of foreign nations (of which Belgium is a prime example), support the notion that certain violations of international law, particularly international human rights law, are so heinous that national courts may entertain prosecutions based upon such acts even when the usual minimum criteria for the exercise of personal jurisdiction (such as a nexus with the act, the offender or the victim) are not met. Under so-called "universal" jurisdiction, any nation may entertain such actions. Section 404 of the Restatement (Third) of Foreign Relations Law would authorize an exercise of universal jurisdiction for the prosecution of certain offenses "recognized by the community of nations as of universal concern, such as piracy, slave trade, attacks on or hijacking of aircraft, genocide, war crimes and perhaps certain acts of terrorism." However, no US court appears yet to have embraced this notion.

CHAPTER SEVEN

CHOICE OF LAW AND THE APPLICABLE LAW

Transnational litigation, by its nature, entails the possibility of applying to a case the substantive law of more than one jurisdiction. Choice of law issues are of course generally endemic to domestic US litigation, due to our federal system. US courts are accordingly accustomed to consulting forum choice of law principles for the purpose of determining, in cases subject to state law, the state whose substantive law should be applied to the case or to one or more issues within it. Transnational litigation, however, invites consideration of the application of foreign rather than sister-state law. Just as the *forum non conveniens* doctrine has heightened interest in transnational litigation, due to the profound differences between litigation in different countries, so too does choice of law have heightened interest, due to the profound differences among the substantive laws that courts in transnational litigation may feel called upon to apply.

The uncertainty and stakes associated with choice of law commonly lead parties to international contracts to include in those contracts express provisions as to the "governing" or "applicable" law. The prominence of such clauses in practice justifies taking them as the starting point for discussion of choice of law in transnational litigation. But it is also necessary to contemplate the possibility that no such selection will have been made, particularly where a tort (or other unplanned transaction) rather than a contract (or other planned transaction) is concerned. The choice of law to be made in the absence of a selection by the parties will be a function of the largely unwritten conflicts of law rules prevailing in the US forum—rules that do not fundamentally differ from those that the forum employs in sister-state conflicts of law situations.

While choice of law clauses play a central role in choice of law determinations, especially in contractual disputes, their importance varies with the kind of litigation at hand. Acting in the exercise of its authority to advance the public interest, a legislature may well enact protective legislation of one kind or another. Such "public" statutory law (public, even though it may specifically create "private" causes of action) includes, for example, the antitrust laws, the securities laws and RICO (at the federal level) and distributor, franchisee or consumer protection legislation (at the state level). As we shall see, it is not at all clear that the parties to a relationship have the power to exclude the application of such a law merely by including in their contract a choice of law clause designating the law of a different jurisdiction.

In determining whether such a statute should or should not be applied to circumstances that seemingly fall within its scope, a court must consider the possibility that application of forum law is "mandatory," in the sense that its application is required, regardless of the strength of the contacts that the case has with another jurisdiction. If the forum considers a local rule of law to be mandatory in this sense, then application of that rule to facts falling within its scope of application cannot be avoided, either through a choice of law clause or as a function of the forum's general choice of law principles. Mandatory rules of law are the subject of a separate section of this chapter.

Even before deciding whether US or foreign law should be applied to a given claim or issue in a case, a court may need to consider whether the American rule of law—be it common law or statutory, be it state or federal—has territorial application to the facts in the first place. This is not lightly to be assumed in transnational litigation. The scenarios to which the potentially applicable US law stands to be applied by definition will present contacts with several jurisdictions. It is entirely possible that a statute is properly interpreted as having a territorially limited sphere of application; in that event, its application to a scenario falling outside that sphere will be impermissibly "extraterritorial." But even if a statute has potential application to multi-state situations, a court may or may not apply it, depending on whether it would be "reasonable" from an international comity point of view to do so.

Where, instead of asserting a cause of action common to the world's legal systems (such as an action in tort or contract), a litigant asserts one that is more or less peculiar to a foreign jurisdiction (as in the case of a special foreign statutory cause of action), the US forum may hesitate to entertain the claim altogether. The clearest cases are claims for the enforcement of foreign tax or penal law; they are universally regarded as ones that only the courts of the jurisdiction that enacted the legislation may entertain. But we need to consider the possibility that the forum will regard other foreign law causes of action, too, as unenforceable by analogy.

Although clearly substantive in its implications, choice of law is treated largely as a paradigmatically procedural issue. As a result, the forum will consult its own choice of law principles, however meager its connection with the dispute. Yet, under *Erie* analysis, choice of law in diversity cases in federal court is uniformly governed by state law. This is the holding of *Klaxon Co. v. Stentor Elec. Mfg. Co., Inc.* (S.Ct.1941). The Supreme Court expressly extended this approach to international cases. *Day & Zimmermann, Inc. v. Challoner* (S.Ct.1975). Odd though it may seem, both from the point of view of the federal interest in "speaking with one voice" and of the interest of other nations, the choice of law to be made by federal courts in transnational diversity actions thus depends on, and varies with, the choice of law principles of the state in which the federal court sits.

Once a US court decides that it is appropriate to apply foreign law to a claim, or to one or more issues in a case before it, it becomes necessary to determine how the tenor of that law is to be determined, who bears responsibility for ascertaining it, and what shall be the consequences of its indeterminacy. This chapter closes on that topic.

CHOICE OF LAW CLAUSES

Just as choice of forum agreements reduce uncertainty as to the competent forum, so agreements on choice of law may reduce uncertainty as to the applicable law. Ideally, they should also designate a body of law that the parties consider to be substantively desirable. Because the stakes of substantive law differences are apt to be even greater in transnational than domestic disputes, choice of law agreements are increasingly to be found in international contracts.

Interpretation of choice of law clauses

Like choice of forum clauses, choice of law clauses may require interpretation as to a variety of issues. As always, one begins with the language of the clause. An initial interpretation question is whether the law referred to in the choice of law clause is the "whole" of that law, including its conflict of law principles, or merely the substantive law rules (or, as they are sometimes called in this context, the "internal law" of that jurisdiction). The parties are presumably free to select either the "whole" or the "internal" law, but a strong (and reasonable) assumption has developed that, in selecting a law, the parties do *not* mean to select its choice of law rules.

See Restatement (Second) of Conflict of Laws, sec. 187(3).

A more serious issue of interpretation concerns the range of matters that the clause covers, that is to say, its scope of application. A question that remains curiously in doubt is the extent to which a choice of law clause covers issues that are arguably procedural. Some procedural issues will not be deemed covered (and presumably could not be). These include rules on service of process, pleading, evidence-gathering, and evidence itself. On other issues having a strong procedural flavor but also clear substantive implications—such as statutes of limitations, burdens of proof, etc.—matters are less clear, and court decisions are not consistent. The same may be said about remedies in general.

But even the range of substantive law claims covered by a choice of law clause may be in doubt. A clause may be so narrowly drawn (e.g., "this contract shall be construed in accordance with the law of ___") that the chosen law applies only to the interpretation of the contract and not to its validity, nor to contractual defenses or to remedies in the event of breach. A somewhat more broadly worded clause (e.g., "this contract shall be governed by [or subject to] the laws of ___") should result in the chosen law being applicable to all contractual matters, including validity and remedial issues. A choice of law clause may be still more broadly crafted (e.g., "all disputes arising out of or related to this contract shall be governed by the laws of ___") so that it covers not only contractual claims in all their aspects, but also other private law claims between the parties bearing a relation to the contract, such as tort, product liability, restitution and the like.

More difficult is the question whether the choice of law clause applies equally to specific statutory claims related to the contract, whether federal (e.g., securities law, antitrust law, RICO) or state (e.g., laws protecting consumers, investors, distributors, franchisees, insured persons etc.). Among crucial questions of transnational litigation, this remains one whose answers are among the most elusive.

When the language of a choice of law clause leaves matters of intention unclear, resort may be had to a body of law as an aid in its interpretation. The Restatement (Second) of Conflict of Laws, sec. 204, states that, generally speaking, the meaning of a contract containing a valid choice of law clause should be determined in accordance with the law designated by that clause. It is unclear, however, whether the forum should also consult the chosen law for purposes of interpreting the choice of law clause itself. In practice, courts commonly interpret choice of law clauses without indicating the precise body of law upon which they rely, leaving the possibility that they relied on the chosen law, on the law that would govern the contract's interpretation in the absence of a valid choice of law, on the forum's own law, or indeed on no particular body of law at all.

Validity of the choice of law clause

Choice of law clauses raise as many "validity" questions as are raised by choice of forum clauses, examined in Chapter 2.

(a) Whose law determines the validity of the clause?

Even if the meaning of a choice of law clause is not in issue, its validity and enforceability may be. To questions of validity and enforceability (as opposed to interpretation), US courts appear normally to apply forum law. In other words, they treat those issues either as if they were procedural, or as if they were issues in which the forum, for some other reason, has a superior interest. The Restatement (Second) of Conflict of Laws, section 187, comment b, supports this approach, at least as to issues of misrepresentation, duress, undue influence, or mistake. Comment d, on the other hand, suggests that issues such as capacity, formalities and "substantial validity" may be governed by the law chosen by the parties, subject to the overriding public policy of a state with a materially greater interest in the issue.

The main alternatives to applying forum law to these issues would be applying (a) the law designated in the choice of law clause or (b) the law that would be applicable to that contract, under the forum's choice of law rules, in the absence of any such clause. The first alternative suffers from an element of "bootstrapping." Why use the law designated in the choice of law clause when it is the validity and enforceability of the choice of that very law that is in issue? While the second alternative has greater logic to it, most courts seemingly find it both simpler and more appropriate to consult the law with which they are most familiar—namely forum law—for making the validity and enforceability determination.

As noted, under *Erie*, federal courts in diversity cases apply the choice of law principles of the state in which they sit. See *Klaxon Co. v. Stentor, supra.* Thus, faced with questions about the enforceability of a choice of law clause, federal courts in diversity cases should apply the law to which the state's choice of law principles point. Once again, however, the forum is likely to make its determination of the clause's validity by reference to some body of federal common law, as if the issue were procedural.

A problem may arise if the parties, having validly made a choice of law, discover that under that law the contract as a whole is invalid. In apparent logic, the contract should be deemed invalid. But the Restatement (Second) of Conflict of Laws urges a different result. According to Section 187, comment e, invalidating the contract on the basis of the law designated in the contract's choice of law clause would frustrate the intention of the parties to make a valid contract. Consequently, the clause will not operate to invalidate the contract, unless, as Section 187(2)(b) expressly provides, the chosen (and invalidating) law happens also to be the law of the jurisdiction with the greatest interest in the dispute and the law that would have been applicable in the absence of the choice of law clause.

(b) Limits on party autonomy

Like choice of forum clauses, choice of law clauses were at one time frowned upon, as private attempts to deprive courts of the right to make a determination that ordinarily is theirs to make, *viz.* identification of the applicable law. Today, however, they are broadly embraced, and enforced as written, though not without reservations.

The common law in some states permits the parties freely to select the law applicable to their contract, but only if the law chosen bears a reasonable relationship to the parties or to the transaction. The impulse behind such a proviso is that the parties should not be able to circumvent the otherwise applicable law by selecting as the governing law the law of an irrelevant jurisdiction. In the same vein, the Uniform Commercial Code, section 1–105(1), provides that the parties may submit their agreement to any law bearing a reasonable relationship to the transaction. Clearly, the forum may also condition application of the chosen law on respect for the forum's own (and possibly a third state's) fundamental public policies.

The Restatement (Second) of Conflict of Laws takes matters in a still more liberal direction, by removing the requirement of a "reasonable relation" between the chosen law, on the one hand, and the parties or the transaction, on the other, at least as to issues in which there is no apparent reason for restricting the parties' contractual freedom. Section 187 of the Restatement does this by distinguishing between those issues which the parties would ordinarily have been free to address through an express provision in the contract, and those issues as to which they do not ordinarily have that freedom. As to the former, the parties apparently may select any law they wish. As to the latter, their freedom is conditional, not only on (a) choosing a law having a substantial relationship with the parties or the transaction, but also on (b) the chosen law not being contrary to a fundamental public policy of a state (including the forum) which has a materially greater interest in the issue and whose substantive law would have been applicable in the absence of a choice. The first category of issues is commonly referred to loosely as "interpretation" issues (including the definition of the parties' contractual rights and duties) and the second loosely as "validity" issues. The distinction is more difficult than may appear.

As in the case of choice of forum clauses (see Chapter 2 *supra*), a choice of law clause may be denied enforcement by the forum on the ground that it is the product of fraud, duress or unconscionability, or is otherwise unfair or unreasonable. That may be difficult to show. See, e.g., *Milanovich v. Costa Crociere. S.p.A.* (D.C.Cir.1992).

Under virtually any choice of law approach, including that of the Restatement (Second), a contractual choice of law may also be overridden by public policy. Thus, even if a choice of law clause is generally valid, its application to one or more issues in the case may be deemed offensive to the public policy of the forum and disallowed. While it is ordinarily the forum's public policy that comes into play, Section 187 of the Restatement, *supra*, provides that the forum may also give priority to the public policy of a third state, where appropriate. See *Triad Fin. Establishment v. Tumpane Co.* (N.D.N.Y. 1985); *Southern Int'l Sales Co., Inc. v. Potter & Brumfield* (S.D.N.Y.1976).

In *Roby v. Corporation of Lloyd's*, discussed at *supra* page 27, the contract designated English law as the applicable law and English courts as the competent forum. When suit under the US securities laws was nevertheless brought in the US, the court respected the choice of forum clause, even assuming that the competent English court would apply English law, rather than US law, to the claim at hand. However, it added that "the public policies of the [US] securities laws would be contravened if the applicable foreign law failed adequately to deter issuers from exploiting American investors." The court found that English law would in fact adequately protect US investors, but if it had not, it presumably would have disregarded both the choice of forum and the choice of law clause insofar as they jeopardized investor protection. The court's reasoning seems to suggest that, had the contract contained only a choice of law clause, but not a choice of forum clause, the court would have entertained the case (subject to the possibility of a *forum non conveniens* dismissal), but would have applied English substantive law rather than the US securities laws in deference to the parties' choice, unless again that law was substantively inadequate, which evidently was not the case. *Roby* has been widely followed in several circuits (see, e.g., *Bonny v. Society of Lloyd's* (7th Cir.1993); *Allen v. Lloyd's of London,* (4th Cir.1996); *Richards v. Lloyd's of London* (9th Cir.1998)).

Although most modern courts do so, not every court takes the view that choice of law clauses, once found to be valid and not offensive to public policy (of the forum or of a third state), are necessarily enforceable as such. An alternative approach, exemplified by the case of *Haag v. Barnes* (N.Y.1961), is to treat the clause as but one factor, albeit a weighty one, in a more general choice of law analysis, aimed at identifying the jurisdiction having the greatest interest in the issue or having the most significant contacts with the parties or the transaction.

CHOICE OF LAW IN THE ABSENCE OF A SELECTION

We have seen that prevailing choice of law methodologies tend to promote respect by US courts for choice of law clauses. Those methodologies must nevertheless also provide for the possibility that the parties will not have selected, or will not have validly selected, a law for cases involving significant contacts with more than a single jurisdiction. By no means do all contracts contain provisions on the applicable or governing law. Moreover, in tort and product liability cases, the parties will ordinarily not have previously entered into an agreement at all, much less on the applicable law.

Federal versus state law

We have seen that, despite the obvious federal interest in ensuring an appropriate choice of law in transnational cases, there is no federal legislation on the subject. Moreover, under *Erie* and *Klaxon Co. v. Stentor, supra*, federal courts in diversity cases follow the state choice of law rules of the state in which they sit. By contrast, federal question cases invite federal courts to apply a federal common law of choice of law. Courts that have embarked on that inquiry show a tendency to follow the approach of the Restatement (Second) of Conflict of Laws, discussed in greater detail below. See e.g., *Liu v. Republic of China* (9th Cir.1989); *Harris v. Polskie Linie Lotnicze* (9th Cir.1987). The contours of what constitutes a federal question case are usually clear. And, in most cases, the choice of law issue does not arise, since the same federal statute (e.g. the securities laws or RICO) that creates the cause of action also defines the substantive law elements of the cause of action. Rarely, a federal statute creates a cause of action without at the same time providing the rules of decision. Such a case presents a federal question, triggering application of a federal common law of choice of law for purposes of identifying the content of the applicable rules of law. See, e.g., *Aaron Ferer & Sons Ltd. v. Chase Manhattan Bank* (2d Cir.1984) (federal common law choice of law rules applicable in actions under the Edge Act).

The Foreign Sovereign Immunities Act has raised a problem in this context since, while the statute establishes subject matter (and personal) jurisdiction, it does not create a cause of action. Accordingly, the Second Circuit does not consider FSIA cases to fall within the federal courts' "federal question" jurisdiction for *Erie* purposes. *Barkanic v. General Admin. of Civil Aviation* (2d Cir.1991). However, the Ninth Circuit has required application of federal choice of law rules, notwithstanding the fact that the cause of action asserted under the FSIA arose under state tort law. *Liu v. Republic of China, supra.* There, accordingly, the court applied the federal common law on choice of law, and by that route proceeded to apply state rather than federal substantive law to define the cause of action.

Despite the differences of view that have arisen in FSIA cases, it is generally agreed that the mere fact that a case is international in character (and perhaps raises a choice between applying US and foreign law) does not render the case a "federal question" case for these particular purposes. See *Day & Zimmermann, supra.* (Recall, however, a recent tendency of courts to treat cases implicating the act of state doctrine or international comity as, for that reason alone, federal question cases. See page 78 *supra.*) Many transnational cases in federal court will therefore be governed by state law. This is so, even in cases governed by the Warsaw Convention, since, according to the Supreme Court in *Zicherman v. Korean Air Lines Co., Ltd.* (S.Ct.1996), the Convention does not itself create a cause of action, and liability and damages are to be determined according to whatever is the relevant domestic law.

Conflicts methodologies

This is not the occasion for a detailed examination of the choice of law methodologies that the various US states have adopted and that are applied by state courts and by federal courts sitting in diversity. There is a considerable diversity among them. Some state jurisdictions still abide by the traditional, strictly territorial, rules, for example that the law governing an action in tort is the law of the place of the allegedly wrongful act, or that the law governing an action in contract is the law of the place of contract (or, alternatively, the place of performance). To this extent, they continue largely to follow the First Restatement of Conflicts of Law.

A number of different, more "modern," approaches have emerged in the academic literature and have been embraced by many state courts. According to an "interest analysis" approach, the applicable law depends on the interests of states in the outcome of a dispute. But interest analyses come in different flavors. Under Professor Currie's original interest analysis approach, the forum would apply its own law only if it has an interest in the outcome of a dispute. If both the forum and another state have an interest, an effort would be made to moderate and reconcile them, but failing that, forum law would apply, without regard to the relative weight of the competing state interests.

Other interest analysis approaches have less of a pro-forum bias, by basically inviting courts to determine the relative weights of different states' interests, and possibly comparing the "impairment" to each state's interests if the other state's law were to be applied. An early international example in the tort field is *Babcock v. Jackson* (N.Y.1963), where New York's highest court decided to apply New York law to an Ontario automobile accident involving two New York domiciliaries on the ground that New York had the greater interest in the issues for decision. Some state courts apply an analogous interest analysis in contract cases.

(a) The Second Restatement

A variant is the approach of the Restatement (Second) of Conflict of Laws, section 6, which, in the absence of a specific statutory directive on choice of law, looks to a broad range of factors, including the needs of the interstate and international systems, the relevant policies of the forum and of other interested states, protection of justified expectations, basic policies in the field of law, certainty and predictability of result, and ease in determining and applying the law. The Second Restatement is also commonly described as having adopted a "center of gravity" approach. In any event, the Restatement does not distinguish sharply between choice of law analysis in sister-state and international cases. Section 10 of the Restatement (Second) merely states that "[t]here may ... be factors in a particular international case which call for a result different from that which would be reached in an interstate case."

For each general branch of law, a most-significant-relationship test is advanced. Thus, respecting torts, Section 145 provides that "[t]he rights and liabilities of the parties with respect to an issue in tort are determined by the local law of the state which, with respect to that issue, has the most significant relationship to the occurrence and the parties ...". In contracts, Section 188 of the Restatement provides that "[t]he rights and duties of the parties with respect to an issue in contract are determined by the local law of the state which, with respect to that issue, has the most significant relationship to the transaction and the parties...." It identifies as among the relevant factors the place of negotiation, the place of contract, the place of performance, the location of the contract's subject matter, and the parties' domicile, residence, place of incorporation and place of doing business, with the understanding that "[t]hese contacts are to be evaluated according to their relative importance to the particular issue." In the case of each such rule, reference is also made to a set of generally relevant factors, set out in Section 6 of the Restatement, *supra*.

Moreover, the Second Restatement brings with it a recognition that not all of the issues in a given case—in tort cases, for example, fault, causation, damages, defenses, vicarious liability, contribution and indemnity—need to be governed by the law of a single jurisdiction. Under a theory of *dépéçage*, different issues in a case may be determined by reference to a different body of law, depending upon the "interests" or "significant contacts" relevant to each issue. The Second Restatement expressly embraces this practice in Section 188, comment d.

Where the prevailing conflicts methodology requires identifying the jurisdiction with the greatest governmental interest in, or the most significant relationship with, the dispute, the court may need to inquire into the substance of foreign law. At least a minimal understanding of the laws competing for application is required in order to identify and weigh the relevant interests or relationships pertinent to this determination. (Another threshold moment that we have encountered at which questions about the substance of foreign law may emerge is, of course, upon a motion for *forum non conveniens* stay or dismissal.)

(b) Forum public policy in the transnational context

As we have seen in other contexts, differences in substantive law among nations tend to make the choice of law issue in transnational litigation generally more salient than in domestic cases, and the determination as to whose law to apply particularly critical. But those differences may sometimes cause courts to "bend" seemingly neutral conflicts rules so as to avoid the application of what may seem to them to be an unsuitable foreign law. This has been especially visible in cases in which US courts face strict foreign law limitations (including fixed ceilings) on the damages recoverable in tort.

In some cases, rather than manipulate the choice of law, courts have simply ruled that public policy concerns of the forum outweigh a foreign country's interest in having its law applied. A good illustration is *Pancotto v. Sociedade de Safaris de Mocambique, SARL* (N.D.Ill.1976), where in a personal injury case arising out of an African safari, the court applied the law of Mozambique to the question of liability, but found that country's ceiling on damages to be offensive to Illinois public policy and thus unenforceable. See also *Marsh v. Burrell* (N.D.Cal.1992); *Perez v. Alcoa Fujikura, Ltd.* (W.D.Tex.1997); *Marriott v. Sedco Forex Int'l Resources, Ltd.* (D.Mass.1993). Yet occasionally a court will apply the foreign law, notwithstanding reservations about its adequacy. In *Tramontana v. S.A. Empresa de Viacao Aerea Rio Grandense* (D.C.Cir. 1965), for example, the court was confronted with the prospect of applying a strict damage limitation in Brazilian law to a wrongful death action against Varig Airlines arising out of an airplane collision in that country. Upon weighing the competing interests, the court concluded that Brazil's prevailed. This result seems to be reinforced by the Supreme Court's decision in *Gasperini v. Center for Humanities, Inc.* (S.Ct.1996), in which it held that even a seemingly procedural forum law provision, which permitted a state appellate court to reduce a trial court damage verdict as excessive, was sufficiently "substantive" for *Erie* purposes to require its application by federal courts sitting in diversity.

Disillusionment with the practicability of neutral principles in choice of law led some authors (but few courts) to simply embrace a "better law" approach, that is, to apply the law that the forum simply considers to be the better rule.

Treaty law

Even in disputes ordinarily governed by state law, the applicable legal principles may be determined by treaty if the US happens to have validly entered into a treaty on the subject. The paradigmatic example is the 1980 UN Convention on Contracts for the International Sale of Goods (CISG), 15 U.S.C.A. App. sec. 52, 19 ILM 671, to which the US is a party. The Convention, applicable to contracts for the sale of goods between parties whose places of business are in two different states both of which are Convention signatories, provides rules of contract law, binding as federal law in both state and federal courts, in all contract cases falling within its scope. Application of the CISG may produce results that differ substantively from those that would follow from the ordinarily applicable state law, including the Uniform Commercial Code. See, e.g., *Calzaturificio Claudia s.n.c. v. Olivieri Footwear Ltd.* (S.D.N.Y.1998); *Filanto, SpA v. Chilewich Int'l Corp.* (S.D.N.Y.1992). However, the parties to a contract may opt out of the CISG through an appropriate choice of law clause.

More generally, treaties are federal law and constitute part of the supreme law of the land (Const, art. VI). Whether a treaty gives rise to judicially enforceable legal claims is another matter. Generally speaking, a treaty will not do so unless it is "self-executing," meaning that it requires no statutory implementation in order to become part of domestic US law. As to this, the courts generally inquire whether the language and history of the treaty, the availability of suitable judicial procedures, and the unavailability of alternative claims, among other things, suggest that the drafters intended immediate applicability. *Islamic Republic of Iran v. Boeing Co.* (9th Cir.1985); *Haitian Refugee Center, Inc. v. Gracey* (D.D.C.1985). But even if a treaty is self-executing, there will be other difficult questions, such as whether the treaty may fairly be construed to give rise to a private right of action, and what might be the appropriate domestic remedies.

MANDATORY RULES OF LAW

We have assumed thus far that the forum will consult its own general choice of law principles in deciding, in the absence of a valid selection by the parties, what substantive law to apply to the case at hand. Those general principles largely take common law form and may lead the court to apply to the case (or an issue in the case) a substantive law other than the court's own. It is possible, however, that the courts of a state will have been specifically directed by the state legislature to apply the forum state's law regardless of the relative strength (or weakness) of the contacts of the case with the forum. Such a direction may be regarded as expressing a *specific*, as opposed to a *general*, choice of law rule, and the state law rule that the court is directed to apply may be regarded as in this special sense "mandatory." If so, the court must give application to that rule of law, whatever may be "the otherwise applicable law." The French term used for legislation that "mandates" its own application in this sense is *lois d'application immédiate*. Unfortunately, it is not always easy to determine whether a statutory provision should be understood as containing a specific choice of law direction. The presence of the phrase, "[t]he present law shall apply to all cases in which ..." may cause a statute to be read in this fashion rather than merely setting out the statute's potential sphere of application.

Often the term "mandatory" is used in a somewhat less technical sense, to describe a rule of law that is imperative, not so much in the sense of overriding general conflict of law principles, as in the sense of overriding the right of the parties to derogate from that rule by agreement (whether through a choice of law agreement or through an express contractual understanding between them). These are rules from which the parties, to put the matter simply, may not by party agreement deviate. Recent years have seen a tendency for laws that might at one time have been considered mandatory in this sense to be made subject to choice of law clauses designating foreign law, provided the selected law substantially protect the interests that would have been protected had forum law been permitted to govern. But this is no more than a tendency.

We tend to assume that the forum will ordinarily apply its own mandatory laws, along with the laws—mandatory or otherwise—of the jurisdiction indicated by the forum's choice of law rules. But, as noted, the possibility is not to be excluded that, in a truly international case, a court will apply the "mandatory" rules of law of yet a third jurisdiction. This has happened, for example, where the forum finds that neither it nor the jurisdiction whose law the parties may have selected has a paramount interest in having its law applied to the case, but that a third jurisdiction does, and that that interest would be frustrated if the law selected by the parties were to be applied. The scenario arose in *Southern Int'l Sales Co. v. Potter & Brumfield, supra*, where a New York court applied Puerto Rico's "mandatory" distributor protection legislation, notwithstanding the parties' otherwise valid selection of a less protective Indiana law as the law governing their contract. The Restatement (Second) of Conflict of Laws, section 187(2), codifies this approach as follows:

> The law of the state chosen by the parties to govern their contractual rights and duties will be applied, even if a particular issue is one which the parties could not have resolved by an explicit

provision in their agreement directed to that issue, unless either:

(a) the chosen state has no substantial relationship to the parties or the transaction and there is no other reasonable basis for the parties' choice, or

(b) application of the law of the chosen state would be contrary to a fundamental policy of a state which has a materially greater interest than the chosen state in the determination of the particular issue and which [is] the state of the applicable law in the absence of an effective choice of law by the parties.

Article 7(1) of the 1980 Rome Convention on the Law Applicable to Contractual Obligations (to which all EU member states are parties) provides in a broadly similar fashion for giving effect to the mandatory rules of law of another country with which the situation has a close connection, notwithstanding the otherwise applicable law.

CONSTITUTIONAL LIMITS ON THE APPLICATION OF FORUM LAW

Does the Constitution ever bar the forum from applying its own substantive law in preference to the law of a "foreign" jurisdiction? There has developed on this issue a body of federal constitutional case law, albeit only in the sister-state context. According to this case law, even if a state has a constitutionally adequate basis of personal jurisdiction over the defendant, it may not constitutionally apply a substantive body of law—including its own—to a case in the absence of a reasonable relationship between that law and the dispute at hand. *Phillips Petroleum Co. v. Shutts* (S.Ct.1985); *Allstate Ins. Co. v. Hague* (S.Ct.1981); *Home Ins. Co. v. Dick* (S.Ct.1930). In *Allstate*, the Court ruled that "[in order] for a State's substantive law to be selected in a constitutionally permissible manner, that State must have a significant contact or significant aggregation of contacts, creating state interests, such that choice of its law is neither arbitrary nor fundamentally unfair."

This case law has been predicated chiefly on the notion of due process. The *Home Insurance* case, *supra*, which involved an impermissible application of Texas law to an insurance policy to be made and performed in Mexico, shows that due process may prevent the courts of a state from applying local law to a case bearing no reasonable relation to that state, not only when its reasonable relationships are with sister states, but also when they are with a foreign country. The Court emphasized that the basis for its decision was due process, and not the "full faith and credit" clause. (In Chapter 5, we considered a somewhat different constitutional limitation on the application of state law, namely the federal constitutional requirement that state law not unduly interfere with the federal interest in good foreign relations and international commerce.)

THE "EXTRATERRITORIAL" APPLICATION OF US LAW

Even where a US court is prepared, as a choice of law matter, to apply domestic law to a given case, it may be necessary to determine the territorial limits on the application of that law. The legislature may have intended a statute of seemingly general application to apply only to situations having one or more specific connections with the enacting state—for example, only where the contract in question was to be performed on the state's territory, or where the buyer is a resident of the state, or where the relevant property is situated on the state's territory. Where this is the case, the statute simply has no application outside of those territorial limits.

Presumption against extraterritorial application of domestic law

Determining the proper territorial scope of application of a US statute is not necessarily a simple matter, precisely because the intended scope may be apparent neither from statutory language nor from legislative history. Yet, courts have recognized (though not invariably followed) a presumption that federal law should not be interpreted as applying extraterritorially, absent statutory language or legislative history clearly indicating that intention. See, e.g., *McCulloch v. Sociedad Nacional de Marineros de Honduras* (S.Ct.1963); *Foley Bros., Inc. v. Filardo* (S.Ct.1949). Thus, courts may feel constrained to give statutes a territorially narrower scope of application than appears from the statute's face. The Supreme Court has reiterated that the presumption against the extraterritorial application of US law applies even in the absence of any conflict between US policy and the apparent policy or interests of the other country or countries in question. See *Sale v. Haitian Centers Council, Inc.* (S.Ct. 1993).

(a) Narrowed statutory construction

The Supreme Court forcefully embraced the presumption against extraterritorial application of US law in the case of *Equal Employment Opportunity Comm'n v. Arabian Am. Oil Co.* (S.Ct.1991). There, a majority of the Court was unwilling to have US laws prohibiting employment discrimination applied to alleged discrimination by a US company against a US employee, where the place of employment was overseas. (Congress subsequently amended the statute to produce a different result.) Cases like *EEOC v. Arabian Am. Oil* illustrate what may be called a "statutory construction" approach to extraterritoriality. Subject matter jurisdiction will then turn on the presence or absence of certain stated contacts with the US and not, at least in principle, on a case-by-case balancing of competing states' interests.

(b) Balancing of factors

In other cases, courts limit the extraterritorial application of US laws, but without adopting a rigid "territoriality presumption." The case of *Lauritzen*

v. Larsen *(S.Ct.1953), involving the Jones Act, is a good example. There the Supreme Court decided that, even though the language of the Act did not foreclose the possibility, the Jones Act should not be applied to the case of a personal injury sustained by a Danish seaman onboard a Danish-owned ship moored in Cuba. The Court reached this result not by insisting on a certain designated nexus with the US, but rather by weighing a broad range of factors—including place of injury, place of contract, flag of the vessel, plaintiff's and defendant's nationality and domicile, availability of a foreign forum, and interest of the forum—connecting the incident with the US, Denmark and other jurisdictions. The contacts with, and interests of, Denmark were found to be so superior to those of the US that the Jones Act should not be held to apply. In a subsequent decision,* Romero v. Int'l Terminal Operating Co. *(S.Ct.1959), the Court declined to apply the Jones Act even though there the injury occurred while the ship was in US territorial waters.*

This balancing of contacts and interests is typical of international antitrust and securities law litigation in US courts. The evolution began with the case of *United States v. Aluminum Co. of America* (2d Cir.1945), in which the Second Circuit, in an influential opinion by Judge Hand, moved beyond the strictly territorial approach that the Supreme Court had previously employed in *American Banana Co. v. United Fruit Co.* (S.Ct.1909). In *Alcoa*, the court permitted the assertion of federal subject matter jurisdiction on the basis of the effects in the

US of acts concededly performed abroad. A more recent example is *Matsushita Elec. Indust. Co. v. Zenith Radio Corp.* (S.Ct.1986). In countless antitrust cases, federal courts have applied the relevant federal statutes to genuinely multinational scenarios, because of substantial effects in the US, thus arousing objections by foreign parties and foreign governments alike (objections fueled by opposition to free-wheeling US discovery and to the availability under the US laws of treble damages). Foreign blocking statutes, treated in Chapter 8, have been part of the response. Due to the criticism leveled at a pure "effects" test in international antitrust, the federal courts in the years since the *Alcoa* case embraced a more subtle balancing approach, not altogether unlike the one followed in *Lauritzen.* Essentially they would determine, on the basis of all the possibly relevant considerations (including contacts with, and interests of, other nations), whether application of the US legislation would be "reasonable." Given its prominence, we explore this approach more fully in the following section.

The "Timberlane" rule of reason

This jurisdictional "rule of reason" test is associated with, and commonly bears the name of, the Court of Appeals decision in *Timberlane Lumber Co. v. Bank of America N.T. & S.A.* (9th Cir.1976). In *Timberlane*, the court confirmed that the US antitrust laws apply to conduct taken in other countries, provided that conduct has substantial actual or intended effects in the US. But that would not be the end of the analysis. Even in the face of substantial effects within the US, the potential interests of other countries, notably the country where the conduct in question occurred or where other substantial effects were felt, might preponderate. In that event, the US territorial effects would not suffice to dictate application of the US antitrust laws. "[I]t is evident that at some point the interests of the United States are too weak and the foreign harmony incentive for restraint too strong to justify an extraterritorial assertion of jurisdiction." In deciding whether this point has been reached,

> [t]he elements to be weighed include the degree of conflict with foreign law or policy, the nationality or allegiance of the parties and the locations or principal places of business of corporations, the extent to which enforcement by either state can be expected to achieve compliance, the relative significance of effects on the United States as compared with those elsewhere, the extent to which there is explicit purpose to harm or affect American commerce, the foreseeability of such effect, and the relative importance to the violations charged of conduct within the United States as compared with conduct abroad. A court evaluating these factors should identify the potential degree of conflict if American authority is asserted.... Having assessed the conflict, the court should then determine whether in the face of it the contacts and interests of the United States are sufficient to support the exercise of extraterritorial jurisdiction.

Under the *Timberlane* analysis, courts, acting essentially out of comity, may decline to apply local legislation to a set of facts that literally come within the legislation's scope of application, where they conclude that it would be unreasonable to do so, in light of all the circumstances, including a possible conflict with the regulatory interests of one or more other jurisdictions having an important connection with the case. *Timberlane* is commonly described as "moderating" or "mitigating" the extraterritorial application of US antitrust law, and it has been widely, but not invariably, followed. See, e.g., *Mannington Mills, Inc. v. Congoleum Corp.* (3d Cir. 1979) (supporting *Timberlane*); *Laker Airways Ltd. v. Sabena* (D.C.Cir.1984) (declining to engage in *Timberlane* balancing where US and foreign policies conflict); *National Bank of Canada v. Interbank Card Ass'n* (2d Cir.1981) (no *Timberlane* balancing when insufficient effect on US commerce).

In its precise sphere of application, the *Timberlane* test has been modified by statute. 15 U.S.C.A. sec. 6(a) exempts from US antitrust law conduct that lacks a direct, substantial and reasonably foreseeable effect on domestic US commerce, or on import or export trade with foreign nations. That the infringing conduct originates in the US or involves US-owned entities operating abroad will therefore not guarantee the application of US law. See *McGlinchy v. Shell Chem. Co.* (9th Cir.1988).

(a) Subject matter jurisdiction versus merits

The *Timberlane* approach makes it difficult, though not impossible, for a court to determine at the outset of antitrust litigation whether it has, or does not have, subject matter jurisdiction. Precisely because of its multi-factor and fact-intensive character, this approach does not lend itself particularly well to disposition of a case at an early stage on subject matter jurisdiction grounds, for example, by a motion for summary judgment. Rather, it may be necessary for a court to treat the jurisdictional question in combination with the merits, necessitating a trial, at least where a *prima facie* jurisdictional showing has been made. See, e.g., *Industrial Investment Dev. Corp. v. Mitsui & Co., Ltd.* (5th Cir.1982).

This indeterminacy is, of course, problematic. We can discern in the international securities law cases an attempt by the courts, even while broadly adhering to the *Timberlane* approach, to introduce somewhat greater certainty and predictability by once again identifying crucial connecting factors. In *Psimenos v. E.F. Hutton & Co., Inc.* (2d Cir.1983), the court applied the anti-fraud provisions of the Commodities Exchange Act to claims by a Greek investor that the defendant had fraudulently procured and managed his account. Although most of the alleged misrepresentations occurred outside the US, the court found the Act to be applicable, on the ground that those misrepresentations culminated in trading transactions executed in the US on the US commodities markets. The court considered that jurisdiction could be exercised on the basis of either a "conduct" or an "effects" test, and found that the "conduct" test for jurisdiction was met, citing leading cases under the Securities Acts to the effect that substantial relevant conduct in the US is sufficient to bring transactions entered into abroad within the reach of those Acts, unless that conduct is purely "preparatory." See *Zoelsch v. Arthur Andersen & Co.* (D.C.Cir.1987); *IIT, Int'l Investment Trust v. Cornfeld* (2d Cir.1980); *Bersch v. Drexel Firestone, Inc.* (2d Cir.1975); *Leasco Data Processing Equip. Corp. v. Maxwell* (2d Cir.1972). In *Alfadda v. Fenn* (2d Cir.1991), the court ruled that RICO could be applied to a securities fraud case as long as the "predicate acts" occurred primarily in the US. (The *Alfadda* case was eventually dismissed on *forum non conveniens* grounds).

(b) Subject matter jurisdiction versus comity

The *Timberlane* decision is not entirely clear as to the basis of its "rule of reason." Under one version, the statute applies to the fullest extent possible, but courts have discretion, in the interest of comity, to mitigate its application. Under a second version, Congress is deemed, in enacting such legislation, to intend it to be applied to transnational scenarios only when "reasonable." But under yet a third version, whatever Congress may have intended, the statute cannot be applied to a transnational scenario when doing so would be unreasonable and thereby run afoul of international law.

The latter seems to be the general import of Sections 402 and 403 of the Restatement (Third) of Foreign Relations Law. Section 402 sets out the general circumstances in which a state has "jurisdiction to prescribe": namely, (a) where the conduct addressed takes place on the state's territory, (b) where the status of persons or interests in things on its territory are concerned, (c) where conduct abroad has or is intended to have substantial effects within the territory, (d) where "the activities, interests, status, or relations" of the state's nationals are concerned, or (e) where conduct abroad is directed against the security or other fundamental interests of the state. Section 403, however, goes on to provide:

> Even when one of the bases for jurisdiction under Section 402 is present, a state may not exercise jurisdiction to prescribe law with respect to a person or activity having connections with another state when the exercise of such jurisdiction is unreasonable.

Section 403 then recites the factors that courts should take into account in determining whether an exercise of prescriptive jurisdiction is reasonable when it relates to a person or activity having connections with another state. These include, but are by no means limited to, "the likelihood of conflict with regulation by another state" (sec. 403(2)(h)). Courts come close to this view when they say that they lack jurisdiction to apply US law extraterritorially if doing so would be unreasonable. See, e.g., *United States v. Javino* (2d Cir.1992).

(c) Hartford Fire Ins. Co. v. California

The Supreme Court's most recent pronouncement on the extraterritorial application of federal legislation, *Hartford Fire Ins. Co. v. California* (S.Ct.1993), sheds some light on the problem. In this Sherman Act case, brought by the attorneys-general of 19 states, plus some private parties, a majority of the Court upheld the Act's application to an alleged conspiracy among US and non-US insurance companies to restrict the coverage of general liability insurance on the US insurance market. In reaching its decision, the majority clearly stated that where an application of the Sherman Act would be impermissibly extraterritorial, not only does the Sherman Act claim fail on the merits, but the court is even without subject matter jurisdiction to entertain it. (For the dissent, Justice Scalia insisted that subject matter jurisdiction could be present, and still the court could decline to exercise that jurisdiction out of international comity.) Most courts do indeed consider that extraterritoriality raises a subject matter jurisdiction as well as a "merits" question. This can make a practical difference. A motion to dismiss for failure to state a claim (under Fed. R. Civ. P. 12(b)(6)) will necessarily fail if there is any genuine issue of material fact, while a motion to dismiss for lack of subject matter jurisdiction (under Fed. R. Civ. P. 12(b)(1)) entitles the judge to weigh the evidence at hand.

On the merits, so to speak, the Court conceded that, in a proper case, the courts could decline out of international comity to exercise Sherman Act jurisdiction over foreign conduct. However, it found this an inappropriate case for doing so, because it was unconvinced of the existence of a direct conflict between the US and the foreign (in this case, UK) policies. Evidently, the majority considered the absence of direct conflict to be a decisive factor. The effect of *Hartford Fire* in this regard is to curtail the role of international comity in deflecting enforcement of the otherwise applicable American legislation.

EXTRATERRITORIAL CAUSES OF ACTION AND EXTRATERRITORIAL APPLICATION OF CONSTITUTIONAL RIGHTS

The preceding section dealt with cases arising under general federal legislation that lends itself on occasion to application to international scenarios. But Congress occasionally enacts legislation specifically targeting certain international scenarios. For this reason, they can be especially controversial from an international relations point of view. The best known is the so-called Helms–Burton Act (more formally, the Cuban Liberty and Democratic Solidarity (Libertad) Act) of 1996, 22 U.S.C.A. sec. 6082. This statute permits anyone owning a claim to property confiscated by Cuba to sue anyone who "traffics" in that property, including purchasing it, and specifically forbids a US court to decline jurisdiction over such a case on act of state grounds. (The Act provides for additional, non-litigation sanctions.) In response, the EU adopted a regulation inviting "clawback" actions in European courts against subsidiaries of US companies invoking the statute, and initiated a complaint with the WTO, while Canada enacted legislation forbidding Canadian companies from complying with certain US prohibitions on doing business with Cuba. In view, no doubt, of such reactions, the US Presidency has suspended the right to sue under Helms–Burton Act for successive six-month periods, as provided for in the legislation. Broadly similar legislation forbids entities to make investments contributing to the ability of certain allegedly "rogue" states to develop their petroleum resources or weapons or aviation capabilities. This measure, too, has drawn international protests.

While Congress occasionally enacts deliberately extraterritorial causes of action, the courts from time to time have had occasion to determine the territorial reach of constitutional protections. In recent decisions the Supreme Court has shown a clear tendency to restrict territorially the scope of application of constitutional rights. The case of *United States v. Verdugo–Urquidez* (S.Ct.1990), illustrates the point. There, the Court ruled that the Fourth Amendment does not apply to searches and seizures of the residence or property of aliens, even when conducted by US officials, if the investigative acts take place on foreign soil. The Court read the term "the people" in the Amendment as limited to US citizens and residents. The Fifth Amendment has similarly been held to provide no protection to aliens outside US territory. *Haitian Refugee Center, Inc. v. Gracey* (D.D.C.1985). Similarly, the Court has ruled that the constitutional guarantee against self-incrimination does not apply when the prosecution to which the party invoking the privilege would be subjected is a foreign prosecution. *United States v. Balsys* (S.Ct.1998).

THE APPLICATION OF FOREIGN TAX, PENAL AND "PUBLIC" LAW

The readiness of US courts to apply foreign law, where general US conflicts of law principles point in that direction, is not invariable. It is true that when the cause of action is a traditionally private one (as in tort or contract), the court will ordinarily be prepared to apply foreign law to the merits of the dispute if forum conflicts rules so indicate. But not all cases represent this scenario.

We have already considered one such scenario. The cause of action before a court may be one that expressly arises out of a specific US (state or federal) statute, thus constituting what is commonly called a "statutory" as opposed to a "common law" claim. In such a circumstance, a US court may give no consideration whatsoever to applying a foreign body of law to the substance of the claim; it will consider the US law "mandatory," in the sense in which that term was used earlier in this chapter (see page 213 *supra*). The court will either entertain the domestic statutory cause of action because the statute "applies" (assuming the case falls within the statute's ambit) or decline to do so. It is unlikely to apply a foreign jurisdiction's comparable statutory cause of action instead.

Conversely, however, the cause of action asserted in US court may be one that specifically arises out of the legislation of a *foreign* jurisdiction. We may consider these claims to be based upon a "foreign statutory cause of action." Here, too, a US court will be inclined either to enforce the foreign cause of action or to decline to entertain it, but not to substitute for it the comparable domestic law cause of action.

In fact, a US court may be unwilling—even categorically so—to enforce a cause of action arising out of certain foreign legislation. In order to appreciate this, we must envision a range of scenarios. At one extreme, the foreign legislation may be readily enforced as such because, while statutory in form, it corresponds closely to a traditional private law cause of action recognized in US law. We find courts willing, for example, to entertain copyright infringement actions both under US law (*viz.* The Lanham Act) and under foreign countries' copyright protection legislation. See, e.g., *Armstrong v. Virgin Records, Ltd.* (S.D.N.Y.2000). Nor will the fact that the foreign cause of action takes statutory rather than common law form (and it likely will because non-common law legal systems will simply not have "common law" causes of action) make much difference.

At the other extreme fall causes of action which will be treated, virtually categorically, as unenforceable in the US because they are deemed to represent an assertion of foreign sovereign prerogatives in which US courts should not participate. Of these, foreign tax and penal law claims are the clearest examples. It is well established that US courts will enforce directly neither the revenue laws nor the penal laws of other countries—a notion advanced by the Supreme Court as early as 1825 in *The Antelope* (S.Ct.1825). The standard explanation for the rule was offered by Judge Hand, concurring in *Moore v. Mitchell* (2d Cir.1929):

> [A] court will not recognize those [liabilities] arising in a foreign state, if they run counter to the "settled public policy" of its own. Thus a scrutiny of the liability is necessarily always in reserve, and the possibility that it will be found not to accord with the policy of the domestic state. This is not a troublesome or delicate inquiry when the question arises between private persons, but it takes on quite another face when it concerns the relations between the foreign state and its own citizens.... To pass upon the provisions for the public order of another state is, or at any rate should be, beyond the powers of a court; it involves the relations between the states them-

selves, with which courts are incompetent to deal, and which are intrusted to other authorities. It may commit the domestic state to a position which would seriously embarrass its neighbor. Revenue laws fall within the same reasoning; they affect a state in matters as vital to its existence as its criminal laws. No court ought to undertake an inquiry which it cannot prosecute without determining whether those laws are consonant with its own notions of what is proper.

Application of the "revenue rule" is straightforward in certain cases. See e.g., *Her Majesty the Queen v. Gilbertson* (9th Cir.1979), involving efforts at the direct collection of a tax liability. But the "revenue rule" has also been applied to bar RICO actions both by Canada and the European Community against a group of cigarette manufacturers seeking damages for lost tax revenues and additional law enforcement costs stemming from an alleged cigarette-smuggling conspiracy. *Attorney General of Canada v. R.J. Reynolds Tobacco Holdings, Inc.* (2d Cir.2001); *European Community v. RJR Nabisco, Inc.* (E.D.N.Y.2002). The fact that the relief sought took the form of recovery of RICO damages, rather than recovery of taxes as such, was held to make no difference. Nor was the court prepared to interpret the RICO statute as abrogating the revenue rule within the scope of application of RICO.

While criminal prosecutions are of course "penal" within the meaning of this rule, this category's outer limits are also difficult to draw. In *Republic of the Philippines v. Westinghouse Elec. Corp.* (D.N.J.

1993), which involved a foreign law claim for punitive damages, the court borrowed for these purposes the criterion, drawn from the domestic recognition and enforcement case of *Huntington v. Attrill* (S.Ct. 1892), "whether the wrong sought to be redressed is a wrong to the public or a wrong to the individual." It declined enforcement.

The question has arisen whether still other foreign statutory causes of action should be assimilated for these purposes to tax and penal claims, and treated as unenforceable in US courts. Sometimes the term "public laws" is used to denote laws which, while not strictly speaking tax or penal, nevertheless are thought of as assertions of sovereign authority by foreign governments and as likewise unworthy of enforcement in US courts. Section 610 of the Restatement (First) of Conflict of Laws provided that a US court would not entertain an action to enforce rights "created by the law of a foreign state as a method of furthering its own governmental interests," and section 611 more specifically provided that they would not entertain an action to "recover a penalty" under foreign law. The Second Restatement, section 89, is more restrained, confining itself to barring the enforcement of "a foreign penal cause of action," and expressing no view on actions by foreign nations to recover taxes.

The case law on the matter is highly fragmentary. Instructive in this regard is *Banco do Brasil S.A. v.*

A.C. Israel Commodity Co., Inc. (N.Y.1963), where the court refused to entertain an action by the Bank of Brazil, a government instrumentality, for damages and for rescission of certain currency exchange contracts, due to their alleged violation of foreign currency exchange regulations. In a later case, *Banco Frances e Brasileiro S.A. v. Doe* (N.Y.1975), the court agreed to hear and decide a similar case where brought by a private foreign bank.

Even if a US court is willing in principle to enforce a given "public" law of a foreign state, there is always a possibility that it will not do so because enforcement would be offensive to forum public policy. See, e.g., *J. Zeevi & Sons, Ltd. v. Grindlays Bank (Uganda) Ltd.* (N.Y.1975), where the offensive Ugandan regulations took the form of an order by the Bank of Uganda canceling all foreign exchange authorizations issued in favor of Israeli companies. This serves as a reminder that forum public policy is always available as a basis for the forum to decline to apply foreign law, however the foreign law is characterized.

Occasionally, courts may decline to enforce a foreign cause of action, not because it is penal or revenue (or even "public") in nature, and not because repugnant to forum public policy, but simply because it requires a form of relief that the forum considers itself unable, remedially, to furnish. An old example is *Slater v. Mexican Nat'l R.R. Co.,* (S.Ct.1904), where the Supreme Court ruled that the lower court lacked jurisdiction to enforce a

Mexican wrongful death statute, due to the fact that the statute contemplated damages in the form of an annuity (or periodic payment), subject to modification from time to time as circumstances might change. This was considered unknown in US practice. It is, of course, difficult, to imagine that the case would be decided in those terms today.

The fact that US courts will not "enforce" the revenue, penal or certain other laws of other countries does not mean that they will refuse to take any note of them. Even if not enforced as such, in the sense of serving as the predicate for a judgment entitling the claimant to the specific remedy contemplated by the foreign legislation, these laws may be recognized for other purposes—either as a defense to some other claim or as a datum relevant to the application of some other legal rule or principle.

PLEADING AND PROOF OF FOREIGN LAW

In US litigation, it may be assumed that a court will apply the domestic law that is relevant to the claims and defenses before it, even when the party asserting the claim or defense has not specifically advanced that law. The court may "adduce" and eventually apply the relevant domestic law with or without the aid of counsel.

This model has traditionally been thought inappropriate for the pleading and proof of foreign law in US courts. The dominant common law approach was to consider the substance of foreign law, for these purposes, as if it were an issue of fact. By that, it was meant that the party invoking foreign law in US litigation bore the burden of specifically asserting the relevance of foreign law and alleging its tenor in the pleadings. As for establishing the foreign law, that burden, too, fell on the party relying on the foreign law. The common law was less clear about the consequences of a failure adequately to plead and/or prove foreign law. Some courts regarded such failure as justifying, if not mandating, the dismissal of the claim or defense at issue. Others treated it as warrant to apply the substantive law of the forum instead. Still others took this as an opportunity to ascertain and apply the corresponding *domestic* substantive law.

More recently, both the Federal Rules (insofar as federal courts are concerned) and state legislatures have intervened to clarify the ground rules for the pleading and proof of foreign law. Federal Rule 44.1 provides as follows:

> A party who intends to raise an issue concerning the law of a foreign country shall give notice by pleadings or other reasonable written notice. The court, in determining foreign law, may consider any relevant material or source, including testimony, whether or not submitted by a party or admissible under the Federal Rules of Evidence. The court's determination shall be treated as a ruling on a question of law.

Due to the freedom thereby given to judges to ascertain foreign law, even without the help of the parties, enactments like Rule 44.1 are sometimes referred to as "judicial notice" provisions. State legislation, where it exists, presents variations on the same themes as Rule 44.1. For example, the New York procedural statute (CPLR, sec. 4411) provides that:

> Every court may take judicial notice without request of . . . the laws of foreign countries or their political subdivisions. Judicial notice shall be taken of matters specified in this subdivision if a party requests it, furnishes the court sufficient information to enable it to comply with the request, and has given each adverse party notice of his intention to request it. Notice shall be given in the pleadings or prior to the presentation of any evidence at the trial, but a court may require or permit other notice.

The California statute is broadly similar, but it makes explicit a requirement that the judge notify the parties if he or she proposes to consult and possibly apply foreign law on his or her own initiative.

Federal Rule 44.1 does not dictate the form in which foreign law needs to be brought to the court's or to other parties' attention. Production may be facilitated through the Hague Convention Abolishing the Requirement of Legalization of Foreign Public Documents, 134 UNTS 189 (1965), to which the US is a party. But, typically, litigators turn to an expert witness (academic or practitioner), who will furnish the court a written expert opinion, usually in the form of an affidavit or declaration under oath, and be available for direct and cross examination either in court or at a deposition. According to the Federal Rules of Evidence (Rule 702), an expert need only possess the requisite "knowledge, skill, experience, training or education." Courts may freely, but seldom do, appoint their own expert under Rule 706(a). Given the problems associated with the use of party-retained experts "doing battle" with each other, one might expect greater use than has been made of the court-appointed expert alternative

Under Federal Rule 44.1, parties that do not promptly raise a claim that foreign law should govern a claim or defense in an action in federal court will be deemed to have waived the application of such law. *Whirlpool Fin. Corp. v. Sevaux* (7th Cir. 1996); *Commercial Ins. Co. of Newark, New Jersey v. Pacific–Peru Constr. Corp.* (9th Cir.1977). Raising the foreign law issue on appeal may be too late. *Ruff v. St. Paul Mercury Ins. Co.* (2d Cir.1968).

On the other hand, a party that has invoked foreign law in a timely and reasonable manner has a right of appeal from the court's refusal to apply that law where the forum's conflicts of law rules point to it. As Rule 44.1 implies, the lower court's determination of the applicable law is fully reviewable on appeal as a matter of law. See *Banco de Credito Industrial, S.A. v. Tesoreria General* (5th Cir.1993). Because it is a question of law, the foreign law issue is also susceptible of determination by summary disposition (see *Instituto per lo Svilup-*

po Economico dell'Italia Meridionale v. Sperti Prods., Inc. (S.D.N.Y.1971)). This device would not ordinarily be available if foreign law were to be considered a question of fact (*First Nat'l Bank of Arizona v. British Petroleum Co., Ltd.* (S.D.N.Y. 1971)). Also, although Rule 44.1 is silent on this particular point, its characterization of foreign law as a matter of law should lead to the result that it is not entrusted to the jury.

Unfortunately, Rule 44.1 does not identify the consequences of a failure adequately to plead and/or prove foreign law; nor does most state legislation do so. Accordingly, the matter is often left to judicial discretion. Courts have responded in a variety of ways. They may find and apply the applicable foreign law on their own initiative, though their readiness to do so will depend on the foreign law's accessibility and intelligibility. They may apply forum law in its place, possibly on the theory that the parties, by failing adequately to adduce foreign law, acquiesced in the forum's application of its own law (and possibly even on the fiction that foreign and forum law may be presumed, in the absence of proof to the contrary, to be identical). See, e.g., *In re Oil Spill by the Amoco Cadiz* (7th Cir.1992); *Interpool, Ltd. v. Char Yigh Marine (Panama) S.A.* (9th Cir. 1989). Restatement (Second) of Conflicts of Law, section 136, comment h, supports this approach. This has even occurred in the face of a contractual choice of law clause designating non-forum law as the governing law. See, e.g., *Cantieri Navali Riuniti v. M/V Skyptron* (5th Cir.1986), where the court applied the forum state's law in certain respects, notwithstanding the parties' selection of a foreign country's law as governing. Rarely these days, a court may simply dismiss a claim or affirmative defense where based on unproven foreign law. The latter seems no longer to be a favored approach. See, e.g., *Vishipco Line v. Chase Manhattan Bank, N.A.* (2d Cir.1981).

Occasionally courts do take advantage of the opportunity that the modern "judicial notice" provisions give them to "find" and apply foreign law on their own initiative. In *Frummer v. Hilton Hotels, Int'l, Inc.* (N.Y.Sup.1969), a New York trial court, absent a showing of UK law on comparative negligence, initially applied New York contributory negligence principles in a tort action properly governed by UK law. In post-trial proceedings, the court on its own motion invoked Section 4511(b) to take judicial notice of the UK's Law Reform Act of 1945, and ordered a new trial to be conducted under that Act's rule of comparative negligence. Even among federal courts, there is a marked difference in attitude toward the court's duty to research and ascertain foreign law. Some circuits appear to require trial courts to make an independent effort, if need be. See, e.g., *Twohy v. First Nat'l Bank of Chicago* (7th Cir.1985). Others do not. See, e.g., *Carey v. Bahama Cruise Lines* (1st Cir.1988).

It is useful to bear in mind that a court's attitude toward finding the foreign law itself (or insisting that the parties do so) may vary depending on whether the foreign law constitutes the governing law (in the sense of providing the court with the applicable rules of decision) or merely functions as a datum (like any other factual material in the case) for purposes of applying the rules of decision supplied by forum law. The case for active judicial intervention is probably stronger in the first scenario. Such a distinction was drawn in *First Nat'l Bank of Arizona, supra.*

CHAPTER EIGHT

TRANSNATIONAL SERVICE AND PRODUCTION OF EVIDENCE

An especially common feature of transnational litigation is the necessity of making overseas service of documents and securing overseas production of evidence. Perhaps more than any other area of transnational litigation, this one entails the direct interaction of legal systems and, more specifically, between courts of different jurisdictions. The subject is accordingly governed to a significant extent by international agreement, raising questions of interplay between treaty and domestic legislation. The subject is further complicated by the necessity, with respect to service and evidence alike, of considering the problems from the perspective of both the so-called "requesting" and "requested" states.

SERVICE OF DOCUMENTS ABROAD

Plaintiffs bringing litigation in the US against a non-resident defendant may be faced with the necessity of making service of process overseas. While service is associated with delivery of the summons and complaint initiating a lawsuit, service may also be required for other procedural acts as well, such as a subpoena to produce testimony or documents or to appear for a deposition. In most jurisdictions, service is a necessary component of personal jurisdiction, but it invariably also serves a notice function, which is itself of due process significance. In making service abroad, parties need to consider questions both of their authority to do so under US law and of their entitlement to do so under the law of the place where service is made. As this chapter and Chapter 10 will show, the enforceability of a US judgment abroad may depend on a foreign court's assessment of the legitimacy of the service performed. This is so whether service on a foreign national is made in the US or on the territory of the foreign state.

However, service on non-residents does not necessarily require service overseas. A non-resident may be physically present in the US, and thus amenable to service locally. A non-resident may also have expressly or impliedly appointed an agent for service of process within the US. In circumstances where a court is prepared to "pierce the corporate veil," or identify "alter egos," for personal jurisdictional purposes (see chapter 2 *supra*), it very likely will also treat service on the affiliate or alter ego as effective.

The Federal Rules

Still, overseas service will often be necessary in litigation in US courts. As to this prospect, the Federal Rules of Civil Procedure are decidedly generous. A new Rule 4(f), added in 1993, privileges "any internationally agreed means [of service] reasonably calculated to give notice." At present, the only such means in the US are the Hague Convention on the Service Abroad of Judicial and Extrajudicial Documents (which the Rule expressly mentions) and the Inter–American Convention on Letters Rogatory. If these "internationally agreed means" are not exclusive (and, of course, if they are not even applicable), then service may be made by any of the other means recited in Rule 4(f).

Assuming a treaty-based means of service is unavailable or, if available, is non-exclusive, Rule 4(f)(2) affords a range of other possibilities, including service as permitted by foreign law, as directed by a foreign authority, by personal service to an individual, or by return-receipt mail. In the case of each means, its availability under US law is conditional on its compatibility with the law of the place where service is effected. In this respect, the Rule represents an advance upon its predecessor rule, the former Rule 4(i), introduced in 1963, which did not expressly require conformity with foreign law for service abroad made by these means. *Umbenhauer v. Woog* (3d Cir.1992). In addition, Rule 4(f)(3) permits service as ordered by the district court, except where prohibited by international agreement. (Rule 4(f)(3) does not however, by its terms, specifically bar a court from ordering service abroad in a fashion that would violate foreign law.)

Service under the Federal Rules of Civil Procedure ordinarily must be made within 120 days of the filing of a complaint. However, this does not apply to service in a foreign country (Rule 4(m)). In addition, the provisions in Rule 4(d) on agreements for waiver of service are equally available in domestic and international cases. The only difference in treatment (other than the length of time—90 rather than 60 days—that the defendant has to respond to a waiver request and to serve an answer) concerns sanctions for an unjustified refusal to waive service. Rule 4(d) permits sanctions, which take the form of cost-shifting, only where both the plaintiff and defendant are located in the US. Despite the absence of any threat of sanctions, a foreign defendant may still decide to give a waiver, if only to reduce the costs (including translation costs) that may ultimately be taxed against it if it loses the suit. In any event, a waiver of service is not considered to be a waiver of objections either to jurisdiction or venue.

State courts, of course, have their own service rules, and they typically allow a variety of modes of overseas service. By way of exception, state courts are required in two circumstances to follow federally-prescribed service rules. First, service in state court must be performed in accordance with the Hague Service Convention in all cases to which the Convention applies. Second, the special service provisions of the Foreign Sovereign Immunities Act (28 U.S.C.A. sec. 1608), incorporated by reference in Rule 4(j)(1) of the Federal Rules, govern service in actions under the FSIA, whether they are brought in state or federal court, and whether service is made in the US or abroad. The FSIA provides one set of means of service on a foreign state or on one of its political subdivisions, and another set for service on an agency or instrumentality of a foreign state. The latter service must be made by notice directly to the agency or instrumentality and not merely the state. See *Filus v. LOT Polish Airlines* (E.D.N.Y.1993). In each case, Section 1608 establishes a priority among the available means.

As in domestic cases in state and federal court, service in international cases must not only be statutorily authorized, but also satisfy due process. That is to say, it must be reasonably calculated, under the circumstances, to give the addressee timely and adequate notice and an opportunity to be heard. *Securities and Exchange Comm'n v. Tome* (2d Cir.1987).

US service under foreign law

Even if overseas service is authorized by the procedural law governing the US court in which an action is brought, parties to transnational litigation need also to consider the legitimacy of such service from the point of view of the law of the place of service. The Restatement (Third) of Foreign Relations Law, section 471(1), provides that "[u]nder international law, a state may determine the conditions for service of process in its territory in aid of litigation in another state, but the state where the litigation is pending may determine the effect of such service."

Foreign states may limit the means of service within their territory in a number of different ways.

For example, performance of service may be restricted to certain officials or methods. Breach of the local rules governing service may also have a range of consequences, some of them potentially serious.

In the first place, irregularity of the service under foreign law will place a cloud over any judgment eventually entered as a result of the proceeding in question. At a minimum, it will jeopardize the eventual recognition or enforcement of the resulting judgment in the state whose rules of service were not respected, and possibly in other states prepared to enforce those rules as a matter of public policy. Under some circumstances, this will impair the practical value of the judgment. In addition, however, the invalidity of the service may in turn render the service ineffective under US law, even when it would otherwise have been unobjectionable. It is true that Congress may expressly authorize service to be performed in a manner that violates foreign law (or international law) and that, if it does so, the violation will not affect the validity of the service for US law purposes. *Umbenhauer v. Woog*, *supra*; *Commodity Futures Trading Comm'n v. Nahas* (D.C.Cir.1984). However, an intent by Congress to authorize service in violation of foreign law is not to be presumed. See *Commodity Futures Trading Comm'n v. Nahas*, *supra*; *Federal Trade Comm'n v. Compagnie de Saint–Gobain–Pont–a–Mousson* (D.C.Cir.1980).

It is also true that, even absent express authorization by Congress, US courts have sometimes upheld the validity of foreign service though the latter was performed in violation of the law of place of service, particularly where the person served abroad is a US national. (See, e.g., *Blackmer v. United States* (S.Ct.1932); *Securities and Exchange Comm'n v. Briggs* (N.D.Ohio 1964).) But there remains a risk that the validity of the service, even under US law, may be impaired. With the 1993 amendments to the Federal Rules, the risk has become especially real, since Rule 4(f) expressly requires that service of US process abroad generally comply with foreign law, thus making its effectiveness depend on such compliance.

Second, an act of unauthorized service on foreign soil may subject the party making service to foreign law sanctions. Disapproval by a state of a mode of service performed on its territory may take a variety of forms. Among strict regimes, Switzerland is perhaps the best known. Service of foreign process in Switzerland, at least on persons resident there, other than through official Swiss governmental channels is forbidden by the Swiss Penal Code (art. 271). Other countries, while not criminally punishing unauthorized service on their territory, have filed diplomatic objections when it occurs. See *Federal Trade Comm'n v. Compagnie de Saint–Gobain–Pont–a–Mousson, supra.*

SERVICE OF FOREIGN JUDICIAL DOCUMENTS IN THE US

We now turn to the service of documents in the US in connection with foreign judicial proceedings. Compared to other states, the US has fairly relaxed rules governing service within the territory. Generally speaking, state and federal procedural laws permit a variety of modes of service in domestic litigation, including private use of the mails, and they do not restrict them when used in connection with foreign judicial proceedings. Service of documents in judicial proceedings is not generally viewed as a function reserved to certain public officials. The parties themselves, rather than designated government officers, are responsible for effectuating service. Fed. R. Civ. P. 4(c)(1). Federal legislation (28 U.S.C.A. sec. 1696(b)) confirms that parties to foreign litigation are basically free to effect service in the US in connection with that litigation.

While it may be the case that US courts have inherent authority to transmit foreign judicial documents for service in US territory, federal legislation expressly confers such authority upon them. The relevant statute—28 U.S.C.A. sec. 1696—provides:

> The district court of the district in which a person resides or is found may order service upon him of any document issued in connection with a proceeding in a foreign or international tribunal. The order may be made pursuant to a letter rogatory issued, or request made, by a foreign or interna-

tional tribunal or upon application of any interested person and shall direct the manner of service.

Requests for US service may also be submitted to the State Department which, under 28 U.S.C.A. section 1781, has authority to deliver them to the appropriate court or agency, typically through the Justice Department's US Marshal's Service.

From the use of the word "may," it is clear that the service authority conferred by sections 1696 and 1781 is discretionary in character. A decision by a court to grant or deny assistance is accordingly subject, in principle, only to judicial review under an abuse of discretion standard. The passage of this legislation was prompted only in part to establish federal judicial authority in this respect; mainly it provides a basis for satisfying a reciprocity on which other States may condition their own willingness to render like assistance. On the other hand, as Section 1696 expressly states, assistance to foreign courts by way of service does not entail any obligation of recognition or enforcement with respect to the resulting foreign judgment.

THE HAGUE SERVICE CONVENTION

In order to convert what is essentially a matter of discretionary cooperation into an international legal obligation, and to avoid the above-mentioned risks, an international agreement of some sort is needed. The 1965 Hague Convention on the Service Abroad of Judicial and Extrajudicial Documents in Civil and

Commercial Matters, 20 UST 361, TIAS no. 6638, 658 UNTS 163, drafted under the auspices of the Hague Conference on Private International Law, is such an instrument. The US signed the Convention in 1965 and ratified it in 1967, effective 1969. The Convention has been held to be self-executing, in the sense of not requiring statutory incorporation before becoming legally effective in the US.

The Service Convention establishes an obligation on the part of contracting States to perform service of documents at the request of another contracting State, subject of course to the request satisfying the conditions laid down in or authorized by the Convention. The Convention does not establish any basis for the exercise of personal jurisdiction; it merely identifies available means of service on the assumption that personal jurisdiction exists.

Workings of the Convention

Under the Convention, each State designates a "Central Authority" responsible for receiving and handling foreign requests for service in civil or commercial litigation, including furnishing proof of service to the requesting state. The US Central Authority is the Department of State, assisted by the Justice Department's Office of International Judicial Assistance. Such requests may emanate from another country's Central Authority, but may also emanate directly from its courts. The Convention also contains rules governing the form and language of requests.

Once in receipt of a request, a Central Authority makes service by one of several means laid down in the Convention: (a) in the same manner as service is made in domestic actions, (b) in the manner specified by the requesting party, or (c) by voluntary acceptance of service. Where service is made in the same manner as in domestic actions, the requested state may require the translation of documents into one of its official languages. It is less likely to do so where service is made by a means that the applicant has requested or where service is voluntarily accepted. The only basis on which the Central Authority of a State may decline to make service is if there is a defect of form in the request or if compliance would entail an infringement of the requested state's "sovereignty or security."

The establishment and functioning of a Central Authority constitutes a minimum obligation. States may, but need not, agree under the Convention to permit service on their territory by certain additional means. These include service through the requesting state's diplomatic or consular agents (arts. 8 and 9), by local judicial officers or other local authorities (arts. 10(b) and (c)), by mail (art. 10(a)), or by any means otherwise permitted by the requested state (art. 19). (The latter provision has permitted the US to continue enforcing its liberal rules on service of process on its territory.) Under Article 21, a State may exclude any or all of these additional means of service. The Convention's main purpose is thus to create a simple and efficient means of making service abroad.

Article 10 in particular is not without difficulty. It provides that if a state does not object, the Convention shall not be deemed to restrict "(a) the freedom to *send* judicial documents, by postal channels, directly to persons abroad." At the same time, the Convention shall not be deemed to restrict "(b) the freedom of judicial officers ... of the State of origin to *effect service* of judicial documents directly through the judicial officers ... of the State of destination," or "(c) the freedom of any person ... to *effect service* of judicial documents directly through the judicial officers ... of the State of destination." Some courts have read Article 10(a) as essentially meaning "effect service" when it says "send," so that direct mail service is deemed effective (that is, unless a state has objected). See *Ackermann v. Levine* (2d Cir.1986). Other courts read "send" in subparagraph (a) as not constituting service, so that only means (b) and (c) are available under Article 10, and even then, only if a state has not objected. The problem has arisen particularly with respect to service in Japan, since Japan has specifically objected to service under both Articles 10(b) and 10(c). See, e.g., *Bankston v. Toyota Motor Corp.* (8th Cir.1989). If service in US litigation is made by mail in Japan, enforceability of the resulting judgment in Japan becomes doubtful.

In prescribing means of service, the Convention is not insensitive to the necessity of actual notice. According to Article 15, a default judgment in a case in which service was made under the Convention may not be entered, unless it can be shown both (a) that service was made in accordance with the local law of the place of service or that it was actually delivered to the defendant (or the defendant's residence) through a method permitted by the Convention, and (b) that the defendant received service in sufficient time to respond. This guarantee of actual notice of service stemmed from a concern that permissible methods of service under the law of some Contracting States (such as *notification au parquet* in France) included deposit of the documents with a government official, without regard to whether or not that official effectively transmitted those documents to the party addressed.

Scope and exclusivity of the Convention

The Convention applies only to "civil or commercial matters." The Convention, however, does not define the terms "civil" or "commercial." Ordinarily this generates no difficulties. But questions have arisen whether certain matters that would be considered civil in US law—such as private antitrust litigation—are in fact "public" rather than civil or commercial, within the meaning of the Convention, and whether punitive or treble damages should be considered "penal" or otherwise non-civil and non-commercial. Similarly, an action in civil court to which a governmental entity is a party may be considered "civil" in this country, but may not be in countries that reserve such actions to special "administrative courts."

Still more problematic is the question as to when "there is occasion to transmit a judicial or extrajudicial document for service abroad." The position of the Supreme Court is that service is not subject to the Convention where it does not need to be made abroad because, for example, it can be made on the defendant within the US in a fashion that is legally effective under domestic law. *Volkswagenwerk AG v. Schlunk* (S.Ct.1988). In principle, the determination of when service abroad is "required" is made by reference to the law of the forum. Only where the defendant cannot be reached through an act of service validly performed within the territory of the US is the Convention applicable. According to Justice Brennan's concurrence in *Schlunk*, Contracting States do not, however, have unlimited freedom to determine that service within the territory vests a local court with jurisdiction over a non-resident defendant.

Courts have enabled the Service Convention to be avoided by permitting local service on foreign defendants in a variety of circumstances. Typically, as in *Schlunk*, they have permitted service on a foreign corporation, not itself present within the jurisdiction, to be performed through service on an agent or alter ego corporation that is itself present, provided that the legal conditions for finding agency or alter ego status are met. However, the courts are divided as to whether service on a non-resident defendant can validly be made by so-called "substituted service," that is, through service on a state official, such as the Secretary of State, appointed by statute to accept service. In *Melia v. Les Grands Chais de France* (D.R.I.1991), the court found that service was complete when substituted service was made on the Secretary of State, and not when the documents were thereafter transmitted abroad. But other courts have construed such "substituted service" as not made until the documents are transmitted to the defendant abroad in cases where the applicable service rule expressly requires transmission abroad. See, e.g., *Davies v. Jobs & Adverts Online, GmbH* (E.D.Va.2000).

The Service Convention has been interpreted in the US as "mandatory" not only in the obvious sense of making the rendering of assistance obligatory in cases covered by the Convention, but also in the less obvious sense of requiring that parties seeking to make service in another contracting State do so through the Convention's channels, and not through any other mechanism that the domestic law of the "requesting" state may allow. In *Schlunk*, the Court interpreted the Convention language ("[the Convention] shall apply in all cases . . . where . . .") as mandating the exclusive use of the Convention in all cases in which it is applicable. In other words, Convention channels are the exclusive means of making service in all cases falling within its scope. Because a party has a right to insist in a proper case on use of the Convention, it has been held reversible error to impose Rule 11 sanctions on a foreign party that refuses waiver of service under Rule 4(d). *Sheets v. Yamaha Motors Corp.* (5th Cir.1990).

If the Hague Service Convention applies and is not followed, the question of remedy arises. Ordinarily, service will be deemed improper and, under Rule 4(f)(1), ineffective, though subject to cure, unless the that would be futile (as where due process minimum contacts are in any event missing). *Rhodes v. J.P. Sauer & Sohn, Inc.* (W.D.La.2000).

As of 1988, the US is also a party to the 1975 Inter–American Convention on Letters Rogatory (or Panama Convention), 14 ILM 339 (1975), and Additional Protocol to the Convention (Montevideo Protocol), 18 ILM 1238 (1979). In many ways, the Inter–American Convention resembles the Hague Service Convention. However, unlike the Hague Convention, it has been held not to constitute the exclusive means of service in cases falling within its scope. See *Kreimerman v. Casa Veerkamp, S.A. de C.V.* (5th Cir.1994); *Pizzabiocche v. Vinelli* (M.D.Fla.1991).

OBTAINING EVIDENCE ABROAD

Compared to overseas service, overseas production of evidence is a decidedly more problematic matter. We begin once again with the scenario of transnational litigation in US court, and the likelihood that one or both parties will find need or utility in obtaining evidence situated outside US territory. Once again, we must distinguish between a US court's authority under its own law to order the production of documents or testimony, on the one hand, and the legality of that production under the law of the place where production may be deemed to be made, on the other.

The Federal Rules

The Federal Rules facilitate the conduct of extraterritorial production, much as they do extraterritorial service, by enabling it to be performed in a wide variety of ways from which the party seeking production may in principle freely choose. To begin with, there is no bar to using the same evidence-gathering techniques that are available under Rule 26 for obtaining evidence located in the US, including documentary discovery (Rule 34), deposition (Rule 30), interrogatories (Rule 33), inspections (Rule 34), physical and mental examinations (Rule 35) and requests for admission (Rule 36). Rule 26(b) authorizes discovery of "any matter, not privileged, that is relevant to the claim or defense of any party," even when the requesting party does not know that the document exists or cannot specifically describe it. "For good cause, the court may order discovery of any matter relevant to the subject matter involved in the action."

Where a party seeking evidence abroad for use in US litigation is unsuccessful in obtaining it voluntarily, it may ask the court to order production under Rule 37, and the court may do so directly if the party in possession of the evidence is subject to the court's jurisdiction. Noncompliance may result, as usual, in the imposition of sanctions, again under Rule 37. On the other hand, a party to whom a discovery request has been addressed may apply to the court for an order limiting the request or excusing noncompliance (Rule 26(c)). In these ways, a court will be called upon to decide either the propriety of issuing a production order or the necessity of placing limits on required production through a so-called "protective order." Issuance of such orders is reviewable on appeal by an "abuse of discretion" standard.

Perceptions of discovery abuse led in 1980 to amendments to the Federal Rules to curb excessive use of discovery devices and to impose discovery discipline on lawyers. See Rules 16, 26(f) and 37(g). In 1993, the Rules were again amended to provide for broad mandatory initial disclosure by each party of discoverable information without discovery paperwork. In 2000, Rule 26 was confined to information "that the disclosing party may use to support its claims or defenses, unless solely for impeachment." Beyond this automatic disclosure, party requests may be made for "any matter, not privileged, that is relevant to the claim or defense of any party.... Relevant evidence need not be admissible at trial if the discovery appears reasonably calculated to lead to the discovery of admissible evidence." For still further discovery, a court order is required.

As to the initial question of a US court's power to order the production of evidence located abroad, there appears to be little doubt. See *United States v. Reagan* (6th Cir.1971). A leading judgment is *In re Uranium Antitrust Litigation (Westinghouse Elec. Corp. v. Rio Algom Ltd.)* (N.D.Ill.1979), where the court ruled that a court may order a person subject to its jurisdiction to perform an act in another state, including the production of documents over which that person has actual control. Courts have taken this position, notwithstanding the general "territorial presumption" in US law, discussed in Chapter 7.

Any doubts on this matter as concerns depositions in particular are dispelled by the fact that Rules 28(b) and 29 specifically identify the means available for conducting discovery abroad. Rule 28(b) offers several alternatives for obtaining evidence, including deposition material, abroad. One such method is a letter of request (on "terms that are just and appropriate"), by which the courts of one country seek the aid of the courts of another in obtaining evidence in the latter's territory. In the absence of a special treaty arrangement, letters rogatory go from court to court or through diplomatic channels. In the latter event, a request will travel from the requesting US court to the Justice Department, from there to the requested state's ministry of foreign affairs, and from there to the foreign court where the evidence is to be taken, pursuant to 28 U.S.C.A. Section 1781. Once taken, the evidence presumably follows the same path in reverse. State courts likewise employ letters rogatory addressed to foreign courts. Because, absent a treaty, there can be no guarantee that letters of request will be performed abroad in the form or manner customary in US practice, Rule 28(b) specifically adds that the evidence yielded by a letter of request "need not be excluded [from admissibility in federal court] merely because it is not a verbatim transcript, because the testimony was not taken under oath, or because of any similar departures from the requirements for depositions taken within the United States under these rules." Such departures presumably also include the absence of cross-examination. Of course, the fact that the evidence need not be excluded on these grounds does not mean that it will not be given less weight on account of them.

Rule 28(b) also permits depositions "pursuant to any applicable treaty or convention." By far the most important treaty on obtaining evidence is the multilateral Hague Evidence Convention, discussed in detail below.

In addition to resorting to letters rogatory issued to a foreign court and/or invoking a judicial assistance treaty (both of which presume cooperation by the country of the place of deposition), parties may under Rule 28(b) employ two additional means: notice (meaning that the deposition is performed before a person authorized to administer oaths under the law of the place of examination, such as US consular officials or certain foreign authorities) and commission (entailing the appointment by the US court of a specific individual to take the deposition). Each means presents certain potential advantages and disadvantages. For example, depositions by notice or commission may be faster, but are useful only if the deposition will be given voluntarily, since in neither case are local means of compulsion normally available. Depositions by notice or commission may, in any event, not be legal in the foreign country. On the other hand, a letter of request or treaty may ensure a degree of coercion by foreign authorities (which may be useful where the witness is recalcitrant and where the US court lacks coercive power over the witness), but may yield depositions that are less useful and possibly less probative. This may be due to their non-verbatim form or to the absence of direct and cross examination.

All of this serves as a reminder that transnational production needs to respect the law of both the requesting and the requested state. If a foreign state objects to the taking of evidence by non-nationals of that state, for example, direct use of an authorized local national or use of a letter rogatory may be the only safe and legal options.

Before ordering production, the court must satisfy itself that the addressee has the requisite control over the evidence. This can be problematic, particularly where the evidence sought is not in the hands of a party subject to the court's jurisdiction, but rather in the hands of one of its affiliates or other closely related entities. In that event, courts look to the addressee's extent of actual control over the affiliate or entity in possession of the evidence. As between especially close corporate affiliates, the court may even assume access to documents. See, e.g., *Japan Halon, Co., Ltd. v. Great Lakes Chem. Corp.* (N.D.Ind.1993); *Cooper Indus., Inc. v. British Aerospace, Inc.* (S.D.N.Y.1984). While courts are fond of pointing out that the generally greater public interest in permitting such discovery in criminal as compared to civil cases (see, e.g., *United States v. Vetco, Inc.* (9th Cir.1981)), a pattern of veil-piercing for these purposes may be observed in civil cases as well.

Production by non-parties

The situation is slightly different where evidence abroad is sought from a non-party to the US litigation, and that non-party is unwilling to produce voluntarily. Federal legislation (28 U.S.C.A. sec. 1783) subjects US nationals or residents, wherever located at the time, to subpoenas in connection with actions to which they are not parties, and the constitutionality of this legislation has been affirmed. *Blackmer v. United States, supra.* Moreover, Federal Rule 45(b) specifically provides subpoena power in such cases.

More generally, Rule 45(a) permits a party to issue and serve a subpoena directly to a non-party (of any nationality or residence) to produce documents or attend a deposition or trial. However, this power is subject to strict limitations. The person to whom the subpoena is addressed must, as a matter of due process, be subject to the personal jurisdiction of a US court, typically measured by minimum contacts. Before ordering production by a person in his or her representative capacity, the court may need jurisdiction over the party represented. See, e.g., *In re Sealed Case* (D.C.Cir.1987). In addition, by the terms of Rule 45, he or she must be located within the judicial district of the court or within 100 miles of the place of production, deposition or trial. Rule 45(e) makes failure by a non-party to comply punishable as a contempt of court. Since only a federal district court can issue a subpoena under Rule 45, a non-party witness, not located in the US, is ordinarily beyond reach. The only significant exceptions are cases where the non-party has a US branch or an officer or agent in the US, or is temporarily in the US at the time of service. In a recurring scenario, bank records are sought from a foreign branch of a bank within the court's jurisdiction. If that branch has control over the records, then, depending on the weight attached to any applicable blocking legislation (see below), production may be ordered. See, e.g., *In re Sealed Case* (D.C.Cir.1987); *Garpeg, Ltd. v. United States* (S.D.N.Y.1984).

In any case, a court will not issue a subpoena against a non-party, or enforce one issued by a party under Rule 45, where it considers the demand to be unreasonable or abusive. The fact that the non-party is located abroad may be an important factor, among others, to be taken into consideration. See *Laker Airways Ltd. v. Pan American World Airways* (S.D.N.Y.1985). So, too, may be the applicability of foreign blocking legislation (see below) or prudential foreign policy considerations. *Id.* Rule 45 also specifically contemplates the issuance of protective orders in connection with subpoenas.

Assuming that issuance of a subpoena to a non-party is proper in all respects, there may be additional complications where oral depositions of foreign non-party witnesses are concerned. The choice is between bringing the witness to the US and conducting the deposition abroad. This is a decision to be made in light of such factors as the procedural advantages of oral examination in the US, the legality and feasibility of conducting a deposition abroad, and the degree of hardship to the deponent.

Jurisdiction to order jurisdictional discovery

The question of personal jurisdiction to order the production of evidence is complicated when the party seeking the order claims that discovery is needed to establish jurisdiction to issue the order. The question that arises is whether a court may order the production of evidence by a party precisely for the purpose of determining whether it has jurisdiction over that party (whether for discovery purposes or otherwise). While the decision to order production or not under these circumstances of uncertainty is ultimately within a court's discretion, the prevailing view is that courts do have the authority to do so. See, e.g., *Insurance Corp. of Ireland, Ltd. v. Compagnie des Bauxites de Guinee* (S.Ct.1982); *Leasco Data Processing Equip. Corp. v. Maxwell* (2d Cir.1972). To justify so-called "jurisdictional discovery," there must generally be a basis for considering the presence of jurisdiction to be reasonably probable. *In re Marc Rich & Co. A.G.* (2d Cir.1983).

"FOREIGN BLOCKING LEGISLATION" AND ITS EFFECTS

US law contains no specific prohibitions on the production of evidence on US territory for use in foreign judicial proceedings. But "blocking legislation"—that is, enactments which basically prohibit compliance with foreign court orders for the production of evidence under certain circumstances—is found elsewhere. Some such statutes purport to avoid undue coercion of witnesses and disrespect for privacy and for the applicable legal privileges, concerns heightened by the fact that evidence-taking in that country is regarded as a public function that only designated public authorities may exercise. Such legislation has undoubtedly also been prompted by objections to what are regarded as exorbitant party-driven demands for discovery in US litigation (as in "fishing expeditions"), particularly when arising in connection with the extraterritorial application of US law. Foreign governments have accordingly invoked "national sovereignty" in their opposition to the performance of US-style discovery on their soil and occasionally responded with diplomatic notes of protest.

Some secrecy laws are longstanding and were not enacted specifically to impede discovery in connection with certain kinds of US litigation. For example, Article 273 of the Swiss Penal Code punishes persons who seek to discover in Switzerland manufacturing or business secrets so as to make them available to a foreign governmental or business organization, or their agent. Switzerland law has also long had bank secrecy legislation, chiefly found in Article 47 of the Banking Act, SR 952.0.

Other blocking legislation is of more recent vintage. Some statutes merely "authorize" government authorities to forbid certain categories of disclosure so that disclosure is permitted, unless and until prohibited. The UK Protection of Trading Interests Act of 1980 (21 ILM 834 (1982)) is an example, as are the Canadian Foreign Extraterritorial Measures Act (24 ILM 794 (1985)) and the Australian Foreign Proceedings (Excess of Jurisdiction Act of 1984 (23 ILM 1038). Other statutes themselves impose a categorical prohibition on disclosure of material in response to foreign production orders, unless permission to comply is sought and granted. They may even require addressees of discovery requests to notify the local authorities. See, e.g., French Law No. 80–538, [1980] O.J. 1799. Probably the first such statute was the Ontario Business Records Protection Act of 1947 (1947 Ont. Rev. Stat. ch. 54), which was a response to a US federal court order addressed to the Canadian subsidiaries of a New York corporation to produce documents located in Canada for use in a US grand jury investigation of alleged Sherman Act violations. *In re Grand Jury Subpoenas Duces Tecum Addressed to Canadian Int'l Paper Co.* (S.D.N.Y.1947).

Still other foreign blocking legislation is sector-or industry-specific, as in the case of banking, petroleum, uranium production and shipping. (For example, shipping-sector blocking statutes were enacted to impede investigations by the US Federal Maritime Commission into alleged anti-competitive and discriminatory practices in international shipping.) When major US antitrust suits alleging worldwide anticompetitive conduct in the uranium industry appeared imminent in the late 1970's, a number of jurisdictions enacted legislation barring disclosure of related documents for use in that litigation.

Foreign blocking legislation can do more than prohibit the furnishing of information to, or for use before, foreign judicial authorities. The UK Protection of Trading Interests Act, *supra*, also bars enforcement in the UK of awards of multiple (including treble) damages, and actually gives parties (apparently whatever their nationality) a UK remedy for recovery of two-thirds of any US antitrust judgment awarded, assertable against the party winning that judgment. The latter is commonly known as a "clawback" provision. While the statute reportedly has never been enforced, it may have on occasion exerted a deterrent effect. The UK is not alone among foreign countries in statutorily barring or limiting enforcement of US antitrust judgments. An Australian statute—the Foreign Proceedings (Excess of Jurisdiction) Act of 1984, *supra*, sec. 9(1)(b)(ii)—permits recovery of the entire amount of an antitrust judgment in a foreign court proceeding that is declared by the Attorney General to be "contrary to international law or inconsistent with international comity or international practice."

Plainly, blocking statutes furnish a basis on which both requests for production and requests for assistance in production may be denied. Arguably, one of the advantages of international agreements on obtaining evidence abroad is a limitation on the invocability of blocking legislation by one contracting State to prevent production at the request of the courts of another contracting State. We shall return to this matter below in the context of the Hague Evidence Convention.

CONFLICTS BETWEEN US DISCOVERY ORDERS AND FOREIGN LAW

The existence of foreign blocking legislation sets up the possibility of conflict between the evidentiary needs of US litigation and the commands of the law of the place where the evidence is gathered. Predictably, such conflict frequently occurs.

A noted example arose out of the uranium antitrust litigation referred to just above. When uranium customers sued Westinghouse for breach of supply contracts, Westinghouse defended on the ground that performance had become impracticable due to a sudden dramatic price increase occasioned by cartel activities on the part of UK, French, Australian, South African and Canadian suppliers. Westinghouse sought discovery in the UK from Rio Tinto Zinc, while instituting its own affirmative antitrust suit. When the US court ordered discovery, the UK Court of Appeal approved it, with some modifications to narrow its scope, and there followed an appeal to the House of Lords, which ruled that the orders should not be given effect on account, among other reasons, of their extraterritoriality. *Rio Tinto Zinc Corp. v. Westinghouse Elec. Corp.* (1978). In Westinghouse's own antitrust suit, Westinghouse moved for orders compelling production under Rule 37. Faced with the uranium-specific blocking statutes of various countries referred to earlier, the court ruled that once personal jurisdiction and control over the documents is established (the latter often being a difficult issue where documents are in the files of corporate affiliates), it could order production, foreign blocking legislation notwithstanding. *In re Uranium Antitrust Litig., supra*. We deal with the consequences below.

Conflicts of this sort may be resolved in a number of different ways. Traditionally, US courts followed a policy of deference to the law of the place of evidence-taking, in the sense of not even ordering discovery abroad where compliance would require violation of foreign law. According to the Restatement (First) of Conflict of Laws, US courts do not even have authority to order production under those circumstances. This reflects a more general international law precept that no nation should order a party to take action forbidden by the law of the place where that action would be taken, or order a party to refrain from taking action in a jurisdiction whose law requires such action to be taken. However, this approach would amount essentially to subjecting the availability of foreign-based evidence in US courts to foreign law, and has accordingly fallen into disfavor. On the other hand, ordering discovery abroad in complete and utter disregard of a local prohibition seems inappropriate and out of step with notions of international comity. Of course, the extent to which comity should play a role will vary in accordance with the US court's assessment of the enacting state's motivations in erecting the barrier to production.

Societe Internationale Pour Participations Industrielles et Commerciales v. Rogers

The Supreme Court decision in *Societe Internationale Pour Participations Industrielles et Commerciales v. Rogers* (S.Ct.1958), signaled a change of approach. The Court there held in effect that US courts do have authority to order production abroad even in the face of blocking legislation, where the claim advances an important policy of US law and the evidence sought is relevant to the prosecution of that claim. (The Court also acknowledged that the degree of flexibility in the blocking legislation could be a relevant factor.) More than that need not be shown. In a separate part of the opinion, the Court turned to the question of the range of sanctions appropriately imposed on a party to the litigation who fails to obey such in reliance on the foreign blocking legislation. The Court ruled that a party should not ordinarily be subject to contempt or to dismissal of its claims or defenses, provided it acted in good faith in failing to comply. This means, in effect, that such a party did not, among other things, "court" the foreign state's prohibition, deliberately place the evidence in a jurisdiction that would prohibit disclosure, or fail to take reasonable steps to secure a waiver form application of the blocking legislation. *Republic of the Philippines v. Marcos* (2d Cir.1989). Having said that, the Court in *Societe Internationale* refused to protect persons, even those relying in good faith on foreign blocking statutes, from all adverse consequences of non-production. More specifically, it held that a court may (though need not) find that the party refusing production failed to carry its burden of proof in the litigation, and may even draw adverse inferences from the non-production.

(a) Production order or not?

The cases following *Societe Internationale* are not entirely consistent. The Court in *Societe Internationale* purposely did not embark upon a balancing of US and foreign government interests in deciding whether to order production or whether (and if so, how) to punish non-compliance. Some lower courts have followed suit. See e.g., *In re Uranium Antitrust Litig., supra,* declining to balance what it considered to be irreconcilable national interests. But other courts have conducted a general balancing operation for either or both purposes. In doing so, older cases relied on Sections 39 and 40 of the Restatement (Second) of Foreign Relations Law. According to Section 39, a state is not precluded from exercising jurisdiction solely because it requires conduct that is subjected to liability under the law of another state having adequate jurisdiction. Where two states require inconsistent conduct of a person, each state should "consider . . . moderating the exercise of its enforcement jurisdiction, in the light of such factors as: (a) vital national interests of each of the states, (b) the extent and the nature of the hardship that inconsistent enforcement actions would impose upon the person, (c) the extent to which the required conduct is to take place in the territory of the other state, (d) the nationality of the person, and (e) the extent to which enforcement by action of either state can reasonably be expected to achieve compliance with the rule prescribed by that state." Thus, they should take into consideration, among other things, the competing interests of the interested jurisdictions and the possible hardship to private parties.

In some cases, the court concluded that the foreign government's interest in secrecy outweighed the US court's need for the evidence. See, e.g., *United States v. First Nat'l Bank of Chicago* (7th Cir.1983). In others, such as *United States v. Vetco, Inc., supra*, the court found the balance of national interests tipping in favor of ordering production. In *United States v. First Nat'l City Bank* (2d Cir.1968), the court, while admitting that exposure to civil as opposed to criminal liability could constitute a sufficient reason for a court not to order production of evidence, found that in the case at hand the balance tipped in favor of issuing the order. This might be due to a range of factors, including the waivability of the privilege, the unlikelihood of criminal sanctions or civil liability, lack of good faith, and the failure of either the US State Department or the German government to intervene. Production having been ordered, non-compliance was punished by civil contempt due to a finding of lack of good faith.

(b) Sanctions or not?

On the question of sanctions, lower courts have followed rather closely *Societe Internationale*'s framework of analysis. Sanctions imposed have included dismissal, contempt, the striking of pleadings, adverse findings, and preclusion of evidence. See, e.g., *Richmark Corp. v. Timber Falling Consultants* (9th Cir.1992) (contempt); *General Atomic Co. v. Exxon Nuclear Co., Inc.* (S.D.Cal.1981) (dismissal and default judgment).

The range of available sanctions is of course reduced where the person failing to produce evidence in reliance on blocking legislation is a non-party. See, e.g., *United States v. Bank of Nova Scotia (II)* (11th Cir.1984); (11th Cir.1982), involving the placement of funds in the Cayman Islands to avoid discovery through reliance on its blocking legislation. Even in cases of bad faith, neither dismissal nor default will be available. Nor is it possible to draw adverse inferences against a non-party, while drawing them against a party may be unjust. A contempt fine will be necessary. In practice, courts hesitate to impose sanctions on non-parties in purely civil cases.

Overall, it is interesting to compare the sophistication of the courts' analysis of foreign blocking statutes with their general treatment of foreign law testimonial privileges. Such privileges have traditionally been regarded as raising procedural questions, thus pointing to the application of forum law. Some courts, however, have acknowledged that privileges also have a substantive, or policy, dimension. In consequence, they have shown a willingness to subject the question of applicable privileges to a general conflict of laws analysis, and thus also apply the privilege law of a suitably interested jurisdiction. Privilege raises difficult choice of law questions. The Restatement (Third) of Foreign Relations Law, section 442, comment d, appears to place emphasis on the law of the place where the communication in question was made.

The Third Restatement

The Restatement (Third) of Foreign Relations Law addresses this entire problem, drawing in part, but only in part, from *Societe Internationale*. Section 442 reads as follows:

(1) (a) A court or agency in the United States, when authorized by statute or rule of court, may order a person subject to its jurisdiction to produce documents, objects, or other information relevant to an action or investigation, even if the information or the person in possession of the information is outside the United States.

. . .

(c) In deciding whether to issue an order directing production of information located abroad, and in framing such an order, a court or agency in the

United States should take into account the importance to the investigation or litigation of the documents or other information requested; the degree of specificity of the request; whether the information originated in the United States; the availability of alternative means of securing the information; and the extent to which noncompliance with the request would undermine important interests of the United States, or compliance with the request would undermine important interests of the state where the information is located.

(2) If disclosure of information located outside the United States is prohibited by a law, regulation, or order of a court or other authority of the state in which the information or prospective witness is located, or of the state of which a prospective witness is a national,

(a) a court or agency in the United States may require the person to whom the order is directed to make a good faith effort to secure permission from the foreign authorities to make the information available;

(b) a court or agency should not ordinarily impose sanctions of contempt, dismissal, or default on a party that has failed to comply with the order for production, except in cases of deliberate concealment or removal of information or of failure to make a good faith effort in accordance with paragraph (a);

(c) a court or agency may, in appropriate cases, make findings of fact adverse to a party that has failed to comply with the order for production, even if that party has made a good faith effort to secure permission from the foreign authorities to make the information available and that effort has been unsuccessful.

Clearly, the Third Restatement embraces *Societe Internationale*'s distinction between a court's decision to order production of evidence covered by a foreign blocking statute, on the one hand, and its decision to impose sanctions upon a party for not obeying such an order, on the other. One reason for bifurcating the analysis is to preserve the possibility of pressuring parties to secure waivers from blocking legislation by foreign governments or by private parties in a position to issue a waiver. A threat of sanctions may in fact be enough to cause production or to secure waivers permitting disclosure by third parties (such as banks), as occurred in *SEC v. Banca della Svizzera Italiana* (S.D.N.Y.1981).

In another example, a grand jury investigating Marc Rich International AG (a Swiss company doing business in the US) for tax evasion issued a subpoena, which the target company moved to quash on grounds of lack of personal jurisdiction and Swiss secrecy (Article 273 of the Penal Code). The court issued the order, relying on Section 40 of the Second Restatement and eventually held the company in civil contempt, imposing fines that were upheld in *Matter of Marc Rich & Co. AG* (2d Cir.

1983). After paying the fine that had accrued, Rich and his associates fled the US and attempted to remove large quantities of documents from the jurisdiction. Although the Swiss government interposed Article 273 of the Swiss Penal Code to order non-production, the grand jury nevertheless handed down an indictment against the company, its successors and individuals (including Marc Rich) for tax fraud, wire and mail fraud, and racketeering. The court refused to lift the contempt order and a plea bargain agreement was eventually reached. *In re Marc Rich & Co., A.G.* (2d Cir.1984).

Like *Societe Internationale*, Section 442(1) admonishes courts to exercise some restraint in ordering extraterritorial discovery. Interestingly, it does so irrespective of the presence or absence of blocking legislation in the foreign state. At the same time, it seems clear from the factors mentioned in subparagraph (c) that the presence of such legislation may well make a difference in a court's disposition to order extraterritorial production. More generally, the Restatement appears to take a somewhat broader range of factors into account in the decision to order extraterritorial production than *Societe Internationale* had enumerated, including the specificity of the request and the availability of alternate sources. Significantly, among these factors is one that could require the court to weigh and compare national interests, *viz.* "the extent to which noncompliance with the request would undermine important interests of the United States, or compliance with the request would undermine important interests of the state where the information is located." A court intent on avoiding a comparison of national interests could interpret Section 442(1)(c) as calling, not for a comparative weighting of the interests, but rather a comparison of the "impairment" to those interests. To do the latter, a court would compare the detriment to the forum's interest in non-production of the evidence with the detriment to the other state's interest in its production.

Whatever its ambiguities, Section 442 has been highly influential in the case law on the issuance of production orders in the face of foreign blocking legislation. In *Reinsurance Co. of Am., Inc. v. Administratia Asigurarilor de Stat* (7th Cir.1990), the Court of Appeals upheld the district court's refusal to order production in light of a Rumanian secrecy law, describing that result as consistent with the Third Restatement. Because of the strength of the Rumanian government's interest, the Court did not even require that a good faith petition for waiver be sought. For a more nuanced application of Section 442, in the context of discovery against a foreign sovereign, see *McKesson Corp. v. Islamic Republic of Iran* (D.D.C.1991).

When it comes to the question of sanctions, the Restatement closely parallels the approach adopted by the Court in *Societe Internationale*. Notably, it invites a court to "make findings of fact adverse to a party that has failed to comply with the order for production, even if that party has made a good faith effort to secure permission from the foreign authorities," though only in "appropriate" cases. This means that a non-producing party may conceivably suffer detriment—even beyond its inability to meet its burden of proof on a claim or defense—even though it is entirely innocent in the matter.

PRODUCTION OF EVIDENCE FOR USE IN FOREIGN JUDICIAL PROCEEDINGS

As noted, the absence of blocking legislation in the US simplifies the production of evidence in the US for use in foreign judicial proceedings. So too does the general absence of any serious restrictions on the gathering of evidence on US territory, whether the forum in which it will be used is domestic or foreign. But production is also facilitated, at least in federal courts, by the existence of legislation expressly authorizing courts to lend their assistance to that production. This legislation is to be found at 28 U.S.C.A. sec. 1782, a provision broadly parallel to 28 U.S.C.A. sec. 1696, examined above in the context of US judicial assistance in the service of documents, and likewise adopted in 1964 on the recommendation of a Commission on International Rules of Judicial Procedure created by Congress in 1958. (Section 1781 permits such requests to be transmitted via a letter of request through the Department of State.)

Section 1782, like Section 1696, is circumscribed. It provides that "[t]he district court of the district in which a person resides or is found may order him to give his testimony or statement or to produce a document or other thing for use in a proceeding in a foreign or international tribunal." Under Section 1782, a production order may be requested either by the foreign court or by "any interested person." The courts have ruled that a foreign proceeding need not yet actually have been instituted; it suffices that an action is contemplated. Predictably, the issue has arisen whether the body in support of whose proceedings a Section 1782 request is made is in fact "a foreign or international tribunal." The prevailing view is that international arbitral tribunals do not constitute courts or tribunals within the meaning of Section 1782, and that Section 1782 assistance is therefore unavailable in aid of proceedings in such a forum. *Republic of Kazakhstan v. Biedermann Int'l* (5th Cir.1999); *National Broadcasting Co. v. Bear Stearns & Co.* (2d Cir.1999).

Ultimately, the assistance authorized by Section 1782, like that authorized by Section 1696, is discretionary, and district court decisions on the matter will therefore be reviewed by a deferential abuse of discretion standard. A factor sure to be taken into account is the burden that compliance with a request would impose upon the requested court. Also relevant will be the potential duplicativeness of the evidence or its more convenient availability elsewhere. In addition, the US court may try to discern how helpful the evidence will be, including to the foreign court itself, in the conduct of the litigation.

A question has arisen as to the weight to be given to the identity of the requester. It would seem that, all else being equal, requests coming directly from foreign courts would get a better reception than requests from "interested" persons, notably the litigants themselves. A leading case is *In re Application of Euromepa SA* (2d Cir.1995). There, the district court had denied a private party request for discovery assistance under Section 1782 in aid of French commercial litigation, on the ground, among others, that granting the request would have the effect of thwarting the French judicial policy of placing evidence-gathering in the hands of the courts rather than the parties and would amount to an interference with the French system. The Second Circuit reversed and remanded on the ground that the lower court had unduly restricted its scope of discretion, cautioning against embarking on an inquiry into foreign law or into the attitudes of the foreign legal system, contrary to Section 1782's purposes. The Court emphasized that the French court had ultimate authority over what evidence could be admitted and what weight it deserved, and that the district court could in any event, under Section 1782 and Rule 26, in the interest of fairness or efficiency, impose reasonable limitations on any discovery it might order. Only in the presence of authoritative proof that a foreign tribunal would reject evidence obtained with the aid of Section 1782, embodied in a foreign country's legislative, executive or judicial declarations that specifically address the use of evidence gathered under foreign procedures, should cooperation be withheld. The court referred to Section 1782's "twin" objectives of efficiently assisting participation in overseas litigation and encouraging foreign courts to follow our example.

Other courts have similarly rejected a number of other more or less categorical reasons for denying a request under Section 1782, including that (a) the country in aid of whose proceedings the request was made does not offer comparable assistance (i.e. lack of reciprocity), (b) the interested party making the request did not first seek the assistance of the foreign court in obtaining the evidence (i.e. failure to exhaust local remedies), and (c) the evidence sought would not be admissible in the foreign court. See *In re Malev Hungarian Airlines v. United Technologies Int'l Inc.* (2d Cir.1992); *John Deere Ltd. v. Sperry Corp.* (3d Cir.1985); *In re Letters of Request from Supreme Court of Hong Kong* (S.D.N.Y.1993). *A fortiori*, courts have declined to examine whether, under foreign law, the foreign court or tribunal had jurisdiction, whether subject matter or personal, in the case before it. A reciprocity requirement, in particular, has been ruled out on the strength of legislative history suggesting that the US sought to encourage international judicial cooperation and was willing to lead the way even without its cooperation being reciprocated.

Perhaps the most controversial basis for denying a request is that the material sought to be discovered in the US would not be "discoverable" in the foreign forum. Some courts have made discoverability of the evidence abroad a prerequisite for ordering its production under Section 1782 (see *In re Application of Asta Medica, S.A.* (1st Cir.1992)), on the theory that parties could otherwise circumvent the foreign state's discovery limitations. But a majority of courts decline to treat this as anything more than "just another factor" in the overall analysis (see *In re Bayer* (3d Cir.1998), *In re Application of Aldunate* (2d Cir.1993)), at least unless and until the undiscoverability of the evidence in the foreign court is clear and based on authoritative proof. One court has suggested that a showing of discoverability might be required where the request under section 1782 emanates from a private "interested party," but not otherwise. *In re Letter Rogatory from First Court of First Instance in Civil Matters, Caracas* (5th Cir.1995).

A foreign court could conceivably enjoin a party before it from seeking assistance from a US court under Section 1782. This in fact occurred in the UK courts, but the House of Lords reversed in *South Carolina Insur. Co. v. Assurantie Maatschappij "De Zeven Provincien" NV* (H.L.1986), on the ground that nothing in resort to Section 1782 offended British public policy or amounted to unconscionability. If such an injunction were to be issued and upheld, however, the "requested" US court would presumably respect that order.

THE HAGUE EVIDENCE CONVENTION

Generally speaking, courts are free not to comply with production requests emanating from another country's courts or litigants. They may be especially reluctant to comply when they find the underlying cause of action, or its seemingly extraterritorial application, objectionable. In order for cooperation in the transnational production of evidence to become mandatory (and for a mutually agreeable means of ordering production to emerge), an international agreement of some sort is once again needed. The 1970 Hague Convention on the Taking of Evidence Abroad in Civil and Commercial Matters, 23 UST 2555, 847 UNTS 231, seeks to achieve this. Under the Convention, the contracting States agree to receive and to enforce production requests duly submitted by other contracting States. Predictably, requests under the Convention must satisfy certain procedural and presentation requirements.

Scope of the Evidence Convention

The Convention is confined to "civil or commercial matters," producing difficulties of interpretation not unlike those that have arisen under the Service Convention. (These include whether tax and administrative law litigation may be regarded as "civil or commercial," or are more properly considered as "public" and outside the Convention's scope.) The Convention apparently contemplates only requests by "judicial," as opposed to "administrative," authorities. On one matter of scope, the Convention, in Article 1, is clear. It applies not only to requests in relation to judicial proceedings that have been "commenced" but also to those that are merely "contemplated."

As far as procedures are concerned, only Chapter 1 of the Convention—dealing with "letters of request" (essentially letters rogatory)—is mandatory upon signatory states, in the sense that they may not derogate from its obligations. For performance, the Evidence Convention (art. 2), not unlike the Service Convention, relies on a "Central Authority" mechanism; a requesting court is to convey its request directly to the relevant foreign Central Authority, rather than to any other authority of the requested State, but the Central Authority may be relied upon to direct the request to the appropriate court within the country.

A related advantage of the Convention has to do with procedures. In the absence of a treaty, a court that responds favorably to a letter of request will likely be inclined to follow its own procedures, particularly as regards the examination of witnesses and the preparation of a record. More specifically, US requests, even if acted upon favorably, may not elicit verbatim transcripts, examination and cross-examination by counsel, or even testimony under oath. The Evidence Convention improves this situation somewhat. While taking as a point of departure the principle that the requested State will ordinarily apply "its own law as to the methods and procedures to be followed," Article 9 requires States to follow special procedural requests made in a letter of request, subject only to two conditions: that the requested procedure not be "incompatible" with the local law and that compliance by the requested court be neither impossible nor impracticable. The

Convention also lays down ground rules on such important questions as the available privileges, stipulating (art. 11) that a witness may invoke not only the privileges provided for by local law, but also those provided for by the law of the requesting state, where compliance with them has been specifically requested.

As noted, the Convention's prime advantage is that it transforms a voluntary act of cooperation into an international obligation, albeit a conditional one. The Convention uses the term "shall" rather than "may," and requires that letters of request be executed "expeditiously" (art. 9). But there is more. Contracting States are also obligated under Article 10 of the Convention to offer appropriate measures of compulsion in support of a letter of request, at a minimum making available the same coercive measures that would ordinarily be made available in a comparable domestic case. As for formal defects in the request (such as failures of translation or required information), while a Central Authority is permitted to decline execution on those grounds (art. 5), it must promptly notify the requesting state of the problem.

The Convention (art. 12) recognizes only two grounds for refusing to comply with a procedurally proper request. One is that the request seeks performance of a non-judicial function. The other is that the requested state regards compliance with the request as prejudicial to its "sovereignty or security"—terms that have received little by way of interpretation in practice. (A possible exception is *Rio Tinto Zinc Corp. v. Westinghouse Elec. Corp.* (1978), where certain members of the House of Lords found that UK sovereignty or security would be jeopardized by assisting a US antitrust action, considered to be "public" in nature as well as in conflict with UK antitrust policy.) In an effort to keep the exception within bounds, Article 12 declares that sovereignty or security may not be deemed to be prejudiced for these purposes merely because the requested state does not recognize a cause of action comparable to the one that gave rise to the request or because the requested state asserts "exclusive" subject matter jurisdiction over the underlying claim.

Among the most contentious provisions of the Convention is Article 23, which was proposed by the UK, and which permits signatory states to declare that they will not execute letters of request "issued for the purpose of obtaining pretrial discovery of documents as known in Common Law countries." The great majority of States (but not the US) have made such a declaration, each one determining for itself in the text of its declaration what it considers as constituting pretrial discovery for these purposes. Some declarations offer no definition, but those that do tend to consider requests for unspecified documents or categories of documents lacking a direct or precise link with the subject matter of the litigation to be requests for pretrial discovery. Such is, in part, the import of the House of Lords decision in *In re Asbestos Insurance* (H.L.

1985), interpreting the UK legislation implementing the Convention and the UK's discovery declaration. Inclusion of Article 23, and the filing of declarations by so many States, reflects suspicion of "fishing expeditions" on the part of US lawyers. However, Article 23 applies to document production only, and not to testimonial evidence. Thus, in a well-known case, the German Ministry of Justice refused to order documentary production pursuant to the Convention, even while ordering personal testimony on the same subject. The orders were upheld by the German courts. *Corning Glassworks v. International Tel. & Telegraph Corp.* (1981).

The Convention establishes two additional methods of evidence-gathering abroad (described below), but these are subject to three important reservations. First, signatory states are permitted to opt out of both of these methods by a declaration to that effect, or through an agreement to that effect between two or more contracting states. Second, the Convention does not require States to make means of compulsion available in connection with these methods. Third, both methods are subject to various limitations. The two additional methods echo two of the alternative methods of evidence-taking permitted by Rule 28(b) (see page 280 *supra*).

The first such alternative entails the taking of testimony by diplomatic officers or consular agents. Under Article 15, consuls may take testimony from nationals of their home state. However, a consul may only take their testimony under the Convention for purposes of actions in the courts of his or her home state, and those actions must be commenced and not merely contemplated. States are also free to require consuls to obtain general permission from the local authorities. Under Article 16, consuls may also take evidence from nationals of the state to which they are accredited, or from nationals of third states, but only under somewhat more restrictive conditions. Once again, the actions in connection with which evidence is taken must actually have been commenced in the courts of the consul's home state. However, the permission that is required before the consul proceeds to take evidence may only be given on a case by case basis, unless the host state has taken the affirmative step of filing a declaration granting general authority.

The second alternative (art. 17) entails the taking of evidence by "commissioners," i.e., persons specifically appointed for this purpose by a court of the requesting state. Similar restrictions apply as to evidence-gathering by consuls. Thus, evidence may only be taken for use in proceedings actually commenced in a signatory state court. Also, as under Article 16, prior approval from the host state on an individual case basis is required, unless that state has by declaration granted general authority to that effect.

Both consuls and commissioners may administer oaths and take any form of evidence not incompatible with the law of the host state or with the terms of the permission granted. Persons giving evidence under Articles 15 through 17 may invoke the same privileges and immunities as apply in connection with letters of request (art. 11) and must, except in the case of nationals of the requesting state, be requested to appear by a notice in the language of the host state. In any event, the request to appear must inform persons of their entitlement to legal representation and of their right not to appear. Although, as noted, States are not required to make coercive means available in support of evidence-gathering by consuls or commissioners, Article 18 provides that states may, by declaration, authorize consuls and commissioners to seek orders from local authorities compelling the giving of evidence.

Exclusivity of the Convention

While the Supreme Court has interpreted the Hague Service Convention as the exclusive vehicle for making service abroad in cases within its scope of application (see page 276 *supra*), and in that sense as mandatory, it has ruled that the Hague Evidence Convention is not the exclusive vehicle for seeking the production of evidence abroad in cases falling within its scope. A divided Court held in *Societe Nationale Industrielle Aerospatiale v. U.S. District Court for the So. Dist. of Iowa* (S.Ct.1987), that the text of the Convention, available legislative history, and policy considerations required that the Convention not be understood as mandating its use, to the exclusion of other available means, in situations covered by the Convention. In other words, the Convention's methods are merely among the options for discovery abroad to which a party to US litigation may have recourse. The majority also rejected the position, that some lower courts had adopted, namely that the Convention should nevertheless be interpreted as requiring its own "prior use" before resort to discovery under the usual methods provided by the Federal Rules of Civil Procedure.

As for considerations of international comity, the majority ruled that their effect on the decision whether or not to require resort (or prior resort) to the Convention is to be determined strictly on the basis of an individualized case-by-case analysis, and not according to any general preference for Convention methods. In deciding whether to require prior resort to the Convention, a court is to make an *ad hoc*, three-prong, inquiry into (1) the nature of the discovery sought, (2) the relevant sovereign interests, and (3) the likelihood that Convention procedures would be effective. The burden of proof appears to lie with the party asserting that the Convention must be used. *In re Perrier Bottled Water Litig.* (D.Conn.1991); *Hudson v. Hermann Pfauter GmbH & Co.* (N.D.N.Y.1987). At the same time, the majority urged courts to exercise "special vigilance" to protect foreign litigants from unnecessary or unduly burdensome discovery by minimizing its cost and intrusiveness and, more generally, by avoiding "discovery abuse." And indeed, even while not requiring compliance with the Convention, post-*Aerospatiale* decisions have shown a willingness to entertain requests that sweeping demands for production be narrowed. See, e.g., *In re Vitamins Antitrust Litig.* (D.D.C.2000); *Great Lakes Dredge & Dock Co. v. Harnischfeger Corp.* (N.D.Ill.

1990); *Benton Graphics v. Uddeholm Corp.* (D.N.J. 1987).

A minority of the Court (in an opinion by Justice Blackmun, concurring in part and dissenting in part) agreed that the Convention did not as such make resort to it mandatory, even as a first resort. However, it took the position that principles of international comity required that, as a general rule, litigants first exploit the opportunities for production under the Convention before proceeding by any other means, including those provided for under the Federal Rules.

The position of the majority in *Aerospatiale*, which has been harshly criticized in foreign government circles as well as in academic writing, both domestic and foreign, reflects deep concern that, with the prevalence of Article 23 declarations, interpreting the Convention as exclusive could deprive litigants in US court, and transnational litigation in the US more generally, of the advantages of ample pretrial discovery. Lower courts have struggled with the individualized comity analysis that *Aerospatiale* invites them to conduct, and the decisions are difficult to reconcile, even on the question of how the burden of proof on the "prior resort" question should be allocated. On the "merits," so to speak, courts have generally shown reluctance to require prior resort to the Convention, particularly where discovery is sought from a party subject to the court's jurisdiction. But this is by no means invariable. Some courts have required prior resort to the Convention (and in so doing sometime expressed a preference for justice Blackmun's position). They are most likely to do so where the addressee is a non-party to the litigation.

The Court's interpretation of the Hague Evidence Convention as non-exclusive plainly binds state as well as federal courts. It is less clear whether the Court's position on international comity, which calls for a case-by-case determination whether litigants should be required to make prior use of the Convention's mechanisms, is similarly binding on state as well as federal courts. By analogy to the act of state doctrine, which (as noted, *supra* page 168) is widely regarded as expressing a substantive federal common law norm, the comity-fueled deference owed to the Convention in the state courts may be subject to the Court's approach in *Aerospatiale.*

Suppose the foreign state where evidence is located is not a Convention state? Assuming production seems called for, courts still face the question of how to order such production, as between use of the Federal Rules and the means, if any, specifically provided for by the law of the foreign state. Courts have assumed that general comity analysis should govern that decision. If they find a conflict between the two sets of procedural norms, they commonly purport to balance the US and foreign state's interests. In *McKesson Corp. v. Islamic Republic of Iran* (D.D.C.1999), for example, the court ordered the government of Iran to permit plaintiff's expert to inspect a government dairy facility in Iran, produce witnesses for deposition, and answer interrogatories.

CHAPTER NINE

TRANSNATIONAL PROVISIONAL RELIEF

Just as transnational litigation may occasion a need for cross-border service and cross-border evidence-gathering, so it may occasion a need for transnational provisional relief. The same purposes that are served by provisional relief in domestic litigation (e.g. ensuring the adequacy of an eventual judgment, preserving the *status quo* pending the litigation) may be served by provisional relief in transnational cases. The difficulty that arises of course is that, in order for relief in transnational cases to be adequate, it may have to exert extraterritorial effects, which may in turn render it objectionable to the affected foreign States. Indeed the very prospect of objections may cause US courts to decline to order transnational provisional relief in the first place, even in situations in which, in entirely domestic cases, they ordinarily would.

Conversely, US courts should expect that from time to time foreign courts, in the context of the transnational litigation before them, will order measures of provisional relief having consequences of some sort in the US. These may be most pronounced when a US court is called upon actually to "enforce" a measure of provisional relief that a foreign court has ordered. Extraterritorial measures may elicit a range of responses in the courts of this country.

ORDERING "EXTRATERRITORIAL" PROVISIONAL RELIEF

US courts in domestic litigation regularly entertain, and grant, applications for provisional relief when equitable circumstances so suggest. There may be a need to protect persons or property from irreparable harm while litigation on the merits is pending, and there may be other reasons to preserve the status quo in the period before judgment is rendered. More specifically, there may be a need to secure a probable judgment. The prime instruments are preliminary injunctions and attachments.

As for preliminary injunctions, the Federal Rules do not prescribe a standard for their issuance. While Rule 65 addresses requirements of notice, duration, form and security, it leaves the question of whether and when a preliminary injunction should issue to the discretion of the courts under traditional equity principles. By way of a state law example, the New York statute (CPLR sec. 6001) expressly provides for provisional relief in the form of attachment, injunction, receivership and notice of pendency.

As for attachments, Rule 64 of the Federal Rules authorizes a federal court to issue such an order if the law of the state where the court sits permits it. In New York (CPLR, sec. 6201), for example, an applicant for an attachment must demonstrate an entitlement, at least in part, to a money judgment against one or more defendant, and also show one of several circumstances, including (a) that the defendant is a non-domiciliary and non-resident, or a foreign corporation not qualified to do business in the state, or (b) that the defendant will assign or remove property from the state with intent to defraud creditors or frustrate the enforcement of an eventual judgment in plaintiff's favor. Generally, then, an applicant must show that it has a good chance of prevailing on the merits and that there is a likelihood that the defendant will dispose of its assets before the eventual judgment can be executed.

In this chapter, we assume that the same general considerations that would in principle justify an order of provisional relief in domestic cases before US courts will be deemed to justify it in transnational cases. We therefore focus on the extent to which the transnational character of the case or of the relief sought might make a difference.

US practice in this area has undoubtedly been influenced by the practice of UK courts, notably the so-called "*Mareva* injunction," whose name derives from the 1975 Court of Appeal decision in *Mareva Compania Naviera SA v. Int'l Bulk Carriers SA* (Ct.App.1975). A *Mareva* injunction is an order restraining a party from removing or disposing of assets found within the jurisdiction, regardless of whether those assets relate to the underlying cause of action. Typically, no notice to the opposing party is required and the injunction will be issued on an *ex parte* basis. The practice of issuing *Mareva* injunctions has been extended so as even to reach assets outside the jurisdiction, provided their owner is otherwise subject to the jurisdiction of the court. *Babanaft Int'l Co. SA v. Bassatne* (Ct.App.1988); *Republic of Haiti v. Duvalier* (Ct.App.1988).

The UK Court of Appeal explored the "extraterritorial" application of *Mareva* injunctions in greater depth in the case of *Derby & Co. Ltd. v. Weldon (I)* (Ct.App.1988). While conceding that a world-wide injunction (and an ancillary order to disclose the location of world-wide assets) is a drastic and potentially oppressive remedy to be granted only in exceptional circumstances, it found such circumstances to be present in that case. These included the fact that the defendants' assets in the UK were wholly insufficient to satisfy an eventual judgment and that the defendants were very likely to dispose of their foreign assets in anticipation of an adverse judgment.

Republic of the Philippines v. Marcos (9th Cir. 1988), is a high-profile example drawn from US practice. This was a suit by the Republic of the Philippines against its former president, his wife and others under RICO and pendent state law claims, arising out of the defendants' alleged investment in the US of fraudulently obtained moneys. The plaintiff sought and was granted a preliminary injunction barring the defendants from disposing of any assets, except as needed to pay their attorneys' fees and meet their normal living expenses. The order targeted assets located not only in the US, but also in the UK and Switzerland. The Court of Appeals sustained the district court's order in view of the likelihood of success on the merits and the risk of irreparable injury. To defeat the argument that the order was impermissibly extraterritorial, the court underscored that the defendants were before the court and that the injunction operated entirely *in personam*, rather than against the overseas assets *in rem*. The Court did not invoke any particular provision of federal law, including the Federal Rules, but rather its inherent equitable power to issue provisional remedies ancillary to its authority to provide final equitable relief.

The *Marcos* case was not unprecedented. In *United States v. First Nat'l City Bank* (S.Ct.1965), an action by the US against a Uruguyan corporation for income taxes owed, the Court had sustained a federal court order enjoining a New York bank from transferring any assets of the corporation held in the bank's Montevideo branch. The Court deemed the branch to be within the court's jurisdiction due to the close control exercised over it by the bank's New York office. Courts in subsequent cases have restricted a party's free use of overseas assets, where the circumstances are found to justify that remedy. *Reebok Int'l, Ltd. v. Marnatech Enterp.*, Inc. (9th Cir.1992); *SEC v. International Swiss Invs. Corp.* (9th Cir.1990); *In re Feit & Drexler, Inc.* (2d Cir.1985).

This growing practice has recently been curtailed, at least in the federal courts, by the Supreme Court's ruling in *Grupo Mexicano de Desarrollo, S.A. v. Alliance Bond Fund* (S.Ct.1999), holding that a district court lacks authority under Rule 65 to issue a preliminary injunction restraining a party from disposing of assets in which the plaintiff has no legal interest. There, upon default by a Mexican holding company in interest payments due, the plaintiff investment fund accelerated payment of the debt and sued for the notes' principal amount. In conjunction with that suit, the plaintiff, alleging that the company was on the brink of insolvency, sought a preliminary injunction restraining it from transferring assets to its Mexican creditors. When the case reached the Supreme Court, a majority ruled that the Judiciary Act of 1789 only conferred on federal courts the equity jurisdiction exercised by the English Court of Chancery at the time of American independence (the *Mareva* injunction only having been established in 1975). According to the traditional English practice, only a creditor who had already obtained a judgment establishing a debt could obtain such relief; otherwise the creditor had no interest cognizable in law or in equity in the debtor's property or in his or her free use of it. The majority ruled that the "new rule could radically alter the balance between debtor's and creditor's rights which has been developed over centuries." The dissenters objected to this "unjustifiably static conception of equity jurisdiction." Some state courts, in determining the availability of an injunctive remedy under these circumstances have followed the majority's view in *Grupo Mexicano*. See e.g., *Credit Agricole Indosuez v. Rossiyskiy Kredit Bank* (N.Y.2000).

In the past, some courts have exercised their injunctive powers to order a party before the court to "repatriate" foreign assets, thereby enabling their attachment. See. e.g., *Inter-Regional Financial Group, Inc. v. Hashemi* (2d Cir.1977). The availability of such a remedy in federal court and certain state courts after *Grupo Mexicano* may be severely curtailed.

Presumably, the availability of local attachments under Rule 64 will continue to depend on state law.

PROVISIONAL RELIEF IN AID OF ENFORCING A FOREIGN JUDGMENT

In its decision in *Shaffer v. Heitner*, *supra* page 51, the Supreme Court suggested that "a State in which property is located should have jurisdiction to attach that property, by use of proper procedures, as security for a judgment being sought in a forum where the litigation can be maintained consistently with [the requirements of due process]." On occasion, US courts have indeed shown a willingness to exercise attachment jurisdiction in aid of execution of a future foreign judgment at the request of party to the foreign proceeding, in much the same way as they do in aid of the eventual execution of a sister-state judgment. See, e.g., *Cameco Indus., Inc. v. Mayatrac, S.A.* (D.Md.1992); *Barclays Bank, S.A. v. Tsakos* (D.C.App.1988).

While the practice of issuing attachment orders over local property to help secure an eventual foreign court judgment may not be particularly well-developed in the US, there appears to be no formal bar to doing so. There is certainly no bar as between states of the European Union, whose Regulation 44/2001 (art. 31) on jurisdiction and judgments, building upon the prior Brussels Convention (art. 24) on that subject, expressly provides that a court lacking jurisdiction to decide the merits of a case may nevertheless entertain a request for provisional relief pending a decision on the merits by a competent court in another EU Member State. Needless to emphasize, the fact that there is authority to afford relief of this sort does not mean that this authority will be exercised in any given case. As with provisional relief generally, the decision is considered to be a highly discretionary one.

The likelihood of enforcement in the US may be enhanced if the foreign court has itself awarded provisional relief, and the party benefitting from it then, so to speak, seeks "enforcement" of the order in the US. This is not unimaginable since foreign courts, like US courts, do award provisional relief in appropriate circumstances in domestic and transnational litigation alike. When a litigant before a foreign court seeks to have such an order of provisional relief enforced in the US, we find ourselves very close to the situation examined in the next chapter, *viz.* efforts by a party prevailing in overseas litigation to have the resulting judgment enforced in the US. The principal difference—which flows from the very nature of provisional relief—is that the order does not reflect a final judgment on the merits (as in the standard enforcement of judgments situation), but rather an interim measure that the foreign court has seen fit, for reasons of justice or utility, to order during the pendency of the litigation. In fact, the instances in which foreign orders of provisional relief are sought to be enforced as such in the US are remarkably few. If they are ordered, there remains a serious question as to whether a US will be willing to enforce them.

Sometimes it is difficult even to determine whether a party to foreign litigation is seeking enforcement of a foreign order of provisional relief or rather a new order "extending" the scope of the previous one. In *Pilkington Bros. PLC v. AFG Indus. Inc.* (D.Del.1984), a UK company that had won an *ex parte* interim injunction against a US company from a UK court then sought parallel provisional relief from a US court. Characterizing the request as seeking enforcement of the UK injunction in the US, the court nevertheless declined the request, chiefly on the ground that the UK order was purely interlocutory and had not been based on a full consideration of the merits of the underlying dispute, but also because of the awkwardness of coordinating parallel orders of two courts over time. To the same effect, see *Cliffs–Neddrill Turnkey Int'l–*

Oranjestad v. M/T Rich Duke (D.Del.1990). Other courts have been much more hospitable to interlocutory foreign court orders. See, e.g., *Nahar v. Nahar* (Fla.Dist.Ct.App.1995), where a Florida court enforced an Aruban court order requiring a decedent's Florida bank accounts to be transferred to Aruba for disposition in accordance with Dutch law. The court declined to distinguish sharply, for enforcement purposes, between final and interlocutory orders of foreign courts.

Among the *Pilkington* court's stated reasons for declining to issue the requested injunction was that doing so might be seen as intruding in a matter before the UK courts in violation of principles of international comity. To the extent that comity is in issue, it may be reasonable to assume that the outcome of a request could vary according to whether it emanates from a litigant in a foreign court or from the foreign court itself. In *de Pacanins v. Pacanins* (Fla.App.1995), a Florida appellate court reversed a trial court's ruling denying a request from a Venezuelan court to freeze funds in Florida belonging to the Venezuelan defendant, pending the outcome of the main action. It ruled that compelling public policy considerations might require a relaxation of the general rule against enforcing non-final orders of foreign courts. The same court had previously taken such a step. *Cardenas v. Solis* (Fla.App. 1990).

In bankruptcy cases, federal law specifically authorizes preliminary relief in aid of foreign judicial proceedings. 11 U.S.C.A. sec. 304 permits a foreign trustee or other representative in bankruptcy to commence an ancillary action in US court so as to ensure that domestic US creditors do not pursue or execute on US assets belonging to the bankrupt entity, pending the outcome of the foreign proceeding. Like US bankruptcy law (11 U.S.C.A. sec. 362), foreign bankruptcy legislation commonly provides, upon filing of the case, for an automatic stay of creditor collection actions world-wide. US courts' hospitality to extraterritorial stay orders by foreign tribunals has surely been enhanced by considerations of reciprocity. See *In re Artimm S.r.l.* (Bkrtcy.C.D.Cal.2002), enforcing an Italian court's order staying collection efforts in US state court by a creditor against the US property of a bankrupt Italian corporation. US courts commonly entertain, and grant, applications for stay of proceedings, both in bankruptcy and non-bankruptcy (e.g. contract) cases alike, pending foreign bankruptcy proceedings. See, e.g., *Philadelphia Gear Corp. v. Philadelphia Gear de Mexico, S.A.* (3d Cir.1994); *Maxwell Communic. Corp. p.l.c. v. Societe Generale* (2d Cir. 1996). Section 304, which contemplates not only stays but also turnover of property to a foreign representative or other appropriate relief, does not, however, make the issuance of ancillary stays mandatory. According to Section 304(c):

> In determining whether to grant relief ... the court shall be guided by what will best assure an economical and expeditious administration of [a bankrupt's] estate, consistent with:

(1) just treatment of all holders of claims against or interests in such estate;

(2) protection of claim holders in the United States against prejudice and inconvenience in ... such foreign proceedings;

(3) prevention of preferential or fraudulent dispositions of property ...;

(4) distribution of proceeds ... substantially in accordance with the order prescribed [by US law];

(5) comity; and

(6) if appropriate, the provisions of an opportunity for a fresh start for the individual that such foreign proceeding concerns.

US courts are much more commonly asked to issue attachment orders or preliminary injunctive relief in aid of the effectiveness of an eventual international arbitral award, a matter treated more fully in Chapter 11. Most courts do not consider entertaining such requests to be inconsistent with the agreement to arbitrate. See, e.g., *PMS Distrib. Co., Inc. v. Huber & Suhner, A.G.* (9th Cir.1988). But some courts have refused to entertain applications for provisional relief (notably pre-award attachments) when the situs of arbitration is elsewhere, if the arbitration is subject to the New York Convention on the Recognition and Enforcement of Foreign Arbitral Awards; they rely upon the language of the Convention (art. II(3)) requiring courts to "refer" the parties to arbitration. See *I.T.A.D. Assocs. v. Podar Bros.* (4th Cir.1981); *McCreary*

Tire & Rubber Co. v. CEAT S.p.A. (3d Cir.1974); *Metropolitan World Tanker Corp. v. P.N. Pertambangan* (S.D.N.Y.1975). Other courts do not read that provision as barring actions for preliminary relief, and have accordingly entertained and sometimes granted such applications. *Filanto v. Chilewich Int'l Corp.* (S.D.N.Y.1992); *Carolina Power and Light Co. v. Uranex* (N.D.Cal.1977). However, even a court that considers itself authorized to afford such relief may decline to award it where the parties had adopted arbitral rules that expressly permit the arbitral tribunal to order preliminary relief or to apply to a local court for relief of that sort. See, e.g., *Simula, Inc. v. Autoliv, Inc.* (9th Cir.1999); *China Nat'l Metal Prods. Import/Export Co. v. Apex Digital, Inc.* (C.D.Cal.2001).

Parties to arbitration may, in addition, fear that by seeking provisional relief in court prior to (and possibly even pending) arbitration, they may be deemed to have waived their right to arbitrate. They can be reassured. All circuits have refused to hold that such an application constitutes a waiver. See, e.g., *Sauer–Getriebe KG v. White Hydrauics, Inc.* (7th Cir.1983).

CHAPTER TEN

RECOGNITION AND ENFORCEMENT OF FOREIGN JUDGMENTS

If transnational litigation has culminated in a final judgment of a foreign court, the prevailing party may very likely seek to have that judgment either recognized or enforced abroad, including in a US forum. Conversely, a US judgment may turn out to be enforceable only abroad or to require recognition there. This is why a party introducing transnational litigation in any court needs, as earlier chapters have stressed, to anticipate the impact of their various procedural decisions on the prospects of the resulting judgment receiving recognition or enforcement abroad.

It is important at the outset to appreciate in this regard the distinction between "recognition" and "enforcement." Starting with the latter, enforcement denotes in effect providing in the judgment-enforcing forum (which we shall, for short, call F2) the very relief that the judgment in the judgment-rendering forum (F1, for short) has awarded. By contrast, recognition simply means treating the foreign judgment as conclusive, i.e. not open to relitigation. The conclusiveness of a foreign judgment arises most squarely when, for example, the plaintiff in F2 seeks to prosecute a cause of action that that party has already prosecuted to an unsuccessful conclusion in F1, or when the defendant in F1, having lost, brings a "mirror-image" action for relief in F2. In truth, recognition and enforcement have just about the same meaning in the transnational context as they enjoy in the sister-state context under the Full Faith and Credit Clause (US Constitution, Art. IV, sec. 1). For example, we may assume that when foreign judgments are recognized, in the sense of being given *res judicata* effect, they are conclusive not only as to those issues actually litigated in the first proceeding, but also as to those which might have been litigated there. *Laufer v. Westminster Brokers, Ltd.* (D.C.App.1987). (On the distinction between recognition and enforcement, see *Victrix S.S. Co., S.A. v. Salen Dry Cargo, A.B.* (S.D.N.Y.1986).)

A threshold question concerns the US jurisdictional basis for an action to enforce a foreign judgment. Clearly, the physical presence of the judgment debtor in the enforcement forum, or the existence of minimum contacts between the debtor and that forum, will suffice. But we must reckon with the possibility that the judgment debtor has no nexus with the enforcement forum other than the presence of assets unrelated to the underlying cause of action. The weight of opinion is that due process permits the exercise of *quasi-in-rem* jurisdiction in such a case, provided the action is one for enforcement only. See *Shaffer v. Heitner* (S.Ct.

1977) ("Once it has been determined by a court of competent jurisdiction that the defendant is a debtor of the plaintiff, there would seem to be no unfairness in allowing an action to realize on that debt in a State where the defendant has property, whether or not that State would have jurisdiction to determine the existence of the debt as an original matter"). See *also Pure Fishing, Inc. v. Silver Star Co., Ltd.* (N.D.Iowa 2002); *Biel v. Boehm* (N.Y.1978); *Lenchyshyn v. Pelko Elec., Inc.* (App. Div. 4th Dept. 2001); Restatement (Third) of Foreign Relations Law, sec. 481, comment h. But see *Jimenez v. Mobil Oil Co. de Venezuela* (S.D.N.Y. 1991), rejecting the exercise of enforcement jurisdiction over US property belonging to the parent corporation of a judgment debtor Venezuelan entity.

FOREIGN VS. SISTER–STATE JUDGMENTS

The above-mentioned clause of the US Constitution guarantees that "Full Faith and Credit shall be given in each State to the Public Acts, Records, and Judicial Proceedings of every other State." This has been understood to mean that the courts of one state in the US will in virtually all respects fully recognize and enforce the final judgments rendered by the courts of sister-states. Restatement (Second) of Conflict of Laws, sec. 93. The Restatement recognizes an exception only in rare circumstances, such as where recognition or enforcement would improperly interfere with important interests of the requested state, where the judgment was entered without adequate personal jurisdiction or an opportunity to be heard, or in the absence of subject matter jurisdiction. The Restatement properly suggests that the judgment also must be final (and probably also not modifiable), must not be too indefinite, and must not have been vacated or had its enforcement enjoined at the place of rendition. Judicial practice suggests a similar array of narrow grounds: lack of personal or subject matter jurisdiction (see *Adam v. Saenger* (S.Ct.1938)), lack of notice or opportunity to be heard (see *Mullane v. Central Hanover Bank & Trust Co.* (S.Ct.1950)), and fraud in obtaining the judgment (see Restatement (Second) of Judgments, sec. 70). Moreover, even these grounds may not be entertained if they were considered and rejected on the merits by the rendering court (see *American Surety Co. v. Baldwin* (S.Ct.1932); *Baldwin v. Iowa State Traveling Men's Ass'n* (S.Ct.1931)).

Case law of the Supreme Court even prevents courts of one state in the US from invoking forum public policy to decline to recognize or enforce sister-state judgments (see *Thomas v. General Motors Corp.* (S.Ct.1998); *Magnolia Petroleum Co. v. Hunt* (S.Ct.1943); *Fauntleroy v. Lum* (S.Ct.1908)). If the judgment of F1 is impeachable, say on grounds of fraud or lack of jurisdiction (personal or subject matter), it may basically only be impeached by way of appeal in the courts of F1 and not at the stage of recognition or enforcement in F2—the major exception being where the impeaching party excusably defaulted in F1.

Obviously, foreign country judgments lie outside the scope of the Full Faith and Credit Clause. The Constitution accordingly guarantees neither their recognition nor their enforcement, whether in state or federal court. If respect is to be owed, the source of that obligation must be found elsewhere.

Although Congress surely has legislative authority to regulate the recognition and enforcement of foreign judgments by both federal and state courts, it has never exercised that authority. Calls are still periodically made for the enactment of federal legislation on recognition and enforcement of foreign judgments that would be considering binding on state and federal courts, and the American Law Institute, as of this writing, is drafting legislation of this sort. Nor has the US become a party to any treaty on the subject although, again, the US is currently participating in negotiations for an international convention on the subject under the auspices of the Hague Conference on International Law. Occasionally, courts have interpreted the "national treatment" principle stated in most bilateral friendship, commerce and navigation treaties as requiring that judgments of the foreign state be received no less generously than sister-state judgments. See *Vagenas v. Continental Gin Co.* (11th Cir.1993).

Under *Erie*, federal courts sitting in diversity apply the principles of foreign country judgment recognition and enforcement adopted by the law of the state in which they sit. *Southwest Livestock & Trucking Co., Inc. v. Ramon* (5th Cir.1999). This body of state law may be common law or statutory, depending on the state. (A good number of state statutes have been based upon a uniform act, the Uniform Foreign Country Money–Judgments Recognition Act, discussed below.) As a result, the matter of recognition and enforcement of foreign judgments remains entrusted to state law.

Highly influential both in the drafting of state legislation and the development of state common law has been the Supreme Court's pre-*Erie* decision in the case of *Hilton v. Guyot* (S.Ct.), decided in 1895. In that judgment, the Court ruled that a party that prevailed in a final judgment in a foreign court was entitled, out of considerations of international comity, to have that judgment enforced in the US, provided:

> there has been opportunity for a full and fair trial abroad before a court of competent jurisdiction, conducting the trial upon regular proceedings, after due citation or voluntary appearance of the defendant, and under a system of jurisprudence likely to secure an impartial administration of justice between the citizens of its own country and those of other countries, and there is nothing to show either prejudice in the court, or in the system of laws under which it was sitting, or fraud in procuring the judgment, or any other

reason why the comity of this nation should not allow it full effect....

Ultimately the Court in *Hilton* denied enforcement of the French judgment, not on any of these grounds, but on the further ground of lack of reciprocity, since it was shown that a French court under analogous circumstances would have allowed the claim to be retried.

As noted, the *Hilton* formula continues to be influential, though the usual rationale is as much finality of litigation as it is international comity. While *Hilton*'s basic approach is widely followed, the reciprocity requirement that proved decisive in that case has been abandoned in many jurisdictions. This is reflected in the Restatement (Second) of Conflict of Laws, sec. 98, comment e, and in the Restatement (Third) of Foreign Relations Law, sec. 481, comment d. Since most recognition and enforcement cases arise either in federal court under diversity jurisdiction or in state court, the courts have not had much occasion to determine whether the federal common law rule expressed in *Hilton v. Guyot* might possibly still be directly applicable as substantive federal common law in federal question cases.

That having been said, it is not excluded that the federal courts might elaborate a federal substantive law on recognition or enforcement of foreign judgments, expressing a uniform federal policy on the matter, much as they appear to have done regarding other issues implicating foreign affairs, such as the act of state doctrine and the "dormant" foreign affairs doctrine, discussed in Chapter 5 *supra.* If the federal courts were to articulate strongly, and in those terms, a common law rule on such a uniquely federal matter, the rule could well be regarded as binding on state as well as federal courts under the supremacy principles. They have not done so.

THE UNIFORM FOREIGN COUNTRY MONEY-JUDGMENTS RECOGNITION ACT

The fact that federal courts follow the international recognition and enforcement policies of the state in which they sit makes it all the more desirable to introduce some consistency among those policies. To this end, in 1962 the National Conference of Commissioners on Uniform State Laws, together with the ABA, has produced the Uniform Foreign Country Money-Judgments Recognition Act, 13 ULA 261, which has been adopted (occasionally with slight modifications) in over 30 states. The Act expressly leaves open the possibility of recognition or enforcement of a foreign judgment in situations outside the Act's scope.

As its full name suggests (and unlike the Restatements), the Uniform Act is confined to "money-judgments," meaning judgments that grant or deny recovery of a sum of money. This does not of course prevent an enacting state from adopting additional legislation providing for the recognition and enforcement of a broader category of foreign judgments. Moreover, the Act pertains only to judgments that are "final and conclusive and enforceable where rendered," even though an appeal is pending or still possible. Though appealable judgments are covered, section 6 permits a court in its discretion to stay recognition or enforcement proceedings until an appeal is decided or the time for appeal has expired.

Despite the fact that only the term "recognition" appears in its title, the Act contemplates both recognition and enforcement. Thus, subject to stated exceptions, a foreign judgment covered by the Act is, according to section 3, both "conclusive" between the parties (i.e. required to be recognized) and "enforceable in the same manner as the judgment of a sister state which is entitled to full faith and credit" (i.e. required to be enforced).

The exceptions as set out in the Uniform Act are limitative. If no ground for non-recognition or non-enforcement is present, F2 will recognize and enforce the F1 judgment, without any reexamination of F1's findings of fact, determinations of law on the merits, or application of the law to the facts—i.e. the merits. Permitting such review would effectively deprive the foreign judgment of the very benefits of recognition. The Uniform Act's exceptions fall into two categories: situations in which the judgment *may not* be treated as conclusive (i.e., mandatory non-recognition) and situations in which it *need not* be so treated (i.e., discretionary non-recognition). As the Act is drafted, the circumstances entering in the first category are: (1) lack of impartial tribunals or respect for procedural due process, (2) lack of personal jurisdiction over the defendant, and (3) lack of subject matter jurisdiction. Those in the second category are: (1) lack of adequate notice of the proceedings, (2) fraud in obtaining the judgment, (3) repugnance of the cause of action or claim to the public policy of the recognizing or enforcing state, (4) inconsistency with another final and conclusive judgment, (5) violation of an agreement to settle the dispute exclusively in another forum, and (6) serious inconvenience of the foreign forum as a place for trial in cases in which jurisdiction over the defendant was based solely on the fact of personal service within the state of the rendering court. The burden of proof is on the party seeking to avoid recognition or enforcement. *Banque Libanaise Pour le Commerce v. Khreich* (5th Cir.1990).

Significantly, the absence of reciprocity is not recognized as a ground for denying recognition and enforcement in either category of exceptions in the Uniform Act. However, some states, in enacting the Act into law, have expressly added lack of reciprocity as a ground. (Where added, it usually, but not invariably, appears as a discretionary rather than a mandatory ground.) A reciprocity requirement also still figures in the common law of some states that have not enacted foreign judgments recognition legislation.

REVIEWING PERSONAL JURISDICTION AND NOTICE

Perhaps the single most common ground advanced for denying recognition or enforcement in F2 to a foreign judgment is F1's alleged lack of personal jurisdiction over the defendant. Closely related to the adequacy of personal jurisdiction is adequacy of notice. *Hilton* and state common law principles require that this inquiry be made as well, when the question is raised. Indeed, foreign judgments have been denied effect where the service was not reasonably adequate to assure notice, even though actual notice was had. See, e.g., *de la Mata v. American Life Ins. Co.* (D.Del.1991).

As noted above, the Uniform Act makes both lack of personal jurisdiction and lack of notice a ground for mandatory non-recognition and non-enforcement. However, the Act usefully goes on (sec. 5) to specify six circumstances in which personal jurisdiction may not be found to be lacking. These are where the defendant (a) was personally served in the foreign state, (b) voluntarily appeared (other than specifically to contest jurisdiction or to protect property from seizure), (c) had previously submitted by agreement to the court's jurisdiction, (d) was domiciled, was incorporated, or had its principal place of business in the foreign state at the time the action was begun, (e) had a business office in the state and the claim relates to business done through that office, and (f) operated a motor vehicle or airplane in the foreign state and the cause of action arises out of that operation. This means that a judgment may not be denied recognition or enforcement on grounds of lack of personal jurisdiction where any one of these circumstances is present. The list in effect functions as a kind of jurisdictional "safe harbor." This does not mean, of course, that if none of those circumstances is present, F1 was necessarily lacking in personal jurisdiction.

Notice an underlying choice of law question: should the adequacy of personal jurisdiction or notice be governed by the law of F1 or F2, or both? The Restatement (Third) of Foreign Relations Law, section 482(1)(b), suggests that the personal jurisdiction standards of both the rendering and the enforcement state must be satisfied. However, the Uniform Act may imply otherwise, since, by specifying the circumstances in which personal jurisdiction cannot be found lacking, the Act suggests that F2 should not concern itself with the question whether or not the personal jurisdiction standards of F1 were satisfied. Although few US courts address the question explicitly, they generally appear to favor exclusive application of F2 (i.e. US) law to that question.

Assuming they apply US law to the jurisdictional issue, US courts show a clear tendency to inquire, not into the conformity of F1's assertion of personal jurisdiction with US *statutory* standards, but rather with US *constitutional* (i.e. due process) standards. In asking whether the defendant had minimum contacts with F1, or whether F1's exercise of personal jurisdiction was otherwise unfair or unreasonable, the US is essentially applying the same jurisdictional due process standards that it uses in sister-state cases. See, e.g., *Ackermann v. Levine* (2d Cir.1986); *Ma v. Continental Bank N.A.* (7th Cir.1990); *Cunard S.S. Co. Ltd. v. Salen Reefer Servs. AB* (2d Cir.1985). Occasionally these standards are found not to have been met. See, e.g., *Thorsteinsson v. M/V Drangur* (11th Cir.1990) (no arrest of vessel in admiralty action); *Koster v. Automark Indus., Inc.* (7th Cir.1981) (no minimum contacts); *Choi v. Kim* (3d Cir.1995) (no notice). Moreover, since the party seeking recognition or enforcement may bear the burden of proof on this question, its failure affirmatively to demonstrate the fairness of F1's jurisdictional exercise may cause recognition or enforcement to be withheld. See, e.g., *Pure Fishing Inc. v. Silver Star Co, Ltd., supra.*

Thus, most US courts appear to assume that they have no business inquiring into whether they would have enjoyed statutory personal jurisdiction over the defendant in a comparable case before them, provided the assertion that was made would not offend US due process. There are exceptions, however. In one careful and detailed opinion, a federal district court limited itself to inquiring whether the assertion of personal jurisdiction made by F1 would have been justified, on the same facts, under the provisions of the long-arm statute of the US state in which it sat. The court found (see page 344 *infra*) that, although that the specific bases of jurisdiction that the Tokyo court asserted were not themselves provided for by F2's long-arm statute, its exercise of jurisdiction, on the facts, was consistent with that statute. *Nippon Emo–Trans Co., Ltd. v. Emo–Trans, Inc.* (E.D.N.Y.1990). (Having reached that conclusion, the court did not additionally inquire whether the jurisdictional exercise might nevertheless offend US due process.)

Rarely, a finding of absence of personal jurisdiction will rest on narrow non-constitutional grounds, such as failure to use the Hague Service Convention, where required. See, e.g., *Arco Electronics Control Ltd. v. Core Int'l* (S.D.Fla.1992). The judgment sought to be recognized or enforced may also be contrary to the parties' agreement to submit the dispute to a different court or to an arbitral tribunal. Both the Uniform Act and the Restatement recognize this as a ground for refusing recognition or enforcement.

Certain interesting questions remain unanswered.

Let us begin by supposing that a party who is doubtful of the foreign court's jurisdiction nevertheless appears in F1. If it fails to raise its jurisdictional defense at that time, it may be deemed to have waived its objection, not only in F1 but also in F2. Within a single legal system, waiver principles might ordinarily operate to prevent a party from "reserving" its objections for the recognition or enforcement stage, but matters are less clear in the transnational context. It may be that the court in

F2 will still feel bound to make the inquiries that its own recognition and enforcement standards require it to make, irrespective of whether F1 had been invited to make them. On the other hand, the possibility of waiver cannot be entirely ruled out. That having been said, there still may be no estoppel on questions of fundamental due process.

Suppose the defendant in F1 raises a jurisdictional defense and loses on that issue. The defendant may be tempted to walk away, so as not to submit to an adjudication of the merits in F1. If the defendant does so, a judgment may well be entered against it in default. (The consequences in F2 of a default judgment in F1 are dealt with below.) The benefit of doing so is that it will not likely be considered by F2 to have "voluntarily appeared" in F1 by contesting the merits and thus to have submitted to F1's jurisdiction. In *Nippon Emo–Trans Co. Ltd., supra,* the US defendant in a Tokyo action unsuccessfully contested jurisdiction over it. Then, while strenuously preserving its jurisdictional objections, it stayed in the action and defended itself on the merits—again unsuccessfully. The federal district court, as F2, consulted the law of the state in which it sat (New York) and concluded that the New York legislature, in enacting the Uniform Act, considered that by defending on the merits in F1 (even upon reservation of jurisdictional objections), the defendant "voluntarily appeared" in F1, with the meaning of the New York statute, and consented to F1's jurisdiction. The court did so reluctantly, finding it "[i]n some ways ... unsatisfying" that the F1 defendant should have in all such cases to choose between surrendering a jurisdictional defense and surrendering a defense on the merits.

There is a risk, however, in walking away from F1. The defendant very likely will incur a default judgment against it in F1, without ever having had its "day in court" on the merits. This is because, as we shall see below, a default judgment will most likely be recognized and enforced in F2, unless the F1 defendant can persuade F2 that the F1 court did indeed lacked personal jurisdiction over it. Absent such a showing, the F1 judgment on the merits will be recognized and enforced in F2, without the F1 defendant ever having been "heard," either in F1 or F2.

Whatever the scenario, we also need to ask whether and to what extent F2 may be tempted to consider itself bound by the jurisdictional findings that the F1 court may have made, particularly when the jurisdictional question was actually litigated there. In other words, even if F2 confines itself to determining whether F1's exercise of jurisdiction is protected by the "safe harbor" provision of the Uniform Act or, more generally, is consistent with US jurisdictional due process, it may treat certain F1 findings as conclusive. Case law indications are few and unclear. There are some indications that, on international collateral estoppel principles, the issue cannot be relitigated. See e.g. *Sprague & Rhodes Commod. Corp. v. Instituto Mexicano Del Cafe* (2d Cir.1977). But other courts do not treat the jurisdictional matter as closed. See e.g., *S.C. Chimexim S.A. v. Velco Enterpr. Ltd.* (S.D.N.Y.1999); *Hunt v. BP Exploration Co. (Libya) Ltd.* (N.D.Tex. 1980). The latter apparently proceed on the assumption that the relevant rules in F2 on the recognition and enforcement of foreign judgments imposes the inquiry upon them.

This question, too, was posed by the court in *Nippon Emo–Trans Co. Ltd., supra*. As noted above (page 342 *supra*), the court there held that, under New York law on recognition and enforcement, the F1 defendant voluntarily appeared merely by proceeding to the merits in F1, even though it contested jurisdiction there and sought to preserve its objections thereafter. In dictum, however, the court considered what preclusive effect, if any, it would give to F1's jurisdictional findings if it were to be willing to entertain the jurisdictional question at the recognition or enforcement stage. Drawing upon the Restatement (Third) of Foreign Relations Law, sec. 482, comment c, the court opined that, while it would treat F1's basic findings of fact as binding, it would not treat as binding F1's legal conclusions on the jurisdictional question, or even its findings on "mixed questions of fact and law" relating to jurisdiction. (Applying that approach, the court found that the Tokyo court's jurisdictional determinations in the case represented "mixed" questions and were thus reviewable. On review, it found that the bases invoked by that court would not support jurisdiction under New York's long-arm statute, but that the basic facts, as found by the Tokyo court, would nevertheless support an ultimate finding that the defendant was "doing business" in Japan.)

IMPARTIALITY, PROCEDURAL DUE PROCESS AND FRAUD

The impartiality of the foreign court and the basic procedural fairness of its proceedings are also a precondition of recognition and enforcement, and their review likewise entails application of US due process standards. The question has arisen whether the due process standard to be applied is the same as the due process standard to which US courts are ordinarily held. There is growing support for the notion that the procedures of foreign courts need only meet an "international" due process standard of basic fairness in order for their judgments to merit recognition or enforcement, while US judicial proceedings are held to a conceivably higher and more elaborate "domestic constitutional" due process standard. See, e.g., *Society of Lloyd's v. Ashenden* (7th Cir.2000).

Occasionally, the integrity or fairness of the foreign court system as a whole is called into question. Thus, in *Bank Melli Iran v. Pahlavi* (9th Cir.1995), the court found that the sister of the former Shah of Iran could not get due process in Iranian courts at the time, if only because she could not appear in person, be properly represented or produce witnesses. Liberian justice for these purposes was found similarly wanting in this context in *Bridgeway Corp. v. Citibank* (S.D.N.Y.1999). By comparison, post-Communist Rumanian justice passed muster. *S.C. Chimexim, supra.*

When it comes to specific procedural complaints, US courts understandably avoid taking a hard look at F1's procedural choices. They repeatedly observe that the mere fact that certain valued practices—e.g. a civil jury, discovery, cross examination, a verbatim transcript, a subpoena power over witnesses, testimonial privileges—may be absent from foreign procedure does not make the resulting judgments unworthy of recognition or enforcement. See, e.g., *Ingersoll Milling Mach. Co. v. Granger* (7th Cir.1987). This, too, was essentially the position taken by the Supreme Court in *Hilton v. Guyot.* At a minimum, however, a foreign judgment will be denied recognition or enforcement where the judgment debtor can demonstrate inadequate notice of the proceedings in the rendering forum. See e.g., *Gondre v. Silberstein* (E.D.N.Y.1990).

Claims of fraud raise somewhat different problems. Unlike specific procedural practices about which reasonable legal systems may differ, fraud in the judicial process is uniformly condemned and universally regarded as a ground, if proven, for vitiating the resulting judgment, at least where the fraud is considered to be "extrinsic," that is, calculated to prevent the judgment debtor from having his day in court, as opposed to "intrinsic," that is, fraud in relation to issues actually litigated in the foreign proceedings themselves, as in the use of perjured testimony. It has been said that the latter should ordinarily have been contestable within the courts of F1. Proof of extrinsic fraud in obtaining a foreign judgment is, in principle, fatal to the latter's recognition or enforcement. *Mata, supra.* In practice, such fraud is scarcely ever established. See, e.g., *Bank of Montreal v. Kough* (N.D.Cal.1977). The distinction between intrinsic and extrinsic fraud is increasingly discredited, however—with the result that either form of fraud will suffice to justify non-recognition and non-enforcement. See, e.g., *Bandai Am. Inc. v. Bally Midway Mfg. Co.* (3d Cir.1985).

JUDGMENTS CONTRARY TO FORUM PUBLIC POLICY

Unsurprisingly, both state legislation and common law principles reserve to US courts the right to deny recognition or enforcement to foreign judgments that are deemed violative of forum public policy. The Uniform Act specifically refers in this regard to F2's *own* public policy, but treats the exception as permissive rather than mandatory.

US courts rarely conclude that foreign country judgments are contrary to forum public policy. The fact that the foreign law differs from or is less protective than domestic law is insufficient. See, e.g., *Southwest Livestock & Trucking Co. v. Ramon, supra* (cause of action for collection on promissory note not in itself repugnant, despite usury under Texas Constitution, though not under Mexican law); *McCord v. Jet Spray Int'l Corp.* (D.Mass.1994) (judgment in conflict with Massachusetts policy against "at-will" employment); *Toronto–Dominion Bank v. Hall* (E.D.Ark.1973) (enforcement of loan guaranty contract giving bank unusually broad rights); *Milhoux v. Linder* (Colo.App.1995) (30–year limitations period not offensive). But this has occurred. A controversial example is *Ackermann v. Levine*, *supra*, where the court refused to enforce in full a German judgment awarding attorneys fees to a German lawyer from his US client, on the ground that forum public policy prohibits enforcing such a judgment in the absence of evidence that the client authorized the attorney to perform the services and that services were in fact performed.

Constitutional law is a likely source of public policy for these purposes. Thus, a number of UK defamation judgments have been denied enforcement in the US on the ground that the UK law principles of defamation under which those judgments were rendered are insufficiently protective of First Amendment freedom of expression, especially where commentary on public figures or matters of public concern is the subject. See, e.g., *Matusevitch v. Telnikoff* (D.C.Cir.1998); *Abdullah v. Sheridan Square Press, Inc.* (S.D.N.Y.1994); *Bachchan v. India Abroad Pubs. Inc.* (N.Y.Sup.Ct.1992). Similarly, in *Yahoo!, Inc. v. La Ligue Contre le Racisme et L'Antisemitisme* (N.D.Cal.2001), a California internet service provider brought suit for a declaratory judgment that a French court order requiring it to limit access to certain Nazi memorabilia on its US auction websites could not be enforced in California. The court ruled the French court order unenforceable because any such order, if issued by a US court, would clearly be inconsistent with the First Amendment.

But a principle need not be "constitutional" in order to furnish a public policy basis for non-recognition or non-enforcement of a foreign judgment. Thus, judgments have been denied enforcement because of a non-constitutional federal principle favoring international arbitration agreements (e.g. *South Ionian Shipping Co., Ltd. v. Hugo Neu & Sons Int'l Sales Corp.* (S.D.N.Y.1982)), or a non-constitutional federal protecting US tax revenues bankruptcy (e.g. *Overseas Inns S.A. P.A. v. United States* (5th Cir. 1990)). Still, it is well established that forum public policy is not to be deemed violated for these purposes merely because the cause of action or substantive legal principles on which a foreign judgment is based are not recognized, or have no analogue, in US law, or because a US court would have reached a different result in such a case. To run afoul of forum public policy for enforcement purposes, the foreign judgment must offend a fundamental or deeply-held policy of the enforcement forum. The case of *CIBC Mellon Trust Co. v. Mora Hotel Corp. N.V.* (App. Div., 1st Dept. 2002), offers a good illustration. There, a New York court enforced a UK judgment entered against two Netherlands corporations, notwithstanding the claim that the UK court violated due process by virtue of its issuance of a *Mareva* injunction (see page 317 *supra*). The court stressed that the Supreme court's disapproval of that type of relief in the *Grupo Mexicano* case (*supra* page 320) was not based on fundamental due process grounds.

OTHER GROUNDS FOR NON-RECOGNITION AND NON-ENFORCEMENT

As noted above, the Uniform Act provides, in addition to lack of personal jurisdiction or adequate notice and violation of public policy, several further grounds for withholding recognition or enforcement of a foreign judgment. But that still leaves open certain issues.

Reviewing subject matter jurisdiction is especially problematic. Both *Hilton* and the Uniform Act treat lack of subject matter jurisdiction, or competence, as a ground for denying recognition or enforcement, even though by definition it invites a US court to reexamine a foreign court's determination of competence under its own law. So too does the Restatement (Third) of Foreign Relations Law, section 482. US courts nevertheless recognize a strong presumption that foreign courts acted within their scope of subject matter jurisdiction as defined by their own law. However, if a foreign court were to entertain a case in which it has no interest, or if the foreign court were to apply its own law to a case in which it has no interest, a US court that is called upon to recognize or enforce the resulting judgment might well refuse to do so on "due process" grounds having a distinct "lack of subject matter jurisdiction" flavor.

Both the Uniform Act and the Restatement also permit non-recognition and non-enforcement when a judgment conflicts with another judgment. However, there is no systemic preference, either in favor of the first or the latest in time. The Uniform Act also makes "serious" inconvenience of the forum an available ground, but this has not been easy to establish.

RECIPROCITY

The Uniform Act rejects the inclusion of reciprocity as a requirement for the recognition or enforcement of foreign judgments. But some US states adopting the Uniform Act have added a reciprocity requirement, typically as a discretionary rather than a mandatory ground. Failure of reciprocity (or, rather, the petitioner's failure to prove reciprocity) is accordingly a basis in some states for withholding recognition or enforcement. See, e.g., *Banque Libanaise pour le Commerce v. Khreich, supra*; *Royal Bank of Canada v. Trentham Corp.* (5th Cir.1981).

THE CASE OF FOREIGN "DEFAULT" JUDGMENTS

Foreign judgments are not unworthy of recognition or enforcement merely because the F1 judgment was entered in default of appearance by the defendant. See, e.g., *Bank of Montreal v. Kough* (9th Cir.1980). Neither the Uniform Act nor the Restatement (Third) of Foreign Relations Law, section 481, comment i, distinguishes between default and contested judgments.

However, it is well established that a defendant who has defaulted in F1 will nevertheless have preserved its right to question F1's personal jurisdiction. The defendant may fully reopen that issue in F2 and expect the F2 court to take a close look. See e.g., *Covington Indus., Inc. v. Resintex, AG* (2d Cir.1980). But which jurisdictional standards will F2 apply in deciding the jurisdictional question? F1's own jurisdictional standards or F2's constitutional jurisdictional standards or, again, both? The answer to that question remains uncertain, precisely because the defaulting party never contested F1's jurisdiction in F1's court. In any case, defaulting in transnational litigation can be a risky strategy. A party who defaults in F1 and incurs an adverse judgment there may subsequently find that F2 sustains F1's exercise of jurisdiction, not only on F1's statutory grounds, but also according to F2's due process criteria. In that event, F2 will then likely proceed to recognize and enforce the judgment (unless of course some independent statutory ground for refusal, like fraud or violation of forum public policy, is present), with the consequence that the defendant will never have taken the opportunity in any court to address the merits, whether as to the facts, the law, or application of the law to the facts.

In the well-known case of *Somportex, Ltd. v. Philadelphia Chewing Gum Corp.* (3d Cir.1971), a US company was sued in the UK by its UK contracting partner. Although the US company, after entering a conditional appearance, sought to withdraw it, the UK Court of Appeal treated the appearance as unconditional. The US company took no further action and a default judgment was entered against it. The US court enforced the judgment, notwithstanding the judgment debtor's claim that the UK court lacked personal jurisdiction under UK law. According to the court, the US company, having "appeared unconditionally," and having been given in that court an opportunity to contest the jurisdictional issue, could no longer question the UK court's jurisdiction. ("In the absence of fraud or collusion, a default judgment is as conclusive an adjudication between the parties as when rendered after answer and complete contest in the open courtroom.") The court did, however, examine whether the assertion of jurisdiction by the UK court met US due process standards, and found that it did. As a result, the court enforced the judgment without the merits of the claim having been contested in either jurisdiction.

REVENUE AND PENAL JUDGMENTS

US courts have recognized foreign judgments across a broad range of civil and commercial disputes, including succession, copyright infringement, bankruptcy and divorce. However, at common law, courts neither recognized nor enforced the revenue or penal judgments of the courts of other nations. The prohibition has largely survived. See. e.g., *Overseas Inns S.A. v. United States*, *supra*; *Her Majesty the Queen v. Gilbertson* (9th Cir.1979). (Note that the Uniform Act categorically excludes such cases from its scope by way of its definition of the term "foreign judgment.") Thus, these quintessentially sovereign claims are, by their nature, not enforceable in the courts of other sovereigns—in the absence, that is, of reciprocal undertakings through international agreement.

Various rationales for the rule have been advanced, including that such judgments, due to their sensitivity, do not tolerate very well the measure of judicial review that recognition or enforcement of foreign judgments necessarily entails. More specifically, refusals to recognize or enforce such judgments on forum public policy grounds would likely ensue, thereby risking international offense. All of these arguments mirror those made in opposition to the enforcement of foreign tax or penal laws and causes of action (see Chapter 7 *supra*).

The traditional prohibition has nevertheless come to be relaxed in certain respects. First, the term penal is generally construed narrowly. A judgment is penal only if it imposes a punishment for wrongdoing against the public (as opposed to against a private party). It does not cover, for example, a judgment for civil damages rendered by a foreign criminal court. See, e.g., *Chase Manhattan Bank, N.A. v. Hoffman* (D.Mass.1987). Moreover, some courts have reformulated the rule in permissive rather than mandatory terms. The Restatement (Third) of Foreign Relations Law, section 483, does so: "Courts in the United States are not required to recognize or enforce judgments for the collection of taxes, fines or penalties rendered by the courts of other states."

While the rule against enforcing revenue or penal judgments could conceivably apply to judgments rendered by foreign courts under the antitrust and other broad regulatory laws of other countries, the question has not arisen, mostly because it is rare for actions seeking enforcement of such judgments to be brought in the US. It is true that US antitrust judgments and US punitive damage judgments may be denied enforcement abroad, but when that occurs, it is couched more in terms of general repugnance to the public policy of the enforcing forum (including complaints of extraterritoriality) than in terms of a specific prohibition against enforcing revenue or penal judgments.

ENFORCEMENT OF NON–MONETARY JUDGMENTS

In the previous sections we have largely envisioned the recognition and enforcement of foreign *monetary* judgments. We have seen that the Uniform Act does not require, though neither does it rule out, the enforcement of foreign *non-monetary* judgments. Enforcement of such judgments is thus basically discretionary with the F2 court. Interestingly, the recognition and enforcement policies expressed in the Restatement (Third) of Foreign Relations, while largely echoing those of the Uniform Act, and are not limited to money judgments.

The reason for possibly treating non-monetary judgments differently is quite simply a concern that their enforcement may place an undue burden on the F2 court. Orders of specific performance or orders of injunctive relief illustrate the problem. A good expression of judicial hesitation in enforcing decrees of this sort may be found in *Pilkington Bros. v. AFG Indus., supra* page 323.

THE COLLATERAL ESTOPPEL EFFECT OF FOREIGN JUDGMENTS

We have noted that recognition of foreign judgments consists of giving them preclusive effect, in the sense of barring relitigation of the underlying claims (or giving the judgments *res judicata* effect). But might preclusive effect also be owed to foreign courts' determinations of specific issues (as if through collateral estoppel)?

The Restatement (Third) of Foreign Relations Law (sec. 481, comment c) reports that judgments of foreign courts ordinarily are given no greater effect in the US than in the country where the judgment was rendered. Thus, some courts make the collateral estoppel effect of a foreign judgment depend strictly on the law of the rendering country as to that matter, and more specifically on whether that the courts of that country practice collateral estoppel and would apply it to the issue at hand (see *Bata v. Bata* (Del.1960). Others are willing, at least in some circumstances, to go beyond the rendering court's law in this respect (see *Carl Zeiss Stiftung v. V.E.B. Carl Zeiss, Jena* (S.D.N.Y.1968).

PROCEDURE IN ENFORCEMENT ACTIONS

Ordinarily, enforcement in the US of a foreign country judgment requires instituting a separate action to this effect, albeit a summary one. The Uniform Act does not contain a statute of limitations and it is assumed that state courts will apply the relevant state statute of limitations, typically the same one that they would apply to a enforcement of a local judgment. But the foreign statute of limitations may still be important if the enforcing jurisdiction happens to require that, at the time of the request for enforcement, the foreign judgment still be enforceable in the rendering jurisdiction. See *Nadd v. Le Credit Lyonnais, S.A.* (Fla.2001), interpreting the Florida version of the Uniform Act as requiring that the statute of limitations for an enforcement action on the judgment in the rendering forum not yet have run.

The Uniform Act provides for enforcement of foreign country judgments "in the same manner as the judgment of a sister state ... entitled to full faith and credit." This has real advantages in those states that have also adopted the 1964 revised Uniform Enforcement of Foreign Judgments Act, 13 ULA 149 (1964). This act enables sister-state judgments to be enforced without instituting a separate proceeding to that effect. Thus, once the foreign judgment is shown to be entitled to recognition, it becomes enforceable. *Guinness PLC v. Ward* (4th Cir.1992). Generally, the summary action entails attaching an authenticated copy of the foreign judgment to the motion. After the court has determined that enforcement is proper, the debtor is generally given a period of time in which to comply. After this time has passed, the court may order the seizure and sale of the judgment creditor's assets.

The burden of proof in establishing that a foreign judgment should be recognized or enforced rests with the party seeking recognition or enforcement. *Shen v. Leo A. Daly Co.* (8th Cir.2000); *Bridgeway v. Citibank*, *supra*. However, if a ground for resisting recognition or enforcement is advanced, the burden passes to the party resisting. In other words, the conditions on recognition and enforcement operate as affirmative defenses, with the burden of proof on the party invoking them. In one influential opinion, it was held that the party seeking enforcement must establish *prima facie* (1) a final judgment conclusive and enforceable where rendered, (2) subject matter and personal jurisdiction, and (3) regular proceedings under a fair and impartial system. Beyond that point, the burden passes to the defendant to show a reason to deny recognition or enforcement. *Ackermann v. Levine*, *supra*.

THE CURRENCY OF FOREIGN JUDGMENTS

In a world of multiple currencies, it is quite possible that a party will bring to a court for enforcement a judgment that is not only "foreign," but that is expressed in a foreign currency. In the absence of a firm statutory or common law rule, the F2 court has a number of options, both as to whether the enforcement forum may give judgment in a foreign currency and as to how the F1 judgment (expressed in foreign currency) shall be converted into F2 currency. A parallel problem arises in US litigation over debts or other obligations or liabilities expressed in a foreign currency.

Traditionally, common law and statutory rules required US courts to enter money judgments in US dollars. The statutory bar has been traced to section 20 of the Coinage Act of 1792, requiring that all court proceedings to be "kept and had" in conformity with the rule that the "money of account" must be expressed in dollars. The repeal of this section in 1982 opened up new possibilities. In this spirit, the Restatement (Third) of Foreign Relations Law (sec. 823) states that US courts are not precluded from giving judgment "in the currency in which the obligation is denominated or the loss was incurred." See also Uniform Foreign–Money Claims Act, 13 ULA 17 (1989), secs. 4, 7. Some states have gone further, as has New York by actually requiring that, where a cause of action is based upon an obligation denominated in a foreign currency, judgment be rendered in that currency.

The general view is that the choice of currency in which to enter judgment is a matter of forum law. The court in *In re Oil Spill by Amoco Cadiz* (7th Cir.1992), one of the first reported US decisions to enter judgment in foreign currency, found it especially appropriate to enter judgment in French francs, since the parties had conducted their commercial activity in the foreign currency, felt the loss in that currency, and could be presumed to have accepted the risk of changes in the value of that currency.

When F2 is invited to enforce a judgment expressed in F1's currency, the interesting question arises as to the date of currency conversion, triggered by fluctuations over time in the relative values of currencies. In principle, the rules on this issue have tended to be treated as matters of substance for *Erie* purposes, and thus governed in diversity actions by state law. The Restatement, section 823, says only that if judgment is given in US dollars, the conversion from the foreign currency in which the judgment was expressed should be "made at such rate as to make the creditor whole and to avoid rewarding a debtor who has delayed in carrying out the obligation." But it fixes no specific moment for determining the conversion rate. In practice, US courts have converted foreign judgments into dollars, variously, as of the date of breach, the date of injury, the date of judgment by the foreign court, the date of institution of the US enforcement action, the date of the judgment granting enforcement, and the date of actual payment. See, e.g., *Delta Foods Inc. v. Republic of Ghana* (D.C.Cir.2001) (date of filing of the enforcement action); *Competex S.A. v. LaBow* (2d Cir.1986) (date of breach, defined as the date of entry of the foreign judgment); Uniform Foreign–Money Claims Act, *supra*, sec. 7(b) (date of payment). Under a more complex approach, the judgment day rule is used where the obligation arises entirely under foreign law, while the breach day rule applies if the cause of action arises under US law. See, e.g., *In re Good Hope Chem. Corp.* (1st Cir.1984).

Occasionally, state legislatures have intervened to adopt, or change, a rule on this matter. The New York Judiciary Law, section 27(b), adopts the date of entry of the enforcement judgment, thus discarding the state's prior common law rule favoring the date of breach. See *Dynamic Cassette Int'l Ltd. v. Mike Lopez & Assocs., Inc.* (E.D.N.Y.1996).

To rid the system of this uncertainty, a Uniform Foreign–Money Claims Act, 13 ULA 47 (1989), has been produced, establishing a uniform method. As to conversion time, the Act comes down in favor of the payment day rule, reasoning that it best restores the aggrieved party to the situation it would have been in, but for the liability-generating act. The Act has been adopted in a number of states and has influenced the case law in others.

RECOGNITION AND ENFORCEMENT OF US JUDGMENTS ABROAD

Transnational litigators may be as interested in the enforceability of US judgments abroad as the enforceability of foreign country judgments in the US. In the absence of any treaty to which the US is a party, the applicable standards will be those in place in the foreign country. Every country sets some limits on the recognition and enforcement of foreign country judgments, including American ones. Under most circumstances, US judgments in civil cases will be received generously. Thanks to the well-established recognition and enforcement policies in the US, even those countries that condition their acceptance of foreign judgments on a showing of reciprocity are ordinarily satisfied by US practice.

Still, some kinds of US judgments run a serious risk of non-enforcement. In this category need to be placed judgments awarding punitive or treble damages (or damages deemed excessive generally) as well as judgments regarded as entailing an excessively extraterritorial application of US law. But even judgments that are "safe" by their nature may run into difficulty on grounds having to do with service, personal jurisdiction or other broadly procedural features of US practice. Here we should place judgments based on "transient" or vague "doing business" jurisdiction, or on improper service.

TREATY REGIMES FOR THE ENFORCEMENT OF FOREIGN JUDGMENTS

Given the potential mutual benefit of foreign judgment recognition and enforcement, the subject is ripe for international agreement. Since 1968, for example, the nations of the European Union have participated in treaty arrangement among themselves (the Brussels Convention) and with the remaining members of the European Free Trade Area (the Lugano Convention), harmonizing rules for the exercise of personal jurisdiction and conditionally guaranteeing the enforcement of foreign judgments based upon a permissible jurisdictional ground. Due to this linkage, the Convention is known as a "double" convention. In the year 2000, these undertakings, as concerns the EU Member States, were transformed into an EU regulation that is directly applicable in the Member State judiciaries. Council Reg. 44/2001, O.J. L 12/1 (Jan. 16, 2001). European nations also have entered into various bilateral judgment recognition treaties with other states.

The US is not at present a party either to bilateral or multilateral judgments conventions, although it has participated since 1993 in the preparation of such a convention under the auspices of the Hague Conference on Private International Law. Like the Brussels and Lugano Conventions, the Hague Convention that is under negotiation is a "double" convention. Differences over a variety of issues—including, but not limited to, US courts' use of a general "doing business" basis of jurisdiction, European states' general acceptance of jurisdiction in tort cases in the place where injury occurred, the exercise of universal jurisdiction, *forum non conveniens* practice, and enforcement of punitive damages awards—have stalled progress. Not even agreement to establish a so-called "grey area," that is to say, a sphere in which specified jurisdictional bases are neither prohibited nor required to be recognized, has broken the logjam.

CHAPTER ELEVEN

JUDICIAL INTERVENTION IN INTERNATIONAL COMMERCIAL ARBITRATION

A hallmark of international arbitration is the submission of transnational disputes to the exclusive jurisdiction of one or a panel of arbitrators acting in the fashion of "private judges." By including arbitration agreements in their contracts, parties to international transactions seek, among other things, to avoid subjecting their disputes to the jurisdiction of national judges. They may also seek to achieve speed, flexibility, expertise, neutrality, confidentiality, and heightened enforceability.

Since arbitration is driven by a purpose to substitute private for public adjudication, one might suppose that disputes arising out of international agreements containing arbitration clauses will not likely find their way into national court. This, however, is far from the case. Even in the presence of a perfectly valid and clearly applicable arbitration agreement, national courts potentially have a variety of roles to play throughout the life cycle of an arbitration. The moments of intersection between arbitral and judicial procedures may occur at different stages of the arbitral process: before commencement of the arbitral proceedings (as in compelling arbitration or determining the arbitrability of disputes), during arbitration (as in assisting arbitration or reviewing arbitral jurisdiction), as well as after an arbitral award has been rendered (as in the vacatur or confirmation of arbitral award or the recognition and enforcement of a foreign arbitral award). One obvious issue that is apt to arise at any or all such moments is the validity or applicability of the arbitration agreement itself.

International commercial arbitration as a whole is far too large a subject for treatment in this volume on transnational litigation in US courts, and is accordingly the subject of a separate Nutshell. But arbitration disputes do represent an important and growing component of the US courts' transnational litigation diet, thus necessitating at least some coverage here. And because international arbitration cases cannot be understood in a vacuum, we necessarily begin with a look at arbitration's overall legal framework. We then turn to consider in a more focused way the principal points of intersection between the judicial and the arbitral process.

INTERNATIONAL ARBITRAL INSTITUTIONS

International arbitration may be either institutional (i.e., organized under the auspices of a more or less permanent arbitral institution, which often enough has its own published procedural rules) or *ad hoc* (i.e., organized for the dispute in question).

Prominent international arbitral institutions include the International Chamber of Commerce (ICC), the American Arbitration Association (AAA) and the London Court of International Arbitration (LCIA). This chapter will refer to the rules of these three institutions at various points. International arbitration is associated with cities having influential international arbitration institutions, and the procedural rules promulgated by these bodies address recurring procedural questions in arbitration: appointment of arbitrators, pleadings, hearings, timetables, provisional relief, and the like. These cities include (besides London) Stockholm, Geneva, Singapore, Hong Kong, and Washington D.C. (Washington is the site of the International Center for Settlement of Investment Disputes (ICSID), which provides facilities for conciliation and arbitration of investment disputes in accordance with the Convention on the Settlement of Investment Disputes between States and Nationals of Other States, 17 UST 1270, TIAS 6090, 575 UNTS 159 (1965). ICSID's procedural rules may likewise be incorporated by reference in arbitration clauses in private contracts, which would not ordinarily be subject to the ICSID Convention.

Although *ad hoc* arbitrations do not take place within the institutional framework of any given international arbitral body, they do not occur in a vacuum. The arbitration agreement will ordinarily designate an arbitral site, with the law of arbitration in effect within that jurisdiction thus providing the applicable legal framework. This body of law is commonly referred to as the *lex arbitri*. Moreover, even when opting for *ad hoc* arbitration, contracting parties are free specifically to incorporate preexisting procedural rules, which will then supply the arbitral ground rules. By far the most frequently adopted procedural rules are those promulgated by the United Nations Commission on International Trade Law (UNCITRAL), known simply as the UNCITRAL Rules, to which reference will be made throughout this chapter. If the parties to *ad hoc* arbitration have failed to designate a set of procedural rules, and do not subsequently agree on one, then the arbitrators will identify or devise their own. Especially in *ad hoc* arbitration, it will be necessary for the parties to have designated a mechanism for appointing the arbitrators in the event the parties cannot agree on their appointment.

It bears emphasis throughout, however, that institutional and *ad hoc* arbitrations alike are subject to the mandatory rules of the place of arbitration. That law may dictate various matters concerning the conduct of the arbitration, such as rules on the number or nationality of arbitrators. However, many rules found in the *lex arbitri* are default rules only, in the sense that the parties may derogate from them by agreement to the contrary. Within the widely-adopted UNCITRAL Model Law on International Commercial Arbitration, 40 UN GAOR Supp. (no. 17), annex 1, UN Doc/A/40/17 (1985), 24 ILM 1302 (1985), truly "mandatory" provisions are very few.

THE INTERNATIONAL ARBITRATION FRAMEWORK IN US LAW

In the US, federal rather than state law governs most issues relating to international arbitration. The principal source is the Federal Arbitration Act (FAA), adopted in 1925 and applicable to contracts respecting interstate and foreign commerce. The FAA establishes the broad procedural framework for the conduct of arbitration in the US, while at the same time announcing a strong federal policy in favor of the enforcement of both arbitration agreements and arbitral awards.

The FAA, codified at 9 U.S.C.A., consists of three chapters. The original and basic Chapter 1 (secs. 1–16) applies generally to agreements and awards affecting interstate or foreign commerce. Chapter 2 (secs. 201–10) implements the 1958 United Nations Convention on the Recognition and Enforcement of Foreign Arbitral Awards, (or the "New York Convention"), 21 UST 2517, T.I.A.S. no. 6997, 330 UNTS 3, while Chapter 3 (secs. 301–01) implements the Inter–American Convention on International Commercial Arbitration. The latter two chapters concern only agreements and awards falling within those Conventions' respective scope.

FAA Chapter 1 is commonly referred to, somewhat misleadingly, as applicable to "domestic" arbitration. In fact, it covers arbitration in foreign as well as interstate commerce. The arbitration that is covered is domestic only in the sense that it does not specifically fall within the scope of the New

York or Inter–American Conventions. The FAA's pro-arbitration bias is best reflected in section 2 of the Act, which provides that, subject to ordinary rules of law and equity for the revocation in any contract, agreements to arbitrate "shall be valid, irrevocable, and enforceable," and in section 9, which declares that, unless vacated or subject to one of several stated grounds set out in the Act, awards shall upon application be confirmed in US court. Other sections of Chapter 1 deal with various aspects of the arbitral process: appointment of arbitrators, judicial assistance to arbitral tribunals in the taking of evidence, awards, inapplicability of the act of state doctrine, appeals, confirmation procedure, correction or vacatur of arbitral awards, etc.

As mentioned, Chapter 2 of the FAA implements the 1958 New York Convention. Although much of the Convention, as its name suggests, is devoted to the recognition and enforcement of arbitral *awards* (see pages 404–421 *infra*), the Convention, like FAA Chapter 1, is also concerned with the recognition and enforcement of arbitration *agreements*. Indeed, Article II(3) of the Convention obligates the courts of signatory states to "refer" the parties to arbitration when seized of a dispute that is subject to a valid arbitration agreement falling within the scope of the Convention. According to the Convention, the only circumstances in which a court may refuse to recognize an agreement to arbitrate, or decline to refer the parties to arbitration, are when the subject matter of the dispute is not arbitrable or when the agreement itself is "null and void, inoperative or incapable of being performed" (art. II(3)).

The Convention, however, has a limited scope of application and, accordingly, so too does the FAA's Chapter 2. To begin with, it applies only to disputes, whether present or future, which arise out of a "defined legal" relationship. In addition, the Convention applies only to agreements that are "in writing." Article I(3) of the Convention also allows states to limit the Convention's application to commercial cases, and the FAA does so.

Finally, the awards that are contemplated must be "made in the territory of a State other than the State where the recognition and enforcement ... are sought." (i.e., foreign awards) or "not considered as domestic awards in the State where their recognition and enforcement are sought" (i.e., "non-domestic" awards). This is the class of arbitration agreements that the Convention requires courts of the contracting States to honor and enforce, and the class of arbitral awards that it requires courts of the contracting States to recognize and enforce. FAA Section 202 elaborates upon this:

> An arbitration agreement or award that arises out of [a legal relationship considered as commercial] which is entirely between United States citizens shall be deemed not to fall under the Convention, unless that relationship involves property located abroad, envisages performance or enforcement abroad, or has some other reasonable relation with one or more foreign states.

US courts have found agreements to arbitrate in the US to be "foreign" for these purposes in various circumstances, such as where both parties are foreign (see, e.g., *Bergesen v. Joseph Muller Corp.* (2d Cir.1983)), where only one party is foreign but the underlying contract was to be performed abroad (see, e.g., *Smith/Enron Cogeneration L.P., Inc. v. Smith Cogeneration Int'l, Inc.* (2d Cir.1999); *Industrial Risk Ins. v. M.A.N. Gutehoffnungshutte GmbH* (11th Cir.1998)), and even where neither party is foreign but the underlying contractual performance is abroad (see, e.g., *Lander Co., Inc. v. MMP Investments, Inc.* (7th Cir.1997)).

Chapter 2 of the FAA implements the New York Convention in all major respects. Sections 206 and 208 (which echo sections 3 and 4 of the FAA Chapter 1, concerning domestic awards), require courts to stay proceedings on issues that are referable to arbitration under the Convention, and to issue orders compelling arbitration, even where the seat of arbitration is located outside the US. Chapter 2 (secs. 203 and 205) creates federal subject matter jurisdiction for these purposes, as well as removal authority from state courts. Implementing the 1975 Inter–American Convention on International Commercial Arbitration (also known as Panama Convention), Chapter 3 of the FAA (secs. 302–04) provides for enforcement of specified arbitration agreements and awards, and sets out procedures similar to those established in Chapter 2 for the New York Convention.

Given its avowed pro-arbitration policy, the FAA constitutes both substantive and procedural federal law. See *Southland Corp. v. Keating* (S.Ct.1984); *Moses H. Cone Memorial Hosp. v. Mercury Constr. Corp.* (S.Ct.1983); *Scherk v. Alberto–Culver Co.* (S.Ct.1974). But, while the FAA remains the basic federal framework, it is not the *exclusive* standard, even as to arbitration under contracts affecting interstate or foreign commerce. The parties' agreement, and the procedural and substantive rules they may be deemed to have adopted or incorporated by reference, also form part of this framework. See *Volt Information Sciences, Inc. v. Board of Trustees* (S.Ct.1989). In addition, most states have enacted arbitration laws of their own (some of them even enacting *international* arbitration laws), which will apply to arbitrations within their territory to the extent not expressly or impliedly inconsistent with the FAA.

The FAA, dating as it does from 1925, is by no means the most modern of national arbitration laws. A good many of jurisdictions around the world have enacted the UNCITRAL Model Law, referred to at page 368 *supra*. Reference will often be made in this chapter to the provisions of this Model Law.

THE ROLE OF US COURTS PRIOR TO THE ARBITRAL PROCEDURE

We adopt a basically chronological approach to the judicial role in international arbitration. At every principal stage, including at the very threshold of arbitration, national courts may be called upon to intervene in one respect or another. Typically, the fashion in which they may do so is rather carefully circumscribed.

Compelling arbitration

In principle, an arbitration commences when one of the parties to an arbitration agreement signifies to the other, either directly or via a chosen arbitral institution, its intent to arbitrate a given dispute falling within the scope of application of the agreement to arbitrate. However, rather than appear in the arbitration, the other party may institute its own action in national court seeking a stay of the arbitration on grounds of the inexistence, inapplicability or invalidity of the arbitration agreement. That party may also institute an action in national court seeking affirmative relief of some kind (e.g. under the securities or antitrust laws, or simply in contract), notwithstanding the arbitration agreement. The defendant in that action (i.e. the arbitral claimant) then typically interposes the arbitration agreement as a basis for a motion to dismiss.

Precisely because a court cannot logically compel arbitration without making at least a preliminary judgment about the existence, scope and enforceability of the arbitration agreement, it will find itself facing issues that go to the heart of the agreement to arbitrate. The decision whether or not to compel arbitration is by no means a simple one.

The FAA requires of course that an arbitration agreement exist, but does not supply criteria for determining whether or not it does. The prevailing view is that the *existence* of an agreement to arbitrate depends upon the substantive law of contract of the jurisdiction indicated by the forum's choice of law rules. This may be the law of a particular US state or of a foreign jurisdiction. Assuming that state law will determine whether an arbitration agreement exists, that law must still not, under the federal policy embodied in the FAA, disfavor arbitration. Thus, state contract law will be inapplicable to the extent that it singles out arbitration agreements for unfavorable treatment. See *Perry v. Thomas* (S.Ct.1987); *First Options of Chicago, Inc. v. Kaplan* (S.Ct.1995); *Mastrobuono v. Shearson Lehman Hutton, Inc.* (S.Ct.1995); *Allied–Bruce Terminix Cos., Inc. v. Dobson* (S.Ct.1995); *Doctor's Assocs., Inc. v. Casarotto* (S.Ct.1996).

According to the decision in *Ledee v. Ceramiche Ragno* (1st Cir.1982), a court presented with a request to refer a dispute to arbitration under FAA Chapter 2 must determine whether there is a written agreement to arbitrate the subject of the dispute, whether the agreement provides for arbitration within a Convention state, whether the agreement arises out of a commercial relationship, and whether one of the parties is not an American national or the matter has a reasonable relation with a foreign state. The language of the Convention (art. II(1)) suggests that the arbitration agreement must be found in a signed contract or in an exchange of letters or telegrams. *Kahn Lucas Lancaster, Inc. v. Lark Int'l Ltd.* (2d Cir.1999).

If all these conditions are satisfied, the court must order arbitration unless it finds the agreement "null and void, inoperative or incapable of being performed," within the meaning of Convention Article II(3)—language that the courts have narrowly construed. *DiMercurio v. Sphere Drake Ins., PLC* (1st Cir.2000). One exception is where the court is sufficiently persuaded that a party has by word or deed waived the arbitration agreement that it decides the waiver issue itself, rather than referring the parties to arbitration over that issue. See, e.g., *S & R Co. of Kingston v. Latona Trucking, Inc.* (2d Cir.1998).

(a) Validity of the arbitration agreement

Similarly, the FAA does not address directly the question of the *validity* of agreements to arbitrate. That question, too, is subject to the generally applicable contract law of the relevant state, whether the issue is fraud, mistake, duress, illegality, unconscionability, or some other ground of invalidity.

Courts commonly distinguish between challenges to the validity of the underlying contract, on the one hand, and to the validity of the arbitration agreement in particular, on the other. Resort is had in this connection to a broad doctrine of "separability," according to which an arbitration agreement is deemed to be separate from, and independent of, the contract containing it. See, e.g., *Prima Paint Corp. v. Flood & Conklin Mfg. Co.* (S.Ct.1967); *Sauer–Getriebe KG v. White Hydraulics, Inc.* (7th

Cir.1983); *Teledyne, Inc. v. Kone Corp.* (9th Cir. 1989). Even a claim of fraud in the inducement is arbitrable, unless the arbitration clause itself was allegedly fraudulently induced.

This means that the court should ordinarily not undertake at this early stage to determine the validity of the underlying contract, but should instead refer the parties to arbitration, thus respecting their intention that that question be determined by the arbitrators, at least in the first instance. The separability doctrine also has the practical advantage of permitting an arbitration agreement to survive the invalidity of the contract in which it is found. That is to say, when, in the course of an ongoing arbitral proceeding, one of the parties questions the validity of the underlying contract, the arbitrators may decide that question for themselves, rather than suspend proceedings in order to obtain a judicial ruling on the issue. This means, too, that if the arbitrators do find that the contract is invalid and unenforceable, they will not thereby have vitiated their jurisdictional power under the arbitration agreement to make that very determination.

Thus, while a court may, when asked to compel arbitration, entertain challenges to the validity of the *arbitration agreement* as such, it should not entertain challenges to the validity of the *underlying contract*, since the latter is within the province of the arbitrators. In *Republic of Nicaragua v. Standard Fruit Co.* (9th Cir.1991), a district court declined to compel arbitration because it found that the document containing the asserted agreement to arbitrate was not a valid contract. The court of appeals reversed on the ground that, while the district court was free to interpret and determine the validity of the arbitration clause as such, it was not free to adjudicate the validity—or indeed even the existence—of the alleged contract containing it, because this was a question properly for the arbitrators, provided the court can make a threshold finding that the document in question at least purports to be a contract evidencing a transaction in commerce. The court did not, however, disapprove of the district court's inquiry into whether an agreement to arbitrate itself existed or was valid (although it disagreed with the district court on the merits of that issue). Most courts do consider it appropriate at this stage to determine the existence and validity of the arbitration agreement as such, assuming it is called into question. See, e.g., *David L. Threlkeld & Co. v. Metallgesellschaft Ltd. (London)* (2d Cir.1991); *Interbras Cayman Co. v. Orient Victory Shipping Co.* (2d Cir.1981).

By no means do all courts accept this sharp distinction between validity of the arbitration agreement and validity of the contract as a whole. Some courts draw a further distinction, among challenges to the contract as a whole, between those going to its existence and those going to its validity. Their reasoning is that the arbitrators should not proceed in the absence of a contract of which the agreement to arbitrate is a part. See e.g., *Interocean Shipping Co. v. Nat'l Shipping & Trading Corp.* (2d

Cir.1972). But others courts go still further, even subjecting the validity (and not merely the existence) of the underlying contract to judicial determination in the context of an action to compel arbitration. See, e.g., *Continental Serv. Life & Health Ins. Co. v. A.G. Edwards & Sons* (M.D.La. 1987). The rationale for this position appears to be that if the contract containing an arbitration clause is indeed invalid, then the arbitration clause itself is necessarily invalid as well. A recent example of this approach is *Sphere Drake Ins. Ltd. v. All Am. Ins. Co.* (7th Cir.2001).

It would thus appear that, by all accounts, the courts have a definite role to play at this early stage in assessing the validity of the arbitration agreement should that question arise. Since parties who have resort to court in a dispute that is arguably subject to arbitration will very likely be prepared to demonstrate the invalidity of the agreement to arbitrate, the courts may be kept busy by this issue.

In the *Ledee* case, *supra*, for example, the plaintiff sought to avoid arbitration of a dispute arising out of the termination of a Puerto Rico distributorship by showing that the agreement to arbitrate such disputes violated a Puerto Rico statute barring out-of-state arbitration of disputes arising out of Puerto Rico distributorships, and was therefore null and void. The Court of Appeals disagreed, citing *I.T.A.D. Assocs., Inc. v. Podar Bros.* (4th Cir.1981), for the proposition that the language "null and void, inoperative or incapable of being performed," within the meaning of Article II(3) of the New York Convention, refers only to those defenses to arbitration agreements "that can be applied neutrally on an international scale." The court gave as examples of such defenses fraud, mistake, duress and waiver, and excluded defenses based on legislation that specifically restricts the application or enforcement of arbitral agreements. See also *Rhone Mediterranee Compagnia Francese di Assicurazioni e Riassicurazoni v. Achille Lauro* (3d Cir.1983), allowing the court also to consider "fundamental policies of the forum state," but not its "parochial interests" or those of a third state (whether a state having a more significant relationship with the dispute, the state of the arbitral situs, the state whose law the parties chose as the substantive governing law, or the state of probable enforcement of an eventual award). The court considered that this rule was most consistent with the Convention's purpose of favoring the enforcement of agreements to arbitrate.

(b) Interpretation of the arbitration agreement

If courts at this stage may examine the validity of the arbitration agreement, they would seem also entitled to interpret it, assuming one of the parties has called the agreement's interpretation into question. However, there is wide support in legislation and case law for another general principle—which often goes by its German name, *Kompetenz–Kompetenz*—according to which arbitrators are to be the judges, again at least in the first instance, of their own competence. This suggests that when a court is called upon to compel arbitration, it should refrain from determining the precise scope of the agreement to arbitrate. Rather, it should compel arbitration in order that the scope of the obligation to arbitrate may in turn be determined initially by the arbitrators themselves. Any doubts as to the scope of arbitrable issues thus should in principle be resolved in favor of arbitration at this stage.

(i) Interpretation questions

The principal issue of interpretation is whether a given dispute falls within the scope of the agreement to arbitrate; a related issue is whether a non-signatory to the agreement should be held to be bound by it. As noted, there is a strong tendency for courts to allow the arbitrators to make such determinations in the first instance, provided there appears to be at least a plausible rationale for considering the dispute to be covered (or the non-signatory party to be bound). See, e.g., *Apollo Computer, Inc. v. Berg* (1st Cir.1989), where the court ruled that, by adopting the ICC Rules, the parties agreed to submit the issue of the arbitrability of their dispute, and not merely its merits, to the arbitral tribunal. Article 6.2 of the 1998 ICC Rules (corresponding to article 8.3 of the prior rules) provides that once a *prima facie* agreement to arbitrate has been shown, issues concerning the existence, validity and scope of the arbitration agreement are for the arbitrators. See also *Teledyne v. Kone, supra*; *Phillips Petroleum Co. v. Marathon Oil Co.* (5th Cir.1986). Under ICC practice, the ICC Court of Arbitration will decide whether there is a *prima facie* case for arbitrability, when that is called into question at the outset. If the ICC Court finds that there is *prima facie* jurisdiction, it will ordinarily order that the arbitration go forward, leaving it to the tribunal to determine ultimately its jurisdiction under the notion of *Kompetenz–Kompetenz*. But, just as surely, there will be cases in which a dispute so patently falls outside the scope of the arbitration agreement (for example, because clearly not arising out of or related to the contract containing the arbitration clause) that the matter should not be referred to arbitration at all. This is even more likely to be the case with respect to claims that the agreement to arbitrate binds a non-signatory.

A good example of an interpretation issue that courts are bound to decide at the very outset is whether the agreement constitutes a "derogation" clause (by which the parties agree to resolve their disputes exclusively by arbitration) or a "prorogation" clause (by which they merely agree to submit to arbitration). The courts have created a powerful presumption—certainly more powerful than in the forum selection clause context—that arbitration agreements mean to be exclusive rather than permissive. Thus, unless the parties clearly manifest a contrary intent, their inclusion of an arbitration clause in a contract will signify that they agree to submit all covered disputes exclusively to the designated arbitral mechanism and not to resort to national court.

On the whole, courts appear to be much readier at this stage to interpret an arbitration agreement for these purposes than they are to interpret the underlying contract. See, e.g., *Republic of Nicaragua v. Standard Fruit Co., supra*, where the Court of Appeals did address the question of coverage and found that the arbitration clause was not too vague to encompass the dispute at hand. To this extent, the separability doctrine once again appears to come into play. The reason is in part theoretical and in part practical. Theoretically, a party should not have to submit its claim to an arbitral mechanism, unless that claim falls within the class of claims to which it had previously consented to arbitrate, the latter being basically a question of contract interpretation which courts are accustomed to deciding. From a practical point of view, too, at the time of an action to compel arbitration, normally no arbitration proceedings are yet underway; thus there is as yet no arbitral panel in place to make these determinations. See, e.g., *Nordin v. Nutri/System, Inc.* (8th Cir.1990); *Mesquite Lake Assocs. v. Lurgi Corp.* (N.D.Cal.1991); *Pollux Marine Agencies, Inc. v. Louis Dreyfus Corp.* (S.D.N.Y.1978). This contrasts with the situation in which the arbitral panel has been constituted and is in a position to act promptly on these issues.

(ii) The Reach of the agreement to arbitrate: the First Options case

As with any exercise in contract interpretation, the language and apparent intention of the parties count. For this reason, the drafting of the arbitration agreement matters. For example, an agreement is more likely to be interpreted as having broad coverage if it refers to any dispute between the parties "arising out of" or "relating to" or "in connection with" the contract, rather than merely "arising under" it. The question can arise in the context of a claim between contracting parties that, while not unconnected to the contract, sounds in tort rather than contract. See, e.g., *Mar–Len of La., Inc. v. Parsons–Gilbane* (5th Cir.1985). But not all courts are willing to calibrate the scope of arbitration according to the precise language of the clause.

The Supreme Court sought to shed further light on the matter in its decision in *First Options of Chicago, Inc. v. Kaplan, supra*. In *First Options*, the Court ruled that the parties are free to allocate to the arbitrators or to the courts jurisdiction both over the question whether a valid agreement to arbitrate was entered into by the parties and over the question whether a given dispute falls within the ambit of that agreement. However, in the absence of express agreement between the parties as to that allocation, certain presumptions operate. Under these presumptions, the courts may independently determine whether the parties made an agreement to arbitrate, unless there appears "clear and unmistakable" evidence of party intent to the contrary. See *AT & T Technologies, Inc. v. Communications Workers of Am.* (S.Ct.1986). On the other hand, the question whether the agreement to arbitrate, once found to exist, covers the particular dispute at hand is presumptively for the arbitrators to make, again unless the parties indicate otherwise.

However, it must be remembered that *First Options* was a case in which the arbitration had already been conducted and an award rendered. The arbitrators had made their determination on both issues—as well as on the merits of the dispute—and the question before the Court was whether, in a court action to vacate the award, a court owes deference to the arbitrators' underlying findings that an agreement between the parties to arbitrate existed and that it covered the dispute at hand. *First Options* does not therefore address the issue of who gets to make these determinations in the first instance, much less at the very early stage of an action to compel arbitration.

(iii) Choice of law governing interpretation

In addressing issues of contract interpretation, courts once again face a threshold question of applicable law. Here too their choices are multiple: the forum's law, the substantive law (if any) expressly or impliedly chosen by the parties to govern their contract, the law indicated by general conflicts of law principles of the forum, and the law of the place of arbitration or of probable enforcement of an award. However, influenced by the federal law context of the FAA, US courts have tended to elaborate a general federal common law of interpretation of agreements to arbitrate. They have often done so, even where, in the case at hand, the underlying contract contained a choice of law clause designating non-US law and where the arbitration clause provided for arbitration outside the US. Such was precisely the case in *Mitsubishi Motors Corp. v. Soler Chrysler–Plymouth, Inc.* (S.Ct.1985).

The federal common law just alluded to has been predictably influenced by the FAA's pro-arbitration bias. See *Mitsubishi Motors Corp., supra*, where the Court ruled that arbitration agreements call for generous interpretation and should not ordinarily be read as excluding the arbitration of statutory claims. See also *Simula, Inc. v. Autoliv, Inc.* (9th Cir.1999); *Riley v. Kingsley Underwriting Agencies, Ltd.* (10th Cir.1992); *Becker Autoradio U.S.A., Inc. v. Becker Autoradiowerk GmbH* (3d Cir.1978). The result, overall, is a broad construction of arbitration agreements and a policy of favoring the submission of disputes to arbitration even in case of doubt.

Federalism aspects of international arbitration in US courts

We have noted that the FAA and the New York Convention embody a federal "pro-arbitration" bias. At the same time, the FAA permits courts to refuse enforcement of arbitration agreements on "such grounds as exist at law or in equity for the revocation of any contract" (FAA § 2), and the

Convention authorizes courts to refuse to compel arbitration where the agreement to arbitrate is "null and void, inoperative or incapable of being performed" (Art. II(3)). The stage is thus set for a possible clash between federal and state law policies.

Although the issue is not settled, it seems that the majority of courts in the US follow a rule that, while the basic issues of contract law arising in agreements to arbitrate (including contract issues of formation and validity) are subject to state law, federal law otherwise governs, including on issues of interpretation. See, e.g., *Rhone Mediterranee Compagnia Francese, supra*; *Kahn Lucas Lancaster, Inc. v. Lark Int'l Ltd., supra*. In this respect, international arbitration is treated no differently than domestic arbitration under the FAA. See *Perry v. Thomas, supra*, confirmed by *First Options*, *supra* ("[w]hen deciding whether the parties agreed to arbitrate ... courts generally ... should apply ordinary state-law principles that govern the formation of contracts").

Supreme Court case law considers the otherwise applicable state law to be unenforceable, as inconsistent with the FAA, to the extent that it discriminates against arbitration agreements as compared to other contracts. See *Doctor's Assocs., supra; Volt Information Sciences, supra; Mitsubishi Motors, supra*; *Moses H. Cone Memorial Hosp., supra.* The FAA thus has been held to preempt state law in various circumstances, such as where it imposes highly onerous conditions on the validity or enforceability of arbitration agreements (see e.g. *Securities Indus. Ass'n v. Connolly* (1st Cir.1989)), prohibits the arbitration of certain disputes (see e.g. *Perry v. Thomas, supra*; *Southland Corp. v. Keating, supra*), or declares certain ordinarily available forms of relief recovery to be unavailable in arbitration (see e.g. *Mastrobuono v. Shearson Lehman Hutton, Inc., supra.*).

The FAA applies to proceedings both in state and federal courts, and bars state courts from applying state legislation that purports to invalidate agreements to arbitrate. *Southland Corp. v. Keating, supra.* In *Allied–Bruce Terminix Cos., Inc. v. Dobson, supra,* the Supreme Court reaffirmed that understanding, while at the same time giving the FAA's scope of application the broadest possible construction. The statutory term in FAA section 2—"a contract evidencing a transaction involving commerce"—is to be read as extending the reach of the Act to the full limits of the commerce clause. More specifically, it is unnecessary that the underlying contract specifically have contemplated interstate commerce, provided it in fact involved an interstate commerce connection. Thus, while state legislatures may seek to create special statutory claims, and to insulate them from arbitration, the FAA will not permit them to do so, at least insofar as interstate commerce is implicated. For a recent case, referring the parties to arbitration over claims arising from an alleged violation of California's Fair

Employment and Housing Act, see *Circuit City Stores, Inc. v. Najd* (9th Cir.2002).

THE ARBITRABILITY OF STATUTORY CLAIMS

As noted, the New York Convention (art. II(3)) excuses a court from referring the parties to arbitration where the agreement to arbitrate is "null and void, inoperative or incapable of being performed." One such scenario arises when the claim lying at the heart of the dispute between the parties is one that is deemed to be "non-arbitrable," i.e. not being legally susceptible to resolution through arbitration. (The term "non-arbitrable" is also sometimes used to denote a dispute that lies outside the scope of the arbitration agreement, properly construed). The arbitrability of a claim, as that term is used here, may arise at various stages of the arbitral process (including the motion to vacate an award or to confirm or enforce an award, both of which are treated below), but here we envisage the situation in which a party seeks to avoid arbitration in the first place on the ground that the underlying dispute by its nature is non-arbitrable. Specifically, Article II(1) of the Convention excuses a court from enforcing an arbitration agreement when the dispute in question is not "capable of settlement by arbitration."

The FAA does not itself determine what is and what is not an arbitrable dispute, within the meaning of these provisions. The question of arbitrability in US litigation will therefore depend upon statutory provisions and public policies. But, as to this issue, there is a prior choice of law question—one that is complicated in that its answer tends to vary according to the stage of the arbitral process at which the issue arises. The choice of law question matters because different jurisdictions treat different categories of disputes as legally incapable of arbitration, typically depending on whether they regard the underlying claims as embodying a powerful public interest and thus requiring judicial rather than arbitral resolution. Their notions of what constitutes a compelling public interest simply tend to differ.

When the arbitrability issue arises at the stage of compelling arbitration, the forum is likely to apply its own law to determine that question. This seems obvious enough when the cause of action whose arbitrability has been called into question arises under the forum's own substantive law as, for example, when a US court determines whether or not a US federal statutory cause of action is subject to arbitration. See e.g. *Mitsubishi Motors Corp., supra*; *Scherk v. Alberto–Culver Co., supra*. The courts routinely hold that federal statutory claims are presumptively arbitrable and uphold agreements to arbitrate such claims unless there are powerful reasons not to do so. The "null and void" exception to the enforcement of arbitration agreements is accordingly narrowly construed. See *Ledee v. Ceramiche Ragno, supra*; *Rhone Mediterranee Compag-*

nia Francese, supra; *Riley v. Kingsley Underwriting Agencies, Ltd., supra*.

But it can also happen that the forum where the action to compel arbitration is brought has to consider the arbitrability of a cause of action specifically arising under the laws of *another* country. In that situation, the forum may elect to decide the arbitrability question in accordance with the law of the place whose statutory cause of action is in issue. As it happens, in all the major US arbitrability cases, the place whose statutory cause of action was in issue was the US. Still, some courts have refused to entertain claims of non-arbitrability under foreign law, even the law of the country where an eventual award is most likely to be enforced. See, e.g., *Meadows Indemnity Co. Ltd. v. Baccala & Shoop Ins. Servs., Inc.* (E.D.N.Y.1991), stating that arbitrability under the Convention should be determined by reference not to any national law, but rather to some "international" standard. As we shall see, the New York Convention (art. V(2)(a)) tries to avoid any uncertainty in choice of law when it comes to the recognition and enforcement of an award. It refers expressly to the law of the country where recognition is sought.

In the US, legislation creating a statutory cause of action seldom expressly declares that the cause of action is or is not arbitrable. Courts thus have to resolve the question by considering any available indicia of congressional intent, as well as the nature and strength of the public policy that the cause of action embodies, At one time, certain major federal statutory claims were considered to be non-arbitrable as a matter of law. In *Wilko v. Swan* (S.Ct. 1953), for example, the Supreme Court, ruling in the absence of any clear legislative guidance on the matter, held claims under the Securities Act of 1933 to be non-arbitrable. Its basis for so holding was statutory language declaring "void" any "condition, stipulation, or provisions binding any person ... to waive compliance with any provision" of the Securities Act. Other federal statutory claims that at one time were held to be non-arbitrable included Title VII of the Civil Rights Act of 1964 (*Alexander v. Gardner–Denver Co.* (S.Ct.1974)) and the Fair Labor Standards Act of 1938 (*Barrentine v. Arkansas–Best Freight System, Inc.* (S.Ct.1981). In both of these cases, the Court emphasized the important "public" rights at stake and the perceived inability of the arbitral process to satisfactorily resolve disputes concerning them.

The non-arbitrability doctrine has undergone an important erosion in US courts in recent years. Distinguishing *Wilko*, the Supreme Court ruled in *Scherk v. Alberto–Culver Co., supra,* that claims arising under the Securities Exchange Act of 1934 and its regulations are arbitrable, at least where they arise in relation to an international transaction. (Subsequently the Court overruled *Wilko* even as to domestic cases. See *Rodriguez de Quijas v. Shearson/American Express, Inc.* (S.Ct.1989).)

Likewise, in *Mitsubishi Motors Corp., supra,* a divided Court ruled that international antitrust claims are arbitrable. So too are claims arising under the Securities Exchange Act and RICO (*Shearson/American Express, Inc. v. McMahon* (S.Ct.1987)). Still more recently, the Court has declared arbitrable actions under the Age Discrimination in Employment Act (*Gilmer v. Interstate/Johnson Lane Corp.* (S.Ct.1991)), the Carriage of Goods by Sea Act (*Vimar Seguros y Reaseguros, S.A. v. M/V Sky Reefer* (S.Ct.1995)), and the Truth in Lending Act (*Green Tree Fin. Corp. v. Randolf* (S.Ct.2000)). Lower courts have followed suit, as in *Kramer v. Smith Barney* (5th Cir.1996), declaring claims under the Employee Retirement Income Security Act (ERISA) to be arbitrable.

The *Mitsubishi* decision was particularly controversial, due not only to the Supreme Court's subjection of antitrust claims to arbitration, but also to the "reservations" that the Court appeared to attach to this holding. In order to meet objections that international arbitrators might prove unwilling or unable to enforce the antitrust laws adequately, the Court in a noted footnote 19, warned that US courts would, upon an application to recognize or enforce an eventual award, decline to do so in certain extreme circumstances:

> There is no reason to assume at the outset of the dispute that international arbitration will not provide an adequate mechanism.... [On the other hand, h]aving permitted the arbitration to go forward, the national courts of the United States will have the opportunity at the award enforce-

> ment stage to ensure that the legitimate interest in the enforcement of the antitrust laws has been addressed. The [New York] Convention reserves to each signatory country the right to refuse enforcement of an award where the "recognition or enforcement of the award would be contrary to the public policy of that country". Article V(2)(b) ... [I]t would not require intrusive inquiry to ascertain that the tribunal took cognizance of the antitrust claims and actually decided them.

The Supreme Court has been criticized for having extended the domain of arbitrability so far that it felt constrained to invite judicial review, at the stage of enforcing an eventual award, of the adequacy of the arbitral tribunal's handling of the antitrust claims in issue. A federal court, in rejecting an argument that arbitration of antitrust claims in Switzerland would deprive the plaintiffs of certain vital remedies, has termed footnote 19 in *Mitsubishi* "dictum" and not binding. *Simula, Inc. v. Autoliv, Inc., supra.*

After *Mitsubishi* and its progeny, it would appear that Congress must expressly declare a cause of action to be non-arbitrable if that is to be the case. Thus, in *Roby v. Corporation of Lloyd's* (2d Cir. 1993), the Second Circuit ordered claims by US investors against Lloyd's arising under the Securities Act, the Securities Exchange Act and RICO to be sent for litigation or arbitration in London, pursuant to a choice of forum clause designating a London court or arbitral tribunal as the exclusive forum for the resolution of disputes. The court said the result would be otherwise only if the investors had been able to show that the remedies and potential damage recovery available in the London fora would be inadequate for achieving the fundamental policies underlying the US statutory protections.

The FAA's powerful (albeit conditional) presumption of arbitrability appears to extend to practically all federal statutory claims. According to the Supreme Court, the FAA's sole statutory exception, for "contracts of employment of seamen, railroad employees, or any other class of workers engaged in foreign or interstate commerce" (sec. 1), is to be read as limited to employment claims in a transportation sector. *Circuit City Stores, Inc. v. Adams* (S.Ct.2001). Outside that sector, employment-related claims will be subject to arbitration where the employment contract contains a suitably drafted arbitration agreement. Such is the case, for example, for employment discrimination claims under Title VII of the Civil Rights Act (*Rosenberg v. Merrill Lynch, Pierce, Fenner & Smith, Inc.* (1st Cir.1999)), claims under the Americans with Disabilities Act (*Topf v. Warnaco, Inc.* (D.Conn.1996)), and the Age Discrimination in Employment Act (*Gilmer v. Interstate/Johnson Lane Corp., supra*). Where, however, Congress has created an agency (such as the EEOC) vested with authority to receive employment-related claims and to investigate and prosecute them, such jurisdiction will not be affected by he presence of an arbitration agreement in the employment contract. *EEOC v. Waffle House, Inc.* (S.Ct.2002).

All of this would suggest that Congress needs to be explicit if, in enacting protective legislation, it means to insulate claims arising under that legislation from arbitration. Thus far, it has not done so. Absent such language, it will be difficult, but by no means impossible, to avoid the obligation to arbitrate a statutory claim.

One way to do so may be to show that the arbitration agreement is itself unconscionable (e.g., because not freely entered into), or is subject to some other fundamental objection rooted in contract law. See, e.g., *Scott v. Borg Warner Protective Servs.* (9th Cir.2003); *Duffield v. Robertson Stephens & Co.* (9th Cir.1998); *Armendariz v. Foundation Health Psychcare Servs., Inc.* (Cal.2000). Another way, drawn from the language of *Mitsubishi* and *Roby*, may be to show that the arbitral forum will not be able to furnish a remedy that is minimally adequate in light of Congress' purpose in enacting the statute. State courts have ruled, for example, that an arbitral forum is incapable of affording the injunctive (as opposed to monetary) relief to which the state statute in question entitles a prevailing claimant. See, e.g., *Broughton v. Cigna Healthplans of California* (Cal.1999). However, the federal courts may not agree, and may not consider such a result consistent with the FAA's "pro-arbitration bias." See, e.g., *Arriaga v. Cross Country Bank* (S.D.Cal.2001).

JUDICIAL INTERVENTION IN THE ARBITRAL PROCESS

Besides enjoying the power to compel arbitration and decide the arbitrability of a given claim, national courts can also participate in the early stages of the arbitral process by assisting in the constitution of the arbitral tribunal. They may be called upon during the life of the arbitration for various purposes, notably to furnish measures of provisional relief or to order discovery.

Judicial assistance in launching the arbitration

We have seen that while US law generally affords parties a large degree of autonomy in structuring the arbitral process, it does make the courts available for compelling arbitration in proper circumstances. The availability of judicial recourse of this sort is properly viewed as supportive of the arbitral process, rather than the contrary.

Another early stage at which courts may help sustain the arbitral process is in the constitution of the arbitral tribunal. A party may have neglected or refused to appoint an arbitrator, where called upon by the arbitration agreement or the applicable rules to do so. An arbitrator may have become unfit or unavailable for service and need replacing. There may be a challenge to an arbitrator's impartiality. Many institutional rules provide specific procedures for the appointment, replacement or challenge of arbitrators. But when the parties have not chosen any institutional rules, or the rules are unhelpful in these respects, resort may be had to the arbitration law of the place of arbitration (the *lex arbitri*). Most such laws provide for recourse to the competent court of the place of arbitration for assistance in accordance with certain stated principles and procedures.

Even once in place and functioning, the arbitral tribunal may occasionally have need of recourse to a court, for example to require discovery or evidence-taking, to compel the appearance of a witness, or even to compel a third party to perform a procedural act. Section 7 of the FAA, for instance, allows arbitrators to request judicial assistance from a US district court in obtaining evidence for use in the arbitration. Apart from the arbitration law of the place of arbitration, the rules of procedure specifically adopted or incorporated by reference by the parties may expressly authorize the tribunal to seek assistance from a local court. Needless to say, a court may refuse to issue or enforce such an order. For example, it may find that the evidence whose production was ordered by the arbitral tribunal is irrelevant (see *Oceanic Transport Corp. of Monrovia v. Alcoa S.S. Co., Inc.* (S.D.N.Y.1954)). On the other hand, a court is not likely to prohibit an arbitral tribunal from itself making the production orders that it deems appropriate, whether for pre-hearing production or production at the hearing. That would be considered inconsistent with the broad authorization to tribunals in the FAA (sec. 7) to issue appropriate orders to appear and produce.

Stanton v. Paine Webber Jackson & Curtis, Inc. (S.D.Fla.1988).

As for provisional relief, modern arbitration laws and rules typically empower the arbitrators themselves to issue preliminary orders as appropriate, for example attaching property in aid of eventual enforcement or issuing a preliminary injunction to preserve the *status quo* pending the award and to prevent irreparable harm to person or property. Once a tribunal is constituted, the parties to the arbitration are accordingly expected to address their applications for provisional relief initially to the arbitral tribunal, with the tribunal in turn empowered, if need be, to seek judicial enforcement of the order.

However, the possibility cannot be excluded that parties to the arbitration will feel they have no choice but to repair directly to a national court in search of provisional relief, notably because it offers the most, and sometimes the only, effective means of implementing conservatory measures during the arbitration process or of backing up orders with means of compulsion. For example, the relief that is required may need to be addressed to a third party over whom the arbitral tribunal has no jurisdiction, or it may necessarily affect persons or property outside the jurisdiction under whose *lex arbitri* the tribunal is operating. Most major procedural rules do contemplate party access to a competent court for provisional relief. See ICC Rules art. 23(2); UNCITRAL Rules art. 26(3); AAA Int'l Arb. Rules, art. 21(3). Depending on where those persons or property are located, a party to the arbitration may have judicial recourse for provisional relief to a national court other than a court of the place of arbitration. And, though they may be hesitant to do so, courts do sometimes issue provisional measures in connection with arbitrations taking place elsewhere.

The New York Convention does not itself deal expressly with the availability of provisional relief, and the courts are in fact divided over whether the Convention permits pre-award attachment. In *McCreary Tire & Rubber Co. v. CEAT, SpA* (3d Cir.1974), the court barred the issuance of court-ordered provisional relief in aid of arbitration, relying on Article II(3) of the Convention, according to which the court of a contracting state "shall ... refer the parties to arbitration." Some state courts have reached a similar result. See *Cooper v. Ateliers de la Motobecane, S.A.* (N.Y.1982).

However, other courts have taken a different view of the Convention. In *Carolina Power & Light Co. v. Uranex* (N.D.Cal.1977), for example, a federal court in California granted a US utility company involved in arbitration in New York with a French uranium supplier a preliminary attachment, pending the arbitration, of a debt owed to the French firm by a third party in California. Courts have also asserted jurisdiction to issue preliminary injunctions, not only to compel arbitration in another forum, but also to preserve the *status quo* pending the arbitration, for example by ordering a party in a trademark licensing dispute not to use disputed packaging until the arbitrators had ruled. See *Borden, Inc. v. Meiji Milk Prods. Co.,* (2d Cir.1990), where the court, having asserted jurisdiction, nevertheless declined on *forum non conveniens* grounds to exercise it.

Interlocutory review of arbitral procedural rulings

During the arbitral process, the tribunal will make rulings on various procedural issues. A party that does not agree with such a ruling may seek interlocutory review of it in a national court, but presumably only in a court of the arbitral situs. As a general matter, however, national courts are reluctant to interfere with the arbitral process and will therefore refrain from conducting interlocutory review of procedural orders or rulings by the tribunal. Invoking Section 10(d) of the FAA, US courts have generally excluded any possibility of such review. See, e.g., *Stanton v. Paine Webber Jackson & Curtis, supra*; *Mobil Oil Indonesia Inc. v. Asamera Oil (Indonesia) Ltd.* (App. Div., 1st Dept. 1977). There are exceptions, however. US courts may, for example, intervene in the event of a challenge to an arbitrator's impartiality.

Whether arbitration is commenced freely by the parties or compelled by a national court, among the first issues likely to arise is, once again, the scope of arbitral jurisdiction. If an arbitral tribunal rules in favor of its jurisdiction, one of the parties may well seek immediate interlocutory review in a local court. Under some national arbitration laws, as well as under the UNCITRAL Model Law (arts. 5 and 16), interlocutory review of this issue is ordinarily available. On the other hand, the FAA does not expressly authorize interlocutory review of jurisdictional rulings by a tribunal, and most US courts have declined to exercise it. See, e.g., *Michaels v. Mariforum Shipping, S.A.* (2d Cir.1980) (quoting *Compania Panemena Maritima San Gerassimo, S.A. v. J.E. Hurley Lumber Co.* (2d Cir.1957)). The principal exception to this rule in FAA practice arises when a tribunal formally issues an "interim" or "partial" award, for example specifically on the jurisdictional question. Such an award, which is deemed final as to the matters decided, may be subject to a vacatur action under the FAA's Chapter 1, as discussed *infra*.

ARBITRAL CHOICE OF LAW

One of the first issues facing an arbitral tribunal relates to choice of law. While the *lex arbitri*, as supplemented by procedural rules that the parties may have chosen, will govern procedural aspects of the arbitration, the tribunal may still need to identify the applicable substantive law. If the arbitration agreement or the underlying contract contains a choice of law clause, the tribunal will ordinarily respect it. This is certainly the case as to the substantive rules of contract relevant to the dispute. But it may happen that the chosen law does not address a particular statutory claim. (For example, a party may assert a US antitrust claim in a dispute arising out of or relating to a contract containing a choice of another jurisdiction's law.) In that event, the arbitrators may apply, as to that particular statutory cause of action, the body of law under which the claim arises. It was on the basis of that assumption that the US Supreme Court in *Mitsubishi* supposed that the arbitral tribunal would apply the Sherman Act, notwithstanding the parties' valid choice of Swiss law as to their contract claims.

If the parties have not designated an applicable law, the arbitrators enjoy some latitude in determining it. They may apply the substantive law of the place of arbitration (as if that represented an implied choice of law), or the conflicts of law rules of that jurisdiction, or the law indicated by the choice of law methodology that they themselves prefer (as called for by ICC Rules art. 13(3)), and possibly even a body of international law, such as the law merchant, consisting of commonly accepted rules of law rather than the rules of a specific jurisdiction.

The parties may stipulate that an arbitral tribunal is to resolve their disputes, not by reference to any preestablished body of law, but to generalized notions of fairness, equity and justice. This intention is not to be presumed, however. The UNCITRAL Model Law (art. 28(3)), for example, allows a tribunal to decide *ex aequo et bono* (or as *amiable compositeur*), but only where the parties have expressly so agreed.

JUDICIAL REVIEW OF THE AWARD

Once an arbitral procedure has ended and the tribunal has issued a final award (or a partial award which is, to that extent, final), the court of the place of arbitration generally enjoys an opportunity—albeit a limited one—to review the award. Either party may request a local court to "confirm" the award, which amounts in effect to reducing the award to a local judgment. Conversely, either party or both may request the court to annul (or "vacate" or "set aside") the award. Most arbitration laws provide standards and procedures by which confirmation or vacatur may be had. In the US, sections 9 and 10 of the FAA reflect a strong policy in favor of confirmation of arbitral awards.

The prevailing party in an arbitration may also seek to have an award recognized or enforced in a jurisdiction other than the one in which the award was rendered. The arbitration law in most legal systems will impose on local courts an obligation to recognize and enforce international arbitral awards, subject of course to certain exceptions. Article 35 of the UNCITRAL Model Law similarly states that "an arbitral award, irrespective of the country in which it was made, shall be recognized as binding and ... shall be enforced," though this obligation, too, is subject to certain exceptions. In any event, the New York Convention (art. III) provides that "each Contracting State shall recognize arbitral awards as binding and enforce them in accordance with the rules of procedure of the territory where the award is relied upon . . . ," again subject to exception.

Confirmation and vacatur of arbitral awards

The national courts of the arbitral situs have an important, and indeed exclusive, role to play in two types of procedure: the vacatur and confirmation of awards rendered locally.

(a) Confirmation proceedings

Most jurisdictions—the US among them—provide a procedure whereby an award rendered locally may be "confirmed." By confirmation is basically meant a reduction of the award to judgment, so that it has the same executory force and effect as a judgment of a local court. In fact, in the US an arbitral award is not self-executing and needs confirmation, or its equivalent, prior to any local enforcement procedure. This is usually accomplished by commencing an action to confirm under FAA Sections 9, 207, or 304, as the case may be. Strictly speaking, US courts are limited to confirming local awards, i.e., awards that were issued in the US, including awards arising out of transnational disputes. A judgment confirming an award, like any other local judgment, may then be enforced locally. Alternatively, it may be brought to the courts of another state for recognition or enforcement as a foreign judgment.

The term "confirmation" in the US is not accurately used when applied to awards issued on the territory, or under the *lex arbitri*, of a foreign jurisdiction. Such awards require judicial "recognition" and/or "enforcement," as discussed below; nor is confirmation of the award indispensable to its effectiveness. Unless vacated, the award remains valid and presumably eligible for recognition and enforcement in the courts of other jurisdictions.

An action by the prevailing party to confirm an award operates, of course, as an invitation to the losing party to challenge the award by having its confirmation denied. An award may be denied confirmation under the FAA on limited grounds. The grounds for denying confirmation are identical to those that would be available in an action to vacate the award under FAA section 10, as discussed below. To the extent that the award whose confirmation is sought is an award that is subject to the New York Convention, FAA section 207 provides that the grounds for non-recognition or non-enforcement are those set out in the Convention, as discussed further below.

(b) Vacatur of awards

For its part, a party that was unsuccessful in the arbitration may commence proceedings in a court of the arbitral situs to "vacate" (i.e., set aside or annul) the award. If vacated, the award becomes unenforceable in the arbitral situs. The award presumably ceases to have any legal effect in that forum and cannot subsequently be confirmed. See *Florasynth, Inc. v. Pickholz* (2d Cir.1984). Its chances of being recognized or enforced elsewhere also become much reduced. Vacatur of an award is most certainly an adequate basis for a denial of recognition or enforcement elsewhere, though, as we shall see, it is not clear that vacatur categorically bars that possibility.

The arbitration law of each state determines in principle the procedure by which, and the grounds upon which, an award—whether domestic or international—may be vacated by a local court. Section 10 of the FAA permits a party to commence an action to vacate a local award and provides limited grounds, such as corruption, fraud, partiality of the arbitrators, excess of arbitral jurisdiction, or non-arbitrability, for doing so. (Section 11 of the FAA also permits the modification or correction of awards under stated circumstances.) While manifest disregard of the law is not a ground for non-recognition or non-enforcement of a foreign award under the New York Convention, and is not specifically set out as such a ground in the FAA, many courts consider it may a proper basis on which to vacate a local award. See, e.g., *Alghanim & Sons v. Toys "R" Us, Inc.* (2d Cir.1997). *Bowen v. Amoco Pipeline Co.* (10th Cir.2001). Manifest disregard is a difficult showing. It is found only where the arbitrators understood and correctly stated the law, but decided to ignore it. *Government of India v. Cargill, Inc.* (2d Cir.1989).

Some courts on vacatur take a fairly close look at local awards. For example, they have reduced local awards on various grounds, including the fact that the award gave double recovery and thus made a materially unjust miscalculation within the meaning of Section 11. See, e.g., *Eljer Mfg. Inc. v. Kowin Dev. Corp.* (7th Cir.1994). Courts have also vacated awards to the extent that they granted punitive damages in an amount so disproportionate as to be irrational. See, e.g., *Sawtelle v. Waddell & Reed, Inc.* (App. Div., 1st Dept. 2003). In any event, FAA Chapter One alone governs vacatur of awards made in the US, except that awards made in the US that are also subject to the Convention are governed in this respect by Chapter Two.

The UNCITRAL Model Law (art. 34) sets out limitatively the grounds for setting aside an award. The party seeking relief must show one of the following: incapacity to arbitrate, invalidity of the arbitration agreement under the law to which the parties subjected it (or otherwise under forum law), insufficient notice or opportunity to present one's case, excess of arbitral jurisdiction, irregular composition of the tribunal or irregular arbitral procedure, non-arbitrability under the law of the forum, and conflict with the public policy of the forum. The Act contains a short (three month) limitations period for bringing such an action.

Recognition and enforcement of foreign arbitral awards

Most arbitral awards do not require judicial enforcement, or even local confirmation, because they are voluntarily complied with in a timely and adequate fashion by the losing party. But, if need be, an award may be confirmed and, if that action is successful, enforced locally in the same manner as a local judgment. It may happen, however, that the losing party lacks assets in the rendering jurisdiction and, if the award is to be judicially enforced, it must be accomplished elsewhere.

The New York Convention facilitates the recognition and enforcement of awards deemed to be "foreign" within the Convention's definition of the term by avoiding the necessity of its prior "reduction" to judgment in a court of the place of arbitration. *Lander Co., Inc. v. MMP Investments, Inc., supra*. As we have already seen (page 371 *supra*), the Convention defines foreign awards as ones that have been made "in the territory of a State other than the State where the recognition and enforcement of such awards are sought," as well as any awards that the State where recognition or enforcement is sought otherwise considers to be non-domestic. The Convention (art. I(3)) expressly permits States to declare that their commitment to recognize and enforce foreign arbitral awards shall be limited to awards rendered on the territory of another contracting State). Many States, including the US, have made such a declaration.

The New York Convention applies to all cases falling within its scope whether brought in state or federal court. The implementing legislation (sec. 205) provides for removal from state to federal court. Should a case remain in state court, the Convention still applies and preempts any inconsistent state law or policy.

The Convention requires contracting States to recognize and enforce foreign awards in the usual manner within those States (art. III), unless one of the limitatively enumerated grounds for non-recognition or non-enforcement is present (art. V). Thus, the Convention treats covered awards as presumptively entitled to recognition and enforcement, placing the burden of proof on the party seeking non-recognition or non-enforcement. Moreover, the Convention states that the enforcement of covered awards may not be made subject to more onerous conditions, including higher charges, than attach to the enforcement of domestic arbitral awards (arts. III, VII). Finally, it expressly permits States to adopt more liberal provisions (i.e. provisions more favorable to the recognition and enforcement of foreign awards) than the terms of the Convention themselves require.

In the same spirit, the US implementing legislation—FAA Chapter 2 (sec. 207)—provides that courts "shall confirm" Convention awards unless one of the Convention's stated grounds for refusal is present. The statute's use of the term "confirm" in this context is unfortunate, since, as we have seen, that term ordinarily refers to actions whose purpose is to reduce an arbitral award to judgment in a court of the place of arbitration, thus giving it the force and effect of a local judgment. In reality, Section 207 means to say that courts "shall recognize and enforce" Convention awards unless a Convention ground for refusal is present.

Significantly, the Convention draws no distinction between awards rendered after participation by both sides and awards rendered, so to speak, on a "default" basis. Moreover, it has been held that Convention awards includes awards of the Iran–U.S. Claims Tribunal, even though the submission to arbitration in such cases was not based on a writing between the parties and even though the awards were not made under a national arbitration law. *Ministry of Defense of the Islamic Republic of Iran v. Gould, Inc.* (9th Cir.1989).

It seems reasonable, in light of our understandings as to the jurisdictional basis needed for enforcing foreign country judgments (see Chapter 10 *supra*) to suppose that the mere presence of local assets will suffice to establish personal jurisdiction in an action to enforce a foreign arbitral award. However, in *Creighton Ltd. v. Government of Qatar* (D.C.Cir.1999), the court refused to entertain an action to enforce a French award against Qatar under the Convention, notwithstanding the applicability of the FSIA's arbitration exception (see Chapter 5 *supra*). The court found that personal jurisdiction, though statutorily present, was constitutionally absent due to the lack of minimum contacts between Qatar and the US sufficient to satisfy due process.

(a) Convention grounds for non-recognition and non-enforcement

Enforcement of an award under the Convention is subject to certain formal requirements. The petitioner must produce a duly authenticated original (or duly certified copy) of both the arbitration agreement and the award. More importantly, Articles V and VI set forth limitatively the grounds on the basis of which a State may refuse to recognize or enforce a Convention award. Refusal of recognition or enforcement is permitted only under certain, rather carefully defined, circumstances, as to which the opponent of recognition and enforcement bears the burden of proof. These include the situation in which:

— the award was rendered pursuant to an arbitration agreement that is invalid under the law applicable to that issue (including, specifically, the case of lack of capacity to make such an agreement) (art. V(1)(a));

— the party resisting recognition or enforcement was not given proper notice of the arbitral proceedings or not otherwise able to present its case (art. V(1)(b));

— the award deals with a matter "not contemplated by or not falling within the terms of the submission to arbitration" (art. V(1)(c));

— the composition or procedures of the arbitral tribunal violated the arbitration agreement or the law of the place of arbitration (art. V(1)(d));

— the award was not yet binding, or had been set aside or suspended by a competent authority either of a court of the place where the award was made or of the place under whose arbitral law the award was made (art. V(1)(e));

— the subject matter of the dispute is "not capable of settlement by arbitration" under the law of the place where enforcement is sought (art. V(2)(a)); or

— the award's recognition or enforcement would be contrary to the public policy of the place where recognition or enforcement is sought (art. V(2)(b)).

Even in the absence of any of the above grounds, a court may suspend proceedings to enforce a Convention award, and order the other party to give suitable security, if an application in connection with the award has been made, or an action is pending, in the country in which, or under the laws of which, the award was made (Convention, art. VI). Although this prerogative is couched in discretionary terms, the Second Circuit reversed as ill-considered a lower court's decision to enforce an Italian arbitral award, rather than suspend proceedings while the award was being challenged in the competent Italian court. *Europcar Italia, S.p.A. v. Maiellano Tours, Inc.* (2d Cir.1998).

Note that the Convention uses the term "may" rather than "must" in connection with the non-recognition or non-enforcement of awards. This means that a court may find that a Convention award falls within one of the stated exceptions to the obligation to recognize and/or enforce, and nevertheless accord it recognition or enforcement. Given the seriousness of some of the stated grounds (for example, denial of an opportunity to present one's case), it seems odd that recognition or enforcement would still be an option. Of particular interest in this regard is Article V(1)(e), permitting non-recognition or non-enforcement of an award that has been set aside by a competent court of the place of arbitration. It has nevertheless been held that the Convention permits a court to recognize and even enforce an award under that circumstance.

The leading case to this effect is *Chromalloy Aeroservs. v. Arab Republic of Egypt* (D.D.C.1996), in which a US court enforced an award rendered against Egypt by a tribunal sitting in that country, notwithstanding the award's having previously been vacated by an Egyptian court. The US court emphasized that the Convention permitted—but did not obligate—it to deny enforcement to an award that had been set aside by a competent court in the place of arbitration. The court exercised its discretion to enforce the award, in partial reliance on Article VII of the Convention, which guarantees parties having an interest in the enforcement of an award the same rights ordinarily provided for by the law of the place of attempted enforcement. The court found that the relevant US law—the FAA—would in fact have ordinarily required enforcement of the award, and so it was entitled to enforcement under Article VII. Moreover, and perhaps more important, the underlying arbitration agreement in the case had provided that the award "shall be final and binding and cannot be made subject to any appeal or other recourse," and in principle should never have been subject to Egyptian court review in the first place. Indeed, most courts continue to refuse to enforce awards set aside in the country of origin, distinguishing *Chromalloy* on the basis of the "no recourse" language just quoted. Thus, a pair of Nigerian awards that had been set aside on various grounds—as beyond the scope of arbitration, as based on the improper admission of parole evidence, as mutually inconsistent, and as lacking in substantial supporting evidence—were denied enforcement on the ground that they had been set aside. *Baker Marine (Nig.) Ltd. v. Chevron (Nig.) Ltd.* (2d Cir. 1999). The court was unimpressed by the argument in *Chromalloy* that Article VII of the Convention requires enforcement of an award, though set aside where rendered, if such an award would ordinarily be enforceable under the FAA, since the arbitration was governed by Nigerian not US law.

(b) US case law on recognition and enforcement of Convention awards

US courts have given the seven grounds for denying recognition or enforcement to Convention awards a very strict and narrow construction so as not to defeat the Convention's, as well as the FAA's, pro-enforcement bias. Three grounds—violation of the right to notice and opportunity to present one's case, the award having exceeded the agreement to arbitrate, and public policy—are especially worth mentioning in this regard.

Courts construing the Convention have granted arbitrators a particularly broad discretion in determining how the proceedings should be conducted. It is therefore extremely difficult for a disappointed party to defeat recognition or enforcement of an award on account of the tribunal's procedural choices on matters such as witnesses to summon, documents to order to be produced, cross-examination to be allowed, or time extensions granted. *Parsons & Whittemore Overseas Co., Inc. v. Societe Generale de L'Industrie du Papier* (2d Cir.1974). A rare example where the attempt succeeded is *Iran Aircraft Indus. v. Avco Corp.* (2d Cir.1992), where the court found that the claimant was denied the opportunity to present its case when the tribunal's chair instructed it in pretrial proceedings not to submit documentary evidence on a matter of proof, only to be replaced by a chair who, along with another replacement arbitrator, found against the claimant for failure of adequate proof on the very point. The courts reiterate that parties to arbitration are not entitled to demand the same procedural prerogatives that they would, absent a commitment to arbitrate, have enjoyed in a domestic court. In order to prevail, the complaining party must essentially demonstrate that the arbitral procedure fell below essential procedural due process standards. In any event, a failure to object to procedural rulings by the arbitrators at the time those rulings were made will almost certainly prove fatal to the raising of those objections at the enforcement stage.

As to claims that a tribunal acted in excess of arbitral jurisdiction, US courts are once again markedly indulgent toward the arbitrators. While an arbitral tribunal's determination of the scope of its jurisdiction is obviously not unreviewable, it tends to be shown considerable deference. Courts have once again invoked the *Kompetenz–Kompetenz* doctrine, this time not so much to support the notion that arbitrators may initially determine the scope of their jurisdiction, as to justify giving those determinations, once they have been made and acted upon, deference at the enforcement stage. For instance, in *Parsons & Whittemore*, *supra*, the court refused to withhold enforcement of a portion of the award apparently granting a sum of money for loss of production, even though the contract by its terms sought to preclude any liability between the parties under that heading, taking the position that so doing would require it to second-guess the arbitrators' interpretation of the contract and understanding of the meaning of loss of production damages. In rejecting an argument that a particular award of damages was not provided for by the arbitration agreement, the court explicitly recognized a presumption that arbitrators have acted within the scope of their powers.

The Supreme Court's decision in *First Options of Chicago, Inc. v. Kaplan*, *supra*, tends to support this view. There, it will be recalled (see page 384 *supra*), the Court ruled that reviewing courts are presumptively to review on a *de novo* basis arbitral rulings as to the existence of an agreement to arbitrate and, in particular, as to whether a particular person is a party to such an agreement. On the other hand, once an agreement is found to exist and to bind a given party, then, on the question of whether a certain dispute falls within the scope of the agreement to arbitrate, a reviewing court presumptively owes deference to the arbitral determination. As noted, these are presumptions only. *First Options* makes plain that the parties are free, through clear contractual language, to overcome these presumptions by allocating primary authority differently as between the tribunal and the court.

The Convention also permits courts to decline to enforce an award that is contrary to the enforcement forum's public policy. The Supreme Court has described this as a "specific application of a more general doctrine, written in common law, that a court may refuse to enforce contracts that violate law or public policy." *United Paperworkers Int'l Union v. Misco, Inc.* (S.Ct.1987). But US courts have proved highly resistant to claims that awards are undeserving of enforcement because offensive to US public policy. Once again using *Parsons & Whittemore*, *supra*, as an example, the court rejected the argument that an award in favor of Egypt should be denied enforcement on public policy grounds due to the fact that the underlying breach of contract was occasioned by political hostilities between the US and Egypt, where the contract was to be performed, and that the US government had withdrawn aid support for the project. For other narrow constructions of the public policy defense, see, e.g., *Northrop Corp. v. Triad Int'l Marketing S.A.* (9th Cir.1987); *Waterside Ocean Navig. Co., Inc. v. International Navig. Ltd.* (2d Cir.1984); *American Constr. Mach. & Equip. Corp. Ltd. v. Mechanised Constr. of Pakistan, Ltd.* (S.D.N.Y. 1987). In *Europcar Italia, S.p.A. v. Maiellano Tours, Inc., supra*, the court refused to find offense to forum public policy in enforcing an award based on an allegedly fraudulent contract. The court found that fraud in the underlying contract (as opposed to fraud in obtaining the arbitration agreement or award) was a matter either decided by the arbitrators or else never raised before the arbitrators, and therefore waived. For rare exceptions, see *Victrix S.S. Co. v. Salen Dry Cargo AB* (2d Cir.1987); *Laminoirs–Trefileries–Cableries de Lens, SA v. Southwire Co.* (N.D.Ga.1980).

The great majority of courts take the view that the Convention's grounds for non-recognition and non-enforcement are strictly exclusive, and that no other ground, however reasonable in principle it may be, may be invoked to avoid recognition or enforcement of Convention awards. The ground that litigants have most energetically advanced, but ordinarily have failed to get the courts to entertain, is that the award was rendered in "manifest disregard" of the applicable law. The manifest disregard doctrine has thus largely been confined to the vacatur of domestic awards. See, e.g., *Avraham v. Shigur Express Ltd.* (S.D.N.Y.1991); *International Standard Elec. Corp. v. Bridas Sociedad Anonima Petrolera* (S.D.N.Y.1990). Thus, blatant—even avowed—mistakes of law and fact by arbitrators will not support a denial of enforcement.

On the other hand, the possibility cannot be excluded that a court will determine that the defendant in a US action to enforce a Convention award lacked minimum contacts with the forum to permit the enforcement action to go forward. Numerous courts have reserved the possibility of dismissing such actions for violation of jurisdictional due process. See, e.g. *Glencore Grain Rotterdam B.V. v. Shivnath Rai Harnarain Co.* (9th Cir.2002); *Base Metal Trading, Ltd. v. OJSC Novokuznetsky Aluminum Factory* (4th Cir.2002). An action to enforce a Convention award has equally been held to be subject to dismissal on *forum non conveniens* grounds. *Monegasque De Reassurances S.A.M. v. Nak Naftogaz of Ukraine* (2d Cir.2002).

Concern over the highly deferential standard of judicial review of awards at the vacatur, confirmation, or enforcement stage has occasionally led contracting parties to draft arbitration clauses so as to invite more searching review. Such clauses may expressly contemplate, for example, judicial review of findings of fact, conclusions of law, or applications of the law to the facts. Predictably, the question has arisen whether the parties may validly do so under the FAA. The issue of "heightened" judicial scrutiny of awards by party agreement is one over which the lower courts are somewhat divided. In *Lapine Tech. Corp. v. Kyocera Corp.* (9th Cir. 1997), the Ninth Circuit in a divided opinion ruled that the parties may indeed contract for heightened judicial, and accordingly reversed the district court for applying the FAA's usual deferential standard rather than the substantial evidence and error of law standard provided for by the parties' contract. The *Lapine* court invoked the overriding principle of party autonomy, citing *Volt Information Sciences v. Bd. of Trustees*, *supra*, and *Mastrobuono v. Shearson Lehman Hutton, Inc.*, *supra*. See also *Gateway Techs., Inc. v. MCI Telecomm. Corp.* (5th Cir.1995); *Fils et Cables d'Acier de Lens v. Midland Metals Corp.* (S.D.N.Y.1984). But other circuits have expressed a different view, namely that while private parties are free to contract for appellate *arbitral* review, they may not contract for appellate *judicial* review. *Chicago Typographical Union v. Chicago Sun–Times, Inc.* (7th Cir.1991).

*

SUBJECT INDEX

References are to Pages

ACT OF STATE DOCTRINE
Generally, 167–70
Balancing approach, 180
Basis, 10, 167–68
Bernstein exception, 176–79, 182
Commercial exception, 175–76
Counterclaim exception, 177–79, 182
Definitional elements, 170–74
Exceptions, 175–80
Federal Arbitration Act, 182–83
Helms–Burton legislation, 182
Hickenlooper Amendment, 181–82
History, 168–69
Individual acts, 173–74
"Public" acts, 171–72
Restatement of Foreign Relations Law, 169–70
Separate identity of sovereign entities, 178–79
Situs requirement, 172–73
Statutory exclusion, 181–83
Treaty exception, 179–80
Validity versus motivation, 174

ALIEN TORT CLAIM STATUTE
See also Human Rights Cases, Torture Victim Protection Act
Applicable law, 202–03
Cause of action, 196–97
"Color" of foreign authority, 201

ALIEN TORT CLAIM STATUTE—Cont'd
Customary international law, 204
Forum non conveniens, 203
Personal jurisdiction, 197–98
Proper defendants, 200–01
Relation to Torture Victim Protection Act, 207
State action requirement, 201–02
Subject matter jurisdiction, 79, 195–96
Suits against foreign officials, 196–97
Suits against foreign states, 200–01
Violation of the law of nations, 198–200

ANTI-SUIT INJUNCTIONS
Generally, 110–11
Basis, 111
"Counter–Anti–Suit Injunctions", 113–14
Covenant not to sue cases, 113
Inconvenience cases, 111–12
Public policy cases, 112–13
Standards for issuance, 114–16
UK courts, 116

ARBITRATION
Generally, 365–66
Act of state doctrine, 182
Ad hoc arbitration, 367–68
American Arbitration Association, 367, 399
Antitrust cases, 392–94
Arbitrability of statutory claims, 389–96
Challenge to the arbitrator, 397
Choice of law governing the dispute, 402–03
Choice of law in the interpretation of arbitration agreements, 385–86
Compelling arbitration, 374
Confirmation of awards, 404, 405–06, 410–11
Constitution of the tribunal, 397
Discovery, 398–99
Employment claims, 393, 395
Ex aequo et bono, 403–04
Excess of arbitral jurisdiction, 407, 408, 412, 417
Exclusivity, 382–83
Existence of arbitration agreement, 374–75, 377–78, 384–85
Federal Arbitration Act, 182, 369–370, 372, 374–75, 386–87, 388–89, 395, 398, 402, 405, 407–08, 410–11, 420–21
Federalism aspects, 386–89
First Options of Chicago, Inc. v. Kaplan, 384–85, 418

ARBITRATION—Cont'd
Forum public policy, 408, 413, 418–19
Grounds for non-recognition and non-enforcement of awards, 412–15
Inter–American Convention on International Commercial Arbitration, 369, 372
Interlocutory review of arbitral procedural rulings, 401–02
Interlocutory review of jurisdictional determinations, 401–02
International arbitral institutions, 366–67
International Center for Settlement of Investment Disputes (ICSID), 367
International Chamber of Commerce, 367, 399, 403
Interpretation of the arbitration agreement, 380–86
Judicial review of the award, 404–21
Judicial role in international commercial arbitration, 374–89, 397–402, 404–21
Kompetenz-Kompetenz doctrine, 380–82, 417
London Court of International Arbitration, 367
Manifest disregard of the law, 407–08, 419–20
Party autonomy to design the arbitration, 373
Party autonomy to enhance the standard of judicial review, 420–21
Personal jurisdiction in action to recognize or enforce award, 411–12, 420
Prima facie agreement to arbitrate, 381
Pro-arbitration bias, 370, 373, 386, 395, 396
Procedural rulings by arbitrators, 401, 416–17
Provisional relief by arbitrators, 399
Provisional relief by courts in aid of arbitration, 326–27, 399–401
Recognition and enforcement of foreign arbitral awards, 404–05, 409–21
Requests for judicial assistance, 398
RICO claims, 393, 394
Securities cases, 392, 393, 394
Separability doctrine, 376–79
State arbitration laws, 373, 387–88
State contract law, 387, 396
State law discriminating against arbitration, 387–89
Status of set-aside awards, 414–15
UNCITRAL Model Law on International Commercial Arbitration, 368, 373, 402, 404, 408
UNCITRAL Rules, 368, 399
United Nations Commission on International Trade law (UNCITRAL), 368

ARBITRATION—Cont'd
United Nations Convention on the Recognition and Enforcement of Foreign Arbitral Awards (New York Convention), 7, 231–32, 370–72, 389, 400–01, 403, 404–05, 408, 409–11, 415–21
US case law on recognition and enforcement of New York Convention awards, 415–21
Vacatur of the award, 406–08
Validity of arbitration agreement, 376–80

CIVIL LIABILITY FOR ACTS OF STATE–SPONSORED TERRORISM ACT
"Flatow"Amendment, 166
Individual liability, 166–67

CHOICE OF LAW
See also Choice of Law Clauses, Extraterritorial Application of US Law, Penal Legislation, Pleading and Proof of Foreign Law, Revenue Laws
Generally, 211–14
Choice of law methodologies, 226–29
Constitutional limitations, 235–36
Erie doctrine, 214, 224–25
Foreign remedies, 254–55
Foreign Sovereign Immunities Act, 225
Forum law as source of choice of law principles, 214
Forum public policy, 229–31, 254
Interest analysis, 226–27
Mandatory rules of law, 232–35
Restatement (Second) of Conflict of Laws, 227–29, 234–35
Rome Convention on the Law Applicable to Contractual Obligations, 235
State law in diversity cases, 214
UN Convention on Contracts for the International Sale of Goods, 231–32
Uniform Commercial Code, 220, 231

CHOICE OF LAW CLAUSES
Application to statutory claims, 217, 222–23
Enforceability, 218–23
Erie doctrine, 219
Interpretation, 215–17
Limits on party autonomy, 220–23
Public policy, 221–22
Scope, 216–17
Validity, 218–23

CUSTOMARY INTERNATIONAL LAW
See also Alien Tort Claim Statute
Source of private causes of action, 209
Source of transnational litigation law, 7

DIPLOMATIC IMMUNITY
Restatement of Foreign Relations Law, 165
US Diplomatic Relations Act, 165–66
Vienna Convention on Consular Relations, 165–66
Vienna Convention on Diplomatic Relations, 165

DORMANT FOREIGN AFFAIRS POWER
Generally, 10, 188–91

ERIE DECISION
Generally, 8–9
Choice of law, 9, 214, 219, 224
Currency conversion, 360
Forum non conveniens, 103–06
Forum selection clauses, 31–34
Recognition and enforcement of foreign judgments, 9, 332–33
Remedies, 230–31

EVIDENCE ABROAD
See also Hague Evidence Convention
Generally, 277
Conflicts between US discovery orders and foreign law, 289–300
Discovery from non-parties, 283–85
Federal Rules of Civil Procedure, 278–79
Foreign blocking legislation, 286–89
Foreign state objections, 281–82
Jurisdiction to order jurisdictional discovery, 285–86
Methods of deposition abroad, 280–82
Production of evidence in US for foreign litigation, 300–04
Restatement of Foreign Relations Law, 292, 295–300
Sanctions for non-production, 294–300
Societe Internationale Pour Participations Industrielles et Commerciales v. Rogers, 291–92
US court authority to order foreign production, 279–83

EXTRATERRITORIAL APPLICATION OF US LAW
Generally, 237
Antitrust cases, 242–43, 246–47
Balancing of factors, 238–40
Extraterritorial application of constitutional rights, 248–49
Helms–Burton legislation, 247–48
Presumption against extraterritoriality, 237–38

EXTRATERRITORIAL APPLICATION OF US LAW—Cont'd
Reasonableness, 243–46
Restatement of Foreign Relations Law, 243–46
Securities cases, 243–44
Statutory construction and required contacts, 238
Subject matter jurisdiction, 243–46
Timberlane rule of reason, 240–46

FEDERAL ARBITRATION ACT
See Arbitration

FEDERAL COMMON LAW
Source of transnational litigation law, 8

FEDERAL RULES OF CIVIL PROCEDURE
Generally, 5
Evidence, 5, 278–79
Personal jurisdiction, 34, 37–39, 56–61
Pleading and proof of foreign law, 6, 256–57, 258–59
Provisional relief, 6, 316–17, 320–21
Service, 5–6, 263–66, 269

FOREIGN BLOCKING LEGISLATION
See Evidence Abroad

FOREIGN SOVEREIGN COMPULSION
Generally, 192–94

FOREIGN SOVEREIGN IMMUNITIES ACT (FSIA)
Admiralty exception, 151
Alien plaintiffs, 160
Applicable law, 123–24, 142–43, 225
Arbitration exception, 146–47
Attachment of property, 154–60
Basis of liability, 122–23
Burden of proof, 128–29
Commercial acts exception, 132–38, 145
Counterclaims, 151–53
Default judgments, 161–62
Definition of "states" and "agencies or instrumentalities", 124–28
Discretionary acts, 143–45
Distinction between "states" and "agencies or instrumentalities", 125–27
Due process, 121
Exceptions to immunity, 128–51
Exclusive basis of state liability, 128

FOREIGN SOVEREIGN IMMUNITIES ACT (FSIA)—Cont'd
Forum non conveniens, 161
History, 118–20
Individual defendants, 127
Personal jurisdiction, 121
Procedural limitations, 122
Property rights by succession or gift exception, 140
Punitive damages, 122
Removal to federal court, 122
Retroactivity, 153
Role of State Department, 119–20
Scope, 5
Service, 265–66
Statutory framework, 120–21
Subject matter jurisdiction, 80–82, 120–21
Takings of property exception, 138–39
Terrorist acts exception, 147–50
Tort exception, 140–45
Venue, 84–85
Waiver, 129–32

FORUM NON CONVENIENS
Generally, 89–93
Application to Alien Tort Claim Statute, 203
Application to enforcement of arbitral awards, 420
Application to statutory claims, 92–93
Available alternative forum, 93–95
Balance of convenience, 95–97
Basis, 91
Change in applicable law, 100–02
Conditions of dismissal, 102–03
Erie doctrine, 103–06
Foreign law as a factor, 98–99
Foreign Sovereign Immunities Act, 161
Plaintiff's nationality, 98–100
Relation to forum selection clauses, 20, 29–31, 93
State courts, 104–06
Statutory exclusion, 31, 92

FORUM SELECTION CLAUSES
Generally, 13–14
Consumer contracts, 23
Derogation clauses, 15
Enforceability, 17–29
Forum non conveniens, relation to, 20, 24, 29–31
Interpretation, 14, 17

FORUM SELECTION CLAUSES—Cont'd
Law applicable to, 17, 21
Parties bound, 16–17
Prorogation clauses, 15
Public policy limitations, 27–29
Requirement of adequate remedy, 23, 25, 27–29
Requirement of reasonable relation, 24–25
Scope, 15–16
State law, 20, 32–33
Statutory exclusion, 26–27
Validity, 17–29

HAGUE EVIDENCE CONVENTION
See also Evidence Abroad
Generally, 7, 281, 305
Central authority, 306
Declarations as to pre-trial discovery, 308–09
Evidence-taking by commissioners, 310–11
Evidence-taking by diplomatic or consular officials, 309–11
Exclusivity of the Convention, 311–14
International comity, 313–14
Letters of request, 306
Means of production under the Convention, 306–07, 309–11
Privileges, 306–07
Procedures, 306
Scope of the Convention, 305–06
"Sovereignty or security" exception, 307–08

HAGUE SERVICE CONVENTION
See also Service of Documents
Generally, 7, 270–71
Central authority, 271
Exclusivity of the Convention, 276–77
Means of service under the Convention, 272–74
Requirement of notice, 273–74
Remedies for violation, 276–77, 341
Scope of the Convention, 274–76
"Sovereignty or security" exception, 272
State court proceedings, 265

HEAD OF STATE IMMUNITY
Generally, 162–67
Restatement of Foreign Relations Law, 164–65

HELMS-BURTON LEGISLATION
Act of state, 182

HELMS-BURTON LEGISLATION—Cont'd
Extraterritorial application of US law, 247–48

HUMAN RIGHTS CASES
See also Alien Tort Claim Statute, Civil Liability for Acts of State–Sponsored Terrorism Act, Torture Victim Protection Act, Universal Jurisdiction
Generally, 195

INTERNATIONAL COMITY
Generally, 183–86
Hague Evidence Convention, 313–14
Hartford Fire Ins. Co. v. California, 246–47
Restatement of Foreign Relations Law, 184–86, 245–46

LIS PENDENS
Generally, 106–10
European practice, 109–10

MANDATORY RULES OF LAW
See also Choice of Law
Lois d'application immediate, 233
Non-derogable rules of law, 233–34
Mandatory laws of third countries, 234
Rome Convention on the Law Applicable to Contractual Obligations, 235

MODEL CHOICE OF FORUM ACT
Declining jurisdiction pursuant to a choice of forum clause, 18–19
Declining jurisdiction notwithstanding a choice of forum clause, 19, 30–31, 93

NEW YORK CONVENTION ON RECOGNITION AND ENFORCEMENT OF FOREIGN ARBITRAL AWARDS
See Arbitration

PARALLEL LITIGATION
See also Anti–Suit Injunctions, *Forum Non Conveniens*, *Lis Pendens*
Generally, 86–89

PENAL LEGISLATION
Application of foreign penal laws, 251–53
Application of foreign public laws, 253–54

PERSONAL JURISDICTION
See also Forum Selection Clauses

PERSONAL JURISDICTION—Cont'd
Actions to recognize or enforce foreign arbitral awards, 411–12
Actions to recognize or enforce foreign judgments, 329–30
Agency-based jurisdiction, 65–68
Aggregation of national contacts, 39, 55–61
Alter ego jurisdiction, 61–65
Corporate affiliates, 61–65
Doing business, 45–47
Due process, 35, 40–44
Federal courts, 34, 37–39
General jurisdiction, 44–49, 67–68
Internet jurisdiction, 53–55
Jurisdiction to order jurisdictional discovery, 285–86
Minimum contacts, 35, 40–44
Persons not subject to state court jurisdiction, 38–39
Product liability cases, 40–42, 50–51
Quasi-in-rem jurisdiction, 51–53
Reasonableness, 45
Relation to subject matter jurisdiction, 82–83
Specific jurisdiction, 38, 49–51, 67–68
State law, 34, 35–37
"Stream of commerce", 40–42, 50–51
"Tag" jurisdiction, 47–49
Venue, 83–85
Waiver, 47

PLAINTIFF'S NATIONALITY
Relevance to *forum non conveniens*, 69, 98–100
Relevance to personal jurisdiction, 68–69

PLEADING AND PROOF OF FOREIGN LAW
Generally, 255
Common law approach, 255–56
Consequences of failure to plead or prove, 259–60
Expert witnesses, 257–58
Federal Rule 44.1, 256–57, 258–59
Foreign law as law, 258–59
Judicial notice, 260
Hague Convention Abolishing the Requirement of Legalization of Foreign Public Documents, 257
New York CPLR, sec. 4411, 257

POLITICAL QUESTION DOCTRINE
Generally, 186–88
Foreign Sovereign Immunities Act cases, 188

PROVISIONAL RELIEF
Generally, 315–16
Authority of US courts to order extraterritorial provisional relief, 316–17, 318–19
Authority of US courts to provide provisional relief in aid of foreign litigation, 321–22
Bankruptcy cases, 324–26
Enforcement of foreign orders of provisional relief, 322–24
European practice, 322
Federal Rules of Civil Procedure, 316–17, 320–21
Grupo Mexicano de Desarrollo, S.A. v. Alliance Bond Fund, 320–21
Mareva injunctions, 317–18, 320
Provisional relief in aid of arbitration, 326–27
New York CPLR, 316–17
UK courts, 317–18

PUBLIC POLICY
See also Arbitration, Choice of Law, Recognition and Enforcement of Foreign Judgments
Basis for non-application of foreign law, 254

RECOGNITION AND ENFORCEMENT OF FOREIGN JUDGMENTS
Generally, 328–29
Claims of fraud, 346–47
Collateral estoppel effect of foreign judgments, 356–57
Currency conversion issues, 359–61
Default judgments, 342–43, 351–53
Distinction between recognition and enforcement, 328–29
Erie doctrine, 332–33
European Union recognition and enforcement principles, 363
Exceptions to recognition and enforcement, 336–37
Federal authority to legislate on recognition and enforcement, 332, 334–35
Forum public policy as a defense to recognition or enforcement, 347–50
Full faith and credit under the US Constitution, 330–32
Hilton v. Guyot, 333–34
Lack of impartial tribunals or procedural due process, 345–46
Lack of personal jurisdiction as a defense to recognition or enforcement, 338–45
Lack of subject matter jurisdiction, 350
Non-monetary judgments, 355–56
Penal judgments, 353–55
Personal jurisdiction in actions to recognize or enforce, 329–30

RECOGNITION AND ENFORCEMENT OF FOREIGN JUDGMENTS—Cont'd
Procedural issues, 357–58
Proposed Hague Convention on Jurisdiction and Enforcement of Judgments, 363–64
Public policy as a defense, 331–32
Quasi-in-rem jurisdiction, 329–30
Reciprocity, 334, 337, 351
Recognition and enforcement of US judgments abroad, 362
Revenue judgments, 353–55
Uniform Enforcement of Foreign Judgments Act, 357
Uniform Foreign Country Money–Judgments Recognition Act, 335–37, 338–39, 351, 357–58
Uniform Foreign–Money Claims Act, 359, 361
Waiver of defects of personal jurisdiction, 341–42

RESTATEMENTS OF THE LAW
Restatement of Conflicts of Law, 11, 19, 217, 218, 219, 220–21, 227–29, 234–35, 259, 290, 330–31
Restatement of Foreign Relations Law, 11–12, 44–46, 48, 164–65, 169–70, 177, 181, 184–85, 198, 208, 210, 243–46, 292, 295–300, 339, 356, 359
Source of transnational litigation law, 11–12

REVENUE LAWS
Application of foreign tax laws, 251–53
Application of foreign public laws, 253–54

SEPARABILITY DOCTRINE
Arbitration agreement, 376–79
Choice of forum clause, 22

SERVICE OF DOCUMENTS
See also Hague Service Convention
Generally, 262–63
Federal Rules of Civil Procedure, 263–66
Foreign law rules on service, 266–68
Foreign Sovereign Immunities Act, 265–66
Inter–American Convention on Letters Rogatory, 264, 277
Requirement of notice, 266
Service abroad, 263–68
Service of foreign judicial documents in the US, 269–70
State law, 265–66

SOURCES OF TRANSNATIONAL LITIGATION LAW
Generally, 4–12

SUBJECT MATTER JURISDICTION
Generally, 70–73
Actions against foreign states, 77
Alienage jurisdiction, 71–77
Corporate citizenship, 76
Diversity cases, 71–77
Exclusive federal jurisdiction, 73
Extraterritorial application of US law, 243–46
Federal question jurisdiction, 71–73, 77–82, 225
General federal question jurisdiction, 77–79
Foreign state as plaintiff, 76–77
Relation to personal jurisdiction, 82–83
Removal to federal court, 72
Specific federal question jurisdiction, 71, 73, 79–82

TORTURE VICTIM PROTECTION ACT
Cause of action, 204–06
"Color" of foreign authority, 205
Limitations, 205–06
Proper defendants, 205–07
Proper plaintiffs, 206
Relation to Alien Tort Claim Statute, 207
Subject matter jurisdiction, 205
Suits against foreign states, 205

TRANSFER OF VENUE
Federal courts, 33–34, 87, 90–91

TREATIES
Generally, 208
As federal law, 208–09, 231–32
Self-executing and non-self-executing, 232
Source of private causes of action, 208–09
Source of transnational litigation law, 7–8

UN CONVENTION ON CONTRACTS FOR THE INTERNATIONAL SALE OF GOODS
See Choice of Law

UNIFORM COMMERCIAL CODE
See Choice of Law

UNIVERSAL JURISDICTION
See also Human Rights Cases
Generally, 210

VENUE
Generally, 83–85
Alien Venue Statute, 84
Foreign Sovereign Immunities Act, 84–85

VICTIMS OF TRAFFICKING AND VIOLENCE PROTECTION ACT
Execution of FSIA judgments, 159–60

†